Ethnic and Religious Diversity in Myanmar

Also Available from Bloomsbury:
The Culture of Giving in Myanmar,
Hiroko Kawanami
Buddhism, Education and Politics in Burma and Thailand,
Khammai Dhammasami
Interreligious Comparisons in Religious Studies and Theology,
Perry Schmidt-Leukel and Andreas Nehring

Ethnic and Religious Diversity in Myanmar

Contested Identities

Edited by
Perry Schmidt-Leukel, Hans-Peter Grosshans
and Madlen Krueger

BLOOMSBURY ACADEMIC
LONDON • NEW YORK • OXFORD • NEW DELHI • SYDNEY

BLOOMSBURY ACADEMIC
Bloomsbury Publishing Plc
50 Bedford Square, London, WC1B 3DP, UK
1385 Broadway, New York, NY 10018, USA
29 Earlsfort Terrace, Dublin 2, Ireland

BLOOMSBURY, BLOOMSBURY ACADEMIC and the Diana logo are trademarks of Bloomsbury Publishing Plc

First published in Great Britain 2022
Paperback edition published 2023

Copyright © Perry Schmidt-Leukel, Hans-Peter Grosshans, Madlen Krueger and contributors, 2022

Perry Schmidt-Leukel, Hans-Peter Grosshans, Madlen Krueger and contributors have asserted their right under the Copyright, Designs and Patents Act, 1988, to be identified as Editors of this work.

Cover design: Tjasa Krivec
Cover image © Kumar Sriskandan / Alamy Stock Photo

All rights reserved. No part of this publication may be reproduced or transmitted in any form or by any means, electronic or mechanical, including photocopying, recording, or any information storage or retrieval system, without prior permission in writing from the publishers.

Bloomsbury Publishing Plc does not have any control over, or responsibility for, any third-party websites referred to or in this book. All internet addresses given in this book were correct at the time of going to press. The author and publisher regret any inconvenience caused if addresses have changed or sites have ceased to exist, but can accept no responsibility for any such changes.

A catalogue record for this book is available from the British Library.

A catalog record for this book is available from the Library of Congress.
Library of Congress Control Number: 2021946147

ISBN: HB: 978-1-3501-8740-5
PB: 978-1-3501-8746-7
ePDF: 978-1-3501-8741-2
eBook: 978-1-3501-8742-9

Typeset by Newgen KnowledgeWorks Pvt. Ltd., Chennai, India

To find out more about our authors and books visit www.bloomsbury.com and sign up for our newsletters

in memoriam
Nehȝinpao Kipgen (1978–2021)

Contents

List of Figures	ix
List of Contributors	x
Introduction *Madlen Krueger and Perry Schmidt-Leukel*	1

Part 1 Politics and Identities

1	The making of a fixed national hierarchy of ethnicity and religion in Myanmar *Mikael Gravers*	9
2	Ethnic minorities and Myanmar's democratization *Nehginpao Kipgen*	36
3	Ne Win's echoes: Burmarization policies and peacebuilding in Myanmar today *Saw Eh Htoo*	50

Part 2 The Case of Buddhism

4	Visual culture and identity: Ethnic and religious diversity in the Eastern Shan State *Klemens Karlsson*	73
5	Tempered Tantrism: Buddhism of exception on the Shan Plateau *Jane M. Ferguson*	92
6	Reflections on religion and identity: With a particular emphasis on Theravāda Buddhism *Perry Schmidt-Leukel*	108
7	Coexistence in Myanmar: Challenges and prospects *Alexander Horstmann*	122

Part 3 The Case of Christianity

8 Christianity in Myanmar: With a particular emphasis on its Indian roots — 141
  Marja-Leena Heikkilä-Horn

9 Problems and challenges facing ethnic diversity in Myanmar: A socio-historical analysis from a Christian perspective — 161
  Samuel Ngun Ling

10 Burmanization and its effects on the Kachin ethnic group in Myanmar — 173
  Layang Seng Ja

Part 4 The Case of Islam

11 Islam and ethnic diversity in Myanmar — 191
  Myint Thein (Nyeinchan Lulin)

12 Civil documentation and discrimination against religious and ethnic minorities in Myanmar — 214
  Myo Win

13 Being a Mon: Buddhist–Muslim relations — 231
  Madlen Krueger

Postscripts

14 Tatmadaw's coup in 2021: The return of totalitarian rule? — 249
  Mikael Gravers

15 Ethnic and religious diversity — 257
  Hans-Peter Grosshans

Index — 273

Figures

3.1	Ideological Foundations of Ne Win's Regime	54
4.1 and 4.2	The Big Chiang Tung Buddha statue (20 metres high) pointing to the town with his index finger	80
4.3	The monument of King Anawrahta and Shin Arahan, Chiang Tung	81
4.4	Temple drum, Chiang Tung	86
4.5	Temple banners, Chiang Tung	86
4.6	Gold stencilling, Chiang Tung	87
4.7	Vihāra, Wat In, Chiang Tung	88
5.1	Sao Myat Portrait	99

Contributors

Jane M. Ferguson is Senior Lecturer in Anthropology and Southeast Asian History at the School of Culture, History and Language at the Australian National University. She is the editor of the *Journal of Burma Studies* and former chair of the Southeast Asia Council of the Association for Asian Studies. She is the author of numerous studies on Myanmar and the Shan in particular, such as *Ethno-nationalism and Participation in Myanmar: Views from Shan State and Beyond* (2016), 'Buddhist Bomb Diversion and an American Airman Reincarnate: World War Folklore, Airmindedness and Spiritual Air Defense in Shan State, Myanmar' (2018) and *Repossessing Shanland: Myanmar, Thailand and a Nation-State Deferred* (2021).

Mikael Gravers is Associate Professor Emeritus, Anthropology, Aarhus University, Denmark. He has conducted fieldwork in Thailand and Myanmar since 1970. His research includes Buddhist and Christian Karen communities, Buddhist monasteries and monks and Hindu and Muslim communities. He is the author of *Nationalism as Political Paranoia* (1999). He has edited *Exploring Ethnic Diversity in Burma* (2007). In 2014, he co-edited *Burma/Myanmar – Where Now?* with Flemming Ytzen. He has published on ethnicity, nationalism, Buddhism and politics, as well as on nature, culture and environmental protection. He has conducted research related to Burma in the colonial archives, British Library and Public Record Office, London. He is currently a senior researcher in the Danish-funded research project *Everyday Justice and Security in the Myanmar Transition* in collaboration with Danish Institute of International Studies (DIIS) and Anthropology, Yangon University.

Hans-Peter Grosshans is Professor of Systematic and Ecumenical Studies in Protestant Theology at the University of Muenster, Germany, researcher at the Cluster of Excellence on 'Religions and Politics', president of the European Academy of Religion and vice president of the European Society for Philosophy of Religion. Two of his major research areas are 'religion in modernity' and 'theological discourses in the global south'. Among his numerous publications are: editor (with S. Ngun Ling, P. Schmidt-Leukel) of *Buddhist and Christian Attitudes to Religious Diversity* (2017); editor of *Lutherische Theologie in außereuropäischen Kontexten* (2017); editor of *Integration religiöser Pluralität: Philosophische und theologische Beiträge zum Religionsverständnis in der Moderne* (2010).

Marja-Leena Heikkilä-Horn is assistant professor at the Mahidol University International College, Thailand. Her research is focused on ethnic and religious diversity in Southeast Asia, with a particular interest in contemporary forms of religion in different Asian regions. She is the author of *Santi Asoke Buddhism and Thai State Response* (1996) and, most recently, *History of Southeast Asia (Kaakkois-Aasian historia* 2020) in Finnish.

Alexander Horstmann is Associate Professor of Asian Studies at Tallinn University, Estonia. He is the editor (with Jin-heon Jung) of *Building Noah's Ark: Migrants, Refugees and Religious Communities* (2015) and (with Alessandro Rippa and Martin Saxer) *Routledge Handbook of Asian Borderlands* (2020). He held positions at the University of Copenhagen and the Max-Planck-Institute for Religious and Ethnic Diversity, Göttingen. He also held visiting professorships in Bangkok, Mandalay, Tokyo, Paris and Kunming. He directed ERASMUS+ exchange programmes from Tallinn University with Department of Anthropology, University of Mandalay. He has been appointed external professor at the Chair of Philosophy of Peace at UJI in Castellón, Spain.

Saw Eh Htoo is a doctoral student at the Peacebuilding Program (Payap University, Thailand). He received his MA in Anthropology at the University of Yangon and his MACS at the Myanmar Institute of Theology. He is the executive director of the Kaw Lah Peace Foundation in Myanmar and an independent consultant for various INGOs and NGOs in Myanmar.

Klemens Karlsson is affiliated researcher at Regional Center for Social Science and Sustainable Development (RCSD), Chiang Mai University, Thailand. He received his PhD from Uppsala University, Sweden in 2000 in the History of Religions. His research has focused on religion and visual culture in South and Southeast Asia. His special interest has been in the so-called aniconic Buddhist art in early India and, more recently, in Buddhist visual culture, history and ethnicity in the borderlands of Upper Southeast Asia, especially concerning Chiang Tung/Keng Tung, Myanmar. He has also had a long career as university and research librarian and recently finished his position as library director at Konstfack – University of Arts, Crafts and Design in Stockholm, Sweden.

Nehginpao Kipgen (1978–2021) was professor and executive director of Center for Southeast Asian Studies, Jindal School of International Affairs, O.P. Jindal Global University. He was also a board member (RC18 – Asian and Pacific Studies) of International Political Science Association. He authored four books, including *Democratization of Myanmar* (2016) and *Myanmar: A Political History* (2016). Kipgen has published peer-reviewed academic articles in *Social Research, International Studies, World Affairs, Journal of Asian and African Studies, Journal of Muslim Minority Affairs, Ethnopolitics, Strategic Analysis, South Asia Research,*

Indian Journal of Political Science, Economic and Political Weekly, Asian Profile, Asian Affairs, International Journal on World Peace and *India Review*. He has also published over 220 articles in various leading international newspapers and magazines in five continents – Asia, Africa, Australia, Europe and North America.

Madlen Krueger is the author of *Das Verhältnis von Buddhismus und Politik in Sri Lanka. Narrative Kontinuität durch Traditionskonstruktion* (2019). She was postdoc researcher in the DFG-sponsored, five-year research project 'Religious Diversity in Myanmar' and is now researcher in the Federal Foreign Office-sponsored project 'Religion, Diplomacy and Peace' at the Forschungsstätte der Evangelischen Studienakademie, Heidelberg, Germany. Her fields of research are religious diversity, religion and politics and Buddhism in India, Sri Lanka and Myanmar.

Layang Seng Ja formerly worked as Burmese-Chinese-Kachin Interpreter at Kachin Independence Organization (KIO) after she got her diploma in Chinese Literature from Yunnan Institute of Language and Literature, Kunming, China. She received her BSc (Botany) from Mandalay University of Myanmar; MDiv from Kachin Theological College and Seminary; MTh in the New Testament Studies from South Asia Institute of Advanced Christians Studies (SAIACS) Bangalore, India. She earned her doctor of theology (DTh) in New Testament Studies with distinction from Lutheran Theological Seminary of Hong Kong. Currently, she is head of the New Testament Department and director of Research and Documentation at Kachin Theological College and Seminary (KTCS) Myitkyina, Kachin State. She is also an executive member of Society of Asia Biblical Studies (SABS). Among her recent publications are *The Pharisees in Matthew 23 Reconsidered* (2018) and "I & II Peter," in *An Asian Introduction to the New Testament* (2021).

Samuel Ngun Ling is principal (president) of the Myanmar Institute of Theology and Professor of Theology. He is former chair of the Dialogue Committees of the Myanmar Council of Churches and the Myanmar Baptist Convention; former president of the Association for Theological Education in Myanmar; former director of Judson Research Center of MIT (2003–10); former editor of the *RAYS MIT Journal of Theology* (1999–2009), *Engagement. Judson Research Bulletin* (2003–9) and the *Myanmar Journal of Theology* (ATEM) (2005–8). Currently he is one of the board of trustees members of the Association for Theological Education in Southeast Asia (ATESEA) (2013–21). Among his publications are *Communicating Christ in Myanmar: Issues, Perspectives and Interactions* (2005) and *Christianity through Our Neighbors' Eyes: Rethinking the 200 Year's Old American Baptist Missions in Myanmar* (2014).

Myint Thein (Nyeinchan Lulin) received his PhD with the thesis *The Problem of Muslim National Identity in Myanmar* in 2012 from the International Institute of Islamic Thought and Civilization at the International Islamic University, Malaysia. He is president of the Al-Azhar Islamic Institute of Mynamar, head of the Peace Cultivation Network (PCN), chair of the Advisory Board of Nyein (Shalom) Foundation, and the president of the Malaysian Alumni Council of Myanmar.

Myo Win was the recipient of the Chevening Fellowship to study conflict resolution at the University of York in 2008 and was the recipient of the 2018 Clyde Snow Justice Award for his efforts towards peace and justice in Myanmar. He has long been outspoken about human rights in Myanmar and has spoken at panels in the UN, the United States, Europe and ASEAN. He has authored reports regarding Myanmar citizenship law and its impact on minority groups. He founded Smile Education and Development Foundation (SEDF) and has served as its executive director and CEO since its inception. The foundation works to empower youth and minority communities promotes and protects the rights of minority groups and advocates strongly for legal reform regarding citizenship and freedom of religion and belief in Myanmar.

Perry Schmidt-Leukel is Professor of Religious Studies and Intercultural Theology, principle investigator at the research-cluster 'Religion and Politics', University of Muenster and president of the European Network of Buddhist-Christian Studies. He has published more than thirty books, including *Understanding Buddhism* (2006); *Transformation by Integration. How Inter-faith Encounter Changes Christianity* (2009); *Buddhism and Religious Diversity*, 4 vols (2013); *Religious Diversity in Chinese Thought* (2013). In 2015 he presented the renowned Gifford-Lectures at the University of Glasgow, which were published in 2017 as *Religious Pluralism and Interreligious Theology*.

Introduction

Madlen Krueger and Perry Schmidt-Leukel

News from Myanmar has often come as a surprise or even shock to those in the West. Apparently, such news falsifies one of the West's cherished romantic ideals: that among all the world religions at least Buddhism is indeed peaceful, tolerant and non-violent, not merely in theory but also in practice. 'Chosen for Peace: only the Buddhists' was the assessment of Johan Galtung, the nestor of Western peace studies (Galtung 1997–8: 440). In 2021, the military coup and its dreadful consequences dominated the news. Yet, many people know little about the background of the coup, its endorsement by nationalist monks and the larger context in which it is situated. Before the coup, the Western world was surprised to learn from the news about the ideological involvement of some nationalist Buddhists in the atrocities against Myanmar's Rohingya Muslims. That the Rohingya are not the only Muslims in Myanmar usually causes astonishment even among educated people, as does indeed the fact that the conflict between Buddhists and Muslims is only one strand of a complex web of tense and recurring violent conflicts between various ethnic and religious groups living inside the borders of this highly diverse country – a nation that came into existence in 1948 after more than sixty years of British colonialism and a brief, but cruel, Japanese occupation between 1942 and 1945.

Many of the tensions in Myanmar can be analysed in terms of different ethnic and religious identities woven into a fateful net of domination and defence, alleged and real threats, humiliation and distrust. Moreover, in this complicated fabric, the borderlines between different religious and ethnic identities are far less clear-cut than one might assume and some like to pretend. People belong to the same ethnicity but to different religions, or to the same religion but different ethnicities. And neither the religions nor the ethnicities are homogenous, stable and neatly sorted entities but are also internally diverse. The construction of, and struggle for, one's own identity, as much as the construction of and struggle against the identity of the 'other', belongs to dynamic processes shaped by past memories and present experiences which often testify primarily to persistent political power games. Concluding that politics in Myanmar simply instrumentalizes religious and ethnic diversity would be too easy, since politics is itself a manifestation and part of the dangerous and frequently disastrous potential of contested identities, of a society in search of a way to live in and with its own diversity, a way that all of Myanmar's diverse people can at least accept or, ideally, benefit from.

One factor in Myanmar's conflict-laden search for its own multifaceted identity is the persistent attempt by powerful forces to establish a hierarchical model of diversity, that is to make the culture of the majority ethnic group, the Bamar (or Burman), the nation's dominant culture, and its religion, Buddhism, the nation's dominant faith – the latter being implemented in Myanmar's constitution of 2008. In practice, even the type of Buddhism that enjoys the privilege of the 'special position' granted by the constitution turns out to be that version of Theravāda Buddhism as practised by the Bamar people. Naturally, the process of Burmanization or Bamanization of the whole country meets with resistance from people of other faiths and ethnicities. So far, the mixed government of Aung San Suu Kyi's elected National League for Democracy (NLD) and the constitutionally empowered military (*Tatmadaw*) had not produced significant corrections to the direction of this process. Democracy thus turned into 'majoritarianism'. Aung San Suu Kyi already argued in one of her early essays that 'rulers must observe the teachings of the Buddha' even in a democratically elected government (Aung San Suu Kyi 1991: 177) and manifest the qualities of a traditional Buddhist monarch (ibid.: 170–3).

To analyse this complex web of diverse identities that are 'dependent upon religio-ethnic-cum-political interests and prerogatives' (Holt 2019: xi), we require a multi-perspectival approach that takes into account various disciplines such as history, political science, social anthropology, religious studies and the theologies of the actors. In a number of cases, the contributors to the current volume employ a combination of several such perspectives in their assessment of the situation and their efforts to envision possible solutions. Hence, the book includes both insider and outsider perspectives.

Part 1 of the book comprises three essays dealing with the close entanglement of ethnic and religious identities on the one hand, and the political development of Myanmar on the other. Mikael Gravers (Chapter 1) underlines the imagined and politically driven nature of 'ethnicity' as a concept in the context of social categorization. He presents an analysis of the political conjunctures which had an impact on ethnic and religious identification, such as colonization and its divide-and-rule administration (showing, for example, that Muslim-Buddhist tensions have some of their roots in this period), Christian mission, Indian immigration, the anti-Indian riots of 1938, racial categorization after independence, the 1982 citizenship law introduced by Ne Win, and the 1978 Rohingya crisis. In his case study, Gravers focuses on Karen State and the effects on Karen Muslims and Karen Hindus of identity politics, nationalism and an ethno-religious hierarchy. Nehginpao Kipgen (Chapter 2) then provides a four-stage overview of the relation between the central government led by a Burman majority and the ethnic groups: from the country's independence to the first military coup in 1962; the years of military rule to the introduction of the seven-step roadmap towards democracy in 2003; the events leading up to the formation of a quasi-democracy in 2011; and the transfer of power to a civilian-led hybrid regime in 2016. As Kipgen argues, addressing the demands of ethnic minorities is not merely important but essential for peace, stability, development and the consolidation of democracy. This is supported by Saw Eh Htoo (Chapter 3), who analyses the principles of Ne Win's politics of Burmanization in more detail. Identifying the foundations of Ne Win's idea of a Burmese nation and his strategies of assimilation, accommodation and alienation, he underlines Ne Win's fateful legacy which still functions as the main barrier to the development of a stable peace in Myanmar.

The chapters in Part 2 focus on Buddhism as a lived spiritual resource on the one hand, and as both an instrument of the Burmanization agenda as well as an expression of a distinct local ethnic identity on the other. It begins with two case studies on Buddhism in Shan State. As Klemens Karlsson (Chapter 4) shows for the Eastern Shan region, the Burmese military government tried, even in an area with its own specific Buddhist culture, to Burmanize the region by imposing symbols of a culturally Burmese version of Buddhism and rewriting history through Burmese sculptures and architecture. It emerges from his discussion that the struggle for and negotiation of identities does not always run in strict parallel to larger religious boundaries. Even internal forms of religious diversity, in this case regional ones, are exploited for political claims to power. The Southern Shan religion is at the centre of Jane Ferguson's chapter (Chapter 5). She introduces and explores the meaning of the exceptional figure, Sao Myat of Möng Pan, who is revered by many Shan people and especially by Shan separatists. Sao Myat incorporated symbolic elements of Tantrism yet kept his status as a Theravāda Buddhist monk. To what extent does reverence for such unorthodox figures reflect an insistence on the need to be and remain different in the face of outside pressures? Through Sao Myat's exceptional biography, Ferguson weaves together two tapestries of meaning: spiritual systems and ethno-national histories. Buddhist doctrinal perspectives on identity are taken up in Perry Schmidt-Leukel's contribution (Chapter 6). After presenting Theravāda Buddhist canonical discourses on individual, collective and religious identity, he discusses the tension between Buddhist nationalism and Buddhist religious exclusivism on the one hand and the traditional Buddhist Not-Self teaching on the other. Drawing on the Buddhist critique of the idea of fixed identities, he points out the doctrinal potential for self-critical Buddhist reflection. Alexander Horstmann (Chapter 7) explores the ambivalent role of Buddhism in Myanmar's development towards a democratic and pluralist society. He evaluates the fateful role of ultranationalist Buddhist movements such as 'MaBaTha' and '969', and their interplay with a political agenda that rejects instead of accepts religious and ethnic diversity. He underlines processes of 'othering' in the context of Buddhist protectionism and examines the impact of such protectionism on categories of religion and boundaries of belonging. Yet, his chapter also points towards various initiatives, including Buddhist ones, that deal with diversity in more peaceful and constructive ways.

The contributions in Part 3 problematize the relation between Christian identity and belonging to an ethnic minority in the multi-ethnic and multi-religious society of Myanmar. Marja-Leena Heikkilä-Horn (Chapter 8) provides an overview of Christianity in Myanmar with a particular focus on its Indian roots and the ways in which various forms of Christian identity are negotiated in relation to their ethnic dimension. She emphasizes the difference between the Christian churches among Myanmar's ethnicities and the churches of the Tamil immigrants who assimilated well, while at the same time preserving their identity of belonging to a larger Tamil cosmopolis. Samuel Ngun Ling (Chapter 9) discusses the situation of Christianity in Myanmar from the perspective of the society's various problems and challenges, in particular its religious and ethnic conflicts being in part created by Buddhist nationalism. He pleads for a theology that empowers Christians to participate actively in the development of a democratic society that is genuinely hospitable to diversity. Layang Seng Ja (Chapter 10) exemplifies the problems of Christian minorities through a case study of the Kachin community. With her overview of the conflict since 1948, she depicts the economic, social and political aspect of Burmanization (or, as she prefers to say, Bamanization) that led to Kachin being a region of crisis and recurrent fighting. As a Christian Kachin theologian, she offers her view of an interfaith theology for conflict-solving and better mutual understanding in Myanmar.

The chapters in Part 4 turn to the Muslim communities of Myanmar and the particular challenges that Muslims are facing. Myint Thein (Chapter 11) outlines the different Muslim communities in Myanmar, their history and the massive discrimination to which they are exposed. He describes in detail the numerous problems that confront Muslim communities on a daily basis in relation to their religious practice and identity. In view of the fact that Muslim communities have supported the Myanmar State throughout history, he calls for unification through diversification to achieve peace and national unity. Myo Win (Chapter 12) deals with Myanmar's complicated system of citizenship and citizenship documentation. Drawing on empirical studies from 2016 and 2017, he demonstrates how the issuing of citizenship documentation has developed into an instrument of discrimination particularly, but by no means exclusively, against Muslims living in Myanmar. Given that the loss of citizenship means being deprived of common rights and social services, he underlines the urgency of a serious reform of the current practice and discusses means of how ethnic and religious minorities may better cope with the situation. Madlen Krueger's (Chapter 13) case study of ethnicity and religion in Mon State deals with the intersection of different ethnic and religious identities. She analyses how the construction of a Buddhist Mon identity, in distinction from Buddhist Bamar, impacts on the perception of the Muslim community and the Buddhist-Muslim tensions.

Each of the four parts combines chapters that give a more comprehensive overview with others that provide particular case studies. Given the complexity of the entanglement of religious and ethnic diverse identities in Myanmar within the changing political context, the volume inevitably remains sketchy. In such a situation, the combination of papers by competent outsiders and informed insiders provides a fuller picture and better understanding of what is going on in Myanmar and points out perspectives that each of the groups involved have on finding more suitable ways of coming to terms with or even benefitting from the nation's diverse nature.

Though all chapters in the main parts of this volume had been completed before the coup d'état of February 2021, they elucidate the broader context of the coup. In the postscripts, Mikael Gravers analyses the military coup, its immediate background and its consequences as of March 2021. Hans-Peter Grosshans offers a conclusion to the volume from the perspective of coexistence and constitutional frameworks in contemporary multi-ethnic and multi-religious contexts. He broadens the view by looking beyond Myanmar and highlights the role of religion within the often tense relation between social cohesion, collective identities and vital group interests.

Initial drafts of the contributions were jointly discussed by all contributors at an academic consultation in Yangon in February 2019, which was part of a larger research project on religious diversity in Myanmar sponsored by the German Research Foundation (DFG) and led by Hans-Peter Grosshans and Perry Schmidt-Leukel, both from the University of Münster, in cooperation with Samuel Ngun Ling from Myanmar Institute of Theology (MIT). The fieldwork for this five-year project was carried out by Madlen Krueger, who also designed and organized the 2019 meeting. We are grateful to David West for his assistance with linguistic copy-editing, to the anonymous reviewers who recommended the book for publication with Bloomsbury Academics and (not least) to Lalle Pursglove, Lily McMahon and their team for their support and commitment throughout a highly professional publication process.

On 2 May 2021, the pandemic tsunami that swept over India claimed the life of our contributor, Professor Nehginpao Kipgen. Editors and authors dedicate the volume to the memory of this highly esteemed scholar and political analyst.

References

Aung San Suu Kyi (1991), *Freedom from Fear and Other Writings*, ed. Michael Aris, London: Penguin Books.

Galtung, Johan (1997–8), 'Religions, Hard and Soft', *Cross Currents*, 47 (4): 437–50.

Holt, John Clifford (2019), *Myanmar's Buddhist-Muslim Crisis. Rohingya, Arakanese, and Burmese Narratives of Siege and Fear*, Honolulu: University of Hawai'i Press.

Part 1
Politics and Identities

1

The making of a fixed national hierarchy of ethnicity and religion in Myanmar

Mikael Gravers

Introduction

Three important dimensions characterize the current political situation in Myanmar: (1) nationalism, (2) categorization of ethnic differences and (3) categorization of religious differences – all three generated in a long historical and political process. These three dimensions often amalgamate in the political rhetoric and in administrative practices. They are also dimensions of conflicts and violence since 1949. The aim of this chapter is to explain *the historical process of ethnic identification* and how the three dimensions determine citizenship for those who are excluded, particularly Hindus and Muslims. This is illustrated by examples from the Karen State. However, it is important to underline that conflicts and violence labelled 'ethnic' and 'religious' are fundamentally political. They do not originate from Myanmar's ethnic and religious diversity but from identity politics during and after colonial rule. Colonial administration created a major cleavage between 'native races' and 'Indian races' in censuses since 1891.[1]

Many have criticized the reproduction of reified ethnicity during colonial rule in analyses of present-day ethnic diversity, as for example Taylor (2004), which is a relevant critique. However, the present ethnic hierarchy and reification of ethnicity are not merely a colonial heritage but embedded in the current strong Burman nationalism, which has further ingrained this categorization into the present social order as discussed below. Nor is reification of ethnic categories merely an anthropological 'invention', although anthropologists were used by British colonial rule.[2] Ethnic categorization became part of the process of making ethno-political boundaries and were internalized by the different ethnic groups. In this chapter, it is argued that the role of nationalism is crucial in this process. The aim of nationalism is to defend a *reified primordial essence* of the national identity often involving not only ethnic identity but also religion. Thus, the analysis has to consider this crucial function in order to understand reification of identities.

Ethnic difference is a political criterion as seen in the official rhetoric in today's Myanmar discourse on ethnicity and peace and in the debate on the term 'Rohingya', a term rejected as ethnonym by the government. Moreover, ethnic armed organizations insist that ethnic groups are termed 'ethnic nationalities' – and not 'ethnic minorities' – signifying that they can claim a state function in a future federation. Still, the core of an ethnic nationality is an imagined common ethnic cultural identity and includes political unity.

This function of ethnicity can be illustrated by the author's personal experience from a conference in Chiang Mai (Thailand) in 2004 on a future federal constitution in Myanmar for the opposition to the military rule.[3] Representatives from all the ethnic armed organizations were invited, and I suggested they should look beyond ethnicity and singular ethnic issues and claims and instead into common democratic principles and common laws in order to argue for a federal constitution – that is, placing democratic principles and social rights before ethnic claims. The naïve anthropologist was kindly instructed about his failure to grasp the importance of ethnicity: 'How can we return to our ethnic constituencies and tell them that ethnicity does not matter?' This shows how ingrained the notion of ethnicity is in the historical and political process. It has become *reified as a political substance*, and this is difficult to contradict after sixty to seventy years of armed struggle. Thus, an anthropological critique of reification easily fails to grasp the situation. As Martin Smith writes with reference to Edmund Leach's study of Kachin, 'ethnic identities should not be considered primordial or innate' (Smith 2018: 28). Leach (1964: 281) wrote that it was futile to record the stereotyped variations because they were almost numberless. This anthropological 'truth' of primordial stereotypes, however, is often surpassed by identity politics.

Critics of reified identities often forget that modern ethnicity and religion have become attributes like *natural and essential properties* of social existence, which have to be defended. This happens in a political process of boundary making. Ethnic stereotypes often become important political means – with references to culture, language, custom, dress, myths, rituals – all the *givens* that can be imagined, endangered and lost. In order to understand why ethnic markers appear as primordial and endangered, I argue that the present ethnic diversity has been absorbed in ethno-nationalism and a hierarchy during a historical process of ethnic categorization. It affects the rights of groups and persons who cannot obtain full citizenship.

Theoretical concepts

'Ethnicity' is an imaginary of the world consisting of diverse ethnic cultures and identities, which are divided by imagined boundaries. Thus, it is not about cultural entities but the differences between cultures that matter, according to Barth (1969) and Jenkins (2008). Ethnic groups need not be homogeneous although conceived as such, and they may live dispersed and mixed as in Myanmar. Thus, ethnicity is not a substance of a group but formed in a complex process of boundary-making that entails fission and fusion, inclusion and exclusion in which we attribute specific cultural and political characteristic to others as a group as well as to its individual members. In other words, instead of studying identity as a cultural substance, we must study the *process of ethnic identification* – both the premises for self-identification and for categorizations made by others (Jenkins 2008). As Roger Brubaker (2004: 41) writes, this invites us to specify the agents that do the identification. Moreover, the process of identification changes direction and elements during different social and political conjunctures.

The process of political categorization of ethnic and religious differences appears as an important global tendency in the twenty-first century and is related to the growing nationalism and populism. Immigration – past and present – and major demographic changes have often fuelled nationalist sentiments and resulted in political violence (see Tambiah 1996, 1997). Immigration often sharpens the laws of citizenship – as in the EU and in Denmark in recent years. In this context, states increasingly apply fixed bureaucratic categorization of people according to ethnicity and nationality, as in Myanmar's official definition of eight 'national races' and '135 indigenous groups' (*taing-yin-tha*). Public categorization is important because it legitimizes identification by state authorities and thus becomes a powerful mechanism. Individuals often internalize such categorization in coping with discrimination and domination (Jenkins 2008). Moreover, state categorization often entails a subjugation, as we shall see in the following.

The imaginary of a nation often contains the same mechanisms as ethnicity. However, nation also refers to a sovereign territory.[4] It includes the primordial facts of people who not only share culture, myths, language and religion but also appear like kindred and blood related. These elements combined with relations to territory, a 'sacred' land, constitute crucial primordial attachment.[5] Sometimes racial logic enters as a dimension arguing that blood and race have to be protected. Moreover, historical memory of a common past, sometimes heroic, is a crucial ingredient. The same communitarian ideology is used in the process of ethnic boundary making. As we shall see, nationalism and ethno-nationalism become instrumental in naming potential enemies and those not belonging to a nation and those who deserve a citizenship. Citizenship is not a general obtainable social right but decided by a national system of ethnic categorization. Administrative practices are marred by a mechanism of exclusion and a 'preventive repression' of claiming citizenship according to Balibar (2015: 66), discussed at the end of this chapter. However, we must maintain that ethnicity and nationalism are not a 'natural' human mode of distinction but a political mode of defining unity, differences and boundaries. A major difference in the way ethnicity and nationalism are perceived now as compared to the past is not only that they attribute a specific substance to persons but also that ethnic categorization is sometimes directly used to specify legitimate rights in relation to a state.

While ethnic categorization is used to generalize all members of a group, ethnic conflicts are rarely seen involving entire ethnic groups. Many remain 'quiet' and avoid involvement in the violent struggle, as Thawnghmung (2013) has demonstrated in her analysis of Karen who avoided the long civil war between Karen National Union and the Burmese army. Still, 'ethnic' conflicts involve ethnic armed organizations, who claim to represent the entire group in negotiation of a future state formation as in Myanmar.

Ethnicity and nationalism in Myanmar's history

In this section, I briefly outline seven significant political conjunctures, which have had an impact upon the process of ethnic and religious identification up to the present:

- colonization,
- Christian conversion,
- Indian immigration and anti-Indian riots 1938,
- divide-and-rule administration and racial categorization,
- the Panglong conference 1947 and independence,

- 1982 Citizenship Law and Ne Win's rhetoric, and
- the Rohingya crisis since 1978.

The Burmese monarchy depended on hereditary local leaders and administrators and never had direct control of the hill populations. The kingdom was a galactic polity in which the royal centre depended on tributary alliances, and ethnic identity did not matter as long as tribute was paid and loyalty persisted. In 1740, Mon and Karen rebelled against exorbitant taxes and re-established a kingdom in Bago (Pegu). In 1757, Burman King Alaunghpaya conquered the Mon kingdom, and his conquest sent thousands of Mon and Karen into Thailand as refugees. Although it was not an 'ethnic' or 'racial' war as such since some Mon were loyal to the Burman king, ethnic differences were involved. Mon language and culture came under pressure (Adas 1974: 19). Today, Mon and Karen perceive the conquest in ethnic terms. The Pwo Karen, among whom I have worked in Thailand, have narratives about having to flee when Burmese armies came through the present Karen State and how they allied with the Siamese king who gave them permission to settle in the western mountains. Those Pwo Karen in Thailand, whose ancestors fled from the Burman, still mistrust 'Bamar who have a crooked heart' as do some elder Karen in Myanmar. Burman kings regarded the Mon and Karen as rebels and not as loyal tributary allied. Nevertheless, if ethnicity was not the reason for the conquest, Alaunghpaya mobilized Burman people in upper Burma against Mon and their Karen allies. It seems as if a Burman ethnic identity evolved during the Kònbaung dynasty (1752–1886), Burma's last dynasty, and that a process of Burmanization began according to Thant Myint-U (2001: 88–92; see also Lieberman 1986: 209). Tributes were not higher for Karen because of their ethnicity but because they did not have stable patron–client relations. The main source of ethnic reification, however, was colonial administration in its divide-and-rule policy.

Colonialism focused on ethnicity in its administration and introduced nationalism. Christian missionaries in Burma relied on colonial protection and mostly converted ethnic minorities, such as Karen, Chin and Kachin. In 1881, missionaries assisted in forming the Karen National Association in order to unite 'all Karen clans' in one national unit. However, one consequence of conversion was that the Burman kings perceived the change of faith as a total conversion of Karen identity to become British or *Kalar*, 'foreigners', as exemplified in the following complaint by a Burmese official to a missionary in 1839: 'This is the way you do to get away the hearts of my subjects, is it? You came and fight us, and get away part of our country, and now you wish to turn away the hearts of the poor, ignorant Karens' (Baptist Missionary Magazine 1839: 105). The result was that 'in the opinion of the Burmese, they had embraced the religion of the Kalas [Kalar] and had become bonâfide strangers, having lost their nationality' (Bishop Bigandet 1887: 4). In my opinion, the reasoning in this citation is crucial for our understanding of ethnic, religious and national identification up to the present time. Thus, to be a Buddhist was to be loyal to the monarchy as the primary political identification. Some Karen assisted the British conquest in 1852. Likewise, missionaries and Christian Karen actively participated in what the British called *the pacification* of Burma against rebels, including monks, from 1886.[6] I suggest this signifies that ethno-religiousboundaries of identification began to imply violence.[7]

Immigration from British India is another important factor in relation to ethnic identification. After 1870, British census shows an increased immigration of labourers to work in the harbour of Yangon and on railways, as well as an increase in the unpopular moneylenders of the Chettiar caste who came to control large agricultural areas in the Delta (Taylor 1987: 142). The latter were one of the reasons for the widespread rebellion in 1930 when former monk, Saya San, mobilized angry Burman peasants. Harvey (1974: 55) writes that Chettiars were depicted as the 'public enemy no. 1' in Burma, and much of the violence was directed against this group. The Burma Census from 1931 (pp. 224–32) registered an increase of Indian immigrants since 1921 of 17 per cent in Arakan but 33.1 per cent in the Delta – and of more than one million migrants of whom only 28 per cent were women. Thus, male Indian migrants often looked for Burman wives. The descendants of 'mixed race' marriages were called Zerbadis (pp. 122, 705 in the 1931 Census) – a term resented by Muslims.[8] These migrants were described as 'Indian races' comprising Chittagonians, Bengalis, Cholas, Hindustanis and Tamils, while local Muslims were categorized as 'Arakan Mohammedans'. Interestingly, 565,609 of the immigrants were Hindus and 396,594 Muslims during this period.[9]

In the 1930s, Indian migrants constituted about 5.4 per cent of the total population (Taylor 1987:126). While many migrants returned to India, others settled permanently. In Karen State, Tamil Hindu and Bengali traders and farmers have integrated in Karen communities along the Thanlwin River since the 1890s. Today many Karen Muslims only speak Pwo Karen. However, in Rangoon over half of the population (63 per cent) around 1930 were Indian immigrants (ibid.: 127; Yegar 1972: 31). The Burman majority perceived them as taking their jobs. In the 1930s, anti-Indian riots occurred as part of the Burman nationalists struggle against colonialism, for example, strikes in the oil district of Yanyaungung (see Yi 1938). The Thakin ('Master') nationalists shouted slogans such as this: 'Revenge for all sacrileges to religion. Master race we are, we Burmans' (Yi 1938: 58).

In 1938, a book published by a Muslim, said to contain critical comments on Buddhism, was reprinted, and the All Burma Council of Young Monks mobilized 1,500 monks and thousands of lay people in Rangoon to stage a protest. The riots left 181 dead, of these 139 Muslims (see Smith 1965: 110–11).[10] During the 1930s, riots began as anti-Indian and had underlying economic grievances. As Harvey (1974: 69) admitted, 'there were one million Indians in Burma. They constituted an acute problem, and it was our doing. There had always been Indians, but never in such numbers until we introduced them.' Then religion also became a nationalist issue, and Muslims were named as 'the enemies of Buddhism' while monks became increasingly aggressive (Mendelson 1975: 211–13). In 1939, after a public focus on mixed marriages, the British issued the Buddhist Women Special Marriage and Succession Act in order to secure Buddhist women married to Muslims inheritance and right to their children in case of divorce or death (Yi 1988: 96; Berlie 2008: 23).[11] These events seem almost parallel the situation in 2012–15 when the 'four race protection laws' were promoted by monks and adopted in order to protect Buddhist women against polygamy. However, the basic issue in the 1930s was immigration from British India.[12]

It is important to note that this historical conjuncture in itself *does not explain* the current anti-Muslim and anti-Hindu feelings and discrimination. However, these feelings of resentment were formed at that time and have been ingrained and sustained within Burman nationalism. They were evoked during U Ne Win's and the ensuing military rule; hence these events can be considered as the foundation of current identity politics. The identity of the migrants became reified as 'foreigners' and 'enemies' but first a brief outline of the colonial categorization.

British administration – divide and rule by racial categorization

British colonial administration adopted the anthropological categorization used by British evolutionary anthropologists, such as James Frazer and Edward Tylor. The Ethnographic Survey of Burma applied the questionnaire from the book *Notes & Queries on Anthropology* (1874) widely used by anthropologists in revised editions until the 1960s. Besides 'racial names', the questionnaire of 402 items began with questions based on biological criteria such as physical appearances and temperaments of races, as well as their moral habits, kinship, customs and so on (see details in Boshier 2018: 300–25). Ethnographic race research and categorization was also used by the army to recruit soldiers from the hills, for example, from Kachin, one of the 'martial races', many of whom served in the Middle East during the First World War (see Sadan 2010: 48).[13] Following the ethnographic surveys, colonial governance came to focus on collective ethnic identities and on customary laws mentioned above as much as on common law.[14] This is an important turn in the process of reification.

British census made a crucial distinction between 'Indian Races' and 'Indigenous Burmese races – Buddhists and others'. The term 'tribe' was used to designate the hill minorities who were considered less developed. From 1922, the colonial government divided the territorial administration in Ministerial Burma (lowlands) and Frontier Areas (hills). The Frontier Areas Administration (FAA) included Chin Hills, Naga, Kachin, Shan States, Kayah (defined as independent 'native states') and Salween District. The FAA was a restricted area for Burmans and directly under the governor's control. FAA's administrator in 1945 was the anthropologist Noel Stevenson who had studied the Chin. He organized a large federation from village tract councils to a federal council for the whole FAA and prepared the Panglong conference in 1947. Churchill's war cabinet had prepared to keep this area as a dominion in case of Burma's independence. Thus, Aung San did not trust Stevenson and his activities. He forced the new Attlee government to retire Stevenson in January 1947 before Panglong convened.

Before independence, the British Burma Army was organized in ethnic battalions of Chin, Karen and Kachin, mostly Christians, and included only a few *Bamar* soldiers. Moreover, Burma's discussions of independence were embedded in a discourse of race/ethnic categories and ideas of ethnic autonomy. Meanwhile, Aung San and the Burman nationalists worked for the unity of the country and its ethnic diversity, while Shan, Kachin, Kayah, Karen and other groups looked for independence or self-rule and opted for the Frontier Areas to be confederated with Ministerial Burma with the right to secession. However, the Panglong conference was for the delegates from the FAA area – not from Ministerial Burma. The Karen from Salween District did not arrive, and only four Karen observers from the newly formed Karen National Union (KNU) arrived on the last day without giving their opinion. A major part of the Karen population lived outside the FAA and were not directly involved in the Panglong discussions. Most delegates seem to have been Shan *saopha* (princes) and Kachin *duwa* (chiefs) from Stevenson's administrative system – as well as a few Chin. Pa-o, Naga, Lahu, Wa and other minorities did not have delegates. The complex situation cannot be described in detail here, but it is important to note that the only paragraph in the Panglong Agreement which deals with the main issue is §6 stating that 'full autonomy in internal administration of the Frontier Areas is accepted in principle'. Although most delegates came from Stevenson's administrative system, they had different opinions on independence either as a dominion or within a Burma confederation. As for the Karen, the Christian dominated KNU wanted an independent state, while the Burma Karen National Association (Buddhist) and the Karen Youth Organization, affiliated with Aung San's political alliance the Anti-Fascist Peoples Freedom League, looked for a state within a united Burma. The British were puzzled by this diversity of political opinions and what they perceived as lack of leadership of Karen. The reason for this perception was the colonial perception of race/ethnicity as constituted of a homogeneous culture, a common leadership and the same political aims.[15] In 1931, the colonial category 'Karen' comprised fifteen different Karennic speaking groups (today twelve groups are listed), which were further divided in subgroups, sometimes united but often divided politically. Today only Sgaw and Pwo are categorized as Karen, but they are two different groups with different languages. However, the KNU used the reified colonial category 'Karen' in one of the memorials their delegation presented in London 1946 and emphasized, 'It is a dream that Karen and Burman can ever evolve a common nationality ... We are a nation with our own distinctive culture.'[16] Thus, ethnicity and ethno-nationalism became dominant features of independent Burma.

The colonial rulers never understood that their own ethnic categorization had divided Burma: 'There is a division of labour along racial lines – they mix but they never combine', as John S. Furnivall wrote (1956: 304). KNU's and Kachin's rebellions and fear of Shan and Kayah's rights to secession after ten years, which were outlined in the constitution of 1947, were the main reasons for General Ne Win's military coup in 1962. It was a conjuncture dominated by fear of disintegration of the union state and of an endangered national identity. Interestingly, during the census in 2014, Karen organizations opposed the use of the Burmese word 'Kayin'. Its connotation of 'wild people' is resented. They asked to be termed 'Karen' – the English translation of Kayin – thus emphasizing the pan-Karen identity above subgroups.

General Ne Win and the Citizenship Law from 1982

'There had always existed a traditional Burmese nationalism arising from Burma's cultural homogeneity', according to Aung San Suu Kyi (1991: 103). She adds that Buddhism obviously played a large part in creating this homogeneity (ibid.: 103) – or perhaps more correctly played a role in creating an imaginary of homogeneity. This *primordial heritage* is crucial in understanding why Burmese citizenship laws strive to include all ethnic groups in one hierarchical system of national identification.

The constitution from 1947 stated, 'There shall be *only one citizenship* throughout the Union.' This included those born in British India who had been in Burma before 1948.[17] Yet the heritage of colonial ethnic categorization and Burman (Bamar) ethnic nationalism was inscribed into later constitutions and the citizenships laws. The law from 1982, introduced under Ne Win's rule, mentions the eight main 'national races' (Bamar, Shan, Kayah, Kachin, Karen, Mon, Chin and Rakhine) and 135 eligible ethnic subgroups who have been living in the territory of Burma before 1823, the start of colonial rule.[18] Citizenship was now divided into three categories. Besides full citizenship, there were two other categories: (1) associate citizenship (the Burmese words means 'guest' citizenship) for those who had citizenship in 1948 and had to make an affirmation of allegiance to the state and (2) naturalized citizenship for those who had been residing in Burma before independence but who had not yet registered (see details in Lall and South 2018: 244–55). Most Muslims and Hindus seem to have had the naturalized citizenship card.

General Ne Win's main concern was about ethnic disunity and the ethnic armed organizations' struggle for independence. The 1980s was the time of the army's 'four cuts' strategy to curb insurgency. Ne Win's views are reflected in his speeches as in the following citation from 1979:

> Today you can see that even people of *pure blood* are being disloyal to the race and country but are being loyal to others. If people of pure blood act this way, we must carefully watch people of *mixed blood*. Some people are of pure blood, pure Burmese heritage and descendants of genuine citizens. Karen, Kachin and so forth, are of genuine pure blood. But we must consider whether these people are completely for our race, our Burmese people: and our country, our Burma. (Quoted in Smith [1991] 1999: 37, my emphasis)

During military rule, especially after the uprising in 1988, the political focus was on national unity and defence of national sovereignty, as in General Than Shwe's speech on Independence Day 1997: 'A race will not safeguard the sovereignty if it lacks patriotic spirit.' He also spoke about safeguarding the cultural heritage, including Buddhism, and the national character (cited in Houtman 1999: 95). Thus, race, ethnicity and nationality merged in a fixed order of categories.[19] It seems as if mixed races are not seen as patriotic in this discourse.

The race rhetoric of *thway-naw* ('pure blood') and *amyo kabia* ('mixed races') connected to 'loyalty' derives from primordial nationalism. Mixed blood implies something impure – not Burman and not reliable. According to Wade (2017: 205), mixed blood is 'bad blood' and persons are considered 'aggressive' – a term often used by monks interviewed by me. This is a typical repetition of allegedly fixed racial substance hierarchically graded by a scale of primordial values. The race rhetoric reminds us of George Orwell's description in *Burmese Days* of colonial race logic as when Flory was asked if Eurasian – in this case, two persons who are half Indian/British and half Karen/British – can join the local British club. His reply was, 'God gracious, no. They are complete outcasts' (Orwell 1977: 117). Thus, the military rule continued the colonial practice of including biological criteria to define ethnicity, whereas modern social anthropological classification avoids such criteria.

Then in 1990, a list of 135 *taing-yin-tha* – 'original people' referring to those ethnic groups who had settled in Burma prior to 1823 – appeared in the newspaper *Workers Daily* as an official list related to the Citizenship Law, but of uncertain origin and flawed (Cheesman 2017: 8; Lall and South 2018: 6).[20] Significantly, four races were listed as 'foreign': Chinese, Muslims and Hindus (both of Indian origin), Europeans, and Americans. This categorization meant that only those among these 'four races', who had obtained full citizenship before, could hope to maintain it. Those with associate or naturalized citizenship, whose descendants were supposed to qualify for full citizenship in the future, would begin to encounter problems, as we shall see below. The official categorization turned out to be a powerful instrument for the post 1988 military regime – and still functions as a fixed hierarchy.

This kind of ethnic/racial categorization means that every individual belonging to a category is ascribed a specific ethnic essence of identity, with no room for exceptions or personal choice when it is inscribed on their identity cards. Ethnicity/race, mixed race and religion is entered on all cards by the authorities, forming the basis for the ongoing bureaucratic discrimination. Many individuals in Myanmar are of mixed ethnic origin. I have met people who were Karen/Bamar or Mon/Bamar who complained that they were not allowed to choose their primary identity. Self-ascribed identity is not permitted.

Bureaucrats decide their identification. The bureaucratic system continues as an important instrument in identity politics during the current conjuncture of 'transition' to democracy.

The 'Rohingya crisis' since 1978

While military rule continued the colonial hierarchy, it excluded those groups which they regarded as unwanted migrants from colonial times, that is, the non-original native ethnic groups.[21] Immigration in the 1920s and the 1930s from Chittagong had created ethnic and religious tensions in Rakhine (Arakan) in the 1940s during the Japanese occupation, resulting in serious riots between Buddhists and Muslims. A small Mujahid rebel organization began to operate after the Second World War. After 1948, the army gradually took control of the administration of northern Rakhine establishing special Burman villages.[22] In 1978, the Burmese authorities, military and police began an identification campaign in order to track down illegal immigration and forged identity papers. The campaign resulted in two hundred thousand Muslims from Rakhine State fleeing to Bangladesh. Most of these returned, and, according to Tonkin (2018: 233), at that time 65 per cent of them had National Registration Cards, which were subsequently replaced or just withdrawn.[23] A similar identification exercise was repeated in 1990–1 sending another three hundred thousand people into Bangladesh.[24] The Rakhine State is one of the poorest in Myanmar with a long time mistrust of the central government among all groups, as well as mutual mistrust between Buddhists and Muslims (Leider 2018; Yegar 1972). If we use the term 'communal violence' – a term commonly used by the colonial rule – we must add that police and military have generally supported the Buddhist side. The communal aspect is determined both by state politics and by the global fear of Islamic terrorism in the current situation.

After the renewed violence in 2012 in Rakhine and the attacks in 2016–17 by the Arakan Rohingya Salvation Army, authorities began to define the Rohingya as Bengali, and the term Rohingya was banned from public statements as an illegally self-ascribed ethnonym. Former president U Thein Sein said they were Bengalis invited by the British colonialists prior to independence (Tonkin 2108). However, the military government issued the 'White Card' (temporary registration of foreigners) to Muslims before the elections in 2015 – presumably in order to solicit votes for the Union Solidarity and Development Party (USDP). This was not popular among the majority after the widespread anti-Muslim riots in 2012–13 and following the 'four race laws' campaign by the nationalist monks of the Ma Ba Tha movement.[25] The white cards were annulled before the elections and became illegal to possess. During interviews at that time, I learned from Burmese contacts the term 'yesterday Rohingya' – that is, recent illegal immigrants who adopted the ethnonym in order to appear as a *taing-yin-tha* ('original people') and get a legal status. Despite the fact that Muslims constitute only about 5–6 per cent of the total population, and even less in the Myanmar Census, there is a widespread imaginary of a major long time illegal invasion. This is often related to the widespread perception that authorities in Rhakine have been bribed by illegal immigrants. During an interview in 2017 with the leading and highly respected monk and Ma Ba Tha Chair, U Tiloka Bhiwuntha (the Ywama Saydaw, Insein), he explained that there is an *invasion* of Muslims in Rakhine:

> The Bengalis displace the host – they are guests in Myanmar and do not respect Buddhist moral precepts (*sila*) and the fundamental truth of Buddhism (*byama so tayà*). They are aggressive and force women to convert, bribe authorities, do not respect our flag and say in prayers they will destroy other religions.

Thus, he continued, Burman have to defend and protect their race and national identity – otherwise they will become a minority and Buddhism will decline. However, he did not condone violence – 'those who use violence are not Buddhists or do not understand Buddhism – we must use dhamma against attacks on Buddhism'. This imaginary of immigrants as 'immoral and aggressive guests' is a dominant argument both for state security and for lay Buddhist's defence of race, nationality and religion. It is widely shared not only by Burman but also among Buddhists from other ethnic groups as well.[26]

While Muslims are discriminated and demonized by some monks, the international critical view on anti-Muslim Buddhism as militant – as in Beech (2019) in *New York Times* –tends to forget the important charity (*parahita*) work of numerous socially engaged monks. They often advise lay people caught in disputes and conflicts who want to avoid authorities and big bribes. They organize dhamma schools and aim at promoting and protecting Buddhism. Some monks in the Karen State found that Ma Ba Tha was 'not necessary'. However, direct critique of Ma Ba Tha is avoided as it could end in an indictment under Article 295a in the penal code for 'insulting a person's religion.

For many people in Myanmar, the fear that Buddhism is in danger is a genuine existential concern connected to a long historical process and to Burman nationalism. Researchers will have to take that seriously. Many in Myanmar may agree that the army acted brutally in 2017, but they consider the Rohingya, other Muslims and Hindus to be foreign, a leftover from colonialism and a danger to Myanmar and to national identity. The current xenophobia is not merely based on the residual resentment against Muslims from the 1930s – it is enforced by the globally shared fear of migration and fear of Islam-related terror. In this context, religion and primordial values are taken as normative in judging other religions and, at times, legitimize not only the use of force but also bureaucratic discrimination and public resentment.

The term *Kalar* is still applied to categorize people deriving from India.[27] Since 1982, it has become increasingly difficult for Hindus and Muslims to renew their identity cards – or even to obtain a nationality verification card, which does not provide citizenship rights but is necessary for travel, loans and contact to authorities. As shown below, there is a collusion of the bureaucratic negative categorization and the common negative ethno-religious classification. The following examples from the author's research in the Karen State in two Muslim and two Hindu communities demonstrate how the Rohingya crisis and the anti-Muslim nationalism have upset the formerly peaceful religious and ethnic coexistence in the Karen State.

Karen Muslims and Hindus

The historical conjunctures briefly outlined above are stages in a long process of ethnic and religious categorization and identification. The exclusion from citizenship of the majority of Hindus and Muslims is a recent development in this process and seems to have the support of a majority of the Buddhist population, as well as of the two main political parties USDP and National League for Democracy (NLD). This has had serious implications for Hindus and Muslims who live integrated in local communities as in the Karen State.

During many interviews, informants among Karen Muslims and Hindus, as well as Buddhist Karen, were convinced that the immigration authorities have an instruction not to reply to applications for a nationality verification card or a renewal of citizenship cards for Muslims and Hindus.[28] In their experience, they never get a reply when they apply even if they had associate or naturalized citizenship before. Informants mentioned that in 2001 they were told that the immigration authorities had stopped issuing identity cards to Muslims. In 2001, there were widespread anti-Muslim riots in Myanmar including the northern Karen State. Hence it might be possible that there was such a general order from the ruling military State Law and Order Restoration Council (see Karen Human Right Group 2002: 5).

In the Karen State, the Karen Muslims, as they identify themselves, are descendants of immigrants from India (Bengal) who married Pwo Karen and settled in Karen villages and towns since 1900 – perhaps before – and became traders and farmers. Hindus in the Karen State, who are also mostly farmers, are of Tamil origin. However, both groups have no idea of where exactly their ancestors came from in India. The Karen Muslims speak Pwo Karen as their main language, and according to their Pwo Karen Buddhist neighbours, the Karen Muslims and Buddhists have lived in relative harmony until the nationalist monks became active.[29] Karen Muslim households engage in the same economic activities and have the same level of income as their Buddhist Pwo Karen neighbours. The two groups have sent donations for each other's festivals and events. They have also worked together in paddy farming, and their houses and households are similar to Buddhist Pwo. Karen Muslims often have more children, but I did not register families with two wives, which was confirmed by the Village Tract Administrator.

The inter village harmony has been disturbed after 2012 when local Ma Ba Tha monks urged Buddhist Karen to put up signs on their houses with four rules:

1. Do not marry Muslims.
2. Muslims are not allowed to own land and houses.
3. Do not buy from Muslims shops.
4. Do not sell to Muslims.

Other larger and red signboards ban *Kalar* from entering some Buddhist villages. Some Christian communities also ban Hindus, Muslims and Chinese traders from settling because they are perceived as controlling all trade. Yet during the crisis in August 2017, Buddhist and Muslim villagers cooperated in vigilance groups following rumours on Facebook of 'a Rohingya infiltration and invasion' – which could be military misinformation. In interviews, Karen Muslims said that they 'did not share the Rohingya's agenda'. Their main concern is to maintain harmony locally and avoid external interference.

I recorded many problems concerning identity papers among Hindus and Muslims. Children generally depend on their father's identification for identity papers. If a man is registered as Karen Buddhist and holds a full citizenship (pink) card, his children can obtain a full citizenship card provided he can pay from two to six lakh Kyat (200,0000–600,000 K = c.140–420$) for a card and has connections who can help at immigration office, although this has become rare. However, if a man had a Karen mother and a Muslim father (i.e. 'mixed race'), he will be registered as a 'Bengala Kayin Islam'. Then he is not likely to obtain a full citizen card. He may receive a turquoise National Verification Card, which allows him to travel and borrow money – but not to work in state institutions. This card was issued in 2016 and states that the holder must apply for citizenship. His children cannot obtain high school examination certificates or enter university. Less than twenty of fifty-seven households in one Muslim village had full citizenship. If a card is lost, it will be almost impossible to get a new one.

The whole process of applying is almost Kafka-like. First, the applicant has to fill in around twenty-six forms, then the applicant must take an oath and swear loyalty to the Union; and Muslim informants said they have to renounce Muslim heritage. They have to pay a secretary, a 'legal supervisor' (court official) and the judge. The person must supply a fingerprint, a blood test, a letter from the village tract administrator (confirming the person's identity from a household list), letters from police and school, as well as their parents' identity papers. Finally, they will have to hire a broker in order to get the paperwork done and file the application before meeting an official who often acts arrogantly asking, 'Who are you?'. We collected many stories of 'tea-money' or 'big money' (*being thjông pado*, in Pwo Karen) to be paid to officials – often without any result – not even a reply after one to three years. As I understood, cards of associated and naturalized citizenship are not reissued anymore in Karen State. Some Hindus and Muslims had or still have the naturalized citizen card (see the Myanmar Census of 2014 on Hpa-an). Immigration officers have been in the villages to register young persons before examinations or for the important household list. Some villagers were in Thailand or not at home – one even forgot to mention her child's name. Persons who are not listed cannot obtain any identity paper and have to stay in the village, almost being a non-person. It was said to be impossible to get an adult's name on the list. However, for Muslims and Hindus it seems to be almost impossible now to obtain any form of ID card even when 'big money' is offered,[30] whereas their fellow Buddhist villagers get their cards and pay less. When Hindus and Karen Muslims enter the immigration office, officials often address them as *Kalar*, despite the fact that Muslims and Hindus resent this classification. This bureaucratic discrimination feels like a stigmatization of people who have lived and worked in Myanmar like everyone else and who have not been involved in illegal activities.

Hindu temples are registered as Buddhist shrines because they include a Buddha statue in line with Hindu gods.[31] However, they still have to apply for permission to do minor repairs of temples often in a long bureaucratic process. Muslims, however, cannot get permission to construct or repair mosques now. They often use Koran schools for prayers, which can provoke protests and interventions from Buddhist monks. Muslim and Hindu funeral places have been expropriated and temple land confiscated from the main Hindu temple in Hpa-an by the army. Both groups need permission for religious festivals or they will face prosecution. Thus, religious freedom is clearly limited although a constitutional right.

Muslims and Hindus often try to pay their way out of traffic accidents or other encounters with authorities.[32] This may confirm the widespread impression that they are wealthy and have power. In Muslim villages, many youngsters leave school and enter a Koran school – because they will never be able to obtain a high school certificate or enter university. Thus, Koran schools and Islam becomes the core of self-identification. Some young men have been studying at an Indian madrasa and returned to become teachers (*mullawi*). This could pave the way for more conservative religious rules and even radical Islamist influences – which again will confirm that they are 'enemy no. one, who want to take global control in the 21st century', as a prominent Ma Ba Tha monk in Hpa-an told me during an interview in 2017. Thus, the identification process tends to reinforce the colonial racial categorization where 'temperament' was registered – for example, when U Tiloka emphasized that Muslims were 'aggressive' or another Ma Ba Tha monk who explained that Muslims of 'mixed race' are 'impolite and bad'. While both groups, Hindus and Muslims, are now in the *Kalar* category of foreign races and suffer from the same discrimination, Muslims are the target of the most hateful rhetoric.[33] Even monks who are not Ma Ba Tha in Karen State supported what they consider as preventive actions against Muslim dominance.

The Myanmar constitution of 2008 provides fundamental rights of equality, liberty and justice for every citizen (The Constitution 2008, chapter 1, §21), and every citizen is 'equally entitled to freedom of conscience and freely to profess and practice religion' (ibid.: §34). Furthermore, §364 states that religion must not be abused for political purposes. It is evident that these constitutional provisions on rights and religion are contradicted in the 1982 Citizenship Law and in the current administrative practices based on the fixed hierarchy of ethnic/racial groups. As demonstrated in the examples above, Muslims and Hindus are excluded from these fundamental social rights, and they are excluded from voting. Most Rohingyia are stateless, and by denial of citizenship cards, Myanmar's others Muslims and Hindus are increasingly prevented from pleading for justice and claiming their social rights. Balibar (2015: 85) describes this as a function of 'preventative repression', and the state uses what he terms 'preventative counter-violence' in Rakhine. Of course, it is legitimate for a state to fight organizations, such as Arakan Rohingya Salvation Army, which use violence against the state. Thus, Daw Aung San Suu Kyi, during her appearance in the International Criminal Court in The Hague 2019, defended her country's right to use force in such a situation, and although she rejected the use of the term genocide, she did not defend the conduct of the army.[34] In Rakhine, the army's use of force and violence was, and at the time of writing (2020) is still, excessively directed against civilians from all ethnic groups. Karen Muslim and other inhabitants in Karen State feared that a situation similar to the Rohingya crisis might develop in Karen State and had profound worries about their future – expressing a deep ontological insecurity.

Conclusion

As demonstrated above, it is obvious that the use of a fixed ethnic hierarchy is applied to trump the constitutional civil rights for a part of the population. Ethno-religious antagonisms are not 'natural' but generated in a long historical process dominated by anti-colonial nationalism and ethno-nationalism in Burma/Myanmar. It is one of the most troublesome issue in the transition to democracy. Moreover, the combination of religion, primordial values and nationalism has created a situation where religious rules and authority sometimes override rule of law.

The present conjuncture, however, is different from the colonial time, and the current resentment against Muslims and Hindus is not merely a colonial legacy and reproduction of earlier animosities as the military has argued (Nyi Nyi Kyaw 2015: 196). Military rule has exacerbated the ethnic and religious divide and failed to decolonize laws. The present government of NLD promised legal reforms, but so far this has not materialized.

The anti-*Kalar* rhetoric and the negative categorization were revived in 2012–17, the period when the military allowed Aung San Suu Kyi and the NLD to participate in state affairs. In order to sustain its control, the military has enforced identity politics and nationalism including the spiritual power of nationalist monks. This Burman nationalism deliberately transmits fear on the social media. It thrives on the general insecurity during the present circumstances of the difficult transition to democracy. This was further emphasized during the election campaign in 2020. The military and its party, the Union Solidarity Development Party, used nationalism in appealing to voters of a foreign intrusion, loss of national identity and sovereignty. The army chief urged people to vote for candidates who protect Myanmar's race and Buddhism and warned against candidates who are Kalar and of mixed race, although the election commission announced that such statements are against the election law and the constitution.[35]

As demonstrated above, the process of ethnic and religious categorization, which began during colonial rule, has resulted in a virtual official exclusion of Hindus and Muslims. Further, these two groups have internalized the official and public negative classification as *Kalar* and use avoidance, self-subjugation and substantial informal payments in a vain hope to cope. They resent the negative identification as a humiliation, subjugation and unfair exclusion. As Jenkins writes, 'the rejected external definition is internalized, but paradoxically, as the focus of denial' (Jenkins 2008: 75). However, it is important to mention that not all who fear Muslims share the most negative and hateful classification. Rather, they don't dare to oppose influential monks when they use such terms – sometimes out of fear for being categorized as 'traitors' or accused of creating disharmony with criticism.

Religious identity and race have become hegemonic in social identification. Thus, the powerful official state categorization has created a fixed hierarchy of race/ethnic categories within a frame of nationalism and a unitary state. It has enshrined Myanmar's ethnic diversity into a reified and fixed system based on primordial criteria. While the foundation of this hierarchy is rooted in the historical process, I suggest that the system of categorization today is sustained by an imaginary of endangered Burman national Buddhist identity, which further appeals to a popular ontological fear influenced by global trends of islamophobia.[36]

Moreover, the long history of violence is ingrained into present day's nationalist imaginary. This imaginary activates and reinforces the primordial nationalist values as described above. Unfortunately, it is not helpful for the peace process or for Myanmar's international relations. It limits individual rights and aggravates the internal security situation when mistrust and fear dominate. Finally, it impedes the integration, representation and rights of ethnic organizations in a federal constitution as explained in Kyed and Gravers (2018). It is time to decolonize the current legal system and practice, which base rights on race, ethnicity and religion, with common social rights and neutral personal identification.

Notes

1 The chapter is based on research conducted in the Danish-Myanmar research project *Everyday Justice and Security in the Myanmar Transition* (2015–20) financed by the Danish Ministry of Foreign Affairs. Fieldwork was conducted in 2017–18 with anthropologist Anders Baltzer Jørgensen and three excellent and dedicated Karen assistant researchers, Saw Say Wah, Saw Eh Dah and Nang Sapphires Tinilar Win. The author has conducted fieldwork in Karen State since the 2012 ceasefire.
2 Among these were Edmund Leach and Col. James H. Green, who both studied Kachin, and Noel Stevenson, who wrote about the Chin. There were plans of a new anthropological department in Rangoon University in 1947, see OIOC file *M/4/2832 FA Anthropology*. Anthropologists are used today in the Ministries of Border Affairs and Ethnic Affairs.
3 The Danish Burma Committee organized the conference based on my proposal. The Danish Foreign Affairs Ministry funded it. The discussion on federalism at that time appeared in several publication from the ethnic actors (see, e.g., Yawnghwe and Sakhong 2004).
4 A long discussion of nationalism is not possible here. Hutchinson and Anthony Smith's reader from 1994 includes contributions of some of the most important scholars. On colonialism and Nationalism, see Chatterjee's (1993) critique of Benedict Anderson's *Imagined Communities*.
5 Shils (1995: 110) mentions that the major religions still carry primordial values and that nationalism is not only aggressive towards foreigners but towards groups in its own society. Yet, why primordial values are still important is 'an enigma still to be resolved', Shils added (ibid.). I believe globalization and migration reinforce primordial values.
6 'Pacification' is a colonial word for counter-insurgency when the British met fierce resistance from Burman rebels. In colonial rhetoric, rebels were 'dacoits', a Hindi word for armed robber gangs.
7 I have discussed conversion and missionary impact in Gravers (2007, 1999). See these texts for references on Christian involvement. Buddhist Karen organized a major rebellion against the British in 1856–60 described in Gravers (2012).
8 See Burma Census 1931, chapter XI on the different 'Indian races' as distinct from 'native races'. There were Muslim communities in Burma before colonial rule (see Yegar 1972). Today, the term 'Zerbadi' is considered as derogatory.

9 According to Yegar (1972: 30), they worked as coolies in agriculture, in railways, river traffic, post offices, mines, army, police, as servants, among other jobs. However, many returned to India after a few years and others came in. They dominated trade and some became a substantial part of Burma's middle class (see Taylor 1981 and Egreteau 2011: 45).

10 Varying figures of casualties appear in the texts. Khin Yi (1988: 97) writes that 1227 persons died and mentions major destructions because of the riots in July 1938. Arson, killings and looting followed the first riots. Cady (1969: 394) writes that 192 Indians were killed and 878 injured.

11 British colonial law used to recognize customary laws of religious communities. The 1939 Act was made more detailed in 1954, and then Bamar customary law overruled Islamic law. See Crouch (2015) for details on the complexity of customary laws in Burma.

12 The number of Indians decreased due to the Japanese occupation in the 1940s and nationalizations in the 1960s when 200,000 returned to India. Yangon has a population of 400,000–500,000 of Indian origin (see Egreteau 2011: 40 for details). Muslims constitute 4–5 per cent of the population in the 2014 census (see The Republic of the Union of Myanmar 2015). However, the figure is probably wrong, as Rohingya Muslims in Rakhine were not enumerated. The Buddhist Women's Special Marriage Law requires approval of interfaith marriages by the township registrar. The Religious Conversion Law requires approval from a local conversion board. The Monogamy Law makes it criminal to have more than one wife. The Population Control Law empowers authorities to limit the number of children in families. It is not clear if the last law has been applied. The Monogamy law has been used in cases of adultery. In Karen State, township administrators said they did not know of cases of conversion or interfaith marriages. If they happen, they are probably not reported to authorities.

13 Boshier (2018: 220) cites the British Major Enriquez who in 1923 listed the races of military value: Burmese, Kachin, Chin, Shan and Karen. Surveys depended on local colonial officers and did not become systematic.

14 On the complex customary laws in Burma, see Crouch (2015).

15 For details on the Panglong conference, see Myanmar Universities Historical Research Centre (1999: 182–214) and the Panglong file M/4/2811 OIOC, British Library. See Walton (2008) for a critical assessment of the 'spirit of Panglong' and the hyped expectation it created.

16 Karen's political future 1945–7, M/4/3023 OIOC, British Library, see further Gravers (1999: 43). KNU boycotted elections, and the rebellion commenced in January 1949. Some leaders in the KNU believed the British would come and help. On the role of ethnic groups and leaders in the complex negotiation 1945–8, see Tinker (1983–4) and Myanmar Universities Historical Research Centre (1999).

17 See Dr Maung Maung (1961: 259, my emphasis).
18 A list of 135 subgroups was published in a newspaper and is inconsistent, see Cheesman (2017: 9).
19 *Luo myo* is translated as 'race/ethnic group', *amyo* as 'race' and *amyotha* as 'nationality'. *Myo*, 'seed', refers to blood ties, kinship (see Myint-U 2001: 88).
20 The number is probably higher. The list seems to order other groups under the main eight 'national races'. Wa, Lahu and Pa-o are listed under Shan while some names are unknown. However, the criteria used are obscure and seem partly to derive from the British census 1931. The British listed 110 languages. The race logic was maintained in the flawed 2014 census; see Callahan (2017) for a critical assessment.
21 The following is a very brief outline of a complex history, for details see Yegar (1972) Tonkin (2018); Leider (2016 and 2018); and Wade (2017).
22 The Mujahid surrendered in 1961. Later a Rohingya Solidarity Organization was formed but became defunct in 1990. Arakan Rohingya Salvation Army (ARSA) from 2016 seems to be organized by a Rohingya from Pakistan/Saudi Arabia and perhaps with relations to Islamist groups. It is not clear how much support it has inside Myanmar and among refugees in Bangladesh. See the detailed report by Martin Smith (2019) on the history and recent developments in Rakhine State.
23 For the different types of registration and citizenship cards in Myanmar, see the contribution by Myo Win to this volume.
24 In 1992, a magazine related to the military published an article entitled "Dhammantaraya Rohingya" meaning that Rohingya are a threat to Dhamma (doctrine). See Nyi Nyi Kyaw (2015: 194). The term dhammantaraya ('dhamma in danger') was used in the 1960 referring to the communist insurgency.
25 One law is on monogamy; two laws demand official approval of marriages and conversion from different religious leaders. The last one is a law on population control. On the *Association for the Protection of Race & Religion*, Ma Ba Tha, see International Crisis Group 2017 and *The Review of Faith & International Relations*, vol. 13 (4) 2015 (special issue on Ma Ba Tha). The organization includes lay people and has a strong nationalist agenda. Some of its monks and followers are connected to the military/USDP. President U Thein Sein supported Ma Ba Tha. The riots of 2012–13 followed the pattern of politically organized nationalist described by Tambiah (1997): a local provocation, rumours creating fear, followed by mobilization of a mob and violence (see Gravers 2015).
26 During fieldwork in the Karen State, we also heard of common resentment against Muslims among Christian Karen.
27 *Kalar*, derives from *Kula* ('race'/'caste' in Pāli and Hindi) and *Gola* in Mon meaning 'inhabitant of India'. In the Karen State, we were told that Hindus used to be called *Galae*, but the word is not used more. In Pwo Karen, Muslims and Hindus are *Khola Seung* – 'black foreigners'. *Khola Wa* or *Khola Engelai* is a European. The

word *Kalar* in Burmese also has a connotation of 'black' (from Hindi *kala*). A *Kalar Gyi* in Burmese is a 'bogey man'. The term also includes Muslims settled before colonization and is regarded as derogative by Muslims and Hindus.

28 The General Administrative Department (GAD) formerly under the military controlled Home Affairs Ministry is in charge of immigration and security. In 2019, the NLD government moved GAD to a new administrative ministry under the presidential office. However, the minister is still a former officer as are many officials. Time will show if this shift means a change in bureaucratic practices.

29 However, some Karen look upon Muslims as being too smart in business and squeezing Karen out of business, and some also share the common negative views. Ma Ba Tha has support from Buddhist Karen in Hpa-an and Ein Du town. The Democratic Karen Buddhist Army under the monk U Thuzana's patronage evicted Muslims and destroyed houses and mosques (see Karen Human Rights Group 2002: 13; Gravers ([2018] 2020), and Gravers forthcoming). In 1980s and 1990s, many Muslims became refugees in Thailand and some joined the Kawthoolei Muslim Liberation Front affiliated to the KNU.

30 For details on payment to authorities, see Gravers and Jørgensen (2020). 'Tea-money' for a service is not as morally offensive as a demand of 'big money'.

31 Hindus are often members of the state recognized *Hindu Buddhist Missionary Association*. Their religion is ostensible not regarded as a danger to Buddhism. In Karen State, Hindus have an influential monk as mentor.

32 See Harrisson (2018) who provides examples of Muslim subjugation and avoidance of conflict in Mon State. Some even obtained membership cards to the military party Union Solidarity Development Party – claiming that it functions better than other ID cards.

33 The situation in Karen Muslim and Hindu communities is analysed in detail in Gravers and Jørgensen (2020).

34 See Kyaw Hpyo Tha (2019). Aung San Suu Kyi said that violations of human rights would be prosecuted in Myanmar. Time will show.

35 See San Yamin Aung (2020). National League for Democracy is depicted as pro-Western and pro-Muslim. Aung San Suu Kyi is said to insult Buddhism.

36 I have discussed this in Gravers (2015).

References

Adas, Michael (1974), *The Burma Delta*, Madison: University of Wisconsin Press.
Aung San Suu Kyi (1991), *Freedom from Fear and Other Writings*, London: Penguin Books.
Baptist Missionary Magazine (1839), vol. 19. (*Journal of Missionary Abbot*), pp. 101–6.
Balibar, Étienne (2015), *Citizenship*, Cambridge: Polity Press

Barth, Fredrik (1969), *Ethnic Groups and Boundaries. The Social Organization of Culture Difference*, Oslo: Universitetsforlaget.

Beech, Hannah (2019, 'Buddhism Goes to Battle: When Nationalism Overrides Pacifism', *New York Times*, 8 July. https://www.nytimes.com/2019/07/08/world/asia/buddhism-militant-rise.html (accessed: 1 September 2020).

Berlie, Jean (2008), *The Burmanization of Myanmar's Muslims*, Bangkok: Lotus.

Bigandet, Bishop Paul Ambrose (1887), *An Outline of the History of the Catholic Burmese Mission from the Year 1720 to 1887*, Rangoon: Hanthawaddy Press.

British Census of India of 1931, vol. XI, part I, Report. Rangoon: Government Printer and Stationery Office (1932). www.burmalibrary.org/ (accessed: 1 October 2020).

Boshier, Carol Ann (2018), *Mapping Cultural Nationalism. The Scholars of the Burma Research Society, 1910–1935*, Copenhagen: NIAS Press.

Brubaker, Rogers (2004, *Ethnicity without Groups*, Cambridge, MA: Harvard University Press.

Cady, John F. ([1958] 1969), *A History of Modern Burma*, Ithaca: Cornell University Press.

Callahan, Mary P. (2017), 'Distorted, Dangerous Data? Lumyo in the 2014 Myanmar Population and Housing Census', *Sojourn*, 32 (2): 452–78.

Chatterjee, Partha (1993), *The Nation and Its Fragments. Colonial and Postcolonial Histories*, Princeton: Princeton University Press.

Cheesman, Nick (2017), 'How in Myanmar "National Races" Came to Surpass Citizenship and Exclude Rohingya', *Journal of Contemporary Asia*, 42 (2): 1–23. doi:10,1080/00472336.2017.1297476,1–23.

Crouch, Melissa (ed.) (2015), *Islam and the State in Myanmar*, Oxford: Oxford University Press, 183–210.

Egreteau, Renau (2011), 'Burmese Indians in Contemporary Burma: Heritage, Influence, and Perceptions since 1988', *Asian Ethnicity*, 12 (1): 33–54.

Furnivall, John S. (1956), *Colonial Policy and Practice: A Comparative Study of Burma and Netherlands India*, New York: New York University Press.

Gravers, Mikael (1999), *Nationalism as Political Paranoia*, London: Curzon Press.

Gravers, Mikael ([2007] 2010), 'Conversion and Identity: Religion and the Formation of Karen Ethnic Identity in Burma', in *Exploring Ethnic Diversity in Burma*, ed. M. Gravers, 227–58, Copenhagen: NIAS Press.

Gravers, Mikael (2012), 'Waiting for a Righteous Ruler: The Karen Royal Imaginary in Thailand and Burma', *Journal of Southeast Asian Studies*, 43 (2): 340–63.

Gravers, Mikael (2015), 'Anti-Muslim Buddhist Nationalism in Burma and Sri Lanka: Religious Violence and Globalized Imaginaries of Identities', *Contemporary Buddhism*, 16 (1): 1–27.

Gravers, Mikael ([2018] 2020), 'A Saint in Command? Spiritual Protection, Justice and Religious Tensions in the Karen State', *Independent Journal of Burmese Scholarship*, 1 (2): 87–119.https://journalofburmesescholarship.org/issues/v1n2/04Gravers.pdf (accessed: 1 September 2020).

Harrisson Annika P. (2018), 'Everyday Justice for Muslims in Mawlamyine: Subjugation or Skilful Navigation?' *Independent Journal of Burmese Scholarship*, 1 (2): 57–85.

Harvey, G. E. ([1946] 1974), *British Rule in Burma 1824–1942*, London: Faber and Faber.

Houtman, Gustaaf (1999), *Mental Culture in Burmese Politics. Aung San Suu Kyi and the National League for Democracy*, Tokyo: Institute for the Studies of Languages and Cultures of Asia and Africa, Tokyo University.

Hutchinson, John, and Anthony D. Smith (eds) (1994), *Nationalism*. Oxford Readers. Oxford: Oxford University Press.

Jenkins, Richard (2008), *Rethinking Ethnicity. Arguments and Explorations*, London: Sage.

Karen Human Right Group (2002), *Easy Target: The Persecution of Muslims in Burma*. https://khrg.org/2002/05/khrg0202/easy-target-persecution-muslims-burma (accessed: 1 September 2020).

Khin Yi (1988), *The Dobama Movement in Burma (1930–1938)*. South East Asian Program Monograph, Ithaca: Cornell University Press.

Kyaw Phyo Tha (2019), 'Legal Team Defended Myanmar to "Best of Their Ability", Daw Aung San Suu Kyi says', *The Irrawaddy*, 19 December 2019. https://www.irrawaddy.com/news/burma/legal-team-defended-myanmar-best-ability-icj-daw-aung-san-suu-kyi-says.html (accessed: 1 September 2020).

Kyed, Helene M., and M. Gravers (2018) 'Representation and Citizenship in the Future Integration of Ethnic Armed Actors in Myanmar, Burma', in *Citizenship in Myanmar*, ed. M. Lall and A. South, 59–86, Singapore: Chiang Mai University Press and ISEAS.

Lall, Marie and Ashley South, eds. (2018), *Citizenship in Myanmar: Ways of Being in and From Burma*, Singapore Chiang Mai Press and ISEAS.

Leach, Edmund R. ([1948] 1964), *Political Systems of Highland Burma: A Study of Kachin Social Structure*, London: G. Bell & Sons.

Leider, Jacques (2016), 'Competing Identities and Hybridized History of the Rohingyas', in *Metamorphosis. Studies in Social and Political Change in Myanmar*, ed. R. Egreteau and F. Robinne, 151–78, Singapore: NUS Press and IRASEC.

Leider, Jacques (2018), 'Conflict and Mass Violence in Arakan (Rakhine State): The 1942 Events and Political Identity Formation', in *Citizenship in Myanmar. Ways of Being in and from Burma*, ed. A. South and M. Lall, 193–221, Singapore: Chiang Mai University Press and ISEAS.

Lieberman, Victor (1986), *Burmese Administrative Cycles. Anarchy and Conquest c. 1580–1760*, Princeton: Princeton University Press.

Maung, Dr Maung (1961), *Burma's Constitution*, The Hague: Martinus Nijhof.

Mendelson, Michael (1975), *Sangha and the State in Burma. A Study of Monastic Sectarianism and Leadership*, ed. John P. Ferguson, Ithaca: Cornell University Press.

Myanmar Universities Historical Research Centre (1999), *The 1947 Constitution and Nationalities*, vol. 1, Yangon: Inwa Publishing House.

Myint-U, Thant (2001), *The Making of Modern Burma*, Cambridge: Cambridge University Press.

OIOC file *M/4/2832 FA Anthropology* (1946), in the Oriental and India Office Collections, London: British Library.

Nyi Nyi Kyaw (2015), 'Islamophobia in Buddhist Myanmar', in *Islam and the State in Myanmar*, ed. M. Crouch, 183–210, Oxford: Oxford University Press.

Orwell, George ([1934] 1977), *Burmese Days*, London: Penguin Books.

Sadan, Mandy ([2007] 2010), 'Constructing and Contesting the Category "Kachin" in the Colonial and the Post-colonial Burmese State', in *Exploring Ethnic Diversity in Burma*, ed. M. Gravers, 34–76, Copenhagen: NIAS Press.

San Yamin Aung (2020), 'Military and USDP Play the Nationalism Card Ahead of Myanmar's Elections', *The Irrawaddy*, 23 October. https://www.irrawaddy.com/elections/military-usdp-play-nationalism-card-ahead-myanmars-election.html(accessed: 1 February 2021).

Shils, Edward (1995), 'Nation, Nationality, Nationalism and Civil Society', *Nations and Nationalism*, 1 (1) (1995): 93–118.

Smith, Donald Eugene (1965), *Religion and Politics in Burma*, Princeton: Princeton University Press.

Smith, Martin ([1991] 1999), *Burma: Insurgency and the Politics of Ethnicity*, London: Zed Books.

Smith, Martin (2018), 'Ethnic Policy and Citizenship in History', in *Citizenship in Myanmar. Ways of Being in and from Burma*, ed. A. South and Maria Lall, 26–58, Singapore: Chiang Mai University Press and ISEAS.

Smith, Martin (2019), *Arakan (Rakhine State). A Land in Conflict on Myanmar's Western Border*, Amsterdam: Trans National Institute. https://www.tni.org/files/publication-downloads/tni-2020_arakan_web.pdf (accessed: 1 September 2020).

Tambiah, Stanley J. (1996), 'The Nation-State in Crisis and Rise of Nationalism', *The Politics of Difference: Ethnic Premises in a World of Power*, ed. in E. Wilmsen and P. McAllister, 124–43, Chicago: University of Chicago Press.

Tambiah, Stanley J. (1997), *Levelling Crowds: Ethnonationalist Conflicts and Collective Violence in South Asia*, Berkeley: University of California Press.

Taylor, Robert H. (1981), 'Party, Class, and Power in British Burma', *The Journal of Commonwealth & Comparative Politics*, 19: 44–61.

Taylor, Robert H. (1987), *The State in Burma*, London: Hurst.

Taylor Robert H. (2004), 'Do States Make Nations? The Politics of Identity in Myanmar Revisited', *South East Asian Research*, 13 (3): 261–86.

Thawnghmung, Ardeth M. (2013), *The 'Other' Karen in Myanmar. Ethnic Minorities and the Struggle without Arms*, Lanham, MD: Lexington Books.

The Constitution of the Republic of the Union of Myanmar (2008), Naypyidaw Ministry of Information.

The Republic of the Union of Myanmar (2015), *The 2014 Myanmar Population and Housing Census*, vol. 2, Naypyidaw. https://myanmar.unfpa.org/en/publications/union-report-volume-2-main-census-report (accessed: 1 September 2020).

Tinker, Hugh (1983–4), *Burma. The Struggle for Independence 1944–48*. 2 vols, London: Her Majesty's Stationery Office.

Tonkin, Derek (2018), 'Exploring the Issue of Citizenship in Rakhine State', in *Citizenship in Myanmar: Ways of Being in and from Burma*, ed. A. South and M. Lall, 222–63, Singapore: Chiang Mai University Press and ISEAS.

Yawnghwe, Chao-Tzang, and Lian H. Sakhong (eds) (2004), *The New Panglong Initiative: Building the Union of Burma*, Chiang Mai: UNLD Press.

Yegar, Moshe (1972), *The Muslims of Burma: A Study of a Minority Group*, Wiesbaden: Otto Harassowitz.

Wade, Francis (2017), *Myanmar's Enemy Within: Buddhist Violence and the Making of a Muslim 'Other'*, London: Zed Books.

Walton, Matthew J. (2008), 'Ethnicity, Conflict, and History in Burma', *Asia Survey*, 48 (6): 889–910.

2

Ethnic minorities and Myanmar's democratization

Nehginpao Kipgen

Myanmar officially recognizes 135 ethnic groups (called 'national races'), which are broadly divided into eight major groups – Bama or Burman with nine subgroups, Chin with fifty-three subgroups, Kachin with twelve subgroups, Kayin or Karen with eleven subgroups, Kayah or Karenni with nine subgroups, Mon with one subgroup, Rakhine or Arakan with seven subgroups and Shan with thirty-three subgroups. For various reasons, there is a serious lack of trust in the central government. Ethnic minorities often doubt the government's seriousness to protect their rights and promote their interests. Because of the chauvinistic ideology of the Myanmar military and the civilian Burman elites, the minorities are reluctant to dissolve their own armed groups and surrender complete control to the Myanmar army. The scope of historical events covered in this study ranges from the country's independence from the British in 1948 to the government of the National League for Democracy (NLD), which came to power in 2016. Analysing the relations between ethnic minorities and the Burman majority, I shall argue that addressing the demands of ethnic minorities is not only important but also necessary for peace, stability, development and the consolidation of democracy.

Ethnicity

'Ethnicity' can be defined as a group of people who identify themselves with a community through a common history, set of cultural values, language, shared beliefs and so on. In the contemporary world order, every society is more or less culturally and/or socially identified through its ethnicity or race. Ethnicity, nationalism and democracy are closely related concepts, and are deeply embedded in the history of Myanmar. The struggle throughout history has been largely about the fight for the recognition of identity and rights. With its 135 so-called 'national races', Myanmar is one of the most diverse countries in Asia. According to the Union of Myanmar's Ministry of Labour, Immigration and Population, the country's population on 2 April 2020 was 54.58 million (28.43 million female and 26.15 million male). The Yangon (or Rangoon) Region had the largest population with 8.39 million, followed by the Mandalay Region with 6.54 million and Shan State with 6.43 million. The least populated region, according to the 2014 nationwide census (Global New Light of Myanmar 2020), was Kayah State with a population of 330,000, followed by Chin State with a population of 520,000 (Lwin 2020).

In Myanmar, all but the Bama or Burman group are considered ethnic minorities. However, the term can be controversial and can be interpreted in different ways. While the Bama or Burman group, which roughly constitutes 60–70 per cent of the total population, is numerically the largest, some say that the term 'majority' versus 'minority' is a misnomer as the other ethnic groups were treated as a separate entity during British rule between 1885 and 1948 (Kipgen 2015a). Minority problems have been so pervasive in Myanmar that some consider the country to be the 'most perplexing' in Southeast Asia (Renard 1987: 255). The issue of ethnic minorities gained momentum after the first Anglo-Burmese war in 1824, when each ethnic group dissociated itself from the Burman group (ibid.: 256). The minorities are commonly referred to as 'ethnic groups' or 'ethnic nationalities' in both informal and formal settings, and they are largely settled in the peripheries of the country (Kuppuswamy 2013).

In this chapter, I will go by the general definition of minorities as the numerically smaller, non-Bama (or non-Burman) population groups of the country – Chin, Kachin, Kayin, Kayah, Mon, Rakhine and Shan. The objective of this chapter is to analyse in four stages the movement of ethnic minorities and their relations with the Burman-majority-led central government: from the country's independence to the first military coup in 1962, from the years of military rule to the seven-step roadmap towards democracy that was introduced in 2003, the events leading up to the formation of a quasi-democracy in 2011 and the transfer of power to a civilian-led hybrid regime in 2016. Historically, ethnic minorities do not trust the Myanmar government to safeguard and promote their fundamental interests, such as culture, language and tradition, since the government is dominated by the majority Bama/Burman ethnic group. Many people from the ethnic minorities also believe that, because of the chauvinistic ideology of the Myanmar military and the civilian Burman elites in the past, their situation could deteriorate even further if the ethnic armed forces are dissolved and the Myanmar army is given complete control of internal security matters (Kipgen 2015b, 2016a and 2016b). Addressing the demands of ethnic minorities – such as for equal rights and federalism – is not only important but also necessary for peace, stability, development and the consolidation of democracy.

Independence and military coup

The formation of the Union of Burma[1] in 1948 was preceded by an agreement between leaders of the frontier areas (now known as 'ethnic minorities') and the Bama or Burman group under the leadership of General Aung San. During a meeting at Panglong in Shan State in February 1947, Aung San persuaded representatives of some ethnic minorities – Chin, Kachin and Shan – to cooperate with the interim Burmese government to speed up the country's independence from the British. The minority leaders agreed to do so in the hope of achieving regional autonomy and the right of secession after ten years of the introduction of the constitution. Chapter X, Section 201 of the 1947 Union Constitution stated that 'save as otherwise expressly provided in this Constitution or in any Acts of Parliament made under section 199, every state shall have the right to secede from the Union in accordance with the condition hereinafter prescribed' (Mang 2012: 171).

The Union of Burma would not have been possible without the support and cooperation of ethnic minorities, who were then known as the frontier people. In fact, Aung San had felt it necessary to convince the minority leaders that the Bamas/Burmans would treat all ethnic groups equally post-independence. To allay the lingering concerns of the non-Burman groups, Aung San said that 'if Burma receives one kyat, you will also get one kyat' (Kipgen 2011: 49). The promise to uphold equality made by the Burman leader, who headed the negotiations for independence from the British government, persuaded leaders from the Chin Hills, the Kachin Hills and the Shan States and led to the signing of the historic Panglong Agreement on 12 February 1947 (Kipgen 2011). Since then, the day has been observed as the country's Union Day, and it is an official holiday. The nation celebrated its seventy-third Union Day on 12 February 2020 (Hlaing 2020). Despite the failure to implement the Panglong Agreement during the first few years of the country's independence, especially on issues related to autonomy and ethnic equality, members of the Chin, Kachin and Shan groups remained loyal to the Burmese government throughout the initial years of communist revolt and of rebellion by the Karen and other groups. However, tensions continued to mount between the Burmese military and ethnic minority groups. And, by the end of the 1950s, there were serious discussions on the right of secession from the Union, with a rebellion beginning in the Shan State in 1959 and in the Kachin State in 1961 (Walton 2008).

Aung San was assassinated in July 1947, a few months before the country's independence. Independent Burma under Prime Minister U Nu tended towards a unitary form of government rather than the federal democracy anticipated. Shortly after the country's independence, the Karen leaders, who were disappointed with the compromises made in the country's first constitution, entered into an armed rebellion against the central government. The Karens had hoped for separate political representation from the British government. The Karen insurgency was followed by demands made by the Mon, the Arakan and the Shan for separate states and/or greater autonomy. The wave of insurgencies and the civilian government's inability to govern effectively led to an eighteen-month-long military caretaker government from 1958 to 1960. The caretaker government unsuccessfully negotiated for the Shan sawbwas (rulers) to relinquish their traditional system of government (Taylor 1979). Since the country's independence, there were dissenting views within the ruling Anti-Fascist People's Freedom League (AFPFL), which led to a party split in 1958. The unstable democracy under the AFPFL government and insurgency movements led by the communists and ethnic minorities were two major reasons why the military coup occurred in March 1962 (Kipgen 2011). Minority leaders blamed the civilian government and the military leadership equally for the coup (Bray 1992). The continued armed conflicts sixty years after independence is a testament to the importance of ethnic minorities in the country's peace, stability and development. Although ethnic armed groups have been relatively weakened by several decades of conflict, the Myanmar army has not completely defeated or overwhelmed them at any point in time (Kuppuswamy 2013).

Seven-step roadmap towards democracy

The Myanmar military has staged a coup twice since the country's independence – in 1962 and 1988. The 1962 coup led to the nullification of the 1947 constitution and the adoption of the 1974 one. Nationwide protests against military rule led to the 1988 coup. The second coup paved the way for the first general election in 1990, but the military refused to transfer power when the NLD won the election on the grounds that the country needed a constitution first. The government called a National Convention, but the NLD and the United Nationalities Alliance (UNA), an alliance of ethnic-minority parties, boycotted the Convention because the proceedings lacked the space for democracy. Because of their refusal to participate in the Convention, the military authorities harassed, arrested and imprisoned several NLD and UNA leaders and party workers (Jain 2006). The international community, particularly the Western nations, exerted strong pressure on the military regime to hold talks with the NLD and other ethnic parties for the country's political future. A meeting then took place between the State Peace and Development Council (SPDC), the military government and the NLD, but this ended without any tangible outcome (Kipgen 2016a).

While the military continued to rule, it simultaneously began a systematic and gradual political transition through a seven-step roadmap towards a so-called 'discipline-flourishing democracy', which was officially introduced in 2003. The seven steps included the following: to reassemble the National Convention, which had been suspended since 1996; to implement requisite tasks step by step for establishing a democratic system when the National Convention successfully concludes; to draw up a draft constitution based on the general concepts and principles discussed at the National Convention; to hold a national referendum on the draft constitution; to hold a free and fair election for the formation of national legislative bodies (Hluttaw); to convene a meeting of elected representatives; and to ensure that leaders, government and authoritative bodies elected by the Hluttaw continue with the task of constructing a new democratic state (Kipgen 2017).

Although the military government had taken different steps to address the country's myriad problems, there was no serious intent to address the grievances of ethnic minorities, including the armed groups. For example, following the second military coup in 1988, the military government signed a ceasefire agreement with some of the armed groups but did not put forward any political solution. Instead of engaging these groups in political dialogue, the government imposed a unilateral political roadmap which it said would lead to a modern, developed and democratic nation. The government exerted great pressure on the armed groups to lay down their weapons or transform themselves into a Border Guard Force (BGF) under the command of the Myanmar army. The military government also told the groups that, if they wished to compete in the

2010 election, they would have to form new political parties that were formally separate from the armed organizations (Core 2009). Only a few of the major groups believed in the sincerity of the government, and groups such as the United Wa State Army (UWSA), the New Mon State Party (NMSP), the National Democratic Alliance Army – Eastern Shan State, the Democratic Karen Buddhist Army (DKBA) and the Kachin Independence Organization (KIO) responded ambiguously to the military regime's invitation (Seekins 2009).

By holding the election in 2010, the Union Solidarity and Development Party (USDP) military government was quite successful in two ways – it won the election with ease and split and weakened the opposition parties. The USDP won 76.5 per cent of the seats across all three levels of the parliament – upper house, lower house and regional legislatures. The NLD boycotted the election because it alleged that the authorities were using undemocratic practices. Since it failed to register for the election, the party was delisted from the officially recognized political parties of the country. The NLD had decided to take such an extreme step as its supreme leader, Aung San Suu Kyi, was still under house arrest. The NLD intra-party division led to a splinter group, the National Democratic Force, which fielded candidates for the election and won sixteen seats. While the ethnic parties that had contested the 1990 election boycotted the 2010 election, new parties were formed and participated in the election. For example, the Shan Nationalities Democratic Party won fifty-seven seats, the Rakhine Nationalities Development Party won thirty-five and the All Mon Region Democracy Party won sixteen (Bünte 2016).

Formation of a quasi-democracy

Regardless of whether it is a military regime or a civilian-led government, the issue of ethnic minorities has remained the country's most significant problem since independence. Realizing the importance of securing peace over democracy and development, the USDP government led by President Thein Sein began to hold talks with ethnic armed groups without any preconditions. The previous SPDC military government had set three conditions before engaging in talks: a ceasefire must be agreed first before any negotiations can start, armed groups should lay down their weapons before entering dialogue and all talks must be held inside Myanmar. The USDP government's initiative was an indication that the authorities had understood the importance of reaching an agreement with ethnic armed groups. On 18 August 2011, President Thein Sein made a pledge to make the issue of ethnic minorities a national priority by dropping the demand made by the previous military government that all ethnic armed groups become border guard forces. The Ethnic Affairs and Internal Peace Committee was then formed to prepare plans for a peace process with ethnic armed groups. The government also announced a three-stage peace plan: the state level, the union level and the signing of a nationwide ceasefire agreement (Kipgen 2015a). The government took all those steps after realizing how important for the country's peace and development is the role of ethnic minorities, including the armed groups.

Following more than two years of meetings, the Thein Sein government, which formally assumed power on 30 March 2011, signed a ceasefire agreement with eight ethnic armed groups on 15 October 2015. However, seven ethnic armed groups refused to sign the ceasefire agreement because they disagreed with who should be part of the peace process and because they still distrusted the semi-civilian government, which was dominated by former military generals. During the signing ceremony, which was attended by hundreds of diplomats, officials and representatives of ethnic armed groups, President Sein said, 'The nationwide ceasefire agreement (NCA) is a historic gift from us to our generations of the future … This is our heritage. The road to future peace in Myanmar is now open' (Slodkowski 2015). Recognizing the need to bring on board the remaining ethnic armed groups for a nationwide ceasefire agreement, the president said that he would continue to try to convince the others. Saw Mutu Say Poe, the chairman of the Karen National Union (KNU), the oldest armed group in the country to sign the ceasefire agreement, said, 'The NCA is a new page in history and a product of brave and energetic negotiations' (ibid.). The eight groups which signed the ceasefire were: the All Burma Students' Democratic Front (ABSDF), the Arakan Liberation Party (ALP), the Chin National Front (CNF), the DKBA, the Karen National Liberation Army-Peace Council (KNLA-PC), the KNU, the Pa-O National Liberation Organization (PNLO) and the Shan State Army – South (SSA-S). The groups which did not sign the ceasefire include the UWSA, the country's largest and best equipped armed group, and the KIO and its armed wing, the Kachin Independence Army (KIA), which resumed armed conflicts following the collapse of a seventeen-year-old ceasefire in 2011 (Ghosh 2015).

The NLD government – a hybrid regime

Like its predecessor, the NLD government, which assumed power on 30 March 2016, made one of its most important priorities the forging of a peace initiative with the country's ethnic armed groups. The NLD government, under the leadership of State Counsellor Aung San Suu Kyi, continued its negotiations with the ethnic armed groups which had not signed during the Thein Sein government. After several meetings, the government signed a ceasefire agreement with two armed groups – the NMSP and the Lahu Democratic Union (LDU) – on 13 February 2018. The signing ceremony was attended, among others, by government officials, the military commander-in-chief Senior General Min Aung Hlaing and representatives of ethnic minorities adorned in traditional costumes. During the ceremony, Aung San Suu Kyi said, in an apparent reference to the criticisms over violence towards the Rohingya refugees, that the 'light of peace … cannot cover the whole country … our country is facing a lot of pressure and criticism from the international community'. Somewhat sceptical of what lay ahead, the LDU Chairman Kya Khun Sar said, 'We believe in Daw Aung San Suu Kyi but we'll have to see what happens on the road ahead, because the government and the military are not very united' (Sargent and Htay 2018). Despite this development, the military insistence on a ceasefire agreement, on the one hand, and its offensive attacks on certain ethnic armed groups, on the other, did not help the peace process. And, in fact, the military's actions pushed the conflicts to another level of uncertainty (Kipgen 2020).

Although political power was transferred to the NLD government in 2016, the result fell short of full democracy. The political structure was designed in such a way that the military could continue to hold a significant degree of authority under the new system of a hybrid regime. Under the 2008 constitution, the military was guaranteed 25 per cent of the seats in both the national parliament and state or regional legislatures. The military appoints one of the two vice presidents and three other important ministers – home, defence and border affairs. Although the president is head of the powerful National Defence and Security Council (NDSC), which has the authority to recommend national emergency under which the military takes full control of all branches of the government, the military representatives form a majority. Of the eleven NDSC members, six are either serving military leaders or their appointees (Kipgen 2018). The 2008 constitution institutionally reduced electoral competition to only 75 per cent of seats. In the 2015 election, the ethnic parties had a chance to form a united force under the new political set-up but performed rather poorly, securing only 11 per cent of the seats in the national parliament due to their disunity. This was a drop of 4 per cent from the 2010 election held under military rule. In their attempt to perform better in the 2020 election, different ethnic parties – Chin, Kachin, Karen, Kayah and Mon – expressed their intention to stand united (Lwin 2018). As of June 2020, the NLD has held 59 per cent of seats in the national parliament, the ethnic parties 11 per cent, the USDP 5 per cent and the military its constitutionally mandated 25 per cent (Aung 2020).

Ethnic parties had performed better in the November 2018 by-election by securing a few seats. Acknowledging its poor performance, the NLD Spokesman Myo Nyunt said, 'We lost five out of six seats in ethnic areas. Ethnic people are not satisfied with our performance on the peace process … This result is a lesson for us. We will come up with a strategy for each constituency for the coming election' (Aung and Lewis 2018). In July 2019, the Union Election Commission approved six new ethnic parties that were the result of mergers – the Kachin State People's Party, the Kayah State Democratic Party, the Karen National Democratic Party, the Chin National League for Democracy, the Mon Unity Party and the Inn National Development Party (Nanda 2019). Despite the NLD government's failure to deliver its promises to ethnic minorities, including federal democracy and a peace settlement, Aung San Suu Kyi reached out to ethnic minorities a few months before the 2020 general election with the primary objective of wooing voters to ensure that her NLD party would remain the single largest political party after the election. In her rally in Shan State on 11 March 2020, the State Counsellor stressed that the country's strength is rooted in diversity; she asked for patience and said, 'We do have a lot of time to move forward, and we get ourselves motivated to improve and develop our country' (Nitta 2020).

Burmanization legacy

While Myanmar has witnessed some concrete changes since the NLD government came to power, the state of politics is still far from what many had anticipated. One important issue that divides the country is the lack of trust between the ethnic minorities and the Burman leadership – civilian as well as military. This mistrust is rooted in the country's independence and the inability of successive Burman-led governments to close the gap. General Aung San had promised autonomy to ethnic minorities, a promise that has not been kept. Moreover, the right to secession granted by the 1947 constitution has not been exercised. And, instead of cultivating the spirit of unity in diversity, successive governments have directly or indirectly attempted to weaken the ethnic minorities and their rights. One such common practice is that of Burmanization, which imposes the Burmese language and culture on ethnic minorities. Many people from the ethnic minorities have shown respect for Aung San largely because of his role in trying to convince the former frontier people to join in the birth of the Union of Burma. His daughter, Aung San Suu Kyi, continues to enjoy significant support among the minorities because of her father's legacy and also partly because of her years in the pro-democracy movement.

However, their support for Aung San Suu Kyi and her NLD government is not unlimited. Many people from the ethnic minorities continue to associate the Burman population, including Aung San Suu Kyi and her NLD government, with the policy of Burmanization or Burman chauvinism, which is a system that Burman-led governments have used against the country's minority groups – in education, repressive laws, religious proselytization and economic exploitation (Gray 2018). This Burman chauvinism was manifested again in 2018 when the NLD government announced its plan to build a statue of Aung San in the Kayah State capital, Loikaw. The statue was erected despite strong protests from locals and ethnic-minority organizations (Aung 2019). The protesters perceived the move as the continued domination of the Burmans over the Kayah population. Several protesters were accused of defamation and incitement and faced legal charges. The protesters believed that it was their duty to fight against the version of history which downplays Karenni autonomy in favour of the role of Aung San. The Karenni Youth Force Protest Camp Committee spokesman, Di Di, said, 'We must have a right to self-determination and a right to regional autonomy. The government must guarantee these rights' (K. E. Aung 2019).

Conclusion

Self-identity plays a very vital role in a state like Myanmar. Belonging to the majority gives a person the privilege to rule, while the minorities struggle to survive. As Myanmar heads towards its envisioned federal democracy, it is important for the leaders, particularly the majority Burman group, to build an environment of inclusivity and to ensure that ethnic minorities have equal rights, not just in theory but in practice, too. Throughout the country's post-independence era there has been insufficient trust between the majority and the minorities. In an attempt to make the country seem inclusive and accommodating, Sao Shwe Thaik from the Shan ethnic group was made the first president of the country in 1948. And, after a lapse of more than five decades, Henry Van Thio from the Chin ethnic group was made the country's second vice president in 2016. However, their appointments, both largely symbolic, have not addressed the country's ethnic minority concerns – namely, autonomy and federal democracy.

Political struggle in Myanmar comprises three basic categories. The first is the Bama or Burman group, which aspires to democracy; the second is the ethnic minorities with their own states but who are fighting for equal rights and federalism; and the third is the ethnic minorities who are fighting for recognition of identity. The ethnic minorities – belonging to the second and third categories – have to fight extra layers besides democracy. The perennial mistrust towards the majority Bama or Burman leadership – both military and civilian – has been exacerbated by the inability to reach an agreement on the country's political future. The continuing armed conflicts are a testament to the decades-old mistrust and lack of political accommodation. Constituting roughly 40 per cent of the population and inhabiting about 60 per cent of the country, the ethnic minorities are essential to the country's peace, stability, development and the consolidation of democracy. Any confidence-building should be holistic and comprehensive, and range from politics to security, from the economy to educational and social reforms, including attitudes towards the minorities. It is the duty of those in power – both military and civilian – to ensure that their decisions and actions do not create a sense of fear and discrimination among the different ethnic groups. The role of independent groups in civil society, including the media, is also important in building unity and cohesion in a society as diverse as Myanmar.

Over the years, and especially starting with the USDP government in 2011, there has been concrete evidence that the central government has realized the increasing importance of the role of ethnic minorities. At the same time, there is also plenty of empirical evidence to suggest that the Burman leadership is hesitant to accept the demands of the minorities, particularly on the question of equal rights and federalism. One example was the rejection by the national parliament, dominated by the Burmans, of the proposal to amend Article 261(b) in March 2020. The Article gives the president the power to appoint chief ministers in the country's fourteen states and regions. Had the bill been passed, it would have allowed chief ministers in ethnic minority states to be elected by the people of the respective states, rather than be appointed by the president (Gerin 2020). This would have undoubtedly given more power to ethnic minorities in choosing or electing their own chief ministers. As the country moves towards democracy, the competition and scramble for power among the Burman elites should not happen at the cost of the minorities. Given its historical nature, the issue of ethnic minorities remains the most critically significant. Therefore, addressing the issue is not only important but also necessary for peace, stability, development and the consolidation of democracy in Myanmar.[2]

Notes

1. Burma was renamed Myanmar by the then State Law and Order Restoration Council (SLORC) military government in 1989. Some in the Myanmar opposition groups, the expatriates and some Western countries continue to use the name 'Burma'. Some argue that Burma should still be used since it was an unelected and undemocratic military government which changed the name without the consent of the people. The United Nations uses 'Myanmar'.
2. The author is grateful for the contributions of Megha Gupta and Shivangi Dikshit, master's students at Jindal School of International Affairs, O.P. Jindal Global University. Both students worked as research assistants at the Center for Southeast Asian Studies (CSEAS), the former from fall semester 2018 to spring 2020, and the latter from fall semester 2019 to spring 2020.

References

Aung, K. H. (2019), 'Aung San Statue Controversy Highlights Vulnerability of Ethnic Minority Identity', *Frontier Myanmar*, 13 February. https://frontiermyanmar.net/en/aung-san-statue-controversy-highlights-vulnerability-of-ethnic-minority-identity (accessed: 5 June 2020).

Aung, S. Y. (2020), 'Myanmar's Suu Kyi Still Barred from Presidency as Proposed Charter Change Fails', *The Irrawaddy*, 11 March. https://www.irrawaddy.com/news/burma/myanmars-suu-kyi-still-barred-presidency-proposed-charter-change-fails.html (accessed: 6 June 2020).

Aung, T. T. (2019), 'Myanmar Activists Charged after Protesting Independence Hero Statue', *Reuters*, 8 February. https://in.reuters.com/article/myanmar-protests/myanmar-activists-charged-after-protesting-independence-hero-statue-idINKCN1PX16R (accessed: 5 June 2020).

Aung, T. T., and S. Lewis (2018), 'Myanmar By-Election Results "a Lesson" for Suu Kyi's Party', *Reuters*, 4 November. https://in.reuters.com/article/myanmar-election/myanmar-by-election-results-a-lesson-for-suu-kyis-party-idINKCN1N90CG (accessed: 22 May 2020).

Bray, J. (1992), 'Ethnic Minorities and the Future of Burma', *The World Today*, 48 (8/9): 144–7.

Bünte, M. (2016), 'Myanmar's Protracted Transition: Arenas, Actors, and Outcomes', *Asian Survey*, 56 (2): 369–91.

Core, P. (2009), 'Burma/Myanmar: Challenges of a Ceasefire Accord in Karen State', *Journal of Current Southeast Asian Affairs*, 28 (3): 95–105.

Gerin, R. (2020), 'Myanmar's Ruling NLD Votes Down Bill on Ethnic Chief Ministers', *Radio Free Asia*, 17 March. https://www.rfa.org/english/news/myanmar/chief-ministers-03172020183612.html (accessed: 6 June 2020).

Ghosh, N. (2015), 'Myanmar Signs Ceasefire Accord with Eight of 16 Ethnic Armed Groups', *The Straits Times*, 15 October. https://www.straitstimes.com/asia/se-asia/myanmar-signs-ceasefire-accord-with-eight-of-16-ethnic-armed-groups (accessed: 15 May 2020).

Global New Light of Myanmar (2020), 'MoLIP Updates Estimated Number of Myanmar Population', *Global New Light of Myanmar*, 2 April. https://www.globalnewlightofmyanmar.com/molip-updates-estimated-number-of-myanmar-population/ (accessed: 23 April 2020).

Gray, D. D. (2018), 'Myanmar Forces Burman Culture on Minorities, Erases Identity', *Associated Press*, 16 March. https://apnews.com/249d72db491a47a79886c43b6085b6d2/Myanmar-forces-Burman-culture-on-minorities,-erases-identity (accessed: 5 June 2020).

Hlaing, A. H. (2020), 'Yangon Celebrates 73rd Union Day', *Myanmar Times*, 12 February. https://www.mmtimes.com/gallery/yangon-celebrates-73rd-union-day.html (accessed: 1 June 2020).

Jain, B. M. (2006), 'Dynamics of Political Transition in Myanmar', *Indian Journal of Asian Affairs*, 19 (2): 1–14.

Kipgen, N. (2011), 'Political Change in Burma: Transition from Democracy to Military Dictatorship (1948–62)', *Economic and Political Weekly*, 46 (20): 48–55.

Kipgen, N. (2015a), 'Ethnic Nationalities and the Peace Process in Myanmar', *Social Research: An International Quarterly*, 82 (2): 399–425.

Kipgen, N. (2015b), 'Ethnicity in Myanmar and Its Importance to the Success of Democracy', *Ethnopolitics*, 14 (1): 19–31.

Kipgen, N. (2016a), *Myanmar: A Political History*, New Delhi: Oxford University Press.

Kipgen, N. (2016b), *Democratisation of Myanmar*, New York: Routledge.

Kipgen, N. (2017), 'Militarization of Politics in Myanmar and Thailand', *International Studies*, 53 (2): 153–72.

Kipgen, N. (2018), 'The Quest for Federalism in Myanmar', *Strategic Analysis*, 42 (6): 612–26.

Kipgen, N. (2020), 'The Three Power Blocs Stymieing Myanmar's Democratization', *The Manila Times*, 22 March. https://www.manilatimes.net/2020/03/22/opinion/analysis/the-three-power-blocs-stymieing-myanmars-democratization/704948/ (accessed: 6 June 2020).

Kuppuswamy, C. (2013), 'Challenging the Reconciliation Process: Myanmar's Ethnic Divide and Conflicts', *Institute of Peace and Conflict Studies*, 1 June, 1–8.

Lwin, N. (2018), 'Ethnic Political Parties Merge to Seek Stronger Representation in 2020 Election', *The Irrawaddy*, 11 September. https://www.irrawaddy.com/news/politics/

ethnic-political-parties-merge-to-seek-stronger-representation-in-2020-election.html (accessed: 22 May 2020).

Lwin, M. (2020), 'Myanmar Population Rises by 10 Million in 25 Years', *Myanmar Times*, 6 April. https://www.mmtimes.com/news/myanmar-population-rises-10-million-25-years.html (accessed: 23 April 2020).

Mang, P. Z. (2012), 'Burman, Burmanisation and Betrayal', *Studies in World Christianity*, 18 (2): 169–88.

Nanda (2019), 'Ethnic Parties Merge in Attempt to win 2020 Election', *Myanmar Times*, 15 July. https://www.mmtimes.com/news/ethnic-parties-merge-attempt-win-2020-election.html (accessed: 22 May 2020).

Nitta, Y. (2020), 'Aung San Suu Kyi Reaches Out to Ethnic Minorities in Election Year', *Nikkei Asian Review*, 1 April. https://asia.nikkei.com/Politics/Aung-San-Suu-Kyi-reaches-out-to-ethnic-minorities-in-election-year (accessed: 22 May 2020).

Renard, R. D. (1987), 'Minorities in Burmese History', *Sojourn: Journal of Social Issues in Southeast Asia*, 2 (2): 255–71.

Sargent, R., and Htay, H. H. (2018), 'NMSP, LDU Formally Sign Nationwide Ceasefire Agreement', *Frontier Myanmar*, 13 February. https://frontiermyanmar.net/en/nmsp-ldu-formally-sign-nationwide-ceasefire-agreement (accessed: 15 May 2020).

Seekins, D. M. (2009), 'Myanmar in 2008: Hardship, Compounded', *Asian Survey*, 49 (1): 166–73.

Slodkowski, A. (2015), 'Myanmar Signs Ceasefire with Eight Armed Groups', *Reuters*, 15 October. https://www.reuters.com/article/us-myanmar-politics/myanmar-signs-ceasefire-with-eight-armed-groups-idUSKCN0S82MR20151015 (accessed: 15 May 2020).

South, A. (2004), 'Political Transition in Myanmar: A New Model for Democratization', *Contemporary Southeast Asia*, 26 (2): 233–55.

Taylor, R. H. (1979), 'Burma's National Unity Problem and the 1974 Constitution', *Contemporary Southeast Asia*, 1 (3): 232–48.

Walton, M. J. (2008), 'Ethnicity, Conflict, and History in Burma: The Myths of Panglong', *Asian Survey*, 48 (5): 889–910.

3

Ne Win's echoes: Burmanization policies and peacebuilding in Myanmar today

Saw Eh Htoo

Introduction

There is a strong polarization in Myanmar between the majority lowland Bamar (or 'Burman') population and the many minority groups in the remote highlands and border regions. Decades of war and separatism have exacerbated this polarization, amplified through an army and government dominated by Bamar. 'Burmese identity' is central to both the majority Bamar and the minority groups, who typically define themselves in opposition to the Bamar. Ne Win's Burmanization[1] policy of the 1960s is one of the key reasons why the government of independent Burma/Myanmar cannot easily resolve decades of tensions even after the 2015 Nationwide Ceasefire Agreement (NCA) and the election of Aung San Suu Kyi's National League for Democracy (NLD).

This chapter looks at the principles and practices of Ne Win's nation-building or 'Burmanization'. This includes Ne Win's policies of supremacy of the Burmese Buddhist culture, a centralized economic system, and his quasi-military[2] government. These policies intensified the ethnic tensions and prolonged the violent conflicts which had already begun in 1949–52, but which had effectively been subject to a ceasefire until 1962, when General Ne Win seized complete power. Ne Win resumed military operations in the geographically peripheral areas of Myanmar where ethnic minorities live, with many people being deported or fleeing to Thailand, China and India over the next sixty years.

General Ne Win (1911–2002) is regarded as one of Myanmar's historical figures. He was one of the 'Thirty Comrades' who fought against the

British and with the Japanese in 1942. He was commander-in-chief of the army during U Nu's civilian premiership (1949–62) and leader of the 1962 coup d'état which brought his Burma Socialist Programme Party (BSPP) to power and made him prime minister and chairman of the BSPP. To sustain his power, he assumed the ancient Burmese policy of pursuing Burmese hegemony, which is now known as 'Burmanization'. In doing so, he drew on the traditional understanding of Burmese kingship rooted in Buddhism, the majority religion of the Bamar. Traditional Burmese monarchs believed that being a Buddhist king was a sign of being a *bodhisatta*, that is, a Buddha to be (Maung Maung Gyi 1983: 20). They had absolute power to rule their people. By drawing on traditional Burmese values and policies, Ne Win attempted to influence Burmese Buddhist people. In order to consolidate his power, he reformed the economy, political structures and ethnic relations in a way shaped by Burmanization policies.

Burmese historians[3] have studied Ne Win from different points of view. While most historians have focused on his use of the military and the strategies that he employed to sustain his regime, only a few scholars have analysed Ne Win's ethnic and economic policy. Yet, understanding how and why Ne Win engaged in his Burmanization policy explains one important reason for Myanmar's persistent armed conflicts; in other words, it points to a significant obstacle to lasting peace in Myanmar: the habitus left by Ne Win's decades of Burmanization.

Ne Win justified his coup by pointing to the need to stop the ongoing civil war, which was reported by major English newspapers around the world. Yet, in Ne Win's own reading, there was more to it: his coup paved the way for his 'Burmese Way to Socialism'. This Burmese Way to Socialism, Ne Win's concept of unification, was codified in the 1974 constitution, which replaced the 1947 constitution. The driving force was Ne Win's insistence on a process of Burmanization that incorporated military rule and socialist economic policies facilitating military rule. In the name of Burmanization, Ne Win's regime nationalized the business sectors and expelled foreigners from Burma. He strengthened the monocultural Burmese army while seeking to defeat the ethnic armies, dozens of which were and still are present in the mountainous peripheries of Burma.[4] The dominance of the ethnic Burmans in Burmese politics was legitimized by tracing this dominance back to the ancient Burma kingdoms. According to Ne Win's historians, all the ethnicities living on the periphery had once been under the control of the Burmese Buddhist kingdom defeated by the British in 1885 (Kyaw Thet 2015). The expulsion of the British in 1947 and the re-establishment of Burmese rule were therefore presented as a kind of restoration of the past. Ne Win's Burmanization policies emphasized that his military government was a continuation of the previous Burmese dynasties,[5] and presented the government as a kind of 'fourth dynasty'.[6]

Understanding Ne Win's regime, its structure and its Burmanization policy is necessary to see the flaws in the current efforts at peacebuilding in Myanmar. In order to analyse the negative impact of Ne Win's regime on Myanmar's present situation, we need to focus on the 'three pillars' of Burmanization policy:

1. National identity is formed by the Burmese Buddhist culture.
2. The national economy needs to be a centralized system, the 'Burmese Way to Socialism'.
3. The national government has to be a quasi-military government, in which the Burmese army plays the central role.

These foundational principles led to a process of assimilation, accommodation and alienation for the one-third of Myanmar's population who were not Bamar. These policies were continued in the 1970s when Ne Win attempted to present his regime as a patriotic institution which had actively prevented the disintegration of the country after independence (P. Kyaw Han 2012: 14).

The liberation of Burmese Buddhist society from British rule had been the ambition held by young Burmese nationalists in the colonial period. As Houtman (1999: 29) has shown, these nationalists considered Mussolini and Hitler as their heroes. After independence, they became national leaders, and Ne Win, also known as *Thakin*[7] Shu Maung, was one of them. According to Kyi Sein Win (2020: 154), it was Ne Win who finally fulfilled Aung San's plan for a free Burma. One of Ne Win's comrades, Senior General Saw Maung (1928–1997), created a link between the Burmese army and the ancient Burmese kings by placing Aung San in their tradition (Ministry of Information 1991: 75). But Aung San was assassinated shortly after independence, and Ne Win's supporters regarded him as the true successor of Aung San, who had brought the country together like the ancient kings (Steinberg 2001: 29). According to Houtman (1999: 94), Ne Win himself attempted to prove that he and his family were of royal descent in order to give legitimacy to his politics of Burmanization. In his efforts to link his regime to the Burmese Buddhist past, Ne Win created a modern nation state in the sense of Anderson's (1983) and Thongchai's (1994) concept of an 'imagined community'.[8]

Ne Win's creation of a historical narrative for a new Burma

Historians and political scientists have argued that nationalist ideologies embed their concept of 'nation' in an account of the past that gives the modern nation a specific identity and the desired legitimacy (e.g. Anderson 1983; Thongchai 1994; Waters 2005). The narrative created by the nationalist ideologies evokes the emotions and patriotism needed to maintain the modern state. According to Anderson (1983: 9–10), the force and function of this mechanism can be seen, for example, in the erection of monuments such as cenotaphs and tombs of the unknown soldier. They represent the national spirit, calling on citizens to defend their nation even to the point of death.

For example, in present Thailand, the Commission for National Identity has defined the Thai nation as consisting of eight elements: 'territory, population, independence and sovereignty, government and administration, religion, monarchy, culture, and dignity' (Thongchai 1994: 4). Similar features can also be applied to Ne Win's concept of the Bamar (or Burmese) nation. The creation and promotion of a specific cultural heritage rooted in the Burmese Buddhist past became a necessary catalyst for nation-building through Burmanization. The imagination and representation of Ne Win's regime as a new empire with ancient roots – the fourth Burma dynasty – reflects what Thongchai calls the 'geo-body theory'. In Ne Win's case, this involves historicized ideologies regarding the preferred religion, that is, Buddhism, the dominance of Bamar language, culture and history, an ethnic-based concept of citizenship, independence and sovereignty, government and administration and especially the leading role of the military.

Ne Win's historians tried to find support for their historical narrative in the works of some historians from the British period. In the early twentieth century, both Western and Burmese historians called attention to the so-called Glass Palace Chronicle (*Hmannan Yazawin*), a work composed between 1829 and 1832, during the rule of King Bagyidaw of upper Burma, that focused on the kingdom of Bagan. Ne Win's historians were intent on asserting the work's 'Burmese-ness', even though the Chronicle itself does not mention any specific ethnic name in its description of eleventh-century Bagan (Shwe Lu Maung 1989: 70). The Chronicle mentions the kings' genealogies and their activities, including their military operations. It describes the city states, regions and dialect, but not ethnicity (Than Tun 2003: 109). Moreover, it actually indicates that the ancient people of Burma, especially in the Bagan era, reflected an

Indian type of civilization Bode (2011). But, in the narrative promoted by Ne Win's new historians, the golden days of supposedly Bamar kingdoms comprise all three previous dynasties leading up to the final unification of Myanmar under Ne Win (Myo Oo 2018: 48–59). This kind of nationalist historiography is almost 'hagiographic' in that it ignores the presence of many other kingdoms and princedoms coexisting with the so-called Bamar kingdoms or dynasties in the territory of later Myanmar. In fact, these kingdoms were linked to each other in a range of semi-feudal relationships with varying power relations and have little connection to modern ideas of ethnicity.

The three ideological foundations of Ne Win's regime (1962–88)

Ne Win named his new military government 'the Revolutionary Council', but in practice he exerted personal dictatorial power. It seems that he initially lacked a clear ideology. He chose some military allies to create his regime and to operate the levers of power. Yet, a default ideology gradually emerged,[9] one based on three principles: a central Burmese Buddhist culture as the nation's cultural identity, a centralized economic system and a centralized quasi-military government. These principles translated into a politics of assimilation, accommodation and alienation (see Figure 3.1). I will now explain this structure in more detail.

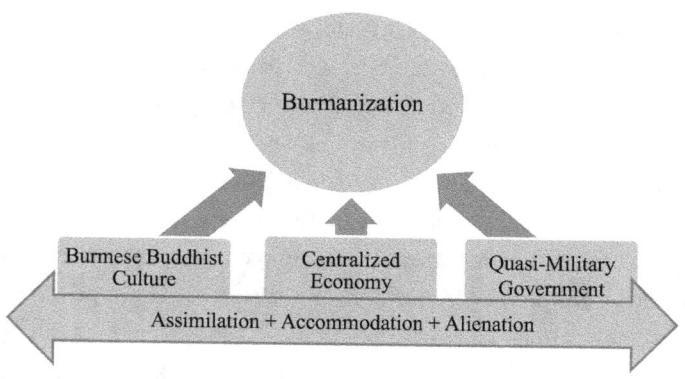

Figure 3.1 Ideological Foundations of Ne Win's Regime.

Building a single culture as national identity (Burmese Buddhist culture)

Ne Win introduced new administrative divisions. The number of non-Bamar states was changed from five to seven (with the creation of the Mon State and the Arakan State), and, in order to balance these, another seven new divisions (or 'regions') were created in the Bamar-speaking areas (see Clarke et al. 2019: 23; Khine Lin 2015: 73). This new map reflected the essence of a We-self *vs.* Others attitude as described by Thongchai (1994: 169–72) for Thailand. In Burma, the 'we-self' was constituted by the two-thirds of the population living in the Bamar heartland of the seven new divisions, who could plausibly align themselves with Ne Win's definition of Bamar/Buddhist identity in terms of heritage, family and culture.

In Ne Win's post-1962 Burma, nationalization became increasingly equivalent to Burmanization. The ethnic-national, mother-tongue-based schools in the ethnic states were nationalized, that is, placed under the centralized Ministry of Education in Yangon (Taylor 2015: 275–6). Burmese supplanted Karen, Kachin, Shan and other languages to become the language of all schools, government offices and other institutions. Under the new regime, all school textbooks were based on Burmese culture and language, effectively erasing ethnic cultures and languages from the national curriculum (Yay 2018: 201). Nationhood was reimagined as Bamar with no other identity or essence. This cultural construct reflected Ne Win's personal vision that decolonizing Burma meant restoring the ancient Bamar culture as the essence of a unified country, which had to be restored after the British policy of divide and rule.

Buddhism was important to Ne Win's new ideology. In the colonial period, Buddhism had lost much of its political influence. The British stopped government subsidies of the temples and the *saṅgha* (the Buddhist order) because they wanted to separate religious organization from the state, while Christian missionaries proselytized to native people through their schooling system (Kyi Win Sein 2015: 2–3). After 1948, Buddhism moved back to the centre. U Nu supported an independent Buddhist order and fostered Buddhism, but also permitted the practice of Christianity and Islam (Kyaw Win et al. 2011: 89). Ne Win, however, viewed the religious diversity of Burma with more suspicion. In 1962, he asserted control over the Buddhist order, with its potential for revolt, forcing all monks to register. The monkhood was brought under military rule (Charney 2009: 119) and ultimately became an ally. Making Burmese Buddhism a central feature of national identity also sharpened the demarcation between 'us and them'. The 'we', the in-group, became the people who lived under the light of Buddhism, the legal people, while the 'they', the insurgents, lived in darkness. Ethnic, religious and political dissenters constituted the out-group irrespective of their ethnic background.

Centralization of the economic system

Under U Nu's rule (1948–62), economic policy can be characterized as laissez-faire market capitalism protected by licensing regimes. State-controlled economic activities hardly existed. Foreign-owned companies from Britain, the United States, overseas China and India ran their businesses in post-independent Burma as a legacy of British colonialism, particularly those dealing with rice production, teak production, gems, oil and the exploitation of natural resources. In accordance with his newly created 'socialist' economic plan, Ne Win nationalized the foreign companies, many of which were controlled by Chinese and Indians (Kyi Win Sein 2020: 186, 192). Nationalization was also applied to non-governmental institutions supported by foreign countries, especially to the extensive Christian missionary system of schools, hospitals, social work and churches (Myanmar Baptist Convention 2012; Kyi Win Sein 2020). Foreign Christian missionaries were expelled. One of the many reasons given was that some missionaries were working as foreign agents (ibid.: 37–8). Whereas 'the departure of foreigners and missionaries did not have much effect on the Baptists for most Baptist church members and leaders were ethnic people …, the nationalization of the church's properties and the implementation of the new socialist system created several unexpected troubles for the Baptists as well as the non-Baptists' (Saw Augurlion 2017: 78).

Ne Win equated capitalism with the colonial system, which is why he felt it was necessary to eliminate both. While he believed that the nationalization of corporations would not have an effect on the different ethnic people because they were mostly farmers and blue-collar workers, he designed the socialist economic plan to promote Burmese businessmen (San Nyein and U Mya Han 2012: 39, 45). As a result of the nationalization programme, both foreign companies and foreigners left the country. Ne Win took the alienation of the country one step further by debarring its citizens from travelling to other countries without official permission. Simultaneously, his centralization, with its focus on Burmese language, Burmese-speaking society and Burmese Buddhist values, inevitably increased animosity between ethnic Bamar and the other ethnic peoples of

Myanmar, despite the fact that most were farmers. Ne Win intended to create a nation centred on the Burmese race, which he regarded as superior.

Quasi-military government

The most important change introduced by Ne Win was perhaps the dominance of the Burmese-speaking military. In the Ne Win regime, almost every cabinet member had a military-service background and connections established at the military academy after independence. Retired military officers with loyalties to Aung San's 'Thirty Comrades' and the Burmese Independence Army were promoted (Taylor 2015: 259), while the veterans of the anti-Japanese King's Karen and Kachin Rifles were drummed out of the military. In designing his dictatorship, Ne Win only trusted men with a military background in the Burma Independence Army and a few ethnic leaders who were there as puppet figures.

Ne Win also appointed government officers for the ethnic states. Even though there were putatively seven non-Bamar states in the Union, all the administrative officers from the governor down were appointed by the central military government in Rangoon (Yangon). Bamar-speaking officials typically had a military background and most were ethnic Bamar, thereby creating a Bamar privilege system (Walton 2012).

Underpinning military control was Ne Win's ideology of Burmese Supremacy (*Mahar Bamar*), which was effective in uniting the seven 'divisions' of central Burma. But this unity was to the disadvantage of the non-Bamar ethnicities in the seven states. The creation of the ideology of Burmese Supremacy privileged the Ne Win regime, since the concept of 'Burmanization' is generally understood to be the result of a 'centre-towards-peripheries' process (Boutry 2016: 105–6). In response, the ethnic armed groups promoted their own vernacular, thus reinforcing the idea of 'we-self vs. others' from a non-Bamar perspective. The crack was so deep that it led to a disintegration in Burma politics and to open revolt in the highlands.

The core procedures of Ne Win's regime

As has been said above, the three ideological foundations of Ne Win's politics translated into three core procedures (assimilation, accommodation and alienation).

Assimilation (Taing Yin Thar See Lone Nyi Nyut Yae)

In his speeches, Ne Win emphasized the myth that all ethnic people in Burma emerged from the same Burmese root. On this basis, he asserted the unifying potential of a 'Burmanized spirit' and presented this spirit as being necessary to establish a united socialist country (Burmese Socialist Programme Party 1964a: 14–19). The result was a politics of assimilation based on the promotion of Burmese Buddhism in the non-Bamar ethnic states, and the replacement of 'foreign missionary education' with state schooling taught mainly in Burmese.

Ne Win's closure of the country was part of his Burmanization agenda. He effectively stopped any foreign support for the Christian Kachin, Karen, Karenni and Chin – support that had developed during the British colonial period (1823–1948). Most of the schools for these ethnic groups were church-based, with the leading staff being missionaries from the United Kingdom and the United States, who also provided healthcare, social welfare and a livelihood. The exodus of Christian missionaries after 1962 decimated education conducted in local languages and English, as teachers and administrators departed. State-sponsored Buddhist missionaries then became active in the ethnic areas. These so-called highland missions (*Taung Tan Tharthnar Pyut*) preached not only Buddhism but also an anti-Western and anti-communist ideology known as Dhamamyal (Pyi Daung Su Thar 1959).

The Ministry of Education in Yangon developed a socialist education curriculum for the whole country. The Burmese Translation Association played an important role in translating English textbooks into Burmese. Promoting the standardized Burmese language (*Bamar Sar*) effectively prevented non-Bamar persons from teaching in formal education unless they could teach in Burmese. This policy reinforced Ne Win's explicit assertion that ethnic people living in border regions lacked proper education and were backward (Burmese Socialist Programme Party 1964a: 31). However, many actually had instruction in their home language through the Christian schools (in the case of the Karen, Kachin, Chin, etc.) or through the older system of Buddhist temple schooling (in the case of the Mon, Shan, etc.). But, in Ne Win's Burmanized world, development and modernity were measured by how well a person spoke Burmese and his or her level of education in a government school.

Ne Win's administration prioritized the Bamar community, and equated trust and loyalty with the government education system (News Editor, *MyanmarAlin News*, 12 December 1979). Non-Bamars, but also Christians and Muslims, were considered outsiders. In contrast to U Nu, Ne Win did not appoint any ethnic leaders to his government. According to Rogers (2015), Christian military officers will not be promoted beyond the rank of major, because they are considered as possible threats. As has been stated by the Burmese scholar Tharaphi Than (2015: 27), the idea that non-Buddhist or non-Bamar people pose a threat to Burmese socio-religious and socio-economic life is deeply embedded in the Burmese mind.

Accommodation (Nay Yar Pay Ah Thi Ah Hmat Pyut Chin)

Broadly speaking, the politics of 'accommodation' means establishing who belongs to Ne Win's new nation and who does not. In 1982, Ne Win's government introduced the Burma Citizenship Law, which reduced the number of legitimate ethnic groups in Myanmar to 135. Any group not or no longer on the list was deemed foreign or foreign-related and deprived of its rights.[10] Historians, social anthropologists and linguists still debate what factors are decisive in determining an ethnic group in Burma (e.g. Tonkin 2018; Ferguson 2015; Steinberg 2001). As I will argue below, linguistic, biological and historical aspects do not lead to clear-cut distinctions. Thongchai and Anderson have both emphasized the cultural construction, that is, the 'imagined' nature, of the concept of 'nationhood'. Thongchai is somewhat critical of Anderson's tendency to give too much weight to such an imagination 'over the operation in human practices', such that 'the newly imagined community seems to be created out of the frictionless propagation of new ideas like inscribing a new language on a blank sheet of paper' (Thongchai 1994: 15). Nonetheless, Ne Win's description of ethnic groups in Burma could indeed be seen as an act of sheer imagination. Its primary foundation seems to lie in serving his political agenda and cementing his political power. This is why, after Ne Win assumed political power, all ethnic groups in Burma were depicted in governmental publications (so-called blue socialist books) in accordance with his ideology of the 'Burmese Way to Socialism'. After 1965, the project of ethnic classification continued and was assigned to the Rangoon Arts and Sciences University (today: the University of Yangon) and especially to the departments of history and anthropology, under the supervision of Ne Win's government (Burmese Socialist Programme Party 1967).

In terms of classification by language, Ne Win's linguists recognized only three basic groups: Mon-Khmer, Tibeto-Burman and Tai-Chinese (Burmese Socialist Programme Party 1964b). But Ne Win's regime recognized eight 'national races', the Bamar, Kachin, Kayah, Karen, Chin, Bamar, Rakhine and Mon, effectively excluding Chinese and Indian groups from Bengal and elsewhere. This categorization was not based on linguistic criteria. In fact, 'the focus on eight major nationality races tended to obscure and confuse the significant diversity that exists within and between non-Bamar communities' (Clarke et al. 2019: 24). Among these groups, only the Mon ethnic group has a single dialect that is used widely. Chin people speak more than fifty different dialects. Karen people also have a large number of dialects, which are divided into eleven groups. Kayah people share the same language group with Karen, but are counted as a different ethnic group. Kachin ethnic groups mostly speak the same dialect, while the Rawang and Lisu speak different languages, but are nevertheless listed as Kachin and distinguished as different clans (Burmese Socialist Programme Party 1964b: 39). The same inconsistency applies to Bamar (Sino-Tibetan) languages. The state did not recognize Danu people, Inthar people or Dawei people as ethnicities on their own but considered them to be ethnically Bamar even though they live in Shan State and the Tanintharyi region, respectively, and speak languages that are not intelligible to each other.

From a biological point of view, the problem of Ne Win's categorization of eight different ethnic groups can be seen in the example of the Shan and the Bamar. Shan State has ethnic groups, such as Pa-O, Wa and Ta'ang, which are considered as Shan but are not related biologically or linguistically to other Shan people. Linguistically, the Pa-O dialect is closer to Karen, but the ethnic group is not included in the Karen group. The language of the Wa and Ta'ang belongs to the group of Mon-Khmer languages, that is, to the same group as the language of the Mon. Regarding the Bamar, there is an ethnic group known as Moken (or Salon) people (also known as 'sea gypsies'), who live in the southern Burma Archipelago and are considered Bamar. This is despite the fact that their language is an Austronesian language, unrelated to the Bamar language, which itself belongs to the Tibeto-Burman language group. Biologically and culturally, the Moken are different from the Bamar (Boutry 2016: 114–17), but they were classed as a proto-Burman group.

Particularly problematic is the attempt to base the categorization on historical arguments. According to Ne Win's regime, some ethnic groups are deemed not to belong to Burma because of their historical roots, as, for example, the Rohingya in Rakhine State (now called 'Bengali' by the government), who are of Indian origin. According to the regime's official categorization in 1965, the Rakhine group includes the Mro (Khume), Kaman, Thet, Maramargyi and Rakhine. They have different dialects and biological features, but were categorized as 'Rakhine' because they had presumably lived in the Rakhine Kingdom in the distant past. For example, the majority of Kama are Muslims of Arab descent, who served Rakhine kings as archers. Mro and Khume speak a Chin dialect, but they are counted as Rakhine because they had lived in Rakhine since the beginnings of the Rakhine Kingdom. Maramagyi are Buddhists, but, despite having similar physical features to Indians, they were also included in the Rakhine group. Similar inconsistencies are found in the ethnic categorization of the Shan. Some Chinese people living in Shan State were not listed in the ethnic group (Burmese Socialist Programme Party 1967 34–5), while the *Shan-Tayouk*, who are also Chinese, are classified as a sub-ethnic group of the Shan (News Editor, *Botataung Daily Newspaper*, 23 February 1973).

The questionable nature of ethnic categorization can also be seen in the persistent variations in numbers. In 1973, Ne Win's government classified 144 ethnic groups. This was changed in 1973, and then again in 1982, when it was fixed at 135 (Kyaw Nay Min (Myo Pya), 2020: 157, 181). However, in 1990, the military government again made some changes to the list, while keeping the number to 135 (News Editor, *Working People Daily Newspaper*, 26 September 1990).

The categorization of ethnic groups in Myanmar is clearly based not on language, biology or history but on political intentions. It served Ne Win's political agenda, as was made explicit in 'The Revolutionary Council's Policy on Ethnicity in Burma', which asserted that ethnic people had been living in Burma since ancient times and were descended from the Tibeto-Burman group (Burmese Socialist Programme Party 1964c: 33–4), that the divisions were the result of British colonial policy (ibid.: 55) and that the time has come to reunify and rebuild the country (ibid.: 69). The other side to accommodation was necessarily alienation, however. People who were not accommodated became foreigners, and regarded as enemies who could not be trusted. This is why, for example, the fact that Aung San Suu Kyi married a foreigner still prevents her from becoming president. It is well known that Ne Win was xenophobic. However, the creation of enemies was also instrumental in his attempt to create a unified Burmese Buddhist nation.

Alienation (Khwe Char Nyin Pae Chin)

The policy of alienation was implemented from the very start of Ne Win's regime for those groups who did not accept the government's new Burmanization policies, including the Kachin Independence Army (KIA), the Karen National Union (KNU), the Karenni National Progressive Party (KNPP) and the New Mon State Party (NMSP). The government used structural and cultural violence, military oppression and exclusion from the development plans against these established regional political parties, who were then seen as state enemies or – as in the case of the Rohingya – were not regarded as proper citizens.

'Insurgents' (as they were called by the government) or 'ethnic armed groups' (as they were called by foreign diplomats) have mostly operated in states on Myanmar's periphery, where the authority of the central government was never fully accepted or implemented. The armed groups resist the government's Burmanization policies as much as the Burmese army fights against them as part of the Burmanization strategy. After all, 'making wars means making the maps' (Thongchai 1994: 14). Where possible, Ne Win's regime used forced labour, relocation, isolation and psychological techniques to Burmanize people. In the 1970s, Burmanization turned into the military's much feared 'Four Cuts Policy', which meant cutting communication, cutting rations, cutting transportation and cutting recruitment for enemies of the state (Than Tin 2009: 347). In practice, it often meant the isolation, invasion and destruction of highland villages.

The Rohingya in northern Rakhine State have been subject to extreme structural, cultural and physical violence since the 1970s. People living there were required to have travel permits from the army to move from one place to another, even within the same region (Berlie 2008: 54). State surveillance was increased and their cultural practices and religious beliefs were labelled as threats to the state. Beginning in 1978, force was used to seize control of northern Rakhine and to Burmanize the Rohingya population, and programmes promoting state education, health and economic and social development were not implemented or supported. Denial of citizenship followed, which was used to rid the country of unwanted people. Operations were undertaken to expel them to Bangladesh (Po Kan Kaung 1992: 90–9).

In other government-controlled areas, people perceived as rebels were arbitrarily imprisoned without trial (Berlie 2008: 55). Those released were placed under surveillance, and their livelihood activities restricted. The citizenship law was used to ensure the 'purity' of those remaining. In 1982, the Ne Win government announced a *ius sanguinis* law to define Burman citizens and to distinguish them from foreigners. So-called mixed-blood people were not deemed full citizens and received at best only temporary residential cards (Khin Maung Kyaw 1971: 114–19). While some of those affected by this law were of Chinese origin, the majority were late descendants of Indian immigrants who had come to Burma to work in the colonial state at the invitation of the British colonial power between 1824 and the 1930s (ibid.: 28–43).

The negative effect of Ne Win's policy on peacebuilding in today's Myanmar

Ne Win's politics still resonate throughout Myanmar (U Aung Htoo 2014: 71–5). Ethnic armed groups are reluctant to enter peace deals with the military and the state government, whom are still thought to follow many of the Bamar-centric features of Ne Win's policy. They believe that ceasefire agreements in 'ethnic-controlled areas' would still serve the military's Burmanization principles (Win Tint Tun 2017: 538–46). To them, ceasefires often appear as attempts by both Burma's military and the new NLD state government to continue diluting the political demands made by ethnic people for autonomy in language policy, school administration and the provision of justice, land policy and other public services.

The handful of trust-building exercises between the government and ethnic armed organizations during the Ne Win years are now seen as pipe dreams that never lasted more than about three years and were brought to a halt by the 'Four Cuts' operations (Maung Aung Myoe 2009: 27–9). Peace talks initiated by the military and the government inevitably failed, leading to the resumption of Burmanization policies, such as the nationalization of schools, the confiscation of lands and the placement of Bamar-speaking military officers in positions of authority. This experience is still vivid in the memory of ethnic people and explains why ethnic armed groups continue to suspect that peace talks are merely strategies to defeat the ethnic opposition. General Ne Win never seriously sought to attain real peace in Burma. Rather, he used 'peacebuilding' as a strategy for his own political agenda. And, despite the fact that this strategy did not succeed during his regime, the military continues to pursue it today. Like a domino effect, Ne Win's insistence on a superior Bamar 'race' led to an increase in ethnic discrimination: ethnic issues of Bamar versus non-Bamar, the perceived 'main' ethnic group vs the sub-ethnic group, the centre vs the periphery. In Ne Win's imagined community of a Bamar-centric nation rooted in the ancient Burmese kingdoms, even such inequalities and acts of discrimination functioned to sustain the imagination. As Anderson (1983: 22) says, the nation 'is imagined as a community, because, regardless of the actual inequality and exploitation that may prevail in each, the nation is conceived as a deep horizontal comradeship' making people 'willing to die for such limited imaginings'. The more the Bamar saw themselves as the main and salient group, the more the other ethnicities emphasized their own identities as different and separate from the Bamar and resisted any attempts to be subjugated to the majority group. 'While the dynamics of division and distrust were certainly present prior to Ne Win's takeover in 1962, they reached new heights under military rule' (Clark et al. 2019: 24). But such 'division and distrust' also grew among the non-Bamar groups themselves. Encouraging this division among ethnic minorities was implicitly part of the 'divide-and-rule' strategy used by the Bamar military from when General Ne Win took over the new country's army in 1948, and particularly after his coup in 1962.

Ne Win's policies also created xenophobic prejudices towards Christianity and Islam, and towards the ethnic groups associated with them. The promotion of Buddhism as the dominant religion was an integral part of his hegemonic politics. Irrespective of history, the Buddhist majority consider Buddhism to be the original, indigenous religion of Burma (Historical Research Committee 2017: 12–15). Other religions, such as Christianity and Islam, and even Hinduism, are regarded as 'foreign'. The merger of Buddhism with Bamar nationalism in Ne Win's policies fuelled inter-religious tensions.[11] Such tensions still echo in current (2019) conflicts such as between Rohingya Muslims and Rakhine Buddhists in Rakhine State, and between the armed organizations of the KNU (led by Christian Karens) and the DKBA (led by Buddhist Karens) (South 2008: 58). The widespread mistrust among the different religious communities of Myanmar makes peacebuilding all the more difficult (see also Ye Hein Aung 2019).

When Ne Win's Burma Socialist Programme Party (BSPP) seized power in 1962, the momentum of Ne Win's political agenda gave many people much hope. But that hope ended when Ne Win transformed the military from a professional organization into a body that protected and implemented his political agenda. The three foundations of his politics – Burmese Buddhist culture, a centralized economy, and military rule – led to the ill-fated policy of one nation, one language, one culture. These three foundations underlay the system that supported militarism in Burma, including the brutal 'Four Cuts' policies of the 1970s. Ne Win's strategies still resonate in the continuing war with the Kachin Independence Army, the expulsion of the Rohingya to Bangladesh in 2017, and the conflict with the Arakan Army in 2019. His Burmanization strategy created conflicts at the time, and still does so today. The flaws in Ne Win's three foundations underlie the seemingly unending tensions and conflicts in the country.

Notes

1 The term 'Burmanization' refers to the domination of other ethnic groups by the Burmese. According to Carol Ann Boshier (2018), the terms 'Burmanized' or 'Burmanization' were first used in *Gazetteer of Upper Burma and the Shan states* in 1899.
2 I call it a quasi-military government because Ne Win constructed his government with military officers whom he could fully trust, but also appointed some civilians.
3 Several Burmese historians such as Maung Maung Gyi, Thant Myint-U, Dr Maung Maung, and Shwe Lu Maung have already written about Ne Win and his regime. According to Maung Maung Gyi, Ne Win and his counterparts adopted monarchical values to build their government. Thant Myint-U focused on modern Burma, where Ne Win's legacy continued with the system of military government. Dr Maung Maung sympathized with Ne Win and asserted that Ne Win's policy was suitable for the country, whereas Shwe Lu Maung held that Ne Win's policy and system created civil war.
4 Since 1949, Burma's periphery has been controlled off and on by dozens of ephemeral ethnic militias and the forces of the Burmese Communist Party and has endured the presence of permanent militaries, such as the Karen National Defence Organization, the Kachin Independence Army, the Mon New State Party, the Shan State Army and colourful rebels (*Young Sone Thabone*).
5 In Burmese historical accounts, the Bagan kingdom is counted as the first dynasty (eleventh to thirteenth century), the Taungoo dynasty (sixteenth to eighteenth century) as the second and the Konbaung dynasty (eighteenth to nineteenth century) as the third dynasty which was followed by British colonial rule.
6 Ne Win's regime was not officially called the 'fourth dynasty'. Yet, the idea was in the air as a result of the attempts to link the Ne Win state to the previous three dynasties. This can also be seen in the fact that Aung San Suu Kyi's followers have continued the narrative by claiming that she is the founder of the fifth Burmese empire, a claim found in various NLD songs and in the speeches of various party members.
7 The title 'Thakin' ('master') referred to the members of the Doh Bamar Association. It carries symbolic meaning in the sense of rejecting the British 'masters'. The real masters of the land are the Burmese people.
8 While differing in theoretical nuance, the two works are complementary. Thongchai's reflections on Thailand also help to understand the recent history of Myanmar.
9 A few of his trusted people were called to design the appropriate ideology, which had to differ from U Nu's ideas and from communist ideology (Kyi Sein Win 2020).
10 The Rohingya are the most obvious example. Considered as one of the ethnic groups of Burma under the U Nu government, they were erased from the list of ethnic groups under Ne Win.

11 In colonial times, religious tensions were largely based on anti-colonialist sentiments. Under Ne Win, religious tensions were deliberately fostered. The anti-Islam book *Ah Myo Pyauk Mar So Kyauk Hsayar* was printed and distributed among government servants in Burma during the time when Ne Win controlled the press and publications department and similar ideas were disseminated in the state newspaper (see Ye Hein Aung 2020: 40). Another book supported by the Burma Socialist Programme Party (BSPP) was *Shwe Pay Lwa*. For example, the lie was spread that Muslim men would receive a reward if they married Buddhist women (see Kyaw Nay Min 2020: 185).

References

Anderson, B. (1983), *Imagined Communities: Reflections on the Origin and Spread of Nationalism*, rev. ed., London: Verso.

Berlie, Jean A. (2008), *The Burmanization of Myanmar's Muslims*, Bangkok: White Lotus.

Bode, Mabel Haynes (2011), *Myanmar Naingan Pali SarPay Thamaing* (= Burmese translation of 'The Pali Literature of Burma', translated by Ashin K Tha La), Yangon: Pan Wai Wai.

Boshier, Carol A. (2018), *Mapping Cultural Nationalism: The Scholars of the Burma Research Society, 1910–1933*, Denmark: NIAS.

Boutry, Maxime (2016), 'How Far from National Identity?: Dealing with the Concealed Diversity of Myanmar', in *Metamorphosis: Studies in Social and Political Change*, ed. R. Egreteau and F. Robinne, 103–26, Singapore: NUS Press.

Burmese Socialist Programme Party Central Committee Headquarter (1964a), *Myanmar Socialist Lansin Party Ei Ah Thwin Ah Pyin* (Characteristics of the Burmese Socialist Programme Party), Yangon: Sar Pay Beik Mann Press.

Burmese Socialist Programme Party Central Committee Headquarter (1964b), *Taw Lan Yay Kaung Si Ei Taing Yin Thar Myar A Paw Htar Shi Thaw Thabaw Hta* (The Revolutionary Council's Perspective and Stance on Ethnic Affairs), Yangon: Sar Pay Beik Mann Press.

Burmese Socialist Programme Party Central Committee Headquarter (1964c), *Taw Lan Yay Kaung Si Ei Taing Yin Thar Myar Apaw Amyin and Ken Yu Chatt* (The Revolutionary Council's Policy on Ethnicity in Burma), Yangon: Sar Pay Beik Mann Press.

Burmese Socialist Programme Party Central Committee Headquarter (1967), *Kachin Taing Yin Thar Yin Kyay Mu Nit Yoe Yar Da Lae Hton San Myar* (Ethnic Culture and Tradition: Kachin), Yangon: Sar Pay Beik Mann Press.

Charney, Michael W. (2009), *A History of Modern Burma*, Cambridge: Cambridge University Press.

Clarke, Sarah L., Seng Aung Sein Myint and Zabra Yu Siwa (2019), *Re-examining Ethnic Identity in Myanmar*, Batambang: Centre for Peace and Conflict Studies. https://

reliefweb.int/sites/reliefweb.int/files/resources/Ethnic-Identity-in-Myanmar.pdf (accessed: 1 October 2020).

Ferguson, Jane M. (2015), 'Who's Counting? Ethnicity, Belonging, and the National Census in Burma/Myanmar', *Bijdragen tot de Taal-, Land- en Volkenkunde*, 171 (1): 1–28.

Historical Research Committee (Department of Historical Research and National Library) (2017), *Myanma Nainganye Thamaing* (Myanmar Political History) *(1906–1930)*, Yangon: Mon Ywer Press.

Houtman, Gastaaf (1999). *Mental Culture in Burmese Crisis Politics: Aung San Suu Kyi and the National League for Democracy*, Tokyo: ILCAA.

Khin Maung Kyaw (1971), *Myanma Nainggan Naingganthar Myar Nit Nainggan Char Thar Myar Pya Tha Na* (The Problem of Myanmar Citizens and Foreigners), Yangon: San Kyawt Yin.

Khine Lin (May Ga Waddy) (2015), *Maha-lumyogyi Wada Ei Maha Aung Pwe Lar? Dutaya Pin Lon Ma The A Nar Guard Pyi Daung Susitho* (Is the Victory of Maha-Bamarism? From the Second Pinlong Toward Future State), Yangon: Renaissance Publishing House.

Kyaw, Nay Min (Myo Pya) (2020), *Myanmar Muslim Ei Thaming Saing Yar A Chat A Let* (Historical Facts about Muslims in Myanmar) *(1909–2019)*, Yangon: Lut Lat Ah Myin Sar Pay.

Kyaw Thet (2015), *Myanma Nainggan Taw Thaming* (History of Union of Myanmar), 2nd ed., Yangon: Yadanapon Books.

Kyaw Win U Mya Han and U Thein Hlaing (2011), *Myanmar Politics (1958–1962)*, vol. 3, Nay Pyi Taw: Department of Historical Research.

Kyi Win Sein (Malcolm) (2015), *Me and the Generals of the Revolutionary Council: Memoirs of Turbulent Times in Myanmar*, Whitley Bay: UK Book.

Kyi Win Sein (Malcolm) (2020), *Taw Lan Yey Kaung Si Ma Sit Arna Shin Sanit Si Tho* (Burmese translation of *Revolutionary Council to Military Dictatorship*), Yangon: Lwin Oo Sar Pay.

Maung Aung Myoe (2009), *Building the Tatmadaw: Myanmar Armed Forces Since 1948*, Singapore: Institute of Southeast Asian Studies.

Maung Maung Gyi (1983), *Burmese Political Values: The Socio-Political Roots of Authoritarianism*, New York: Praeger Publishers.

Ministry of Information (1991), *State Law and Order Restoration Council Chairman Commander-in-Chief of the Defence Services General Saw Maung's Addresses*, Yangon: Myanmar Alin News and Guardian New.

Myanmar Baptist Convention (2012), *Myanma Nainggan Nitchin Khariyan Thar Tha Nar Thaming* (The History of Myanmar Baptist Churches) *(1963–2012)*, Yangon: MBC Press.

Myo Oo (2018), 'Myama Thamaing Yay Thar Ni Ta Sit Choe (The Turning Point of Myanmar Historiography)', *Bulletin of Ethnic Study*, 1: 48–59.

P. Kyaw Han (2012), *Tawlan Yay Kaungsi and Kyuntaw* (The Revolutionary Council and Me) *(1962–1974)*, Yangon: Myowaddy Books.

Po Kan Kaung (1992), 'Dhammayal Rohingya (The Danger of the Rohingya)', *Myatt Khin Thit Journal*, 25: 87–104.

Pyi Daung Su Thar (1959), 'Dhammayal (Threat to the Dhamma)', *Ministry of Information*, 8 (6–7): 2–23.

Rogers, Benedict (2015), 'The Contribution of Christianity to Myanmar's Social and Political Development', *The Review of Faith & International Affairs*, 13 (4): 83–99.

Saw Augurlion (2017), *Christian Existence and Issues Related to Nationalism and Religious Identity in Post-colonial Myanmar*, Yangon: MIT Judson Research Centre.

Shwe Lu Maung (1989), *Burma Nationalism and Ideology: An Analysis of Society, Culture and Politics*, Dhaka: University Press.

South, Ashley (2008), *Ethnic Politics in Burma: State of Conflict*, London: Taylor & Francis.

Steinberg, David I. (2001), *Burma: The State of Myanmar*, Washington, DC: Georgetown University Press.

Taylor, Robert H. (2015), *General Ne Win: A Political Biography*, Singapore: ISEAS.

Than Tin (2009), *Sit Hsin Yay Pyi Sit Hsin Yay* (Personal Experience: Operation after Operation), Yangon: Ar Mann Thit.

Than Tun (2003), *Myama Thamaing Shar Pon Taw* (In Search of Myanmar History), Yangon: Daung Book.

Tharaphi Than (2015), 'Nationalism, Religion, and Violence: Old and New Wunthanu Movements in Myanmar', *The Review of Faith & International Affairs*, 13 (4): 16–33.

Thongchai, Winichakul (1994), *Siam Mapped: A History of the Geo-Body of a Nation*, Honolulu: University Hawai'i Press.

Tonkin, Derek (2018), 'Exploring the Issue of Citizenship in Rakhine State', in *Citizenship in Myanmar: Ways of Being in and from Burma*, ed. A. South and M. Lall, 222–63, Chiang Mai: CMU Press.

U Aung Htoo (2014), *Nyein Chan Yay Sit Tan* (Peace Analysis Paper), Yangon: Shwe Kyae.

U San Nyein and U Mya Han (2012), *Myanma Nainggan Yay Ah Pyaung Ah Leh* (Myanmar's Political Transition) *(1962–1974)*, vol.2, Nay Pyi Taw: Department of Historical Research.

Walton, Matthew (2012), 'The "Wages of Burman-ness:" Ethnicity and Burman Privilege in Contemporary in Myanmar', *Journal of Contemporary Asia*, 43 (1): 1–27.

Waters, Tony (2005), 'Why Students Think There Are Two Kinds of American History', *The History Teacher*, 39 (1): 11–21.

Win Tint Tun (2017), *Ah Maung Du Hte` Ka Bama Pyay* (Burma in The Darkness), Bloomington, IN: AuthorHouse UK.

Yay, Patrick (2018). *Agony to Agony. Part One: In Search of Tranquility*, UK AuthorHouse.

Ye Hein Aung (2019), *Lu Mu Tha Ha Zarta Phit Mu and Patipakha Phit Yat Myar Ar Leylamu* (A Case Study on Social Harmony and Conflict among Human Society), Yangon: MCRS.

Newspapers

"Pyi Daung Su Myanmar Naing Gan Taw, Pyi Taung Su Taing Yin Thar Lumyo 144 Myo", *Botataung Daily Newspaper (Burmese)*, 23 February 1973.

"To Draw the Citizen Law, Considering Loyalty, and Monitoring the Mixed Blood", *Myanmar Alin Newspaper (Burmese)*, 12 December 1979.

"Pyi Daung Su Socialist Thamata Myanmar Naing Gan Taw, Taing Yin Thar Lumyo Su Poung 135 Myo", *People Working Daily Newspaper (Burmese)*, 26 September 1990.

Part 2

The Case of Buddhism

4

Visual culture and identity: Ethnic and religious diversity in the Eastern Shan State

Klemens Karlsson

Introduction

Identity and a sense of belonging are important in a world of ethnic and religious diversity. Identity is a complex and multilayered phenomenon. Humans have many identities: gender, religion, work, ethnicity, language, just to name a few. Identity is a feeling of belonging to a group of people who have something in common. Belonging to a religious or an ethnic group is essential for many people. A sense of belonging to a specific geographic place, the place of domicile or place of birth, is essential for many people in engendering a sense of their own unique identity.

Ethnicity is not a permanent and unchanging condition. Ethnic groups constantly redefine themselves and are similarly redefined by others. Southeast Asia is a region of constantly shifting ethnic boundaries. Ethnicity cannot be treated as a primordial given (Santasombat 2001: 13). Already Edmund Leach argued that ethnic groups transferred themselves from one language group to another, pointing out that 'large sections of the peoples we now know as Shan are descendants of hill tribesmen who have in the recent past been assimilated into the more sophisticated ways of Buddhist–Shan culture' (1954: 39). According to Ashley South, 'the nature and significance of ethnicity, and other categories of identity, have changed over the centuries – often according to political and economic circumstances' (2008: 4).

The concept of 'ethnicity' has long been questioned as an analytical tool. How useful is a concept if it signifies only a moment in an ongoing cultural process? At the same time as 'ethnicity' as a concept has been identified as problematic in academia, it has become increasingly important in the real world. In a country with 135 officially recognized ethnic groups, more than fifty years of armed struggle between the Burmese military and a large number of 'ethnic' rebel groups and armies, it is important, I believe, to respect people who consider themselves as belonging to a particular ethnic group. 'We must evaluate what ethnicity signifies for those who claim it' (Shneiderman 2015: 6). An ethnic group is a socially constructed community that often defines itself by its origin or language, and thus, a chosen history is one of the main elements in creating a self-definition of the group and prescribing its boundaries to others. Ethnic identity, religious identity and identification with a place of living are sometimes very difficult to separate. In the example below from the Eastern Shan State of Myanmar, we will become aware of identity as a multilayered phenomenon were ethnicity and religion are closely connected to a place of belonging. Further, this chapter will show how visual culture and material objects may be important as identity markers. Religious objects, statues and architecture may contain symbolic meanings of identity that give people a sense of belonging and uniqueness in a world of religious diversity. But at the same time, visual and material aspects of religion can be used in conflicts and as a potential for violence and hate.

In Myanmar there is a widespread saying: 'To be a Burmese is to be a Buddhist' (Bechert 1984). As a consequence, religions such as Christianity and Islam are sometimes seen as a threat to Burmese identity, exemplified by some Burmese Buddhist monks in the so-called 969 movement.[1] The strong link between religious and ethnic identity has, on occasion, increased the opposition between two warring partners in a conflict. The fusion between religious and ethnic identity has been important during the long conflict between the Burmese military and minorities in border areas. The fusion of religious and ethnic identity is not only significant in conflicts including different religions, but also important in conflicts involving one and the same religion. This chapter will focus on Chiang Tung, a faraway corner of northeast Myanmar, bordering China, Laos and Thailand. It will emphasize the fusion of religious and ethnic identity and pay attention to the unification of visual culture and identity in a world of conflicts and religious diversity. I will argue in this chapter that the Burmese military government uses Buddhist visual culture as a way to Burmanize a local Buddhist minority culture.

Visual culture and material religion

According to David Morgan, members of an imagined community 'need symbolic forms such as songs, dance, images, and food to allow them to participate in something that is larger both spatially and temporally than their immediate environment' (Morgan 2005: 59). Making images or venerating and offering before them is a form of motion that allows believers to connect with the sacred, but it is also a way to establish a sacred space and a religious environment. Beautiful objects can attract people and make them feel that they are close to something sacred. Nevertheless, a religious object is not only sacred. Religious objects must be seen in a much wider context. They play a part in social constructions of a common culture and constitute a binding element for group membership. Beautiful well-known objects can attract people and can make people feel that they belong to a unique community. This applies in Myanmar as well. Religious objects, statues and sculptures arouse strong emotions. People kiss them, cry before them, go on journeys to them, are calmed by them, sit in contemplation before them, feed them, but sometimes even mutilate and destroy them out of hate. Examples of iconoclasm are many from the Christian history of Byzantine and Reformation, but there is also more recently destruction of religious statues. The Bamiyan Buddha statues of Afghanistan were so hated by the Taliban iconoclasts that they had to be destroyed even if there were no Buddhist people living in the country any more. The Bamiyan Buddhas point to an old history and told an alternative way of life the demolishers didn't want to accept. Just as important, the destruction of this old religious statue included in UNESCO's World Heritage Site created a desired attention worldwide. 'We are different! We are special.' This was the message they sent to the world by destroying the Buddhas of Bamiyan.

As far as I know, there has never been a religion without visual expressions. All forms of religion are, in a certain sense, cultural, whereas not all forms of culture are religious. It is unlikely that Buddhism would ever have become a world religion without its Buddha images and awesome religious buildings. Theravāda Buddhists from different regions and countries have, more or less, the same doctrines and scriptures. But visual expressions and rituals tell another story. Burmese Buddhist sculptures and temples have specific symbolic expressions, quite distinct from their Thai counterparts. The same with Christianity. The different Christian denominations share, more or less, the same doctrines and texts, but the visual expression is quite different between a Greek orthodox church and a Baptist one in the American Deep South. It is unlikely that Christianity would have become a world religion without the symbol of the cross and the great variety of depictions of the Christ.

Religious belief has a powerful potential of becoming the preeminent banner or symbol in whose name people organize themselves inwardly and understand their relations with other groups outwardly. Religion, in other words, is one means by which a group's 'inner' and 'outer' are defined and maintained (Morgan 2005: 115). David Morgan (2005) has emphasized visual expressions like Sallman's Head of Christ and the American flag as a way to express a common identity. People dress in a special way to express identity. Often, they don't think about their own identity markers but take it for granted. They are born and grow up with it as a natural world view. But they also grow up and realize that foreign people dress and behave differently. 'Why are they not normal? Why do they look different? Why do they behave differently?' Without deeper understanding between group of people of different ethnic, language or religion, visual expressions make people see others as 'not like us', 'not normal'. Rumours about other people often start with appearance and behaviour. They do not look and behave as we do. They look strange, and talk and behave strangely. People tend to think that their own culture has always been the same. 'Every person is born into a pre-existing imagined order, and his or her desires are shaped from birth by its dominant myths' (Harari 2014: 128). But, of course, culture is not static. Culture changes, not much at the same time, but little by little over generations. At the same time, people like to be special. Members of a small religious community may think that they are not like the others. A common way to express your exceptionalism is to use visual expressions. See, for example, the clothing among the Amish and the Hare Krishna movement or hair style among Sikh men and Buddhist monks. Visual aspects of religion may become important in conflicts. As religious objects, statues and architecture can make people feel angry and act aggressively. A striking example is the Bamiyan Buddha statues in Afghanistan, mentioned above. The iconoclasts demolished the large Buddha statues in purpose to rewrite history, pull down what stands for a different world view and to get maximum media attention.

In my home country Sweden, religious freedom is strongly accepted by the majority of citizens. Nevertheless, if someone wants to make their religion visual, it can result in negative reactions. There have been many examples of protests when Muslims want to build mosques in the centre of cities and towns. People express that they don't want to have foreign buildings in their neighbourhood. 'People are free to practice their religion, as long as they do not express it openly.' The visual can be perceived as dangerous. There have been examples of people who normally are very peaceful and tolerant, but become aggressive towards the visual appearance of a foreign religion. In the following example from the Eastern Shan State, we will see how Buddhist objects, statues and architecture have been used for a political purpose to express identity and rewrite history.

Visual Burmanization of a Buddhist community

Chiang Tung (also spelled Keng Tung, Kyaingtong), in the Eastern Shan State of Myanmar, is the historic borderland between the powerful cultures of the Burmese, Chinese and Siam/Thai. Chiang Tung was established during the late thirteenth century when the Tai people under the leadership of King Mangrai of Chiang Rai/Chiang Mai conquered the region from the Lua people, a Mon-Khmer Palaung speaking people.[2] The majority of people living in Chiang Tung are named Tai Khuen, or simply Khuen, and consider themselves as an ethnic group alongside Tai Lue, Tai Dam and others in the large group of Tai-speaking people. Chiang Tung became an important city state (*mueang*) in Lan Na during the fourteenth and fifteenth centuries. Lan Na was not a nation state in the sense of a firmly connected political unit. It was more a cultural concept and consisted of a few large and many smaller provinces or city states (*mueang*). They were connected via intricately knitted relationships with one another and with the central and most important city state, Chiang Mai. Theravāda Buddhism was imported from the island of Lanka to Chiang Tung during the golden age of Lan Na culture in the fourteenth and fifteenth centuries. Buddhist monks from Southeast Asia took the dangerous trip all the way to the island of Lanka (now called Sri Lanka), stayed there for years of studying and for reordination. Finally, they went back home with the objective of reforming the local *saṅgha* with the support of the local ruler.

From the sixteenth century, Chiang Tung became more dependent on the Burmese rulers and got involved in the long rivalry between the Burmese and the Siamese. Thai history books describe the two hundred years between 1558 and 1774 as the Dark Age, when Lan Na was conquered by the Burmese Toungoo (also Taungoo) dynasty. This is surely an overstatement, because much of local ordinary life went on as usual and most of the time it was only indirectly controlled by the Toungoo kings. Although after 1774 the Burmese lost most parts of Lan Na, Chiang Tung still remained dependent on the Burmese rulers. Siam send troops against Chiang Tung several times during the middle of nineteenth century. One of Chiang Tung's rulers, Sao Mahakhanan, turned his back on Siam and asked for help from the Burmese to drive away the Siamese and rebuild and repopulate Chiang Tung. The borders between the contemporary nation states in upper Southeast Asia owe their existence largely to the later colonial state-making, which often divided people who share much of the same culture and language. Chiang Tung was included in the British empire in 1890 as a part of the so-called 'Frontier Areas', administrated separately from 'Burma proper'. It had a kind of independence and was ruled by the traditional *saopha* ruler under British protection.

During the military coup 1962, the local ruler (*saopha*) of Chiang Tung was put in prison. The military (*Tatmadaw*) was, from now on, and for more than fifty years, the only ruler of Chiang Tung and the rest of Burma/Myanmar. The long struggle for independence by many minority groups had started already before, but was intensified after the military coup. Fighting for independence or autonomy went on for long time in Chiang Tung and the rest of the Shan States. After the so-called 8888 Uprising (8 August 1988) and the election in May 1990, the new Burmese military government, State Law and Order Restoration Council (SLORC), realized that they could not win the struggle against ethnic resistance movements with weapons alone. The government started the Border Area Development Programme, which later (in 1992) became the Ministry for the Progress of Border Areas and National Races. Part of this program were various ceasefire agreements. In 1989, the first ceasefire was arranged between SLORC and armed rebel groups. It was specifically organized by Khin Nyunt, who was then the chief of military intelligence. Between 1989 and 1995, further ceasefire arrangements were brokered with about twenty-five rebellious groups. The Border Area Development Programme built road infrastructure, schools and hospitals in rebel-occupied territories.

Another important ethnic policy of the military was to use culture and religion to include minority regions in the history of Burma/Myanmar, a trend that can be seen very clearly in Chiang Tung. They wanted to reposition the history of Chiang Tung more closely in the history of the Burmese empire. One example of rewriting history through replacement of local visual culture is the deliberate destruction of a royal palace (*haw*) for the ruler (*saopha*) of Chiang Tung, which had been standing in the centre of the town since the fourteenth century. The last palace was built in 1905 by Sao Intaleng, who was the *saopha* for thirty-eight years (1897–1935) during the British time. The palace, built in a typical British-Indian style with pinnacles and towers, was inspired by Intaleng's visit to the Delhi Durbar in 1903, during the celebration of the succession of Edward VII and Alexandra of Denmark as emperor and empress of India. For the Burmese rulers, the palace must have been a reminder not only of the former independence of Chiang Tung State but also of the British colonial times. It was considered dangerous for the military regime and was therefore totally demolished in 1991. The official reason given for the demolition was the alleged need to build a hotel at that place. But it is obvious that the military wanted to get rid of this old visual symbol of the ancient independent city state (*muaeng*) of Chiang Tung. Local people protested against the destruction and refused to cooperate in the demolition. Hence the military had to use workers from other parts of Myanmar. Today, there is a superstition amongst the locals that the hotel is haunted.

During the same time, the Burmese military initiated a systematized Burmanization of Chiang Tung and other minority regions. They sought to include minority regions within Burmese culture and the history of the Burmese empire. They extended the Burmese sacred Buddhist homeland to this far away corner of the country with sacred objects, statues and architecture. One of the most sacred religious building in Myanmar is the Shwedagon Paya in Yangon. It stands out as a symbol of Burmese Buddhism and culture. Therefore, the Burmese realized that it could be used in minority regions to remind people to which country they belong. Today, there is a copy of Shwedagon at each 'entrance' of the Eastern Shan State, from China and from Thailand. One copy was built in Mongla, the border town to China, and another copy was made in Tachileik, the border town to Thailand. The one in Tachileik was built in 1993 and includes typical Burmese stylistic elements, like the eight planetary shrines associated with the days of the week, the Hamsa bird and a statue of the Buddhist monk Upagopta.[3] Close to the border in Tachileik there is also a huge statue of the Toungoo dynasty King Bayinnung. It was Bayinnung who conquered the whole of Lan Na in the middle of the sixteenth century, and all the city states (*muang*) had to pay tribute to him. The statue, standing very close to the border gate to Mae Sai, reminds the Thai people who cross the border of the Burmese power.

Thein Sein, the first civilian president of Myanmar since 1962, was very active in the Burmanization of Chiang Tung. Between 1997 and 2001, General Thein Sein was the highest commander of the Triangle Regional Military Command in Chiang Tung. Later he became the prime minister (2007–11) and, from 2011 to 2016, Myanmar's president. During the years he spend in Chiang Tung, he and his wife were very active in connecting Chiang Tung with Burmese culture.

Thein Sein and his wife are responsible for the big Buddha statue that still stands on one of the hills near Chiang Tung, pointing to the town with his index finger. The statue is twenty meter high and illuminated at night, easily seen all over town (see Figures 4.1 and 4.2).

The statue is much larger than the nearby Catholic church. The construction of the statue started in 1998 and was finished in 2000. During the consecration ceremony, no locals were invited, and there is a superstition that the image will

Figures 4.1 and 4.2 The Big Chiang Tung Buddha statue (20 metres high) pointing to the town with his index finger. Photos by the author.

Visual Culture and Identity

Figure 4.3 The monument of King Anawrahta and Shin Arahan, Chiang Tung. Photo by the author.

bring bad luck. The statue standing on the hill aims to combine two legends, one local Tai Khuen legend and one recently constructed legend made up by the Burmese military. According to the local legend, during his lifetime the Buddha visited the place that later would become Chiang Tung and predicted that a Buddhist prosperous town would be established there. This legend is well known to local people and transmitted in local chronicles, such as the *Chiang Tung Chronicle* (Sāimöng Mangrāi 1981: 211–12). The latter legend tells of an old Burmese Bagan monastery, supposed to once standing on the hill. Relics and *sarira* stones from the Bagan times (ninth to thirteenth centuries) are claimed to have been found on the hill.[4] The supposed Bagan-time monastery is, with all probability, made-up to claim a Burmese origin of Chiang Tung Buddhism. No archaeological evidence has been presented, and it is a well-known fact that Buddhism was introduced to Chiang Tung from Lanka in the fourteenth and fifteenth centuries. Local chronicles and inscriptions do not mention any Bagan influences in Chiang Tung. This remaking of the sacred Buddhist geography of Chiang Tung was not received positively by local people. They became very sceptical of this military-made Buddha statue and consider it was not properly consecrated and therefore not worthy of veneration. At one of his visits to Chiang Tung, the famous Thai Buddhist monk Khruba Bunchum (see more below), who has been living long time on both side of the Thai Myanmar borders, warned local people not to look in the face of the statue. He has long been popular among local ethnic minorities and is considered as a *ton bun* monk, that is, as a monk who has accumulated great merit (*bun*) and perfections (*barami*) in this and his previous lives. Local people think it was an omen when the statue was hit by lightning shortly after the construction and the index finger broke. Therefore, many people avoid the area of the statue.

Several years later, a statue of the Bagan King Anawrahta (eleventh century) together with the monk Shin Arahan was constructed close to the standing Buddha (see Figure 4.3). Shin Arahan is believed to have converted the king and brought Theravāda Buddhism to Bagan. The statue is therefore an additional attempt to emphasize the alleged Burmese origin of Buddhism in Chiang Tung. This statue shows the king on his knees in front of the standing monk, holding a manuscript in his both hands. 'The true faith of Theravāda Buddhism was introduced to Bagan by Shin Arahan, during the reigns of the first four Bagan kings', is inscribed at the pedestal of the statues. It is obvious that this monument had been erected to emphasize Burmese Buddhism and national culture in this minority region. It had been built in 2012 or early 2013 but had disappeared without any traces in 2015. I was told that local people were dissatisfied and complained about the statues. According to some locals, a thunderstorm damaged the monument, while others suppose that the destruction was done deliberately. It was, however, the military who took it away and prepared the ground in such a way that no traces remained. Superstitious beliefs by the military may have been a reason why they did not rebuild it.

There are further examples of Burmese authorities interfering with or instrumentalizing Chiang Tung culture. I will just mention shortly that those who were in charge as the highest commander of the Triangle Regional Military Command in Chiang Tung involved themselves with both the Mahāmuni (*Maha Myat Muni*) Buddha sculpture and the celebration of Songkran (*Thingyan*), Tai New Year, in April. The Chiang Tung copy of the famous Mahāmuni Buddha near Mandalay was made by the initiative of the Khuen ruler Sao Intraleng during colonial times in the 1930s. It was an early form of Burmanization, but on the initiative of the Tai Khuen themselves. Since the 1990s the military commander grabbed power over the sculpture and had his and his wife's names inscribed on top of the image to the effect that local people, when bowing down in veneration of the Buddha, also bow before the commander. Furthermore, at the annual celebration of Songkran, the military commander had taken the symbolic role of the traditional Tai Khuen ruler (*saopha*) and blessed the drum with seven hits with a golden stick. The twenty-four-hours long drumming by the Tai Loi people together with the huge procession down to the river are the essence of the Songkran festival. The main purpose behind the celebration is to ensure fertility, protection and prosperity for the imagined Tai Khuen nation and the traditional Chiang Tung State (Karlsson 2013). The Burmese military commander thus took the symbolic role of the traditional Tai Khuen ruler (*saopha*), both at the Mahāmuni image and at the Songkran festival. The Burmese military authorities express themselves as rulers of Chiang Tung.

The examples above clearly show how religious visual culture can be used in conflicts to express national or ethno-religious identity. Visual culture is a language quite different from written texts. Observing or venerating visual objects involves other emotions than reading a text. Shwedagon Paya, the standing Buddha statue, and the statues of King Anawrahta and Shin Arahan are all witnesses to an attempt to rewrite the history of Chiang Tung and to include the area in a Myanmar national identity dominated by Burmese culture. The examples of the Mahāmuni Buddha statue and the Songkran festival also show the way the military uses symbolic language to express their sovereignty. The question of how local people perceive these Buddhist objects made by the military is complex. The objects were obviously addressed to the local Tai Khuen people who are already long-established Buddhists. The rationale for this use of Buddhist objects was therefore not a missionary one. Instead, these Buddhist objects signified identity: religious, ethnic and national identity. As we will see in the following, Buddhist identity among the Tai Khuen people in Chiang Tung is closely connected to their own ethnic identity, to the place where they are living and to its long and violent history. To better understand the reason behind the use of Burmese Buddhist visual culture by the military, we must therefore look more carefully at the specific tradition of Buddhism and visual culture in Chiang Tung.

The uniqueness of Chiang Tung Buddhism

Buddhism in Chiang Tung has its roots in the culture of Lan Na, not in the old Burmese Bagan culture. As already mentioned, Theravāda Buddhism was imported from the island of Lanka to Chiang Tung during the golden age of Lan Na culture in the fourteenth and fifteenth centuries. Local Buddhists are still very well aware of this and are proud of the unique independent Buddhist *saṅgha* of Chiang Tung. The *saṅgha* of Chiang Tung does not follow the practice of the Burmese *saṅgha* in every respect, which, for example, can be seen in that the Buddhist full moon days do not always fall on the same days in Chiang Tung and the rest of Myanmar. The *saṅgha* of Chiang Tung still observes old calendar traditions from Lan Na time.

The Buddhist tradition of Lan Na has of course not been unchanged, although Buddhists claim that their tradition comes directly from the words of the Buddha himself. From a historical perspective, we can observe that every religious tradition undergoes changes, sometimes more drastic, other times more slowly. The changes have been less drastic in Chiang Tung compared to those parts of Thailand which once also belonged to the city states (*mueang*) of Lan Na, but became part of the nation of Siam in the beginning of the twentieth century, when Bangkok used education and religious reforms to expand to the north. At that time, Siam was surrounded by colonial powers. The British occupied Burma and the French settled in Indo-China. The Siam government managed to stay free from western colonizers, but they embraced a colonial policy themselves against the north. Ratanaporn Sethakul argues that 'Western colonialism was a catalyst for the full colonization of the North into Siam' (Ratanaporn 2018: 81). This process of incorporating the north into Siam took several decades, starting with the Chiang Mai Treaty of 1874, and has been described by many scholars, such as Keyes (1971), Swearer (1999), Bowie (2017) and Ratanaporn (2018).

Bangkok authorities realized that political centralization was not enough to forge national unity. Religion and culture were necessary in the process to establish national unity. By imposing the Sangha Administration Act of 1902, they standardized the *saṅgha* and incorporated the Buddhist tradition of Lan Na into the national *saṅgha* being under direct control of the state (Ratanaporn 2018: 84). Without control of the *saṅgha*, King Chulalongkorn had been unable to control the provinces. King Cholalongkorn's half-brother, Prince Wichirayan, was the main architect of the changes. The 1902 Sangha Act created the Council of Elders (*Mahathera Samakhom*) and brought the *saṅgha*s from all parts of the kingdom under its control. This new hierarchical structure of the *saṅgha* included every village and monastery in the kingdom, and the *saṅgha* became part of the programme of national integration, steered by Bangkok (Khammai Dhammasami 2018: 132, 143–4). The Act also pursued the educational policy of assimilating the people into Siamese culture and simultaneously preventing young children from being Christianized in the missionary schools (Ratanaporn 2018: 88). One circumstance that made the implementation of the reforms difficult was the language differences. There were differences in pronunciation, vocabulary and script between Siamese and the Tai language in the north. The Siamese Thai language had many more loan words from Pali, Sanskrit and Khmer, compared to northern Tai (Kam Mueang or Tai Yuan) spoken among Lan Na people. Therefore, northern monks were sent to Bangkok to study with the intention that they would bring new educational forms back to Lan Na (Ratanaporn 2018: 88). Recitation in regional dialects was discouraged and reforms were made to regularize ritual chants in Pali. In the 1940s, the government even authorized the burning of palm-leaf manuscripts written in the Lan Na (*tham*) script (Swearer 1999: 203). To sum up, the Sangha Act of 1902 incorporated all monks into one national structure, established a hierarchical principle of authority with the Council of Elders at the top and established a national system of clerical education. This colonization of the north brought every principality in the former Lan Na to the national state of Siam, except those that were outside the border of control, that is, Chiang Tung and Chiang Hung (Sipsong Panna) who belonged to the British and the Chinese.

At the same time as Lan Na Buddhism was integrated into the national Thai *sangha*, the British conquered Burma, including Chiang Tung. Unlike the authorities in Bangkok, the British did not interfere with religious affairs and the Shan States came to belong to the so-called Frontier Areas, still ruled under British protection by the traditional *saopha* rulers. The old traditional Buddhist culture in Chiang Tung continued to flourish during the British period, unlike that of its neighbours in present day north Thailand which were drastically changed by the authorities in Bangkok. Hence Buddhism in Chiang Tung not only preserved but also evolved much of its traditional character through the colonial period until today.

One important specific feature of the Chiang Tung Buddhist tradition is the use of the *tham* script, once used all over Lan Na. This *tham* script is used both for Pali and the local Tai Khuen language. It is used for a local Buddhist calendar and Buddhist literature with a rich tradition of Jataka tales, both traditional Pali *jātaka*s and local *jātaka*s. Neither Burmese nor monks from the Shan States outside Chiang Tung can read *tham* script. And because they cannot read Pali written in *tham* script, monks from Myanmar have difficulties in cooperating with Chiang Tung monks. Also, there is a great difference between Burmese and Tai languages, which have developed quite distinct ways to pronounce Pali texts. Therefore, it is next to impossible for Burmese and Tai Khuen monks to jointly perform ritual recitations.

Figure 4.4 Temple drum, Chiang Tung. Photo by the author.

Figure 4.5 Temple banners, Chiang Tung. Photo by the author.

Visual Culture and Identity

Figure 4.6 Gold stencilling, Chiang Tung. Photo by the author.

According to Ratanaporn Sethakul, the traditional Lan Na *saṅgha* was built on the basis of 'seniority, charismatic qualities, and lineage, i.e. the relations of teachers and ordained students' (Ratanaporn 2018: 84). This corresponds in many ways to the present state of the *saṅgha* in Chiang Tung. Authority in the *saṅgha* comes from seniority, which means the number of years in Chiang Tung *saṅgha* since ordination, not from some standard monastic education system.

There is no official government control of the *saṅgha*. Instead, there is one head monk called Ayatham, who is selected by the local Sangha Council, without any interference by the Burmese authorities. One important duty of the Ayatham is to be the expert on the Chiang Tung Buddhist lunar calendar. The monks of Chiang Tung are proud of their calendar from Lan Na times, and believe it is more original than the calendars of neighbouring peoples. It is the responsibility of the Ayatham to make calculations for each new year and to determine the dates of the full and new moon and all the Buddhist celebrations during the coming year. This calendar does not correspond to the Burmese Buddhist calendar. Therefore, the new moon or full moon days do not always fall on the same days in Chiang Tung and the rest of Myanmar. In 2019, for example, only full moon days in February, April, June and August

Figure 4.7 Vihāra, Wat In, Chiang Tung. Photo by the author.

fell on the same day in Chiang Tung and the rest of Myanmar. There have been arguments against the traditional use of the Khuen Buddhist calendar. Local Burmese authorities want Buddhists in Chiang Tung to follow the national Buddhist calendar, as the rest of Myanmar. The present Ayatham has completely resisted all such attempts.

Veneration of charismatic holy monks are still a living tradition both in Chiang Tung and Northern Thailand. One of the most respected and adored monks who fits in this tradition is Khruba Bunchum, whom I mentioned above. He was born a Thai citizen and ordained in the Thai monastic order, but has spent long time in Myanmar and served as an abbot in the eastern Shan State (Amporn 2017: 191). His transnational characteristics has made him popular among ethnic minorities and have a high reputation in Chiang Tung which he continuously visits. This *ton bun* tradition of *khruba* monks is central to the Buddhist tradition of Chiang Tung and north Thailand, and people make pilgrimages to such a person in order to be in his presence and receive some of his merit.

Buddhist visual culture with roots from Lan Na culture are quite distinct compared to Burmese Buddhist culture. The Buddhist visual culture in Chiang Tung has much in common with Northern Thailand. Temple drums, temple banners, gold stencilling on the inner walls and teakwood pillars are some of its features (see Figures 4.4, 4.5 and 4.6).

This visual Buddhist culture of the Lan Na tradition is clearly different from the Burmese culture, but also from the rest of the Shan States and can make people feel that they belong to a unique community. One of the most obvious differences between Chiang Tung and the Shan States west of Salween are the structural design of the monasteries. Shan monasteries are very much influenced by Burmese design. Most of them consist of one single building on stilts that serves as both a residence for monks and a temple with a sheltering Buddha image in a wide hall. The floor is usually divided into three different heights, separated by about 15–20 centimetres. The lowest level is for lay persons and next for monks. In the middle of the building on the highest level is the central Buddha statue (Robinne 2003: 75–92; see also Murakami 2012 and Cheong 2016). A very distinctive feature is the high and complex roof. The Burmese influence is very much evident in these Shan Monasteries. In contrast, a Chiang Tung monastery forms a monastic complex consisting of several connected buildings such as *vihāra*, *ubosot* and *chedi* and is similar to the structure of the monasteries in Northern Thailand (see Figure 4.7).

Conclusion

Religion is not only a matter of belief. Religion is about identity. Who am I, who are we and who are they? In a world of ethnic and religious diversity, religious identity is a sense of belonging to something bigger than the individual. The examples we just looked at display a strong link between religious and ethnic identity. The fusion between religious and ethnic identity has been important during the long conflict between the Burmese military and minorities in border areas. My chapter emphasizes this fusion of religious and ethnic identity in the dispute between the Burmese military and a Buddhist minority group in the Eastern Shan State.

The unique Buddhist tradition with its roots in Lan Na and a very special visual culture make Chiang Tung and its people very distinct compared to the rest of Myanmar. Therefore, the construction of copies of the Shwedagon Paya, the large standing Buddha statue, and the statues of King Anawrahta and Shin Arahan, all made by the Burmese military, are witness to the attempt of including Chiang Tung more closely in a collective Myanmar national identity, shaped by Burmese culture. It can be described as a visual Burmanization. As has been shown, the introduction of Buddhist architecture and statues was not for missionary purposes. Chiang Tung Buddhism belongs to the Theravāda tradition just like Burmese Buddhism. Instead, the purpose was to implant Burmese culture in this minority area. Shwedagon Paya is used as a model because it stands out as a symbol of Burmese Buddhism and culture. Further, the standing Buddha statue and the statues of King Anawrahta and Shin Arahan had been erected to connect Chiang Tung with the Buddhist tradition of Bagan, often called the 'First Burmese Empire'.

Notes

1 The 969 movement is a radical religious movement known for promoting anti-Muslim sentiment. Its chief proponent is a monk named Wirathu.
2 This Lua ethnic group (Mon-Khmer, Palaung Austroasiatic language) is also mentioned in literature as Lawa. Other names for them used in different chronicles and inscriptions are Damila, Milakkha and Kha (slave). The Wa people living on both sides of the Myanmar/China border have their origin in this Lua people who had to escape from the Tai conquerors.
3 Upagupta (or Shin Upagutta) is a great cult figure in Myanmar. He is venerated as a protective figure endowed with magical powers. He is commonly depicted sitting cross-legged with a hand tilted into an alms bowl and looking up at the sky.
4 The relics are believed to have been enclosed in the statue and the *sarira* stones are exhibited in bottles at a small museum close to the statue.

References

Amporn, Jirattikorn (2017), 'Khruba Bunchum: The Holy Man of the Twenty-First Century and His Transnational and Diverse Community of Faith', in *Charismatic Monks of Lanna Buddhism*, ed. P. T. Cohen, 191–216, Copenhagen: NIAS Press.

Bechet, Heinz (1984), 'To Be a Burmese Is to Be a Buddhist: Buddhism in Burma', in *The World of Buddhism*, ed. H. Bechert and R. Gombrich, 147–58, London: Thames and Hudson.

Bowie, Katherine A. (2017), 'Khruba Siwichai: The Charismatic Saint and the Northern Sangha', in *Charismatic Monks of Lanna Buddhism*, ed. P. T. Cohen, 27–57, Copenhagen: NIAS Press.

Cheong, Conan (2016), 'The Art of Shan State', in, *Cities and Kings: Ancient Treasures from Myanmar*, ed. Stephen A. Murphy, 74–86, Singapore: Asian Civilisations Museum.

Harari, Yuval Noah (2014), *Sapiens: A Brief History of Humankind*, London: Vintage Books.

Karlsson, Klemens (2013), 'The Songkran Festival in Chiang Tung: A Symbolic Performance of Domination and Subordination between Lowland Tai and Hill Tai', *Tai Culture*, 23: 50–62.

Keyes, Charles F. (1971), 'Buddhism and National Integration in Thailand', *Journal of Asian Studies*, 30 (3): 551–67.

Khammai Dhammasami (2018), *Buddhism, Education and Politics in Burma and Thailand: From the Seventeenth Century to the Present*, London: Bloomsbury.

Leach, Edmund R. (1954), *Political Systems of Highland Burma: A Study of Kachin Social Structure*, London: Athlone Press.

Morgan, David (2005), *The Sacred Gaze: Religious Visual Culture in Theory and Practice*, Berkeley: University of California Press.

Murakami, Tadayoshi (2012), 'Buddhism on the Border: Shan Buddhism and Transborder Migration in Northern Thailand', *Southeast Asian Studies*, 1 (3): 365–93.

Ratanaporn Sethakul (2018), 'Lanna Buddhism and Bangkok Centralization in Late Nineteenth to Early Twentieth Century', in *Theravada Buddhism in Colonial Contexts*, ed. T. Borchert, 81–100, New York: Routledge.

Robinne, François. (2003), 'The Monastic Unity: A Contemporary Burmese Artefact?', in *The Buddhist Monastery: A Cross-Cultural Survey*, P. Pichard and F. Lagirarde, 75–92, Paris: École française d'Extrême-Orient.

Sāimöng Mangrāi, Sao (1981), *The Pāḍaeng Chronicle and the Jengtung State Chronicle Translated*, Ann Arbor: Center for South and Southeast Asian Studies, University of Michigan.

Santasombat, Yos (2001), *Lak Chang: A Reconstruction of Tai Identity in Daikong*, Canberra: Pandanus Books.

Shneiderman, Sara (2015), *Rituals of Ethnicity: Thangmi Identities between Nepal and India*, Philadelphia: University of Pennsylvania Press.

South, Ashley (2008), *Ethnic Politics in Burma: States of Conflict*, New York: Routledge.

Swearer, Donald K. (1999), 'Centre and Periphery: Buddhism and Politics in Modern Thailand', in *Buddhism and Politics in Twentieth-Century Asia*, ed. I. Harris, 194–228, London: Pinter.

5

Tempered Tantrism: Buddhism of exception on the Shan Plateau

Jane M. Ferguson

Introduction

'Sao Myat was the only monk in the world to have kon ho zaw ki (dreadlocks). He would always be smiling, and I heard Shan people say that they have seen him floating as far away as Chiang Dao District (Chiang Mai Province, Thailand). He is special and important to the Shan', said Sai Sai, a Shan cultural educator. The Shan State, the largest in Myanmar, incorporates tremendous historic, cultural and geographic diversity. Following the Burmans, the Shan are the largest predominantly Buddhist ethnic nationality in Myanmar. People in paddy-agriculture based Shan State have practised Theravāda Buddhism for centuries, in tandem with their Burman, Lanna (Northern Thailand) and Lao neighbours. The precolonial political units can be characterized as rice paddy-agricultural Theravāda Buddhist fiefdoms ruled by hereditary princes or *sao pha* (Burmese: *sawbwa*). Burmese Buddhism has been noted for its doctrinal variance, and the Shan State perhaps even more so. Shan Buddhist practices and ideas of political and cultural prestige have often been schematized according to geography, with the Salween River dividing the 'cis-Salween' states on the West, from the 'trans-Salween' states to the East. The former cis-Salween states are located close to the Burmese heartland and therefore more involved with Burmese spheres of cultural, political and religious influences. The trans-Salween states, being located in Eastern Shan State, at a crossroads with Yunnan (China), Laos and Lanna (Northern Thailand) are oriented towards those influences. The generalization is instructive for an initial understanding of the political and cultural dynamics in this complex, cellular area. However, it is also geographically determinist and could be seen to suggest that Shan practices would be mimetic or derivative of those of their powerful neighbours. That which is not characterized as derivative is automatically classified as 'local', whatever that might be taken to mean; often it is the catch-all for any practices not ostensibly connected with a dominant school or the cultural hegemony of a political power. This has often been the burden of those which are exogamously labelled 'animist'. Finally, the geographic distinction could foreclose the possibility that practices in certain areas of the Shan State resonate with those much further afield and even those which are survivals of former systems long extinct in neighbouring polities.

During the 1970s, an exceptional religious figure gained fame in the city of Möng Pan, Southern Shan State: a Buddhist monk named Sao Myat (1943–1980). He is still revered by many Shan people in Southern Shan State as well as in Thailand, but particularly among some groups of Shan separatists. In addition to being a Theravāda Buddhist practitioner, his spiritualism incorporates symbolic elements and capacities of Tantrism. As Shan informants iterate, he is the only Buddhist monk in the world to have long, matted hair or dreadlocks. In addition to purported abilities to hover in the air, Sao Myat, after passing, had attained arahant status (i.e. an enlightened Buddhist monk) and self-mummified. Following Sao Myat's self-mummification, his dreadlocked preserved body was put in a glass case and enclosed in a pagoda monument on top of a hill near Möng Pan. Today his corpse is venerated as a near-Buddha relic or supernatural object.

It is Sao Myat's non-orthodox qualities – and his series of remarkable accomplishments and supernatural skills – that give him his special and unique strength and, conversely, reaffirm the position of Buddhism in Shanland; the exception presents complicated symbolic fringes to its very orthodoxy. Indeed, the special significance of his very ordination as a monk could be seen as an assertion of the Möng Pan monastery abbot's sovereignty over the spiritual domain of the area: he could decide to permit Sao Myat's ordination without requiring that he complete the conventional ritual of shaving his head. As a figure with spiritual matted locks, what does it mean to Buddhism that Sao Myat was admitted to ordination? In turn, how can we understand spiritual networks across Shanland that see him as a translocal *weikza* (Burmese sorcery or wizardry) rather than as a Shan 'deviation' or a 'local' manifestation of Tantrism?

Following some general remarks about the history of Shan States and the local historiography of Möng Pan as part of the Theravāda oecumene, in this chapter, I will discuss the situation for Shan sovereignty and religious sponsorship as part of the Frontier Areas in British Burma and later postcolonial contested sovereignty. Then, the chapter considers the ways in which twentieth-century political contestation has also created religious sponsorship which raises questions about the nature of so-called 'state-religion' relationships in a place where there are multiple, often overlapping, sovereignties. Finally, I will analyse the religious symbolism and importance of Sao Myat, as reputably the only Theravāda monk with matted locks. His ability to 'self-mummify' following death is also considered in relation to his abilities in life. Although this chapter does not seek to argue that the Shan context alone generated Sao Myat's 'remarkable-ness', as it were, there is an uncanny relationship between political contestation, exceptional monks and unique religious practices. This situation is partly connected to the cellular nature of Shan political affiliations. They have served to preserve certain practices which are not considered part of mainstream Myanmar Buddhism today and to reassert the importance of being remarkable and unorthodox in the context of many kinds of outside pressures.

Stating Shan Buddhism

In the study of religious practices in Southeast Asia, the role of the state and of state power have frequently been overdetermined. Because of their relationship with the majority nation, minority groups' practices in Thailand, for example, are sometimes not studied as part of Buddhism. Or, when their religious practices are considered, they are studied in terms of either mimicry or resistance (Hayami and Kataoka 2016). The cis-Salween Shan States offer a challenging case study. Seen as Myanmar Buddhists, sometimes their practices are equated with Burmese Buddhism (and evidence is ample) although, as ethnically and culturally Tai, there may be the expectation that they practise forms of Buddhism more associated with those of Thailand. As religion(s) have been understood as discrete systems of meanings or schools, as with state regulations based on Western notions, comparative religion studies are also facilitated (Kataoka 2012: 361). Within this paradigm, the expansion of text-based religions, in general, coincides with the tentacles of state-building practices; part of the ideological leviathan as it were. Often in histories of nation-building and religion, we are presented with stories in which non-orthodox practices are marginalized, seen as organic and local. It is the very fusion of previous spiritual belief with the incoming text-based structures which give the religion its local connection. There are numerous historical examples in Burma and Southeast Asia, from the incorporation of the *nats* (the remaining spirits of local places or individuals who died violent deaths) into a standardized pantheon, making use of various religious motifs as political legitimation (Collins 1998: 106; Keyes 1977: 72). Research about the ways in which supernaturalism, ghosts, *phi* (meaning ghosts in Thai), *nats* and *weikza* and their various comrades and enemies are incorporated into Theravāda Buddhist practice in Mainland Southeast Asia is also well established (Spiro 1967; Brac de la Perriere 2009; Brohm 1963).

Symbolic incorporation and re-signification are hardly new nor revolutionary, but the process offers a useful lens to understand religiosity, politics and state-building, particularly in an area like the Shan Plateau, where the twentieth century has brought seemingly endless wars and ongoing political and ethnic contestation. A quick caveat, however: I am not saying that these practices are intrinsically 'Shan' or that ethnicity forms a discrete category for organizing spiritual practices in these areas. The label can belie other kinds of social difference or lead to a heuristic tag which distracts from the ways people understand their own practices. Understanding Buddhist – or any religious – practices according to ethnic categories intrinsically limits our lens to understanding how people actually practise religion in the here and now, and what it means to their daily experience. How ethnic communities make meaning and perceive their practices as their own, that is, how they 'own them', can make these practices appear to be connected to ethnonationalism, especially for outsiders. Because of the political situation in which ethnic identity is given primacy, studies of religious practices among that group run the risk of overdetermining the role of ethnicity in those practices. In other words, ethnic names can sometimes be used as facile labels for cultural practices not necessarily connected to ethnic identity.

Because of their location, geography and political economy at the crossroads of numerous cultural and trade networks, people in the Shan Plateau have had a long history of pursuing belief systems and practices beyond the orthodoxy of the *saṅgha* and of the powers to which they have been vassal states. At the same time, there is a cellular organization of political power, allowing for a relatively high degree of local political autonomy (Ferguson 2021). Despite centuries of adoption of Theravāda Buddhism and literacy, the cellular political organization of Shan States has never put a large premium on cultural or bureaucratic homogeneity, the tremendous variety of Shan written scripts offering evidence of this (Sai Kam Mong 2004: xiv).

Situating Möng Pan on the Shan Plateau

Möng Pan is one of the smaller Shan principalities, consisting of approximately 3,000 square miles. It is located in Southern Shan State with its southern border abutting Mae Hong Son Province in Northwest Thailand. The town got its name because of the pond in its southwest: the pond has an island in the middle of it, making it appear as if it were a rotary; *pan* (in Möng Pan) means mix or rotary in Shan. Möng Pan is just to the west of the Salween River and therefore considered one of the cis-Salween states (but had trans-Salween dependencies), though a small part of Möng Pan is technically on the east side of the Salween. The *sao pha* (prince) of Möng Pan has maintained relationships with the *sao pha* of Möng Nai (its immediate neighbour) as well as with Keng Tung in Eastern Shan State and Lanna (Northern Thai) principalities.

Compared to other Shan States, Möng Pan is not very old. It was founded in the eighteenth century as a trading town, during the time of King Alaungmintaya, founder of Burma's Konbaung Dynasty (eighteenth to nineteenth century). Möng Pan, via Möng Nai, was a vassal state to the Burmese at the time of the fall of Mandalay in the third and final Anglo-Burmese war in 1885. In addition to rice paddy agriculture, Möng Pan has valuable teak and in the caves are deposits of saltpetre. At the time of British annexation, Möng Pan was ruled by *Sao Pha* Hkun Htun (r. 1858–86) and soon thereafter Khun Leng (r. 1886–8) and Khun Num (r. 1888–1918) (Simms 2017: 217). As with other Shan States, Theravāda Buddhism is the principal religion in the area, and given its location and vassal status in the eighteenth and nineteenth centuries, it was symbolically oriented towards Burmese ways of practice, although with a great deal of variation and incorporation of other practices.

As the British had declared that all of the former vassal states to the Konbaung Crown would become part of the colony, the Shan States were zoned as part of the Frontier Areas. However, the process of annexation to the empire was violent and difficult, with Möng Pan at one point being burned down and abandoned of its inhabitants (Simms 2017: 2016).

Following the annexation and restoration of the town, the *sao pha* of Möng Pan was allowed to maintain a large degree of political autonomy. With the removal of the Burmese king by the British, the public lost their principal sponsor of the Buddhist religion; for the Shan States this was not the case. *Sao phas* were the major benefactors and supporters of the local temples and sponsored Buddhist festivals replete with food, music and entertainment. While the Burmese Buddhist devotees saw the British imposition as the cause of a decline of the *sāsana*, the Buddhist religion, this sentiment was not shared by people in the Shan States.

During the late nineteenth century, using ethnonationalist rhetoric of racial and cultural similarity between the Thais and the Shan, the Siamese government had entertained the possibility of annexing some of the Shan States, but the racial argument was insufficient for the British in the negotiation of borders between British Burma and Siam. During the Second World War, however, in exchange for their pact with the Japanese, Thailand 'received' two Shan States: Möng Pan and Keng Tung; the *sao pha* of these two states were infuriated, as Thai Soldiers were sent to occupy these two Shan principalities. Following the end of the war, the two Shan States were transferred back to Burma.

At independence in 1948, the Shan State was amalgamated as part of the Union of Burma but with the constitutional caveat that the State had the right to separate after ten years, provided it was the will of the population to do so. In the interim, the hereditary *sao pha* maintained a degree of autonomy, but with the ongoing internal conflicts (outside armed groups in Shan State in the 1950s included the Communist Party of Burma, the Kuomintang and increasingly the Burma Army) the situation became more and more tenuous. In 1959, during General Ne Win's military caretaker regime (1958–60), instead of having the promised referendum regarding withdrawal from the Union, there was a forced buyout of the Shan *sao phas*, who surrendered their political autonomy to the Burmese central authorities. The Shan State has been part of the Union of Burma, now Republic of the Union of Myanmar, ever since and is also the location of one of the longest ongoing internal conflicts in modern history.

Turning to history according to Möng Pan lore, there is less emphasis on the political influence or domination of other more powerful groups. Local histories about Möng Pan tell of the mythical and cultural contributions of its residents and finally signal the importance of Shan movements for political autonomy. First of all, rather than use a more conventional division of precolonial, colonial and postcolonial history, Möng Pan's historiography is situated according to three eras:

1. 'Yi Saeng Gaw Era' (*Ban Sao Nang Yi Saeng Gaw*),
2. 'Great Teacher Kaw Li Era' (*Ban Sao Ku Maw Long Gaw Li*), and finally
3. 'Num Süek Harn Era' – Brave Young Warriors (*Ban Num Süek Harn*).

For the local schema for Möng Pan history, the first era represents the founding myth for the town, the second, that of a scholar emerging during a period of instability (including a period of twenty year abandonment of the town). The final era, that of the Num Süek Harn 'Brave Young Warriors' era, is crucial for considering the biography of Sao Myat.

In brief: Num Süek Harn 'Brave Young Warriors' was an armed Shan liberation movement which formed in 1958, the tenth anniversary of Burmese independence and the time promised for which the Shan State would have the option to withdraw from the Union. Möng Pan was an important town in relation to this history of resistance, as it was part of a key corridor to trade and support from Thailand and would also be a source of funds and recruits for the ongoing fight against Burmese government encroachment. In relation to the biography of Sao Myat, this last era is important not only because of the fact that Sao Myat's fame spreads at this time but also because his aura and his exception are a narrative that is important to Shan ethnonationalists until today.

The smiling dreadlocked monk

The story of Sao Myat, like the mysticism that he represents, is a blend of straightforward biography and remarkable events. I have amalgamated the following biography from the stories of Shan interlocutors and photos of the placards at Sao Myat's shrine in Möng Pan. He was born in Wan Waw Som Village outside of Möng Pan on Saturday, 28 August 1943 to parents Lung Sayay Gaw Ya and Pa Nyo. The local village headman, Sao Kham Sai named him Sai Ga Kham; he was one of two children. His sister's name was Nang Oo.

When Sai Ga Kham was ten years old, he started to study Southern Shan-Tai and Lanna scripts with the abbot at a local monastery. Two years later, as is typical for a Buddhist son, Sai Ga Kham made merit on behalf of his parents and became a novice monk, staying in the monastery in that position for another two years; his novice name was Sang Nanta (the term *sao sang* being Shan for novice). He continued his studies and tutelage as the disciple of various abbots at different temples in the Möng Pan area. When he was eighteen, he studied with Saya Santasiri. The following year, he transferred to Mwe Taw temple in Möng Pan, where he continued to study and to practise insight meditation.

At the age of nineteen, in order to practice meditation more intently, he left the monastery and went to the forest. As part of his dedication to otherworldly

Figure 5.1 Sao Myat Portrait. Disclaimer: Efforts were made to find the copyright holder of this image.

matters, he stopped grooming himself: no more haircuts or cutting his fingernails or toenails. Some villagers looked at him as eccentric or crazy. Rather than eat normal food, he ate the leaves of *mon lam* plants (it is a species in the arum family) which gave him the strength to carry on. He moved to a spot on a mountain top to continue his meditation.

During his meditation sessions on a mountain top, there was a series of remarkable events, evidence of his insight and later auspiciousness and exceptional abilities. In one of the incidents, a horse that had come up the mountain fell and died adjacent to where Sao Myat was sitting in meditation. The horse lacked an owner, so nobody came to retrieve the horse's corpse. It started to rot and decompose. The putrid stench did not distract Sao Myat from his meditation, and he continued in meditation until the dead horse was but a pile of bones.

In another remarkable event, a pack of wolves ascended the mountain to Sao Myat. They bit at each other and bit at him. However, Sao Myat's aura of *metta* (loving kindness) and smile subdued the wolves. Despite having been bitten, there was no evidence of injury on Sao Myat's skin. Finally, he was able to maintain intense meditation during a heavy storm, and following a few minutes, the rain started to let up around his body.

By 1967, Sao Myat had not been speaking to others for several years. He returned to Mwe Taw temple, and according to several interlocutors, the abbot said, 'Have sympathy for this figure of a monk who has been out in the sun and the rain, exposed to the elements. We shall welcome him to the temple.' Other laymen were inspired by his story, and at that time he acquired the new name *Sao Myat* (Lord Pinnacle) *Kon Ho Yao* 'Lord Myat of the Long Hair'. Devotees noted that he had an exceptionally wide smile, and it was sometimes unclear to them what he was smiling about.

He died in August of 1980 at the age of thirty-six. I surmise it to be malaria or some other kind of fever. Although he died in Möng Pan, it was said that a layperson in Chiang Mai, Northern Thailand, had seen his figure and even took a photo of him as souvenir evidence.

Sao Myat's remarkable endeavours did not end with his death. Without the injection of any embalming fluid, rather than rot, his corpse self-mummified. According to the story, this was a demonstration of his supernatural power: his body could resist the normal rotting that a corpse usually experiences. It is regarded as evidence that his body completely lacked the normal human polluting components, such as bile, urine or faeces, and as a result of his meditational achievements and deep insight which led to a purified countenance. Three years after his death, Sao Myat's self-mummified corpse was taken as a sacred relic by lay people.

Devotees established a hilltop shrine for him outside of Möng Pan, where a golden pagoda has been built around the glass case containing his self-mummified corpse. At the platform level of the pagoda are windows, so devotees can look through and see Sao Myat's corpse in the glass case in the middle of the pagoda. Surrounding the shrine are offerings, framed photos of Sao Myat, as well as a concrete statue of him, replete with his long hair and wide smile. The name of the hilltop pagoda is the *Kyong Sao Myat Kon Ho Yao*, 'Temple of Long-Haired Sao Myat'. However, there have been sightings of his luminescent aura in Chiang Dao (a district in Chiang Mai Province) and many believers have photos of him on their Buddha altar shelves in their homes. This particular image (see Figure 5.1 was sold for such a purpose and reads at the bottom, 'Sao Myat Möng Pan'.

Untangling the spiritual meanings of Sao Myat

As a remarkable individual, the figure of Sao Myat challenges our understandings of religious doctrine and power in upland Southeast Asia.

He is at the intersection of Tantrism, Buddhism and what is called *weikza* in Burmese, or supernatural wizardry. Most immediately noticeable is Sao Myat's hair. Rather than have a shaved head as is expected as part of the Buddhist ordination ritual, he has matted, locked hair; when he returned to the temple after his years in the forest, he was not required to shave his head to reintegrate.

Commonly referred to in English as dreadlocks, the matted locks of hair have a long history of practice in Asia, which is often associated with Tantric Buddhism, in Burmese referred to as *Passayana* or Vajrayana Buddhism. In brief: Tantric Buddhism was a movement which emerged in Hinduism and Buddhism in the first millennium CE, incorporating magic and antinomian practices, often focusing on worldly needs of lay people rather than their ultimate liberation or higher rebirth. Within mainstream Buddhism, Tantrism is usually seen as 'heretic' and in Buddhist Studies often as 'tribal', peripheral or shamanic (Gellner and Gombrich 2015: 889). In Tibet, from the beginnings of Buddhism as practised there in the eighth century, there is evidence of nonordained tantric masters (Tibetan: *ngakpas*) tying their matted locks above their heads in topknots (Bogin 2008: 99). Joffe (2019) has examined how Tibetan *ngakpa* holders of specific tantric Buddhist vows consume alcohol and have sex (though not within a monastery). They are often hired as ritual specialists (Joffe 2019: 11). The matted hair is referred to as tantric yogic 'retreat hair', which for the Tibetan *ngakpas* signifies one of the main elements of naturalness (Joffe 2019: 194).

Obeyesekere (1984) has written about the Buddhist/Hindu ecstatic 'priests and priestesses' who wear their matted hair as part of their otherworldly demeanour and ritual significance in the pilgrimage town of Kataragama, Sri Lanka. In Southern India, there are female ecstatics who adopt the matted locks of hair, known as *jade*, as evidence of the presence of the goddess Yellamma (Ramberg 2009). In reference to Hindu ascetics, the meaning of the hairstyle has been interpreted as 'abodes of divinity, as symbols of unrestrained sexuality, and as phalluses' (Bogin 2008: 85). Within Sao Myat's legend, there is no mention of sexuality or power in the hair; the abbot still made an exception and did not require that he shave his head, which raises the issue regarding the contrast in significance between shaving versus growing matted locks.

The shaving act is part of the process of becoming a novitiate through the adoption of a new kind of personhood, which Sao Myat had done when he had entered the temple as a *sao sang*. However, because of his matted locks, Sao Myat was not a lay person seeking to become a monk: he was another kind of ascetic becoming a monk. In taking this kind of powerful hair, the Tantric adept uses the matted locks as a force for making spiritual progress (Lang 1995: 34). While the shaven head in Buddhism and the matted locks in Hinduism are both supposed to represent chastity, they are not the same; Hindu chastity involves withholding sex in the interest of conserving semen, while in the case of Buddhist monks or nuns the shaving of hair is as sign of renunciation (Lang 1995: 32). These particular characterizations, however, perhaps belie the diverse ways in which the ideologies might be interpreted. Gananath Obeyesekere's interpretation of matted locks as sexualized has been critiqued as a result of his own sexualized gaze (Lang 1995: 33). Edmund Leach argues that for ritual situations, long hair signifies unrestrained sexuality while short hair indicates restricted sexuality and a shaven head is celibacy (Leach 1958: 154).

Sexuality and masculinity can be part of the story for understanding the meaning of the shaved head as well. According to the Buddha legend, Prince Siddhartha, after departing from his family and the palace, cut his long hair as a sign of renunciation and becoming an ascetic. The cutting of the hair for the person ordaining as a monk or nun recreates this as a phase in the Buddha's life, but also serves to demarcate one's change in status. A nun, for example, has rejected a form of worldly beauty and by shaving her head ostensibly removes that particular form of temptation (Lang 1995: 35). There is the corollary point, however, for the young boy, the ritual of shaving the head to become a novice will signal a start to self-consciousness of masculinity; the importance of the repeated shaving of the head while in the monastery is an ongoing commitment. In relation to sexuality, however, 'just as one's hair can regrow, so can one's sexual desire re-emerge' (Keyes 1986: 73).

But these other interpretations do not explain what the matted hair would have meant to Sao Myat or to his followers. In addition to Sao Myat, there is evidence of matted-haired mystical figures in Shan State. For example, in her book, *Shans at Home*, Leslie Milne described and photographed a 'Hindu Mendicant' who travelled to the Northern Shan village of Nam Kham in 1907. This man renounced his home and family and travelled to the Shan areas via Tibet and Manipur. The Shan abbot allowed him to stay at the monastery, and the local Shan respected him as an ascetic (Milne 1970: 57). Milne's photograph of this Hindu ascetic shows him in meditation and with matted locks of hair.

Former Shan United Revolutionary Army (SURA) veterans referred to the matted locks as *kon ho saw ki*, or 'Zawgyi' hair. The Shan term *saw ki* is cognate with the Burmese *zawgyi*, which is now best known as a particular figure, because of his incorporation as a *dramatis personae* in *zat pwe* theatre and *yok the thabin* puppet shows. The figure is the Burmese appropriation of an Indian yogi, often a master of occult practices using his powers for non-Buddhist ends (Ferguson and Mendelson 1981: 65). Today, in the computing world, it is possible that younger generations recognize Zawgyi principally as the name for an encoding system for a Burmese script computer font. The meaning of the hair, however, as explained by more than one Shan interlocutor, was that the matted locks prevented the power conserved in the body from escaping though the ends of the hair. Another interlocutor told me that there is a Shan State Army soldier who wears *kon ho zawki* 'supernatural hair'. In contrast, Sao Myat's story of acquiring the matted hair is associated with a departure from the worldly concerns of looking after his body (which also included his finger and toenails) and not with an effort of keeping his power inside his body; on the other hand, that his hair became long while he meditated is more than coincidence. It represents his ability to acquire depth of insight, just as his ability to continue meditation despite the rotting corpse of a horse putrefying in front of him.

Speaking of putrefying, an important reason for the continued veneration of Sao Myat is that upon death, he self-mummified. The ability of a corpse to self-preserve is proof of special spiritually advanced capacities, and there is evidence of belief in this capacity across Buddhist Asia, including Southeast and East Asia. In Japan, there are reports of at least eighteen self-mummified monks throughout the country. Their technique for self-mummification involves a special diet of a toxic cap, fasting or drinking only saltwater and isolation in purifying the body to prepare for enlightenment. They are referred to as *sokushinjobutsu* in Japanese, or the notion of attaining Buddhahood in this body, as originated from Kukai's (774–839) branch of Shingon Buddhism (Krummel 2015: 786; Martin, n.d.).

There is often a connection between the materiality of the corpse and what is seen as the movement to the next abode. In some places in Burma, for example, it is a ritual practice to put a coin in the mouth of the deceased as fare for the ferry the person will need to take (Spiro 1982: 250). Let's hope there is no demonetization in the nether world. In Northern Thailand, Charles Keyes has observed that the corpse of a monk or high-status laity will be dehydrated and kept for months prior to cremation; the corpse of a religious person will not carry along with it a potentially malevolent *phi* or ghost (Keyes 1987: 185–6). Within Buddhism in Myanmar today, there are other preserved corpses that are venerated as holy figures or relics. For example, in Magwe Region, Ngape Division, Sitha Kywe Village, is a preserved corpse of a Sayadaw which is stored in a glass box for veneration. Interestingly, the corpse is still wearing spectacles. Similarly, the Cambodian monk Ven Keum Vang died in 1988 and was put in a bamboo casket. A year later, his corpse was found not to have decomposed. Upon the discovery, the corpse was put on display in the monks' eating hall and attracts visitors who donate and make merit (Marston 2006: 497). While self-mummification, although amazing, is not a unique accomplishment of Sao Myat, the fact that he took his matted locks with him as part of the mummification object to be venerated is remarkable. Another aspect of the hair on the relic is that it could be the symbolic association with the Buddha. As Leach pointed out, the standard images of the Buddha depict him in clothing and posture like a celibate monk but with tight curls, which, as Leach argued, denotes the Buddha's 'supreme fertilising power' or 'potency' (Leach 1958: 159). By venerating the relic of Sao Myat and Sao Myat's hair, the devotee may get the 'whole package' as it were.

Conclusions and systems of exception

For a remarkable figure like Sao Myat, the ways in which Tantrism and Theravāda Buddhism have spun together to make a dreadlocked monk might not have happened anywhere except in Shan State. He represents a tapestry of elements in himself, but his body is venerated as a Buddhist relic. Local reverence created this figure, and within Möng Pan historiography, his heroism is located in the era of the Num Serk Harn, or the movement which sought to take Shanland back from its Burmese occupiers.

Justin McDaniel (2012) has made the important point that when studying Buddhist practice in Southeast Asia, we should pay more attention to Southern Chinese and Sanskrit literary sources rather than just calling non-Theravāda/non-Pāli elements simply 'local, or indigenous or even animist' (McDaniel 2012). I could not agree more. There are also the ways in which local political powers and historiographies create new kinds of sovereignties about these new fusions. In contrast to the magical figure of the *weikza* or form of alchemy or wizardry, the monk is often considered to be much more reserved and restricted by the *thila* (Burmese; Pāli: *sīla*) or precepts that he keeps (Rozenberg 2015: 26; Ferguson and Mendelson 1981: 63, 65). But as we can see from Sao Myat, the monk can still possess *weikza* hair. Incidental to that, Sao Myat is characterized by his smile – in contrast to the widespread expectation of a monk displaying no strong signs of emotion.

These unique experiences and special features, one might argue, are what separates these monks from the *sangha* orthodoxy, making them exceptional. But on the other hand, they remind us that religious ecumenism is how most state-building projects established; Sao Myat became exceptional as both a monk and as an ascetic; attaching him to Möng Pan's historical eras and later his reverence by Shan State Army soldiers makes him all the more attached to Shan sovereignty. Studying the different histories and ontologies of Sao Myat's resonance is an interesting exercise in the history of spiritual travels and networks, but it does not necessarily explain what he means to Shan people today and the relationships that are built through his veneration and reverence. In this sense, although the paradox of the monk with dreadlocks might be seen by some as not 'really' a monk, it is all the more important for the Shan people today who venerate his mummified body or keep framed photos of him on their home altars: Sao Myat's ability to be an exception to tradition creates an aura about him and the matted locks; it makes the meaning of the hair perhaps more powerful than the abbot who ordained Sao Myat. The very exception implies a supernatural quality (Spiro 1996: 4). But also, the ability to recognize it and make it meaningful might only happen in a place like Möng Pan.

References

Bogin, Benjamin (2008), 'The Dreadlocks Treatise: On Tantric Hairstyles in Tibetan Buddhism', *History of Religions*, 48 (2): 85–109.

Brac de la Perriere, Benedicte (2009), 'An Overview of the Field of Religion in Burmese Studies', *Asian Ethnology*, 68 (2): 185–210.

Brohm, John (1963), 'Buddhism and Animism in a Burmese Village', *Journal of Asian Studies*, 22 (2): 155–67.

Collins, Steven (1998), *Nirvana and Other Buddhist Felicities: Utopias of the Pali Imaginaire*, Cambridge: Cambridge University Press.

Ferguson, Jane M. (2021), *Repossessing Shanland: Myanmar, Thailand and a Nation-State Deferred*, Madison: University of Wisconsin Press.

Ferguson, John P., and E. Michael Mendelson (1981), 'Masters of the Buddhist Occult: The Burmese Weikzas', *Contributions to Asian Studies*, 16: 62–89.

Gellner, David N., and Richard Gombrich (2015), 'Buddhism', *International Encyclopedia of the Social & Behavioural Sciences*, 2: 1378–86.

Hayami, Yoko, and Tatsuki Kataoka (2016), 'Rethinking "Religion" from the Margins', *Kyoto Review of Southeast Asia*, 19 (n.p.). https://kyotoreview.org/issue-19/rethinking-religion-from-margins/ (accessed: 28 May 2020).

Joffe, Ben Philip (2019), 'White Robes, Matted Hair: Tibetan Tantric Householders, Moral Sexuality, and the Ambiguities of Esoteric Buddhist Expertise in Exile', unpublished PhD thesis, University of Colorado, Boulder.

Kataoka, Tatsuki (2012), 'Introduction: De-institutionalizing Religion in Southeast Asia', *Southeast Asian Studies*, 1 (3): 361–3.

Keyes, Charles F. (1977), *The Golden Peninsula: Culture and Adaptation in Mainland Southeast Asia*, New York: Macmillan.

Keyes, Charles F. (1986), 'Ambiguous Gender: Male Initiation in a Northern Thai Buddhist Society', in *Gender and Religion: On the Complexity of Symbols*, ed. Caroline Bynum, Stevan Harrell and Paula Richman, 66–96, Boston: Beacon Press.

Keyes, Charles F. (1987), 'From Death to Birth: Ritual Process and Buddhist Meaning in Northern Thailand', *Folk*, 29: 181–206.

Krummel, John W. M. (2015), 'Embodied Implacement in Kukai and Nishida' *Philosophy East & West*, 65 (3): 785–808.

Lang, Karen (1995), 'Shaven Heads and Loose Hair: Buddhist Attitudes toward Hair and Sexuality', in *Off with Her Head! The Denial of Women's Identity in Myth, Religion and Culture*, ed. Howard Eilberg-Schwartz and Wendy Doniger, 32–52, Berkeley: University of California Press.

Leach, E. R. (1958), 'Magical Hair', *The Journal of the Royal Anthropological Institute of Great Britain and Ireland*, 88 (2): 147–64.

Marston, John (2006), 'Death, Memory and Building: The Non-Cremation of a Cambodian Monk', *The Journal of Southeast Asian Studies*, 37 (3): 491–505.

Martin, Alex (n.d.) 'Eternal Saints: The Art of Self-Preservation', *The Japan Times*. https://features.japantimes.co.jp/sokushinbutsu/ (accessed: 29 May 2020).

McDaniel, Justin (2012), 'Encountering Corpses: Notes on Zombies and the Living Dead in Buddhist Southeast Asia', *Kyoto Review of Southeast Asia*, Issue 12. The Living and the Dead. https://kyotoreview.org/issue-12/encountering-corpses-notes-on-zombies-and-the-living-dead-in-buddhist-southeast-asia/ (accessed: 28 May 2020).

Milne, Mrs Leslie, Mary Lewis Harper Milne and Wilbur Willis Cochrane ([1910] 1970), *Shans at Home: With Two Chapters on Shan History and Literature*, Bangkok: White Lotus Press.

Obeyesekere, Gananath (1984), *Medusa's Hair: An Essay on Personal Symbols and Religious Experience*, Chicago: University of Chicago Press.

Ramberg, Lucinda (2009), 'Magical Hair as Dirt: Ecstatic Bodies and Postcolonial Reform in South India', *Culture, Medicine and Psychiatry*, December, 33 (4): 501–22.

Rozenberg, Guillaume, *The Immortals: Faces of the Incredible in Buddhist Burma*, trans. Ward Keeler (2015), Honolulu: University of Hawai'i Press.

Sai Kam Mong (2004), *The History and Development of the Shan Scripts*, Chiang Mai: Silkworm.

Simms, Sao Sanda (2017), *Great Lords of the Sky: Burma's Shan Aristocracy*, Asian Highlands Perspectives 48.

Spiro, Melford E. ([1970] 1982), *Buddhism and Society: A Great Tradition and Its Burmese Vicissitudes*, Berkeley: University of California Press.

Spiro, Melford E. ([1967] 1996), *Burmese Supernaturalism*, New Brunswick: Transaction Publishers.

6

Reflections on religion and identity: With a particular emphasis on Theravāda Buddhism

Perry Schmidt-Leukel

Sketching the problem

One of the twentieth-century pioneers of interfaith dialogue, the Indian-born Muslim Hasan Askari wrote about his experience of the partition of India:

> The country where I was born and where I grew up was a country of many races, languages, cultures and religions, and it had been so for many centuries. And yet something had gone wrong during my lifetime, so wrong that those who had been neighbours for generations became, overnight, aliens and enemies and what followed on the eve of the partition of India and afterwards was so baffling and heart-rending that many were compelled to question their very humanity, whether it really existed, and how was it that our religious heritage, in spite of its towering claims to moral and spiritual truths, was unable to prevent us from behaving as beasts, thirsty of one another's blood, *and all in the name of this or that 'religious' identity.* (Askari 1991: 120, emphasis mine)

When Hasan Askari says that the atrocities during the Indian partition were committed in the name of 'religious' identity, he refers to the religions that were primarily involved in the partition, that is, to Hinduism, Islam and Sikhism. However, his point is more general: religions often function as decisive markers of collective identities so that conflicts between different social or ethnic groups are also represented, and carried out, as conflicts between religious communities or, more precisely, in the name of religious identities. Yet what is the link between individual identity, collective identity, religious identity and the potential for conflict?

Personal individual identities are composed of many different factors, such as gender, family status, job, social position, language, colour, ethnicity, nationality, religion and so on. Obviously, identity is a complex and multilayered phenomenon and never one-dimensional. Yet, even if identity is composed of many different factors, it remains selective. Having a particular identity means that I am not everything. There are features that I do not regard as part of my identity. If I am black, I am not white. If I am female, I am not male. To be sure, some people's identity may not easily fit into such simple 'either-or' categories. And a number of people will have, in various respects, several identities at the same time: having two or three jobs, being fully bilingual, having two or more nationalities including passports and so on. But even then, one cannot be everything. Apparently, identity always excludes something that is not regarded as part of one's identity, *something that is other* and *someone who is other*.

Most of the features that constitute one's identity make one a member of different social collectives. This is true of our gender, profession, class, colour, ethnicity, nationality, religion and so on. Identity is always influenced and co-constituted by social collectives providing one with a feeling of belonging. My identity is rooted in, grounded and protected by some larger collective identity. Jonathan Sacks (2002: 47) is probably right when he says, 'To surrender the lonely self to something larger, more powerful and elemental, is one of the deepest instincts of mankind.' Tribe, ethnicity, nationality and religion can function as protective envelopes that give shelter and roots to one's identity. Conflicts between different collectives are therefore often perceived as conflicts between different identities – an aspect which can easily aggravate conflicts between collectives.

Given that identity is never one-dimensional and never unilateral, that is, given that identities are complex and constituted by various collective belongings, one strategy to deal with identity conflicts is the establishment of *hierarchies of values*. Which of the various bonds that constitute one's identity is most important? For example, there may be a conflict between two siblings. But alongside their different individual identities, they are united in their common identity as members of the same family. If their family has a conflict with another family, the siblings may give more weight to their family identity than to their individual differences. As a result, they may postpone their dispute and stand together in defence of their family. Similarly, conflicts between different ethnicities within one nation can sometimes be softened if people consider their belonging to one nation as more important to their identity than their different ethnic belongings. Similarly, conflicts between different nations can be more easily appeased if the idea of belonging to one global family of human beings is seen by all as more important than their belonging to different nations. The danger of slogans such as 'America first' is precisely that it might give national identity priority over the identity of belonging to one global family.

Religions tend to claim for themselves the highest rank in any hierarchy of values. If there is a conflict between different religious identities, to which higher identity could one take recourse in order to appease or reduce such conflicts? If conflicts between different collective identities assume the form of religious conflicts, it gets rather difficult to settle them. Either religions are relegated to some lower rank in the hierarchy of identity formation – which is something that religions are usually inclined to reject. Or the resources for conflict resolution have to be found within the religions themselves. But this is not that easy either. In religions, the exclusion that is inevitably connected to the demarcation of identity is often combined with a derogatory view of the religious other. An interreligious and international consultation process that was carried out in 1993–4, long before 9/11, investigated the role of religions in violent conflicts (see Kelsay and Twiss 1994). Summarizing one of the findings, Sumner B. Twiss (1998: 156) states,

> Religions provide individuals and groups with a sense of identity, a place in the universe, oriented to some notion of a special reality, truth, or authority considered ultimate in some sense. In so doing, they foster a sense of group feeling that motivates not only behavior important to personal and social integration (cooperation, sharing, mutual respect, altruism) but also behavior that draws lines between an 'us' (the in-group), who have the truth, know the good, and live rightly; and 'them' (the out-group), who do not share these characteristics, or at least not fully.

This 'sense of group difference and superiority', says Twiss, can easily result in 'a considerable potential for violence and abuse against any out-group that challenges the in-group about its worldview, territory, values, or way of life' (1998: 156). 'Othering', to quote Jerryson and Frydenlund (2020b: 265), can thus function as 'the justification and catalyst for violence.' Simultaneously, seeing the other, the 'out-group', as an enemy can strengthen the collective identity of the 'in-group'. Often collectives need to produce their enemies in order to reinforce their own identity.

Looking at Myanmar will immediately demonstrate that there is a close link between identities and conflictual tensions. In Myanmar, as John Clifford Hold rightly states, 'for many, majoritarianism is synonymous with democracy'. With the majority being Bamar (Burmese) Buddhists, Myanmar is seen by them as 'essentially a Buddhist country' (Holt 2019: xiv). This understanding of

Myanmar's identity is supported by an indigenous historiography transmitting the 'belief that Burma's national purpose is none other than to perpetuate the original and purest forms of the Buddhasasana' (Holt 2019: 25). If other religions, such as Christianity and Islam, are seen as a threat to such Burmese Buddhist identity, the use of force can be justified politically and religiously as an act of defence: 'We must keep Myanmar Buddhist! If we are weak, our land will become Muslim', says the Buddhist nationalist Ashin Wirathu (quoted in Holt 2019: 10), and the government can be perceived, and indeed present itself, 'as the defender of a primarily Burmese Buddhist state' (Holt 2019: 21).

As has been pointed out repeatedly, this type of Buddhist nationalism is by no means confined to Myanmar.[1] Comparing Buddhist anti-Islamic movements in Sri Lanka and Myanmar, Benjamin Schonthal (2016: 252) summarizes,

> On both sides of the Bay of Bengal, Buddhist nationalist groups describe their purpose as the protection and promotion of Buddhism through preaching about the importance of Buddhist values, history, education, sacred sites, and ceremonies. At the same time, these groups regularly insist upon the need to neutralize threats to Buddhism. They routinely single out Myanmar's and Sri Lanka's Muslims as chief among these threats.

Against this background, it is not surprising that in Myanmar, as in Sri Lanka and Thailand, the political discourse of the Buddhist majority is dominated by Buddhist categories. Hence it is worth to take a closer look at Theravāda Buddhism's traditional analysis of identity and consider the question to what extent an emic perspective, a view from within this particular tradition, entails some aspects which may shed their own light on the relationship between religion and identities and might perhaps enable or even foster a more self-critical attitude based on the Buddhist critique of the self.

A Theravāda Buddhist analysis of identity

A central part of the Buddhist doctrinal repertoire is its teaching of 'Not-Self' (Pāli: *anatta*, Sanskrit *anātman*). While there is still significant scholarly debate about the original meaning of this teaching, some aspects are clear and beyond dispute. Early Buddhism counts five factors that make up an individual human being. One of them, *rūpa*, is of material nature and denotes the physical body. The other four are of a mental nature: feeling (*vedanā*), perception (*saññā*), formations (*saṅkhāra*: including will and karmic inclinations) and finally consciousness (*viññāṇa*). When the Buddha teaches that none of these personality factors should be regarded as the 'self' (Pāli: *atta*, Sanskrit: *ātman*), this must not be mistaken as the denial of a soul in any materialistic sense. The Buddha (as portrayed in the canonical scriptures) is far from denying the mental dimension of human beings by reducing them to bodily functions, as some contemporary neurophysiologists are inclined to do. Instead, the Buddha points out that all of the five constituents, the body and the mental factors are subject to permanent change. Therefore, they should not be mistaken as a permanent, immutable self or eternal soul, that is, as something that—from a Buddhist perspective—would be similar to the concept of the *ātman* in the *Upaniṣads*.[2]

The main point of the Not-Self teaching, however, is not theoretical. The teaching rather relates to a soteriological practice or spiritual attitude (see Schmidt-Leukel 2006: 36–7). In the Not-Self Sermon the Buddha advises his followers to regard each of the five personality factors as 'this is not mine, this I am not, this is not my self (*atta*, *ātman*)'.[3] By looking at the personality factors in this way, one will gradually overcome any attachment, become dispassionate and finally liberated. This implies that the opposite attitude in relation to these factors, that is, the usual unenlightened self-understanding, is a form of attachment. Actually, viewing the physical and mental factors as one's possession ('this is mine'), or as constituting one's identity ('this I am') or even as one's true eternal nature ('this is my *ātman*'), is assessed as the strongest forms of attachment. A key idea of Buddhism is that any attachment to the transitory, impermanent things of the world will inevitably lead to frustration and suffering. This is seen as particularly true of attachment to the five personality factors. Clinging to them by regarding them as 'mine' or 'ego' or '*ātman*' will only lead to suffering. Hence the first of the Four Noble Truths concludes, 'Attachment to the five factors is suffering.'

According to the Pāli *Tipiṭaka*, the Buddha illustrates this teaching by a rather drastic image: if one watches gardeners in a public park carrying off and burning the grass, sticks, branches or leaves, would one think: 'They are carrying off and burning me?' Surely not, for one will not be attached to the garden waste and will not regard it as one's self or as belonging to one's self. In the same way, one should not regard the five personality factors as one's self or as belonging to one's self. Then their transitory nature will not become a source of suffering (*Majjhimanikāya* 22; Bodhi and Ñāṇamoli 2001: 234–5):

> Whatever is not yours, abandon it; when you have abandoned it, that will lead to your welfare and happiness for a long time. What is not yours? Material form is

not yours. ... Feeling is not yours. ... Perception is not yours. ... Formations are not yours. ... Consciousness is not yours. Abandon it.

An important, though frequently neglected, aspect of the Buddhist teaching about suffering is its social dimension. Attachment does not merely lead to the private experience of suffering, to one's own suffering, but is also the reason behind the infliction of suffering upon others. According to the *Mahādukkhakkhandha Sutta* (*Majjhimanikāya* 13), attachment is the ultimate reason behind all sorts of quarrels, conflicts, hurting others and even wars. According to the *Sevitabbāsevitabha Sutta* (*Majjhimanikāya* 114), the mental subtext of all immoral behaviour is self-centeredness manifesting itself as greed and hate. Or as it is said in *Dhammapada* 291, 'he who seeks his own happiness by inflicting pain on others, being entangled by bonds of enmity, cannot be free from enmity'.

The antidote, non-attachment, consists in the development of a different kind of 'self'. As Steven Collins (1982) and Peter Harvey (2004) have shown in their detailed studies, the texts of the Pāli *Tipiṭaka* display a dynamic usage of the self-concept. Once the Buddhist practitioner understands that none of the personality factors constitutes an immutable eternal self, and that the idea of a 'self' is a psychological construct expressive of one's clinging or self-centeredness, a new selfless self can be developed. As Peter Harvey (2004: 54) summarizes, 'indeed, the most developed self is one which is, precisely, known as Selfless and I-less'. The canonical scriptures occasionally refer to the one who has developed this selfless self as one with a 'great self' (*mahattā*) or one who has a 'developed self' (*bhāvit-atto*). His mind (*citta*) has become 'great' or even 'immeasurable' because this mind is no longer limited and confined to his ego-self (see Harvey 2004: 54–63; Collins 1982: 188–95). This conception is of crucial ethical significance. Already the spirit of the so-called Golden Rule points in the direction of an extension of the self by regarding others as equal to oneself, as expressed in the *Suttanipāta* 705 (Bodhi 2017: 277):

'As I am, so are they;
as they are, so am I',
having taken oneself as the criterion,
one should not kill or cause others to kill.

But developing an immeasurable self implies even more. According to Buddhaghosa's authoritative account of the Theravāda Buddhist teaching in his *Visuddhimagga*, extending lovingkindness and compassion to all beings means to see them 'without making the distinction "This is another being"'

(*Visuddhimagga* 9:47; Ñāṇamoli 1999: 301). Buddhaghosa's interpretation is in line with the *Metta-Sutta*, highly popular in Theravāda Buddhism, which says that one should extend lovingkindness to the whole world by regarding and treating all beings in the same way as a mother relates to her child (*Suttanipāta* 143–52). The relation between a mother and her child is a very symbiotic one. She clearly relates to her child as to herself. In this sense, Peter Harvey is right when he says that the 'Arhat', that is, the enlightened person, 'is in several places described in such a way as to suggest that he has broken down all barriers between "himself" and "others"' (Harvey 2004: 60).

A rather challenging example of this kind of selfless self-attitude is provided by the contemporary Vietnamese Buddhist Master Thich Nhat Hanh in his famous poem 'Please Call Me by My True Names' where he compassionately identifies both with the victims and the perpetrators in various contemporary situations of violence and suffering (Nhat Hanh, n.d.). I suggest that this attitude – and the Buddhist analysis of identity standing behind it – may indeed throw some helpful light on the interconnection between religion, identity and the potential for conflict and could be constructively employed in the inner-Buddhist discourse, as I will expound in my final point.

Buddhist religious identity as a problem

Given the Buddhist Not-Self teaching, one may assume that a Buddhist religious identity in any negative, excluding sense should be virtually impossible. Buddhist social activists have argued that the Buddhist critique of the individual self-centeredness can and should also be applied to collective identities. The critique of an 'ego' would then turn into the critique of a collective ego, a 'wego', as David Loy (2006: 46) has pointedly called it:

> In fact, many of our social problems can be traced back to this deluded sense of collective self, this 'wego', or group ego. It can be defined as one's own race, class, gender, nation …, religion, or some combination thereof. In each case, a collective identity is created by discriminating one's own group from another. As in the personal ego, the 'inside' is opposed to the other 'outside', and this makes conflict inevitable.

From this perspective, phenomena such as Buddhist nationalism or strong links between Buddhist and ethnic identity would appear to be a contradiction in terms. How should it be possible to claim that being Thai, or being Sinhalese, or being Burmese is to be Buddhist (see Schmidt-Leukel 2017b: 79, 82, 102, 155; Holt 2019: 275), if a key notion of the Buddhist teaching is to reject this kind of 'wego', that is, this collective self-centred identity construction? But as Buddhist history and current conflicts demonstrate, things are not as simple as that. And the problem is not just one of the gaps between a high moral or spiritual ideal on one hand and on the other hand a practical reality that inevitably falls behind this ideal. The problem is deeper, and it lies within the Buddhist teaching itself.

As careful historical research has shown, the use of the term 'Theravāda Buddhism' as a label for a Buddhist denomination is a rather recent phenomenon (Skilling et al. 2012). It became widespread only in the twentieth century. However, different forms of Buddhism have existed presumably from the very beginning of Buddhism onwards. The probably earliest use of the term *theravāda* is found in the Sri Lankan chronicle *Dīpavaṃsa* which was probably composed in the fourth century CE. Here *theravāda* does not refer to a particular Buddhist community or denomination but to a particular set of Buddhist teachings. The term *theravāda* designates these teachings as the true teachings of the Buddha and sets them apart from other versions of Buddhist teachings. These are blamed as not having preserved the Dhamma in the same purity and completeness. Therefore, these other versions of the Buddhist teaching are compared to thorns on a tree, whereas the *theravāda*, the 'teaching of the Elders', is likened to a good and large banyan tree, that is, the kind of tree under which the Buddha experienced his awakening (Skilling et al. 2012: 42–3, 462–3). Hence it is, according to the *Dīpavaṃsa*, essential to belong to that group which alone is in possession of the true teaching.

Rivalry among Buddhist groups is an old phenomenon, going back to the origins of Buddhism (see Schmidt-Leukel 2021). The same is true of the rivalry between Buddhists and non-Buddhists – despite the fact that some early Buddhist texts warn precisely against such rivalry. Strife between different religious groups is explained as arising from their 'lust for views, bondage [to it], fixation [on it], obsession [by it], holding firmly [to it]', an attitude that the truly wise person should abandon (*Aṅguttaranikāya* I 66–7; Bodhi 2012: 157–8). Regarding one's own faith with the thought 'only this is true, anything else is wrong' is severely criticized at several canonical places (*Majjhimanikāya* 95, *Canki Stutta*; see also *Suttanipāta* 832, 837, 843). Nevertheless, Buddhists did engage in precisely this kind of rivalry, and this is already documented in the canonical texts themselves. Especially the beliefs and practices of Vedic Brahmanism are heavily criticized, ridiculed and treated in highly polemical and derogatory ways (Schmidt-Leukel 2008: 147–9). The Vedic Rishis, that is, 'seers' (*ṛṣi*), are blamed as people who did not see at all. They had no success in meditation and hence impressed the ordinary people by composing the Vedas (*Dīghanikāya* 27, III 94).[4] Those who follow them are called blind men following the blind (*Dīghanikāya* 13, I 239). In one place, the Buddha compares the Brahmins of his time to wild dogs and the dogs fair better in each point of the comparison (*Aṅguttaranikāya* III 221–2). The light brought by the Buddha's contemporary rival teachers is compared to the light of glowworms, while the light brought by the Buddha is compared to the bright light of the sun. And 'when that illuminant arises, the glow worm's light is quenched and shines no more' (*Udāna* 6:10; Ireland 1997: 93). The very Not-Self teaching is itself presented as part of a polemical argument against the understanding of the *ātman* in other, presumably Upanishadic, schools. Their views are designated as 'utterly and completely foolish' (*Majjhimanikāya* 22, I 139; Bodhi and Ñāṇamoli 2001: 232). Thus, the canonical texts of the *Tipiṭaka* are not fully consistent in their attitude towards the religious other (see also Harris 2013). As the reputed contemporary Theravāda Buddhist scholar Mahinda Palihawadana (2001: 9) once stated, it would be 'intellectually dishonest' to deny that 'some texts, a few even in the canon, show not merely a critical, but also a triumphalist and adversarial attitude towards other religionists'.

In the course of Buddhist history, interreligious polemics at times turned into open hostilities and even violent clashes. To quote Palihawadana (2001: 10) again, 'At crucial periods in Sri Lankan history, segments of the Buddhist Sangha adopted a nationalist stand and condoned the politics of violent confrontation in relation to non-Sinhala groups who were perceived as threats to the dominance of Buddhism in the country.' I would like to highlight Palihawadana's observation that the use of violence was condoned as an *act of defence*. Actually, it was and is not merely condoned, but justified. The idea is to protect the teaching of the Buddha against the real or perceived threat coming from other religions by defending, even violently, the country or nation which understands its own vocation as one of preserving and transmitting the Dhamma in its pure version. Similar ideas are also found in the history of Buddhism in Myanmar. In the *Glass Palace Chronicle*, the defeat of the so-called Ari lords (presumably followers of a Mahāyāna or Tantric version of Buddhism) is justified by describing them as a threat to the king's new patronage of Theravāda (Tin and Luce 1923). More or less the same logic is operative in contemporary forms of Buddhist nationalism. This has been demonstrated convincingly by Tessa Bartholomeusz (2002) in her study on the Buddhist justification of the ethnic war in Sri Lanka as, thus the title of her study, an act 'in defense of Dharma'. More recently, a number of studies have shown that this logic of defence is also at work in anti-Muslim sentiments among various Myanmar Buddhists.[5]

But is it possible to protect and defend the Buddhist Dhamma by the use of violence and by subscribing to a logic that goes against the content of the Dhamma or at least against significant strands of its content? Even if one adopts the argument that in a real world it is at times inevitable to defend the Dhamma by means of force, the crucial question is still whether other religions are to be regarded as a threat to the Dhamma. Buddhists, also within the Theravāda school, do not concur on this issue (Schmidt-Leukel 2017a and 2020). While some Buddhists regard other faiths as entirely unwholesome and not leading to liberation at all, others feel that other religions do contain at least some positive elements which may help their members to make some advancement on their personal path to liberation. Still others, as for example the influential Thai Theravāda Buddhist Bhikkhu Buddhadāsa (1906–1993), went even further. Having made himself familiar with Hinduism, Christianity and Islam, Buddhadāsa held that the essence of liberation, the transcendence of self-centredness, is found in one way or another at the heart of all the major religious traditions (Buddhadāsa 1967: 12–39 and 1989: 168–9).

According to Buddhadāsa, the one path of liberation contains several components. Hence it is possible that it appears in different forms. Buddhism, for example, puts its emphasis on 'wisdom' (*paññā*), Christianity on 'faith' (*saddhā*) and Islam on 'will-power' (*viriya*). But, says Buddhadāsa (1967: 13), 'each religion comprises all the three ways; … each religion does have all the principles of truth (Dhamma) which man requires, such as trust (faith), will-power (energy), wisdom, loving-kindness (mettā), generosity, selflessness, egolessness, etc.' From this he concludes (1989: 169),

> Nowadays, however, people have misunderstood the purpose of religion to the extent that they have split off into a great many hostile groups. The conflicts among them have given rise to social problems the world over. In many cases, adherents of different religions cannot even communicate with one another anymore.
>
> The people in these opposing groups are going against a universal religious precept in that they are all being selfish and are governed by a 'me' and 'mine' kind of thinking, which conflicts with the universal principles of religion.

From this perspective, religious diversity will not be seen as a threat to Buddhism but as an opportunity for mutual spiritual enrichment and encouragement. Buddhist identity would not be preserved by fighting other faiths but by overcoming any form of self-centeredness, including its appearance as a collective Buddhist 'wego'. Instead, Buddhist identity would be preserved and practised by engaging with the religious other as 'if he were not another', to paraphrase the instruction from Buddhaghosa's interpretation of *mettābhāvanā*, that is, the mental development of lovingkindness. The hallmark of a nation that wants to honour Buddhism would then be its hospitality, and not its hostility, towards religious diversity. Will such implications of the Theravāda 'Not-Self' teaching have a chance to impact the inner-Buddhist discourse in Myanmar? Some indication of this may be spotted in those Buddhist voices who question the compatibility of the Buddha *dhamma* with Burmese nationalism. But they seem to be waning (Holt 2019: 226–49).

Notes

1 On the complex and often discussed phenomenon of Buddhist nationalism, see, for example, Berkwitz (2008); Keyes (2016); Gravers (2014 and 2015); Walton and Hayward (2014). Berkwitz (2008, 74–6) provides on overview on the scholarly debate. For Buddhist-Muslim tensions across some Theravāda countries see Jerryson and Frydenlund (2020a).

2 We can and should leave the question open to what extent early Buddhist polemics against the *ātman* as found, for example, in *Majjhimanikāya* 22 do justice to Upanishadic ideas or not.

3 *Saṃyuttanikāya* III, 66–8: 'n'etaṁ mama n'eso'ahm-asmi na m'eso attā'. See also Bodhi (2000, 901–3).

4 The text speaks of *ganthe*, which according to the commentary refers to the Vedas. See Gombrich (1990: 27).

5 See, for example, Gravers (2015); Schonthal (2016); Kyaw (2016); and Holt (2019).

References

Askari, Hasan (1991), *Spiritual Quest. An-Interreligious Dimension*, Pudsey: Seven Mirrors.

Bartholomeusz, Tessa J. (2002), *In Defense of Dharma. Just-War Ideology in Buddhist Sri Lanka*, London: RoutledgeCurzon.

Berkwitz, Stephen C. (2008), 'Resisting the Global in Buddhist Nationalism: Venerable Soma's Discourse of Decline and Reform', *Journal of Asian Studies*, 67 (1): 73–106.

Bodhi, Bhikkhu, and Bhikkhu Ñāṇamoli (2001), *The Middle Length Discourses of the Buddha: A Translation of the Majjhima Nikāya*, 2nd edn, Boston: Wisdom Publications.

Bodhi, Bhikkhu (2000), *The Connected Discourses of the Buddha: A Translation of the Saṃyutta Nikāya*. Boston: Wisdom Publications.

Bodhi, Bhikkhu (2012), *The Numerical Discourses of the Buddha: A Translation of the Aṅguttara Nikāya*, Boston: Wisdom Publications.

Bodhi, Bhikkhu (2017), *The Suttanipāta: An Ancient Collection of the Buddha's Discourses Together with Its Commentaries*, Boston: Wisdom Publications.

Buddhadāsa, Bhikkhu (1967), *Christianity and Buddhism*, Sinclaire Thompson Memorial Lecture. Fifth Series, Bangkok: Sublime Life Mission.

Buddhadāsa, Bhikkhu (1989), *Me and Mine: Selected Essays of Bhikkhu Buddhadāsa*, ed. Donald K. Swearer, Albany: SUNY.

Collins, Steven (1982), *Selfless Persons: Imagery and Thought in Theravāda Buddhism*, Cambridge: Cambridge University Press.

Gombrich, Richard (1990), 'How the Mahāyāna Began', *The Buddhist Forum*, vol. 1, ed. Tadeusz Skorupski, 21–30, London: SOAS.

Gravers, Mikael (2014), 'Politically Engaged Buddhism – Spiritual Politics or Nationalist Medium?', in *Burma/Myanmar – Where Now?*, ed. Mikael Gravers, Ytzen Flemming, 293–322, Copenhagen: Nordic Institute of Asian Studies.

Gravers, Mikael (2015), 'Anti-Muslim Buddhist Nationalism in Burma and Sri Lanka: Religious Violence and Globalized Imaginaries of Endangered Identities', *Contemporary Buddhism*, 16 (1): 1–27.

Harris, Elizabeth J. (2013), 'Buddhism and the Religious Other', in *Understanding Interreligious Relations*, ed. David Cheethamn, Douglas Pratt, David Thomas, 88–117, Oxford: Oxford University Press.

Harvey, Peter ([1995] 2004), *The Selfless Mind: Personality, Consciousness and Nirvāṇa in Early Buddhism*, London: Routledge.

Holt, John Cliffort (2019), *Myanmar's Buddhist-Muslim Crisis- Rohingya, Arakanese, and Burmese Narratives of Siege and Fear*, Honolulu: University of Hawai'I Press.

Ireland, John (1997), *The Udāna and the Itivuttaka: Inspired Utterances of the Buddha and the Buddha's Sayings*, Kandy: Buddhist Publication Society.

Jerryson, Michael, and Iselin Frydenlund, eds (2020a), *Buddhist-Muslim Relations in a Theravada World*, Singapore: Palgrave Macmillan.

Jerryson, Michael, and Iselin Frydenlund (2020b), 'Buddhist, Muslims and the Construction of Difference', in *Buddhist-Muslim Relations in a Theravada World*, ed. M. Jerryson and I. Friedenlund, 263–97, Singapore: Palgrave Macmillan.

Kelsay, John, and Sumner B. Twiss (eds) (1994), *Religion and Human Rights*, New York: Project of Religion and Human Rights.

Keyes, Charles (2016), 'Theravada Buddhism and Buddhist Nationalism: Sri Lanka, Myanmar, Cambodia, and Thailand', *The Review of Faith and International Affairs*, 14 (4): 42–52.

Kyaw, Nyi Frieden Lund (2016), 'Islamophobia in Buddhist Myanmar: The 969 Movement and Anti-Muslim Violence', in *Islam and the State in Myanmar. Muslim-Buddhist Relations and the Politics of Belonging*, ed. Melissa Crouch, 183–210, New Delhi: Oxford University Press.

Loy, David (2006), 'Wego: The Social Roots of Suffering', in *Mindful Politics: A Buddhist Guide to Making the World a Better Place*, ed. Melvin McLeod, 45–54, Boston: Wisdom Publications.

Ñāṇamoli, Bhikkhu (1999), *The Path of Purification (Visuddhimagga) by Bhadantācariya Buddhaghosa*, Seatle: BPS Pariyatti Editions.

Nhat Hanh, Thich (n.d.). 'Please Call Me by My True Names'. http://wtf.tw/ref/nhat_hanh.html (accessed: 30 March 2020).

Palihawadana, Mahinda (2001), 'The Impossibility of Intolerance: A Buddhist Perspective', *Dialogue N.S.*, 28: 1–17.

Sacks, Jonathan (2002), *The Dignity of Difference: How to Avoid the Clash of Civilizations*, London: Continuum.

Schmidt-Leukel, Perry (2006), *Understanding Buddhism*, Edinburgh: Dunedin Academic Press.

Schmidt-Leukel, Perry (2008), 'Buddhist-Hindu Relations', in *Buddhist Attitudes to Other Religions* (ed.) Perry Schmidt-Leukel, 143–71, St. Ottilien: EOS-Editions.

Schmidt-Leukel, Perry (2017a), 'Theravāda Buddhist Approaches to Religious Diversity: An Overview', in *Buddhist and Christian Attitudes to Religious Diversity*, ed. Hans-Peter Grosshans, Samuel Ngun Ling and Perry Schmidt-Leukel,59–75, Yangon: Ling's Family.

Schmidt-Leukel, Perry, ed. (2017b), *Buddhist-Christian Relations in Asia*, St. Ottilien: EOS Editions.

Schmidt-Leukel, Perry (2020), 'Paths of Liberation? Theravāda Buddhist Attitudes to Religious Diversity', in *Buddhist Responses to Religious Diversity: Theravāda and Tibetan Perspectives*, ed. Douglas Duckworth, Abraham Vélez de Cea, and Elizabeth J. Harris (eds.), 46–2, Sheffield: Equinox.

Schmidt-Leukel, Perry (2021), 'Buddhist Accounts of Religious Diversity', *Studies in Interreligious Dialogue* 31 (2): forthcoming.

Schonthal, Benjamin (2016), 'Making the Muslim Other in Myanmar and Sri Lanka', in *Islam and the State in Myanmar: Muslim-Buddhist Relations and the Politics of Belonging*, ed. Melissa Crouch, 234–57, New Delhi: Oxford University Press.

Skilling, Peter, Jason A. Carbine, Claudio Cicuzza and Santi Pakdeekham, eds (2012), *How Theravāda Is Theravāda? Exploring Buddhist Identities*, Chiang Mai: Silkworm Books.

Tin, Pe Maung, and G. H. Luce (1923), *The Glass Palace Chronicle of the Kings of Myanmar*, London: Oxford University Press.

Twiss, Sumner B. (1998), 'Religion and Human Rights: A Comparative Perspective', in *Explorations in Global Ethics: Comparative Religious Ethics and Interreligious Dialogue*, ed. Sumner B. Twiss and Bruce Grelle, 155–75, Boulder: Westview Press.

Walton, J. Matthew, and Susan Hayward (2014), *Contesting Buddhist Narratives: Democratization, Nationalism and Communal Violence in Myanmar*, Honolulu: East-West Center.

7

Coexistence in Myanmar: Challenges and prospects

Alexander Horstmann

In this chapter, I explore the challenges to peaceful multi-ethnic and multi-religious coexistence and some practices and strategies of progressive forces in Myanmar that point in the direction of a more peaceful and democratic culture of multi-religious coexistence. For this, it is necessary to investigate the political imaginaries that shape the politics of belonging in the new Myanmar (Schober 2008). Communal relations in Myanmar remain strained. Indeed, in the past decade the level of inter-communal violence in Myanmar has reached a new height (Cheesman 2018; Galache 2020; Sadan 2016; Wade 2017). The way forward would be towards what Stewart, Seiple and Hoover (2020: 1) have called 'covenantal pluralism' – that is a form of pluralism that 'acknowledges the complex challenges presented by deep diversity and offers a holistic conception of the structures and norms that are conducive to fairness and flourishing for all, even amidst stark differences in theologies, values, and lifestyles'. Can the emerging public space in Myanmar be used to establish a consensus on covenantal pluralism? In pursuing this question, I will give special attention to the Buddhist contribution and draw on a decade of my own ethnographic research and teaching in Myanmar.[1]

'Multiculturalism' has faced mounting pressures in Myanmar. Political monks, in alliance with other well-resourced nationalist organizations, have worked to create an atmosphere of 'othering' any group that is not Buddhist and/or not part of the dominant Bamar ethnic group. The mobilization of hatred against the religious other constitutes an organized burden for the future of inter-communalism in Myanmar. Yet there are also nascent structures and norms embodied by various communities of practice that work against hatred and strive towards covenantal pluralism.

For achieving the vision of peaceful coexistence, it will be necessary to establish a constitutional framework that protects religious minorities from harm. At the same time, it will also be necessary to create an atmosphere of common struggle against discrimination and defamation that would support a thriving civil society in which community leaders of different faiths can work together towards a better and more peaceful society. There are some organized efforts to promote these kinds of aspirations in Myanmar today. For example, we see young educated professionals and former student activists joining international NGOs who together with Western peace activists make substantial efforts to empower an emerging civil society in Yangon. But apart from organized civil society – and as such, much less visible to outside observers – constructive interactions within and between faith groups can be found in the 'everyday life' of the neighbourhoods rather than in formalized structures or the vertical power of the state. For religious freedom to take roots in Myanmar, different faith groups need to get together in the neighbourhoods in order to support respect for human rights, democratic participation, the social mobility of the ethnic minorities and the recognition of their citizenship as well as their religion.

Ethnic and religious minorities have suffered under decades of military rule, economic ruin and international isolation (Fink 2009; Rogers 2012). Civic organizations used the opening of civic space and social media since 2011 enthusiastically – but so did Buddhist nationalist activism (Wade 2017). Nine years after the opening, Myanmar is again isolated in the world after the military operations and atrocities against the Rohingyas in Rakhine, Western Myanmar, and the frustration of seeing perpetrators (both military elites and Buddhist vigilantes) go largely unpunished. But there are also signs of hope for a rapidly developing civil society and for democratization.

Religion seems to play a crucial role in this bitter contestation over Myanmar's identity and direction, as a new generation of political monks instrumentalize Buddhism to abuse their power and authority in the name of protecting Buddhism. Religious freedom is of central importance in multi-religious Myanmar and shape not only identity but also citizenship, social mobility and belonging in a contested imagined community. The State Counsellor and foreign minister Aung San Suu Kyi has disappointed many by endorsing and re-fostering the ideology of national race instead of helping to dismantle it. Thus, an embrace of covenantal pluralism in Myanmar would constitute an important step not only towards genuine religious freedom but also towards inter-communal peace.

It will be essential to recognize the diverse identities that have been and continue to be part of Myanmar and to redefine belonging by giving recognition and equality to all ethnicities and all religions.

The rise of Buddhist nationalism and the othering of minorities in Myanmar

From an academic point of view, Myanmar provides an intriguing case study to investigate the role of religious actors in continuous processes of state-building and the question of belonging in a multicultural/multifaith nation (Cheesman and Farrelly 2016). Understanding the historical context is crucial for the state of religion and its relationship to secularism and prospects for a robust pluralism in today's Myanmar. Myanmar is not only overwhelmingly Buddhist; it is one of the least secular societies in the world. The period from 2011 to 2020 has seen a revitalization of Buddhist nationalism and Buddhist symbols, against the expectations that democratization would lead to a decline in religion. As the revitalization of Buddhism is closely tied to the perceived threat to Buddhism posed by other religions as well as secularism, Iselin Frydenlund has called the new phenomenon 'Buddhist protectionism'. As Frydenlund explains, the nationalist organizations also benefit from the widening of public space to introduce new legislation (Frydenlund 2017 and 2018). The race and religion laws provide a powerful tool to use law to advance the political agenda of 'Buddhicizing' the state.

Political monks have successfully used the Buddhist courts to sentence for blasphemy and insult those progressive Buddhist intellectuals and Buddhist monks who want to open up Buddhism for religious critique (Frydenlund 2019). In today's Myanmar, a contradiction prevails between a special position of Buddhism as the majority religion and the strict separation of religion and politics. Officially, the use of religion for political or electoral purposes is banned, yet the political salience of religion is obvious. The ban of the monkhood from political participation and voting does not exclude the monkhood from political mobilization. Quite the opposite, in order to understand the political position of the large parts of the Buddhist monkhood one needs to consider their feeling of a Buddhist disenfranchisement. Moreover, the Buddhist court system (*vinacchaya*) in Myanmar (introduced after the 'Saffron Revolution' in 2007), which is unique to Myanmar, constitutes a particular Buddhist legal culture, in which the Sangha and not parliament has absolute authority in all doctrinal matters relating to Buddhism (Frydenlund 2017 and 2018; Walton 2015 and 2017).

Beginning in 1962 with the military regime of Ne Win, decades of military rule and isolation have created an atmosphere of fear in Myanmar, not least on the part of the religious minorities. The military junta tried to legitimize itself as a protector of Buddhism. It invested in Buddhist monuments and monasteries and supported Buddhist missionaries to convert the minorities in the hills to Buddhism (Learman 2005). The ideology of the military regime was ultranationalist, militaristic, chauvinistic and xenophobic. The regime heavily discriminated against minority religions, occasionally closed mosques and churches or dismantled religious symbols (such as crosses), and delayed or denied the permission to build new mosques or religious schools or to renovate old ones. The regime further put Islam and Christianity under strong surveillance and denied the churches and mosques material support from international networks. Moreover, the ultranationalist agenda of the military junta amplified the ethnic differences by subjecting the population to racialized citizenship. Citizenship was hierarchically constructed and put the Buddhist Bamar at the apex of society, while minorities were put at a lower level. Citizenship in Myanmar is differentiated according to racial categories. Muslims were handed identity papers designating them as Indian or Bengali (Indian or Bengali Islam), thereby limiting their citizenship status and making them vulnerable to discrimination.

The Muslim Rohingya in the west of the country experienced the worst: they were considered alien and were denied basic citizenship rights, effectively becoming stateless (Galache 2020). The Rohingya were branded as the dangerous other: extremist monks would see them as a dangerous intruder who would impose themselves on Burmese territory, outnumbering the Buddhist population in Rakhine. The most extremist monks, like the Islamophobic monk Ashin Wiratu, construct the Rohingya as a 'Muslim savage' and as a threat to Buddhist women or children (Wade 2017). Powerful forces in Myanmar have long politicized ethnic and religious difference and have called the ethnic minorities barbarians, terrorists and fundamentalists who want to take away Burmese souls from the Buddhist community.

The military and populist forces have dehumanized the Rohingya, depriving them of all citizenship rights, restricting their movement, denying them educational opportunities and making their life generally miserable. In 2016 and 2017, the military engaged repeatedly in what international human rights organizations called a textbook example of ethnic cleansing that included ruthless slaughtering, executions, mass rape and mass arson in Rakhine. This was followed by a low-intensity campaign of terror and starvation, killing Rohingya women and men and children, driving approximately eight hundred thousand Rohingya across the border to neighbouring Bangladesh, where they have had to dwell in hopelessly overcrowded camps. In addition, some one hundred thousand people were internally displaced, mostly residing in Internally Displaced People (IDP) camps, without access to basic health services or humanitarian aid (Wade 2017). The Gambia has initiated a case of genocide allegation before the International Court of Justice in The Hague and the court has decided that the Rohingya constitute a protected group under genocide and that Myanmar must take precautions to prevent further violence against them. This court decision, which is not binding, has been perceived within Myanmar as an inappropriate Western intervention into the country's internal affairs. And the plight of the Rohingya does not receive much sympathy from the leading political party National League for Democracy (NLD), nor from former human rights champion and State Councellor and foreign minister, Aung San Suu Kyi. Quite the opposite, on the question of the Rohingya tragedy, Aung San Suu Kyi decided to back the military. As State Councellor, she herself came to The Hague to defend Myanmar against the allegations, admitting some wrongdoings but rejecting genocide. She was widely celebrated at home for defending Myanmar against the allegations.

Secularization, modernization and liberalization has put fragile democracy in Myanmar in a political paradox. The 2008 constitution states a remarkable separation between religion and politics. It bans the use of religion for political purposes. Buddhist monks are neither entitled to vote nor to form political parties. This political disenfranchisement has motivated the ultranationalist wing of the Sangha to use the enormous popularity of their leading monks to dominate the Buddhist political discourse in public space. After 2011, the '969' movement[2] that called for the countrywide boycott of Muslim shops and the MaBaTha[3] declared their intention to protect the beloved Buddhist religion *sasana* and the Buddhist Bamar from internal and external enemies and to promote Buddhist education (Dhamma) and Buddhist values. Such goals found wide resonance among Buddhist communities across the country, including ethnic minority Buddhist communities. The MaBaTha has built bases in monasteries throughout the country and has joined the Buddhist missionaries who were sent out by the government. The movement can be conceptualized as neo-traditionalist in the sense that it works hard against institutional differentiation brought about by secularization (Frydenlund 2019) and as an expression of racializing nativism against the diversification and Westernization brought about by globalization.

Ideologically, the 969 'buy at Buddhist shops only'-movement and the MaBaTha have spread hate speech against Muslims and the Rohingya and have done much to prepare the physical violence that followed the anti-Muslim hate speech in public and in social media. As such, the MaBaTha, together with the military and well-resourced nationalist organizations, form an alliance and a power network to roll back Myanmar from the path to democracy and covenantal pluralism, instrumentalizing resentments as well as feelings of insecurity among Buddhist communities, monks and nuns.

Constitutional change in the direction of democratic reforms has of course raised hopes, but the military has claimed the ministry of home, ministry of defence and ministry of border affairs and keeps control of the finances. In addition, military personnel constitute one quarter of all members of parliament in both houses. One person who wanted to change this state of affairs was Ko Ni (1953–2017), a lawyer, a reformer and close political advisor of Daw Aung San Suu Kyi. As Ko Ni walked out of Yangon airport on a sunny January afternoon in 2017 to greet his grandchild, he was shot dead by a hired gunman. The murder was conspired by two former military officers and possibly backed by military circles who hated Ko Ni for at least two reasons. One is that he dared to confront the powerful generals by attempting to reform the constitution and squeeze the military. He believed in democracy and in the charisma of his patron, Daw Aung San Suu Kyi. Second, he was Muslim and thus hated by the nationalist monks and by the nationalist military. His death sent a frenzy signal to the Muslim and ethnic communities about the limits of democratic change. Ko Ni had received death threats for months. However, he believed in the protection by Suu Kyi and in democracy.

The ethnic cleansing of the Rohingya and the assassination of Ko Ni as well as violent ethnic riots against Muslims in Yangon, Lashio and Mekthila shattered the dream of ethnic reconciliation and sent a signal to democratic dissidents that the military is powerful and not willing to concede easily to democratic reforms. Moreover, the propaganda and crimes revitalized the xenophobic element that characterized military rule all along. There is little solidarity in Myanmar with Muslims or Rohingya, but plenty of hate speech in social media. The reaction of Daw Aung San Suu Kyi was especially disappointing. Instead of condemning the crimes, she remained silent. After the murder of her close advisor Ko Ni, she did not even attend his funeral and did not comment on the crime for months.

These developments have frustrated democratic minds in Myanmar, undermined trust and constituted a great hurdle to communal relations. Monks enjoy enormous prestige in Myanmar and most of the lower middle classes hold that the Muslims and the Rohingya are responsible for the trouble. The high command of NLD decided to endorse no Muslim candidate at the 2015 general elections for the only reason that the NLD feared alienating Buddhist voters (Frydenlund 2017 and 2018). In a way, Suu Kyi and the NLD have helped to prepare the ideological ground for the impunity of discrimination on a religious basis. Instead of highlighting the contributions of Muslims to society, the government shares the widespread resentment against the 'Islamization' of Myanmar, although Muslims in Myanmar are only 2.3 per cent (or 1.2 million people), the Rohingyas not being counted in the census.

Sino-Burmese people are also in an increasingly vulnerable position. The pressure to assimilate and to blend into Burmese society is high. Sino-Burmese today want to believe that anti-Chinese violence is a thing of the past, but anti-Chinese resentments are rising. Even if Sino-Burmese blend in more smoothly into Burmese society, they try to become as Burmese as possible to avoid anti-Chinese resentment or discrimination (see Roberts 2016). With the 2011 political liberalization, there were high hopes among democracy activists and ethnic minority politicians alike that Myanmar would move towards a path where fundamental questions about representation in the state, and autonomy and protection of basic human rights, could be discussed. However, recent developments have put these expectations on hold. Lack of rule of law means that ordinary Burmese have limited opportunities for seeking justice in the legal system (Cheesman 2015: 277–8). Muslims have been selected as a scapegoat (Crouch 2016a), but Christians have also been increasingly targeted as 'foreign agents'. Violent acts have happened both against Muslim and Christians, and both mosques and churches have been targeted.

As for the legal domain, the MaBaTha has successfully pushed for a new law to protect 'race and religion'. The law seeks to regulate marriages between Buddhist women and non-Buddhist men, to prevent forced conversion through state control, to abolish polygamy and extramarital affairs and to promote birth control and family planning in certain regions of the country (Walton, McKay and Mar Mar Kyi 2015). Of crucial concern to the MaBaTha and the Buddhist-protectionist movement 969 was the alleged 'Islamization' of Myanmar and claims of violations of 'religious freedom' for Buddhists. It is important to understand that 'religious freedom' is not interpreted here in a Western sense as freedom of religious practice but as the defence of Buddhism perceived to be weak against its external threats. Despite the earlier wave of political liberalization and legal reform, the Parliament and the President passed this legislation, which implies increased regulation of religion. This was prepared by a public referendum, directly organized and campaigned for by MaBaTha monks, which received massive public support, especially from Buddhist women. As Myanmar lacks a law against domestic violence, Buddhist women felt that they would need the laws to get protection and many Buddhist women were afraid of sexual harassment or sexualized violence by Muslim men. On the other hand, the laws were met with strong opposition from various religious groups and civil society organizations, as well as from local ethnic and international human rights organizations and political parties who argued that the laws would deteriorate interreligious relations at a politically sensitive and uncertain period in Myanmar's history (Crouch 2016b; Frydenlund 2017 and 2018).

In her assessment of the impact of such Buddhist-protectionist laws, Melissa Crouch (2015 and 2016b) has come to a surprising conclusion. The Buddhist 'race and religion' laws build on the history of Buddhist law that was preoccupied with regulating the position of women. The laws follow the rhetoric of the anti-Muslim 1939 Buddhist Women Special Marriage and Succession Act. The laws stipulate that an interreligious marriage is to be governed by Buddhist law in terms of property, guardianship and divorce. The concern of the monkhood was that Buddhism of Buddhist wives would be the weaker religion and that women were forced to convert to Islam. According to the monks, Islamic men would marry more than one wife and force their children to become Muslims. But it turned out that the new laws against polygyny were used by Buddhist women against their unfaithful Buddhist husbands and not against Muslim men. This was because polygyny was more common among Buddhists than among Muslims. Ironically, and against its original intention, the laws demonstrated the inequality of Buddhist women and men and led to a revenge of betrayed Buddhist women on their unfaithful husbands. Thus, MaBaTha monks stated, 'We wanted to catch the "rabbit" (Muslim men), but instead we caught a "cat" (Buddhist men)' (Crouch 2016b).

In short, Myanmar's 'democratization' has entailed some degree of political liberalization and legal reform, but also ethno-religious conflict, restrictions on religion and rising Buddhist nationalism. During the 2015 election campaign, MaBaTha monks came to be associated with the military-allied Union Solidarity and Development Party (USDP), and the role of the movement upon Myanmar's democratization is at best ambiguous (Frydenlund 2017 and 2018). After the shift in power in the 2015 elections in favour of the NLD, the Ministry of Religious Affairs has turned against MaBaTha and its aggressive hate speech. Subsequently MaBaTha has changed its name (The Buddha Dhamma Charity Foundation) and taken a slightly lower profile. Civil society organizations and international NGOs continue to observe and document MaBaTha's hate speech and materials undercover, in order to raise consciousness and to counter its influence by means of education.

Diversity and its denial in Myanmar

In contrast to the hegemonic discourse of Bamar Buddhist homogeneity, diversity is not a new phenomenon in Myanmar. Indeed, in some places it is a way of life with neighbourhood relations historically ingrained into the social fabric of everyday life. Located in mainland Southeast Asia and neighbouring India, China, Thailand and Bangladesh, Myanmar has been diverse for centuries. It has received many cultural influences due to a long history of immigration especially in the colonial capital, Rangoon (now Yangon) and in the urban centres of Mandalay. There are 135 officially recognized indigenous groups living in all parts of Myanmar including the frontier regions of the country. While the heartland of central and upper Myanmar is overwhelmingly Theravada Buddhist, the Chin in Northwestern and Kachin in Northern Myanmar are overwhelmingly Christian, having received the gospel from American Baptist missionaries (Ngun Ling 2014). Other important religions include Hinduism and Islam. Hinduism (or Brahmanism) was introduced to the Burmese kingdoms from Northern India, while Islam was introduced from the Middle East but also from Southwest China. Arabs and Persians were warmly welcomed to trade in Burma and encouraged to take Burmese wives. South Asians used to work in the guard of the Burmese army. Chinese Muslims escaped from persecution and established businesses in Mandalay. Other religions in multi-religious Yangon include Judaism and Baha'i as well as local cosmologies, movements and cults. The Armenian Baptist community of 1,300 people settled in Rangoon in the nineteenth century with a special rapport to the Burmese royal court.

However, the Burmese king was the guardian of Buddhism, and the ruling monks oversaw the harsh rules which severely punished conversion of a Burman to other religions. Hence, the conversion of the ethnic minorities in the nineteenth century, such as the Karen to Christianity, caused violent persecution of the converts. The Karen converts to Christianity were instrumental in converting Kachin and Chin in the mountains of Northern and north-western Myanmar. The military regime of Ne Win and the follow-up military government State Law and Order Restoration Council (SLORC) reinforced the Buddhist nationalist ideology and turned against the ethnic minorities. The military government called ethnic minorities 'barbarians' in order to legitimate violence and atrocities against them. This resentment goes back to colonial times when the Karen Christians collaborated with the British Empire in hope of liberation from the domination by Buddhist nationalists. This historical context explains why Christianity was regarded as a foreign religion. Under military rule, the strict passport control did not allow Christian pastors to travel abroad, and there were restrictions in the import of Christian literature. The Christianized ethnic minorities fared better under British colonial rule, only to be subdued again by the postcolonial state.

The revitalization of Buddhist mission efforts in Karen, Chin and Kachin states, run by the Department for the Propagation of Religion under the ministry of religion (mainly Buddhism) and the MaBaTha, can be interpreted as efforts to reconvert people to the Buddhist centre and to expand Buddhist nationalism among ethnic minorities. The MaBaTha and the Buddhist missionaries have partly succeeded in what the state never achieved: they were able to mobilize ethnic minorities, such as the Buddhist-Shan and the Buddhist Karen against the Rohingya and against Islam.

Therefore, the development and integration of the ethnic minorities remains a daunting task, as they work through ethnic armed organizations that understand themselves as religious armies. The historical context is crucial to understand the tensions between the faiths in today's Myanmar. Resentments against foreigners were building up in colonial times when the country was governed by the British Empire and recruited Chinese and Indians to replace Bamar labour, to fill the colonial bureaucracy and to spur commerce. It is in this time that great anxieties of a declining Bamar Buddhist culture were building up in the new middle class, including civil servants in the British-governed bureaucracy. Significant resentment was rising against Indians, resulting in anti-Indian riots and violence after independence. As such, the anti-Muslim violent riots in 2013 had their predecessors in those earlier anti-Chinese and anti-Indian riots. All riots were legitimized by the assumption that the Indian, Chinese and Muslim others could not possibly be Burmese and should not benefit from the privileges of Burmese citizenship. Equally resented was the perceived alliance of ethnic minorities with the British, such as the Kayin and Kachin who served in the colonial army, resulting in rampage and slaughtering of minorities, including Chinese, by the Burmese Independence Army just after the retreat of the British (Gravers 1993). Revitalization of racialized nativism in Myanmar builds on the chauvinist resentments that grew in British Burma, where the directed influx of foreign labour was perceived as a threat to indigenous society, its morality, its identity and its religion.

The MaBaTha has used the pejorative term *Kalar* extensively. While the term was originally coined to identify strangers of any kind (including Europeans), it is now heavily used as a form of othering against Muslims and Rohingya. Unfortunately, the term *Kalar* is very widespread in political discourse today. The term is not only used by extremists but also by NLD members of parliament, as I witnessed in interviews, as well as by taxi drivers. Racialized attitudes are not isolated extremist opinions but widely shared across class lines in Myanmar society. As the atmosphere in public space turns aggressively against Rohingya and against Muslims, NLD politicians do not want to be associated with them, even as some of their strongest and most popular campaigners, in Mekthila or Mandalay, are Muslims. Public statements by former democratic activists from the 88 Generation (or '8888', the generation of the uprising from 8 August 1988) student group, such as the highly venerated Ko Ko Gyi who speaks of a justified fear of the Arakan Buddhist population, further fuel the othering of the Rohingya. Ko Ko Gyi had spent in total seventeen years in prison (partly in solitary confinement) for his leadership in the student protest movement but accepted membership of the government's Rakhine Investigation Commission to investigate the sectarian violence in Rakhine State. In early June 2012, Ko Ko Gyi accused 'neighbouring countries' of fuelling the unrest in Arakan State and stated categorically that the 88 Generation group will not recognize the Rohingyas as an ethnicity of Burma. Ko Ko Gyi, who also founded his own political party (the Four Eight Party), thus forms part of a widely held conspiracy theory that portrays the Rohingya as troublemakers, when they are actually the main victims of the violence.

Beyond the immediacy of the ethnic cleansing of the Rohingya lies the more historically entrenched and embedded problem of a deep-seated Islamophobia – in the constitution, in the law and in the hostile attitudes of politicians and ordinary folk.

Signposts of pluralism

The politics of religion in Myanmar today are, in the aggregate, hardly encouraging vis-a-vis the ideal of religious freedom and peaceful interreligious relations. Still, this does not mean that the situation on the ground is beyond hope. Indeed, I have witnessed first-hand many everyday embodiments of covenantal-pluralist potential – microcosms of what may someday come to characterize Myanmar more broadly. One example is a project that I have been carrying out with the help of 'ERASMUS +' and in close association with the University of Mandalay, looking at interfaith efforts of reconciliation. This project is akin to the concept of everyday justice, brought forward by Helene Maria Kyed at the Danish Institute for International Studies (DIIS) (Kyed 2018). In many cases, local actors have developed their own frames of justice provision in the context of state violence and the absence of justice provision in areas that have endured years of armed violent conflict. Religion can provide a strong frame of legitimation for ethnic and religious minorities in the ethnic frontier regions as well as a basis for everyday conflict resolution and social justice.

When I was teaching in Mandalay in 2018 and 2019, students told me about their friendships from different communities living in Mandalay. They learned to see Mandalay from a new lens. One student in geography prepared a drawing of a neighbourhood where four buildings of different religions stand side by side: a Buddhist monastery, a Tamil Hindu temple, a Chinese Buddhist temple and a Christian church. He also introduced us to the friendly communication between the houses of worship, inviting religious leaders to festivities of their respective communities. Some students reported about their friendships emerging in school, where they saw each other with open minds and hearts, without being aware of racial, ethnic or religious stereotypes.

In Mandalay, Muslims of mixed marriage are often well integrated. As they wear the same clothes as other Burmans, they are not easily recognizable as Muslims. As many Muslims in the middle class have Buddhist friends, they naively speculated in communication with me that they would not be targeted by the Bamar mob, because they have not had such an experience and because they feel well integrated. For some, it was shocking to hear of attacks for no reason, as they have had no negative encounters so far. They thought that only Rohingya are targeted and ignored the violent riots erupting in Yangon, Mekthila, Mandalay and Lashio.

There are many couples of Buddhist men and Muslim wives living peacefully in Mandalay. They perform marriage ceremonies with their families according to religious standards but do not impose a religious faith on their children, giving equal weight to both the Buddhist monastery and the Islamic mosque to study Dhamma and the Qur'an. But many Burmans are concerned that Buddhism is the weaker religion, willing to compromise and that Islam will eventually win, expanding in Myanmar society. In the current xenophobic climate, Muslims generally put their heads down to be invisible. Mixed couples are particularly vulnerable for harassment and remain silent about their faith. Love relations between Buddhists and Muslims show that social relations across faith remain intact, but constant spread of propaganda by ultranationalist movements puts enormous pressure on them.

There are encouraging signs of a new vision of global citizenship embodied and promoted by certain civil society groups. The goal of such civic organizations throughout Myanmar is to establish a social climate in which new values of liberalism, humanism, democratic law and a strong constitution protect minorities and their religions. In Yangon, there are student activists, artists and international NGOs that promote human rights and interfaith communication. These community leaders invest in multifaith relationships and in education to build bridges between Buddhism, Christianity and Islam.

For example, the Muslim NGO 'Smile' provides workshops to train Muslims in Myanmar to behave in a way that promotes friendship and mutual understanding with their Buddhist neighbours. In the religious field, there are Buddhist monks, Christian priests and Muslim clerics in Mandalay who are deeply interested in leveraging the potential of their religions to promote peace via inter-religious dialogue. In 2018, the Interreligious Dialogue Training Centre has been established with the support Vienna based KAICIID.[4] Buddhist, Christian, Hindu and Muslim religious community members are appointed as fellows who attend a rigorous, but joyful, training to become multiplicators and promoters of global learning.

Another good illustration of the promotion of dialogue is the Myanmar Institute of Theology (MIT). The MIT is a private college and Baptist seminary run by senior Christian leaders from the minority regions, especially Chin, Kayin and Kachin. Since 2000, the MIT also offers, in addition to its traditional theology programs, a program in liberal arts with a wide range of courses in English and other languages, computer sciences, business management, public administration, tourism management, social work and so on. Courses are offered in English and Burmese. The atmosphere in the classroom is full of companionship and solidarity. The students are educated to become community leaders and are equipped with strong Christian ethics and a good dose of cosmopolitanism. Many of the students come from humble social backgrounds, but they receive fellowships from the foundation or have jobs in the school (kitchen, cleaning, admin, etc.) to pay their fees. Unfortunately, the certificates are not recognized by the Myanmar department of education. The president told me that the students are very skilled in English, general communication, public relations and computer sciences and easily find jobs with international organizations and NGOs in Myanmar.

A similar college that offers great opportunities for students coming from poor and marginalized minorities and regions of the country is Paung Daw Oo International University in Mandalay, run by a charismatic Buddhist monk. Paung Daw Oo offers similar disciplines as MIT but focuses on Buddhist ethics instead of Christian theology. While many alumni from MIT serve as pastors in churches, students of Paung Daw Oo emphasize Buddhist teachings and often continue Buddhist studies in a Buddhist college or Buddhist University. Both MIT and Phaung Daw Oo encourage students to develop skills in communication and critical thinking. Both colleges are pathbreaking in the way that they attract students from rural backgrounds, where poor families are generally not able to afford education. Phaung Daw Oo offers a general program in social studies, called 'bridging'. Through bridging students can achieve a level of education that allows them to apply at general high schools and universities. Students generally receive a warm meal and stay in dormitories. I was personally involved in supporting a local project establishing elementary schools in impoverished Shan State, from where students went on to continue their education in Phaung Daw Oo.

More broadly, one can find encouraging examples of counter-mobilization and counter-messaging against MaBaTha's campaign to promote Buddhist nationalism. Some civil society groups used the social space that opened after 2011 for a flourishing of interfaith activities, some of which were built on efforts to bring humanitarian aid to the Delta. New organizations arose, partly supported by the international community, such as Religions for Peace Myanmar, a branch of the global Religions for Peace. After the NLD's 2015 win, the government supported a series of large interfaith rallies around the country, led in large part by Catholic Cardinal Charles Bo. The rallies were seen by many as efforts to counter Buddhist national activism and to constrain MaBaTha's social influence.

Conclusion

Unfortunately, the above examples of cosmopolitan learning and multifaith engagement in a covenantal-pluralist spirit remain in a minority position in Myanmar as a whole. The MaBaTha is still strong and has set up Dhamma schools that promote an exclusive and xenophobic ideology. As such, while there are signposts of covenantal pluralist potential in Myanmar today, a great deal of work remains to be done.

As I have tried to show, religious pluralism is tied to the establishment of a civic culture, to peace education and to full citizenship for all people in Myanmar. For this, it will be necessary to act both vertically and horizontally. *Vertically*, the government bears a huge responsibility in promoting peace in a society where social mobility and recognition are still heavily influenced by ethnic and religious origins. The government needs to spur necessary reforms of the constitution to protect vulnerable minorities and advance decentralization to distribute educational resources more fairly. Christian colleges or Islamic madrasah and their certificates should be widely recognized by the government. The government needs to decolonize religion and to decolonize its own racializing behaviour towards non-Bamar minorities in the country as manifested in multiple practices of institutionalized racism, discrimination, harassment and exclusion. Equality before the law and equal opportunities of social mobility are conditions of a diverse, open and tolerant society.

Horizontally, civic groups should be supported in their efforts to build more schools and to spread education, especially among the disadvantaged population in the outer regions. Education initiatives should incorporate themes of covenantal pluralism and cross-cultural religious literacy. Community centres should be built in every locality, and the initiative to build public libraries everywhere should be widely supported. A flourishing culture of multifaith dialogue and a culture for peace would not only protect religious minorities from discrimination but also open windows of opportunity for a gravely wounded multicultural nation. This essay has followed the suggestion that ethnographically grounded research can help us to identify and appreciate real-world examples of ways to get a bit closer to the vision of a robust covenantal pluralism.

Notes

1 I have done extensive anthropological fieldwork in Mandalay, in Yangon, in Karen state, have visited Shan State and have established a European Union-funded 'ERASMUS +' exchange program with the University of Mandalay. In this program, I taught a project course on 'Everyday Multiculturalism' in Mandalay to encourage the students to look at their own city from a new lens. I also organized a photo exhibition on intercultural, inter-religious and interethnic friendship. The exhibition offered rich opportunity to discuss different family genealogies and cultural and religious backgrounds, shedding light on the hidden diversity in the classroom and beyond.

2 The three digits of 969 refer to the so-called three Jewels of Buddhism: Buddha, Dhamma and Sangha: The first 9 stands for nine special attributes of the Buddha, the 6 for six special attributes of his Dharma (Pāli: Dhamma = the Buddhist teaching) and the last 9 represents nine special attributes of Buddhist Sangha (the monastic community).
3 MaBaTha is an acronym for *Ah-myo Batha Thathana Saun Shaung Ye a-Pwe* or the 'Organization for the Protection of Race and Religion'.
4 KAICIID (King Abdullah bin Abdulaziz International Centre for Interreligious and Intercultural Dialogue) is an intergovernmental organization, recognized by the United Nations, with its main seat in Vienna, Austria. While the work of KAICIID has found praise from other religious communities, it has also been subject to critique due to its close connections with Saudi Arabia.

References

Cheesman, Nick (2015), 'That Signifier of Desire, the Rule of Law', *Social Research: An International Quarterly*, 82 (2): 267–90.

Cheesman, Nick, and Nicholas Farrelly (eds) (2016), *Conflict in Myanmar: War, Politics, Religion*, Singapore: ISEAS.

Cheesman, Nick (ed.) (2018), *Interpreting Communal Violence in Myanmar*, New York: Routledge.

Crouch, Melissa (2015), 'Constructing Religion by Law in Myanmar', *The Review of Faith & International Affairs* (special issue on religion in Myanmar), 13: 1–11.

Crouch, Melissa (ed.) (2016a), *Islam and the State in Myanmar: Muslim-Buddhist Relations and the Politics of Belonging*, Delhi: Oxford University Press.

Crouch, Melissa (2016b), 'Promiscuity, Polygyny, and the Power of Revenge: The Past and Future of Burmese Buddhist Law in Myanmar', *Asian Journal of Law and Society*, 3 (1): 85–104.

Fink, Christina (2009), *Living Silence in Burma: Surviving under Military Rule*, London: ZED.

Frydenlund, Iselin (2017), 'Religious Liberty for Whom? The Buddhist Politics of Religious Freedom during Myanmar's Transition to Democracy', *Nordic Journal of Human Rights*, 35 (1): 55–73.

Frydenlund, Iselin (2018), 'The Birth of Buddhist Politics of Religious Freedom in Myanmar', *Journal of Religious and Political Practice*, 4 (1): 1–15.

Frydenlund, Iselin (2019), 'Protecting the *Sasana* through Law: Radical Buddhism and Religious Freedom in Transitional Myanmar', in *Religion, Secularism and Democracy in South-east Asia*, ed. Vidhu Verma, 194–212, Delhi: Oxford University Press.

Galache, Carlos Sardina (2020), *The Burmese Labyrinth: A History of the Rohingya Tragedy*, London: Verso.

Gravers, Mikael (1993), *Nationalism as Political Paranoia in Burma: An Essay on the Historical Practice of Power*, London: RoutledgeCurzon.

Kyed, Helene Maria (2018), 'Introduction to the Special Issue on Everyday Justice', *Independent Journal of Burmese Scholarship*, 1 (2): 1–21.

Learman, Linda (2005), *Buddhist Missionaries in the Era of Globalization*, Honolulu: University of Hawai'i Press.

Ngun Ling, Samuel (2014), *Christianity through Our Neighbour's Eyes: Rethinking the 200 Years Old American Baptist Missions in Myanmar*, Yangon: Myanmar Institute of Theology Press.

Rogers, Benedict (2012), *Burma: A Nation at the Crossroads*, London: Rider Random House.

Roberts, Jayde Lins (2016), *Mapping Chinese Rangoon: Place and Nation among the Sino-Burmese*, Seattle: University of Washington Press.

Sadan, Mandy (ed.) (2016), *War and Peace in the Borderlands of Myanmar: The Kachin Ceasefire, 1994–2011*, Copenhagen: NIAS.

Schober, Juliane (2008), 'Communities of Interpretation in the Study of Religion in Burma', *Journal of Southeast Asian Studies*, 39 (2): 255–67.

Stewart, Christopher, ChrisSeiple, Dennis Hoover (2020), 'Toward a Global Covenant of Peaceable Neighborhood: Introducing the Philosophy of Covenantal Pluralism', *Review of Faith & International Affairs*, 18 (4): 1–17.

Wade, Francis (2017), *Myanmar's Enemy Within: Buddhist Violence and the Making of a Muslim 'Other'*, London: ZED.

Walton, Matthew J. (2015), 'Monks in Politics, Monks in the World: Buddhist Activism in Contemporary Myanmar', *Social Research*, 82 (2): 507–30.

Walton, Matthew J. (2017), *Buddhism, Politics and Political Thought in Myanmar*, Cambridge: Cambridge University Press.

Walton, Matthew J., Melyn McKay and Daw Khin Mar Mar Kyi (2015), 'Women and Myanmar's "Religious Protection Laws"', *Review of Faith & International Affairs*, 13 (4): 36–49.

Part 3

The Case of Christianity

8

Christianity in Myanmar: With a particular emphasis on its Indian roots

Marja-Leena Heikkilä-Horn

Introduction

Christianity arrived in contemporary Myanmar through two different roads – with the Indian immigrants moving into the country during the British colonial era when Burma was part of the Indian Raj. The other road was through the Western missionaries, many of whom originally also arrived via India and approached particularly the highlanders of Myanmar like Kachin and Chin groups. The Indian Christian population of Myanmar can find religious solace in various congregations and groups: Catholicism, Methodism and Lutheran Protestantism. The Roman Catholic Church has deep roots in Southern India, and the South Indian Catholic congregation in Myanmar is well established and loyal to its own church. The South Indian non-Catholic Christians can be found in the Lutheran and Methodist churches. The Tamil and other South Asian Christians are well connected with their fellow believers both in India and in other parts of Southeast Asia. The Tamils of Myanmar are a diverse group divided into various religious communities of Hindus, Muslims and Christians. Many of them have been assimilated and 'Burmanized' in the sense that they use Burmese names as is common among all assimilated migrant groups in Myanmar. Most of them also have Myanmar citizenship. At the same time, they have preserved their language, culture and traditions within each different religious community.

This chapter looks at Christianity in Myanmar with a particular emphasis on its Indian roots. It further highlights some more recent developments of the Chin Lutheran Churches as well and their interaction with the Tamil Lutheran Church. The chapter is based on earlier literature on the Indian communities in Burma,[1] as well as interviews and observations on the Tamil Christian communities conducted by the author since the early 2000s.

Historical background

Ancient Hindu, Buddhist, Jain and Muslim influences from the Indian subcontinent on modern Southeast Asia is a profoundly studied subject (Coedes 1944; Majumdar 1948). The existence of contemporary South Asian communities with Indian roots is a less studied subject and clouded in controversies. The mainstream narrative is that the Indian migrants were 'imported' to the British colonies particularly to the present-day Myanmar and Malaysia, including Singapore. Indian communities existed also in French colonial Indochina as well as in the British colonies in East Asia particularly in Hong Kong.

The earliest studies on the Indian communities in Burma and Malaya were usually conducted by the British colonial officials themselves (Andrew 1933; Baxter 1941; Pearn 1946). These early authors were predominantly concerned with the impact of Indian labour on the local economy. The general conclusion was that 'Burma', implicitly meaning the British colonial economy in Burma, had substantially benefitted from the industrious and diligent Indian migrants.

The Indian studies on the 'Indian' communities in Southeast Asia by Usha Mahajani (1960) and Nalini Ranjan Chakravarti (1971) also take a pragmatic approach to interpret the 'Indian' communities as a resource for the economic growth during the British colonial era and beyond. Kernial Singh Sandhu edited an informative volume on 'Indian Communities in Southeast Asia' (1993) with several articles on various South Asian groups in Burma as well.

Indian migrants under British administration

The Indians started to migrate to Burma as soon as the British had won the First Anglo-Burmese War (1826). It is worth remembering that the 'British' military forces often consisted of Indian 'Sepoys' (professional infantrymen), some of whom settled permanently in the newly-occupied territories in Akyab – present-day Sittwe in Arakan (now Rakhine) – and in Southern Burma in Tenasserim, particularly in Moulmein. The influx of Indian migrants was defended by reports such as the one by Michael Symes,[2] where he points out that there were already in 1795 numbers of people from Manipur (today at the Indian-Myanmar border) – including prisoners, dancers, musicians and Brahmin astrologers in the court of

Table 8.1 Indian Migrants to Burma (1931)

Race	Males	Females
Hindustani	105,840	19,214
Oriya	55,986	1,902
Tamil	58,823	25,504
Telugu*	108,701	23,026

*Another Dravida language widely spoken in the British 'Madras Presidency', which covered areas from present-day Tamil Nadu and Andhra Pradesh.
Source: Chakravarti 1971: 24, table 2.10 (applied only to four groups)

Table 8.2 Indian Migrants: Origins (1931)

Districts of origin	Immigrants
Ganjam (Orissa)	49,000
Vizagapatam (Andhra Pradesh)	36,000
Godavari (Andhra Pradesh)	26,000
Tanjore (Madras/Tamil Nadu)	14,000
Ramnad (Madras)	13,000

Source: Chakravarti 1971: 26, table 2.11 (applied only to presumed Telugus and Tamils)

Ava. There were, however, very few Indians in Rangoon (Yangon) until the end of the Second Anglo-Burmese War (1852), when a 'full-scale Indian immigration into Burma began' (Mahajani 1960: 2). Before the Second Anglo-Burmese war, in 1838, there had been nineteen Indians in Rangoon, twelve of them Parsis from Bombay engaged in shipbuilding and trade in timber and cheap cottons. In the 1881 Census of India, the entire population of the British-administered territory in Burma, excluding Arakan, was over three million, and 4 per cent were of Indian origins (ibid.).

During the first phase of British administration, the Indian communities preferred to educate their children in separate schools for different linguistic communities such as Bengali, Hindi, Tamil and Telugu schools. The communities also followed separate personal laws, Hindu laws for Hindus and Muslim laws for Muslims. Chakravarti injects a critical comment suggesting that 'an Indian was therefore at liberty to spend his whole life in Burma, from cradle to grave, without having much social contact with Burmans' (Chakravarti 1971: 9–10).

The question what is meant with an 'Indian' in the case of migrations to Burma is ambiguous in the early reports and was further complicated with the British shifting the criteria of an 'Indian' from language to 'race'. An 'Indian' became a generic term hiding the linguistic and religious identities of the population in Burma (Heikkilä-Horn 2009: 147–8).

Chakravarti (1971) also points out that the first two censuses of India including the Burma Province, taken in 1872 and 1881, respectively, covered only parts of Lower Burma occupied by Britain. Upper Burma was initially conquered in 1886 but was 'pacified' and placed under British Indian administration only years later, hence censuses 1891 and 1901 still suffered from similar bias as the two first ones (Chakravarti 1971: 13). Only the censuses of 1911, 1921 and 1931 can be regarded as being somewhat more reliable in terms of covering wider parts of the British-Indian 'Burma Province'.

Since 1900, annually approximately 250,000 Indian immigrants moved to British Burma. By the year 1921, there were one million Indians living in Burma, of whom estimated 50 per cent were Muslims. Total population of Burma was eleven million. In the peak year 1927, about 480,000 Indians migrated to British Burma. Indian population was concentrated in the capital city Rangoon, which accommodated 4,425 Muslims in the year 1869. By 1872 the number had more than doubled to 11,671. In the year 1872, only 16 per cent of the population of Rangoon was Indian; by 1901 it was around 50 per cent. In 1911, a peak was reached when 56 per cent of the population of Rangoon was of Indian origins. Same percentage was reached in 1941 (Tin Maung Maung Than 1993: 586).

Interestingly, the British census takers in 1931 invented a new method in breaking down the numbers of the Indian immigrants into four hybrid groups:

1. Indians born in Burma,
2. Indians born outside Burma,
3. Indo-Burmese races, and
4. Anglo-Indians.

With this division, the numbers of the 'Indian' population could be reduced to smaller units and thus appeared less alarming. At the same time, identity markers such as language groups and religious identities were obscured (Heikkilä-Horn 2009: 147–8).

The situation in the capital city Rangoon tells another story. Rangoon was truly an Indian city and much praised as such by the British Sir J. George Scott, using the pen name Shway Yoe in his book *Burman* published in 1882. He suggested that the old Burmese capital Mandalay was screaming to be annexed by the British, so that it could become like Rangoon, which 'now ... has broad smooth roads beautifully laid out public gardens, abundant street lamps, spacious mercantile offices, mills, schools, jails, hospitals, clubs and halls' (Shway Yoe 1963: 547). Shway Yoe marvels at the multiethnicity of Rangoon:

> There are Chinese, Japanese, Malays, Siamese, natives of India of all parts, Bengalis, Madrassis, Panjabis, Parsis, Persians, Suratis, together with Armenians, Jews, English, French, Germans, Italians, Greeks, and all the European nationalities mixed up with the native races, Burmese, Talaings, Shans, Karens, but they are all kept in order by the strong arm of the law, which is the same for the rich and the poor. (Ibid.: 548)

He contrasts this to the Burmese-administered Mandalay. Mandalay is full of other

> nationalities; Chinamen, ... bearded Surati with solemn face and Jewish tricks of trade; the Palaung from the north; ... the stalwart Shan with baggy blue or white trousers and tattoo marks down to his ankles; ... heavy, easy-going Karen, lithe, treacherous Kachin ... Mandalay had become an asylum for insolvent debtors, runaway soldiers and sailors, and unlucky adventurers from British territory, just as Rangoon used to be for India in the old Burman days. (Ibid.: 546)

Hence, for the British Rangoon was a modern, positively multi-ethnic city, whereas Mandalay was a 'medley' where different nationalities lived in disarray.[3]

Census of India 1931 breaks down the numbers of Indian migrants to Burma by race and sex. The biggest group were 'Hindustanis' which presumably refers to Hindi-speakers from northern India (see Table 8.1).

Chakravarti is compelled to admit that the capital city of colonized Burma, Rangoon, 'housed more foreigners (predominantly Indians) than Burmans' (Chakravarti 1971: 19). More than 66 per cent of Rangoon's population was composed of immigrant races, Indians constituted about 53 per cent of the city's population. Chakravarti emphasizes that Rangoon 'was developed into one of the most prosperous and beautiful cities of the East' and adds that this was achieved 'mostly by Indian capital and almost entirely by Indian labour' (ibid.: 20).

Census of India 1931 presents a table on the Indian districts from where the largest number of Indian immigrants originated: the largest groups were Telugus from Ganjam, Vizagapatam and Godvari and Tamils from and Tanjore and Ramnad (see Table 8.2).

One of the most controversial Indian migrant groups were the Hindu Tamil moneylenders and bankers of the Chettiar caste who made fortunes in Burma and elsewhere in the colonized Southeast Asia. The official Chettiar narrative reiterates that their fortunes were ruined by the Japanese occupation 1941/2 when they had to leave Burma. According to the Chettiars, ultimately their properties vanished in the nationalization policies in the 1950s of Prime Minister U Nu's semi-socialist government (Turnell 2009). The picture looks different in Chettinad in Tamil Nadu, where there are some 70,000 opulent palaces in grandiose Venetian style in over twenty different villages in the Chettiar land. Many of these palaces are now open to the tourists, and the home museums tell a tale of wealth and economic success in Burma.

The Burmese antipathy towards the Indian community was triggered as well by the wealth of the Chettiars as by the violence of the Sepoy military police. Yet, as often happened in the European colonies, the popular rage was directed towards the scapegoats, usually migrants as visible representatives of the hated colonial power, rather than against the British.

It is also worth noticing that when the middle-class Burmese may have resisted the power of the upper-class Indians, at the same time there was a growing well-organized Indian labour movement in the 1930s, and the Burmese attacks against the Indian workers played in the favour of the British authorities who feared all organized political movements against their administration in Burma. The fatal battles between the Burmese and the Indians in the riots of 1930 and particularly 1938 neatly served the British interests in disciplining the Indian labour force in accordance with the British colonial divide and rule policies.

Period of the independence movements

Initially the two countries' nationalist movements were closely intertwined. Burmese nationalists were inspired by the Indian National Congress (INC) and some Burmese nationalists were members of the INC until the 1940s. There were allegedly also links to the Hindu Mahasabha, as a Burmese monk U Ottama – born in Arakan – was the president of the Hindu Mahasabha for three years (Mahajani 1960: 35). The methods adopted against the British were non-violent and peaceful, boycotts and strikes (or *hartals*) in Gandhian style were favoured. The Burmese politicians talked about 'Home Rule' and 'Swaraj' like their Indian colleagues. For a period of time, the Burmese nationalists believed gaining increasing independence in tandem with India but finally opted for separation from India, which was finalized in 1937, with the Burma Act of 1935. With this partition of British India, the pressure on the Indians either to remain Indian or become Burmese increased.

With the separation of Burma from India, several new laws were issued and interpreted as harmful to the Indian economic interests in Burma. Many of the laws indeed aimed at protecting the Burmese peasants against Indian moneylenders who could confiscate their lands in case they defaulted the payments. The landownership of the non-cultivators was also to be limited, the acreage was to be limited, the rents that could be collected from the tenants were to be limited, acts which were all perceived harmful particularly for the Chettiar interests. The Immigration Agreement of 1941 established some new rules in terms of accepting Indian labour force; it was made mandatory to have a passport with a visa permitting the entry; cohabitation with a Burmese woman would lead to a cancellation of the permit; however, Indians who were born and bred in Burma could establish a claim to domicile (Mahajani 1960: 88–9).

Burmese authorities – still under the British rule – started to put pressure on stopping or at least limiting the influx of Indian migrant workers to Burma. This attempt to limit the Indian presence in the Burmese economy was bitterly criticized by the media and lawmakers in British India.

Arrival of Christianity to the Indian subcontinent

As the history of Christianity in Burma is intimately intertwined with the introduction of the Christian gospel to India, it is worthwhile to look into the situation on the Indian subcontinent. Christianity prides itself with a very long history on the Indian subcontinent. Most narratives would start with AD 52, when allegedly one of the apostles of Jesus, St Thomas, arrived in Kerala and introduced the new gospel. This is regarded as the birth of the Syrian Orthodox Church in India. Historically, the origins of the Syrian Orthodox Church in Kerala can more firmly be traced back to the fourth century AD.

One of the earlier Christian denominations that spread from India to Burma was the Armenian Church. The Armenian Church was established in India presumably in the early 1600s. Armenian merchants founded a base in Madras (now Chennai) in present-day Tamil Nadu in Southern India, where they built churches and established a press to publish an Armenian journal, which predominantly propagated for an independent Armenian state. The

Armenians of Madras were trading with Russia and England. St Mary Orthodox Church was constructed in 1712 on Armenian Street in the downtown British-controlled areas of Madras in a settlement called George Town. In the colonial racial parlance, that part of the city was known as the 'white town'.

Some historical narratives indicate that the Mughal emperor Akbar (1556–1605) would have invited the first Armenians to settle down in Agra. Most of the early Armenians were from Persia (Sarkissian 1987). An additional incentive for Armenian settlements in India was a special agreement with British East India Company (EIC), signed in London on 22 June 1688, granting trading privileges to the Armenians and 'equal rights' with the British subjects regarding freedom of residence, travel, religion and unrestricted access to civil offices.[4]

The Roman Catholic Church established itself permanently with the Portuguese conquerors, after Vasco da Gama had found his way to India (1498) and was followed by other adventurers representing the Portuguese Crown such as Afonso de Albuquerque and Francois Xavier. The Roman Catholic Church is a minority church in present-day Tamil Nadu but has nevertheless a volume of roughly twenty million Catholics in India, which translates into approximately 2 per cent of the population. Besides Goa and Kerala, Tamil Nadu is the strongest state in terms of Roman Catholic presence. India has the largest Catholic population in Asia after the Philippines.

Another church that arrived in British Madras was the Lutheran Church. It arrived with the German Bartholomäus Ziegenbalg (1682–1719). Ziegenbalg and another German priest Heinrich Plütschau were ordained as Royal Danish Missionaries by the court chaplain of King Frederik IV of Denmark and they were sent to India in 1705. The two arrived in Tranquebar on 9 July 9 1706, which is regarded as the beginning of the Lutheran Church in India. In May 1707, five adults were baptized, the foundation stone of the 'Jerusalem Church' was laid down in August 1707 and the first translation of the New Testament into Tamil was published in 1711. In 1718, the construction of a new church was started, by the name 'New Jerusalem Church'. This church is well preserved and restored in Tranquebar (Jeyaraj 2003: 82–3; Schönbeck 2012: 9).

Several Lutheran churches were established in Southern India in the 1700s. The first native Lutheran minister with the baptismal name of Aaron was ordained in 1733; the second – a Catholic convert by the name Diogo – followed in 1741. By then, thirty-five years of Lutheran mission ad resulted in some 3,800 individuals having been baptized in Tranquebar and Tanjore (Schönbeck 2012: 10).

The early missionaries were closely linked to the European economic and colonial interests in India. The Danish government asked the Danish clergy of the Zion Church in Tranquebar to function as pastors and missionaries. Danish interests in the region were, however, quickly deteriorated and Danish Missionary Society concentrated its efforts and finances to support William Carey's college in Serampore. William Carey (1761–1834) had joined four other missionaries who moved to the Danish settlement of Fredriksnagar. This was the beginning of the Serampore Mission and Press which became a very influential institution; not least by publishing translations of the Christian gospel in practically all Indian languages (ibid.: 12). The British EIC was emerging as the most powerful player on the Indian subcontinent and pushed the other European trading companies out. In 1845, Tranquebar was sold to England, while the Royal Tranquebar Mission in 1847 was transferred, by special royal request, to the Lutheran Dresden Mission Society, soon to be renamed the Leipzig Missionary Society (ibid.: 11). According to Jayaraj, the church properties were handed over to the Leipzig Evangelical Lutheran Mission (LELM) in Germany (Jayaraj 2003: 90).

Jayaraj concludes that the cooperation between the Western missionaries and the local Tamil Christians did not always run smoothly. The Tamils were treated as objects of study and became nameless numbers as converts in the Western reports. The Western missionaries held monopoly on knowledge about the Christian missions in India but did not share their knowledge with the locals. The economic gap was wide, when the Western missionaries were living in large comfortable mansions surrounded by servants, whereas the local Tamil Christians were eking out existence in modest huts (ibid.: 92).

In 1919, the Tamil Evangelical Lutheran Church (TELC) was officially established when different German, Danish and Swedish Lutheran missions joined together. A Swedish missionary Ernst Heuman was ordained as the first bishop of TELC with the title Bishop of Tranquebar. The origins of the Tamil Lutheran Church go back to the German Leipzig Mission and the Sweden Mission.

After the LELM had changed its name to Tamil Evangelical Lutheran Church (TELC) in 1919, the Church of Sweden Mission in 1921 offered its cooperation in church administration. In 1977, the Evangelical Lutheran Mission of Lower Saxony, Germany, joined TELC as a partner. At the early 2000s, TELC had about 500 congregations with 110,000 members. The headquarters are located in Tiruchirappalli in Tamil Nadu. The Church of South India (CSI) was established in 1947 uniting various Protestant and Anglican churches. Today it is a member of the Anglican Communion and with its about 3.8 million adherents the second largest church in India. Still, with its more than seventeen million members – of whom some four million follow the Syrian Orthodox Church – the Catholic Church of India is by far the largest among the Christian Churches in India. Altogether Christians make up 2.1 per cent of the population of India, while the percentage of Christians in Tamil Nadu is almost three times as high, that is, 6.1 per cent (Schönbeck 2012: 17). Christianized Tamil immigrants brought their faith with them when they settled in Burma.

Arrival of Christianity to the Indian 'Province of Burma'

There were two different patterns in introducing Christianity to Burma: either systemic Christian proselytizing carried out by Western missionaries usually based in India or Christianized migrants moving from the Indian subcontinent to Burma. The Christian proselytizing targeted particularly the highlanders in the areas, which now would be regarded as border areas populated by various ethnic minorities such as Karen, Karenni, Kachin and Chin. The Indian Christians migrated during the British colonial era to larger cities such as Rangoon, Moulmein and Mandalay and established churches where they settled down. The origins of Christianity in areas like Syriam and Bassein are also linked to the economic opportunities the British opened in these cities.

One of the first Christian immigrant groups to Burma were the Armenians, who trace back their presence in Burma to the seventeenth century. An Armenian tombstone, found in Syriam (near Yangon) in the old British Oil Company (BOC) compound, originates from 1725.[5] There is also anecdotal evidence about Armenians working as advisers for the king in Mandalay during the reign of the King Mindon (r. 1854–78). The first Christian mission to arrive in Burma was the Roman Catholic Barnabite Mission in 1722. There had been some earlier attempts that had brought Sebastian Manrique to Arakan between the years 1629 and 1643. The Barnabite Padre Vincenzo Sangermano (1758–1819) visited Ava and Pegu. Both have provided us with some of the first Western description of the society there.[6]

The first missionary to reside in Burma, in Loikaw, was an Italian priest, Padre Bartolomeo Peano, who has described his life and visits to the Padaung in Pekhon, in present-day Kayah State (Gheddo 2007: 207–8). The Padaung author Pascal Khoo Thwe (2002) describes how an Italian missionary, Padre Carlo, who actually was on his way to China, was captured by Pascal Khoo Thwe's grandfather. After some confusion, he was asked to stay in the village for the rest of his life and he 'in due course converted the whole village to Catholicism' (Khoo Thwe 2002: 25).

The French Catholic missionary Paul Bigandet (1813–94) was also based in Burma for some fifty years. His headquarters were located in St John's Cathedral in Rangoon. He describes the development in his book from 1887, *History of the Catholic Burmese Mission* (Bigandet 1887).

The missionary work was significantly boosted on the Indian subcontinent by the interests of the EIC to expand its tea plantations to the northeast. Hence was formed a concentration of predominantly British missionaries in the Assamese highlands and in the Danish colony known as Frederiksnagar in Serampore. This was the area where British Baptist missionary William Carey worked. His son Felix Carey was sent to Burma after the British opened the eastern frontier, but much to the disappointment of his faith brothers in Serampore, Felix Carey ultimately joined the royal household in Ava and served the Burmese king.

In 1807, the English Baptists opened a mission in Burma without much success. The first permanent Baptist mission was founded in 1813 by an American. The first well-known missionary was Adoniram Judson, whose name has survived in Myanmar in Judson Church inside the Yangon University Campus and in a classic Burmese-English dictionary. Judson was based in southern parts of present-day Myanmar and worked only among the ethnic Burman, Mon and Karen groups.

Other missionaries followed Judson. Among all the Western nationalities, the Swedes were surprisingly active. The first Swedish-born missionary was Johanna Anderson (b. 1856) who migrated to America and was appointed for service in Burma by the Women's American Baptist Foreign Mission Society in 1888. During her first term, she taught at the mission school in Toungoo (also Taungoo). After her, other Swedish-born missionaries followed; one of the most famous ones was Ola Hanson (b. 1864). He migrated to America and converted to the Baptist faith. He was ordained in 1890 and appointed by the American Baptist Foreign Mission Society to the northern parts of Burma, populated by the Shan and the Kachin. Ola Hanson and his wife Minnie arrived there in December 1890. The study of Kachin mythology turned out to be useful for proselytizing. The Kachin myths about creation, death and a flood could be reinterpreted in Christian terms. The most useful myth was the myth about the 'lost book', which a 'white man' will one day bring back. Ola Hanson decided to take the role of the 'white man' and give the Kachin their 'lost book'.

The Kachin did not have a written language, thus Ola Hanson created a written language for the Kachin language based on the Roman alphabet. By 1911, he was able to complete his first version of the New Testament translation. In 1926, he had completed the Old Testament as well. According to Bertil Lintner (1997), the Kachin thus reclaimed their 'lost book', and they were beginning to become 'civilised' once again as predicted in their myth (Lintner 1997: 74). In 1906, the American Baptist Missionary Press published *A Dictionary of the Kachin Language* compiled by Ola Hanson. Another famous Swedish missionary to the Kachin Land was Herman Tegenfeldt, who wrote the book *The Kachin Baptist Church in Burma* (1974). By 1956, the church had seven thousand members.

The first missionaries who attempted to enter the Chin areas were Roman Catholic priests in 1864. They were escorted out of the area that time but returned in 1884 to Kalaymyo in present-day Sagaing Region, where they encountered some ethnic Chins. American Baptist missionaries Arthur and Laura Carson succeeded in 1899 to establish a mission station in Hakha. According to Lian Sakhong (2003), the couple was 'invited' by British colonial officers (Sakhong 2003: 119).

They were followed by some other American missionaries. The first Chin converts in 1904 were two couples from Tedim. Christianity gradually spread among the Chins but was also challenged by indigenous cults. According to F. K. Lehman (1967), 'roughly 70 percent of the Chins are non-Christian; most are animists, but some, especially on the Arakan side are at least nominally Buddhists. Only about 22 percent are Baptist, real or nominal, and a few percent more are Protestants or of other denominations or Roman Catholics' (Lehman 1967: 97).

The British and American missionaries targeted particularly minorities such as the highlanders thus choosing the same strategy as used in Assam and Northeast India. By Christianizing ethnic minorities, who often had been suffering under various forms of dominance at the hands of the ruling lowlanders, Christianity was politicized and essentialized as the raison d'etre for the mobilization of ethnic elites to demand autonomy or independence from the central state. The EIC did not particularly promote Christian missionaries although some individual EIC officials may have entertained some sympathy for them. The general policy was not to get involved in the religious affairs of the population of India. Lowlanders being Hindus and Muslims in India and Buddhists in Burma, the highlanders turned out to be more receptive to the new spiritual ideas, which were often incorporated into the existing spirit pantheon.

Indian churches in Burma

The Indian migrant population settled down in the cities and towns in 'Burma Proper', meaning in the areas under direct British rule, and also in the rural areas in the Delta, where the British started industrial scale rice production by opening a new rice frontier in the Delta. Large numbers of labour force were needed and thousands of Tamils and other South Asians settled down in the Irrawaddy Delta region.

The Roman Catholic Church

The Roman Catholics in Burma constitute about 1 per cent of the population. The heaviest concentration of Catholic population can be found in Rangoon (Yangon), Dalla, Moulmein (Mawlyimyine) and Hpa-an. Catholicism is also strong among the Kayah and Kayan people in Kayah State, where there are two magnificent Cathedrals in the state capital Loikaw. In addition, there are vibrant Catholic congregations in Mandalay, Maymyo (Pyin Oo Lwin), Taunggyi and Lashio with magnificent cathedrals.

There are some exclusively Tamil Catholic cathedrals in Myanmar, such as St Anthony in Yangon visited by Pope Francis in 2017. Other more mixed Catholic churches but still predominantly frequented by the Tamils are St Mary's and St John's in Yangon. The Catholic St Xavier's Church in Mandalay is regarded as a Tamil church. The Dalla Catholic church as well as the Moulmein, Kyauktan and Syriam Catholic churches are predominantly Tamil, as are the nunneries, orphanages and boarding schools connected to them.

Pope Francis visited Myanmar on 27–30 November 2017, which strongly boosted the visibility of the Catholic Church. Charles Maung Bo (b. 1948) had been nominated as the cardinal of the Catholic Church of Myanmar, and he has visited the Vatican several times as the first ever Myanmar-based cardinal. The Pope's visit of the St Anthony Cathedral may have empowered the Catholic Tamil community, which now is quite openly emphasizing the community's ethnic and ethnolinguistic identity and has been teaching Tamil language to the children during the school breaks since 2013. Also, the Cardinal has encouraged the preservation of ethnic minority languages, culture and tradition, hence both Karen and Tamil language programmes have been launched in various parishes of the archdiocese.[7] Many ethno-religious minority communities have, in fact, been teaching their own languages for decades, but it appears to be only now that they would publicly mention it to the foreign media.

The Bethlehem Lutheran Church in Yangon – a case study

There are several Lutheran churches in present-day Myanmar. One is dominated by the Indian Tamils, the others by the Chin people.

Bethlehem Lutheran Church was established in 1878 in Madras by Germans. The German missionaries came to Burma and the first wooden church was built on the place where the Yangon Railway Station is currently located. There was also an orphanage, a clinic and a chapel in the church compound. In 1921, the British decided to build the railway station and the Lutherans had to be relocated. They were given a piece of land further north across the railway on the Thein Byu Street, and it is included on the Yangon Heritage List drafted by the city authorities. The church is dominated by the Tamil-speaking Indians, but outside the church there is a signboard stating that the preaching is conducted also in Telugu, Burmese and English.

Until 1962, every five years a new pastor was sent from India to Burma and the congregation paid his salary. In 1962, Reverend Jenson Andrew's father was the assistant manager in a British construction company and functioned at the same time as the church secretary. After the military coup d'etat in 1962, foreign missionaries had to leave Burma, and as Indian citizens some reverends had to leave the country in 1964. In 1964, when the Berlin Wall was built, the links to the East German Leipzig Mission were severed, and the Swedish Lutheran Church took over the Madras mission station and hence the support of the Bethlehem Lutheran Church in Yangon.

The American Lutheran Church (ALC) had been working among a Telugu community, whom the Tamils perceived as being of lower caste and social standing. When the Americans had to abandon their mission in Burma, the Tamil Lutheran Church somewhat grudgingly included the Telugus in their congregations. The majority of the Telugus had left to India as non-citizens but a few Telugus remained in Burma. There used to be seven hundred Telugu people worshiping in the ALC on U Ba Wa Street, whereas Bethlehem Lutheran Church had about eight hundred Tamils. Approximately six hundred Telugus and four hundred Tamils left Burma in the early 1960s to return to India. Only one hundred Telugus remained, and they needed to be included in the Tamil church. The Telugus sold their church for thirty dollars to Assembly of God (AoG). After that the Telugus had no place to worship and joined Bethlehem Lutheran Church. The priest there started to preach also in Telugu.[8]

Reverend Jenson took over the Bethlehem Lutheran Church in 1980. He studied civil engineering against his own wishes; according to his own narrative, he wanted to study medicine. He worked thirteen years as engineer but studied also in the Anglican Seminary for three years. He went to Madurai in Tamil Nadu to attend the Tamil Nadu Theological Seminary and received a bachelor of divinity and thus became the assistant pastor.[9] Reverend Jenson had two sons and one daughter. The daughter is married to a Singaporean Tamil and one of the sons Jan Philip has also studied theology in Hong Kong and has acted as the assistant pastor of Bethlehem Lutheran Church. The other son, Luke Andrew initially studied business administration but is currently interested in furthering his studies in Lutheran theology.[10] Both sons play the organ in the church. The daughter used to run the Sunday school.

Reverend Jenson had been active in the Myanmar Indian Churches (MIC), which meets every three months. MIC constitutes of an educational committee, which teaches vocational skills to the members. A women's fellowship takes care of mothers and hospitals and organizes meeting for mothers, whereas youth fellowship supports and guides the youth who have finished school already. This group is led by the Assistant Pastor Jan Philip. Children's ministry is responsible for the Sunday school.

The Church has vital links to the Tamil Christians in Malaysia. Every March, eighteen Tamil Methodists come to visit the about 1,500 children whom they help to attend school in Myanmar. They donate 100 USD per year to each child. Many of these children live in Dalla. The project has been going on since 2001.

Bethlehem Lutheran Church engages in ecumenical activities among the churches. On Saturday evenings, there are ecumenical services in each church including the Salvation Army and the Insein Baptist Church. Indian churches have ecumenical services once in six months.

Bethlehem Lutheran Church has eighteen outreach centres up to Moulmein and North Dagon, including Karen people and Burmese. They are also active across the river in Lathaya. There is a modest Lutheran Church in Dagon. In Mandalay and in Maymyo, the Lutherans worship inside the Anglican Church.

Bethlehem Lutheran Church organized a 'Peace, Justice and Reconciliation' meeting on 16 January 2012 to 'pray for peace and religious unity'. Various religious leaders participated, including Hindus, Muslims, Buddhists, Christian congregations, Sikhs and some representatives of the 1988 student generation. This was followed by further similar meetings organized by different religious communities.[11]

Non-Indian Lutherans

As the ethnic Chins are divided into sixty-three different subgroups – carefully categorized by the British colonial authorities, not surprisingly – the tiny Chin Lutheran church is split into several factions. There are, in fact, three separate Chin ethnic Lutheran churches; Lutheran Church of Myanmar, Myanmar Lutheran Church and Mara Evangelical Church.[12]

The Lutheran Church of Myanmar (LCM) was established by an ethnic Lushai Reverend Lal Sawi Thanga in 1995 after he had left the Baptist Church. The sermons are conducted in Mizo language.[13] Reverend Martin Lalthangliana's father, Lal Sawi Thanga, was born in Mizoram in India, but it was still easy to cross the border to Burma in 1958.

The church is not linked to the Bethlehem Lutheran Church. Reverend Martin criticized the Bethlehem Lutheran Church, for instance, for not having a mission expansion programme. But they share the Lutheran doctrine with Bethlehem Lutheran Church. The Chin Lutheran Church was not a member of the Myanmar Council of Churches until 2012. They had approached the Council in 2005 but were allegedly rejected by the Bethlehem Lutheran Church. The Chin Lutheran Church blames the Tamil Lutherans for not being open to 'other people'. Bethlehem Lutheran Church is dominated by the Tamils. Although, according to Reverend Martin, the number of Tamils declined, the Reverend of Bethlehem Lutheran Church was not trying to expand and reach out to other people. Since 2000, the Bethlehem Lutheran Church is a member of the Lutheran World Federation (LWF), while the Chin Lutheran Church became a member in 2010, after struggling to get the membership for ten years.

Besides the LCM, there is also the Myanmar Lutheran Church (MLC) established in 1998 by the Lutherans in Singapore. It is closely allied with the Lutheran Church in Malaysia. In the beginning, there were only five members, Reverend D. Andrew Mang Lone, his wife and their three children. In 2016, the church had 3,500 members, 17 ordained pastors, 23 evangelists, 14 congregations with various activities, according to their own information. The church was initially established to serve the Khumi ethnic group, but later the ministry incorporated also Asho Chin, Hakha Chin, Burmese, Karen and Rakhine. The administrative headquarters is located in Yangon with sub-headquarters in Paletwa, Southern Chin State.[14]

Additionally, there is the Mara Evangelical Church (MEC) from 'Maraland' in Mizoram, India. After a split for seventeen years, it reunited in 1987. According to their own information, they have 196 local congregations in 'Maraland' and other regions among the ethnic Chins.¹⁵ Most likely, the number is relatively high due to the system of 'house churches' which is typical for the newer Myanmar Lutheran Church and the Mara Evangelical Church. There appear to be several reasons why the Chin Lutheran Church is split into three different subgroups. A Chin Methodist official somewhat jokingly pointed out that the Chin churches are divided into 'clans'.¹⁶

The four Lutheran churches have increased their cooperation during the last years and during the Covid-19 pandemic. Luke Andrew from the Bethlehem Lutheran Church works as a coordinator for the Evangelical Lutheran Church in Myanmar (ELCM), that is supported by the European Lutheran churches.

Concluding Reflections

Members of the Indian Tamil population of Myanmar practise a variety of religions; Hinduism, Islam, Catholicism, Methodism and Lutheran Protestantism. Particularly the Roman Catholic Church in the larger cities of Myanmar has its historical origins in Southern India. The non-Catholic Tamil Christians belong to the Lutheran and other Protestant churches.

It is worth noticing that there are Tamil priests in various parts of modern Myanmar. Tamil pastors are running the Catholic Churches in Dalla, Kyauktan, Maymyo (Pyin Oo Lwin) and Lashio. There are also Tamil Catholic nuns working around the country in schools and orphanages from Dalla to Kalaw. A Tamil family has also been keeping the Yangon Armenian Church until it was abruptly reclaimed by the Armenian Catholicos Karekin II in 2014.

The Tamil pastors and nuns are very visible on the field but not in the church administration. The Christian seminars and higher positions in the hierarchy are more frequently occupied by Chin Christians, such as the Methodist Bishop Zothan Mawia and the rector of Myanmar Institute of Theology (MIT) Samuel Ngun Ling.

The South Indian churches in Myanmar remain totally unpoliticized – contrary to many ethnic churches – for various reasons. The Tamil identity is not based on religion but rather on the language and on their shared history in Southern India. Tamil identity in Myanmar has been even boosted in recent years, according to some media reports. The Tamils – just like the other ethnolinguistic groups in Myanmar – have been teaching Tamil language to the children and youngsters during the school holidays. This has been conducted for decades despite the harsh military dictatorship ruling the country.

All Christian churches have also been able to preserve active contact to their fellow Christians in other countries. The Bethlehem Lutheran Church has good contacts with the Lutheran missionaries and priests based in Bangkok. They also have active connection to the Tamil Lutherans in Malaysia from where priests have visited them regularly for decades. The contacts to the Indian Lutheran churches have also remained intact, and the Bethlehem Lutheran Church welcomed an Indian priest on Sunday 16 December 2018, while this author attended the service.

A politicization of an ethnic group would demand, according to most scholars, some shared economic interests, a shared territory and a politicized elite to present the demands in the name of the group. Paul Brass (1991), as a scholar on South Asia, emphasizes 'elite competition' as a thriving force of politicization of an ethnic group. This has not taken place among the Tamils of Myanmar although one could see a concentration of South Indian population in a place like Dalla as an example.

As the identity of the Tamil community in Myanmar is not based on their religious affiliation, contrary to many of the highlander groups like Chins, Kachins and their subgroups, the Tamils have assimilated considerably well in Myanmar. This article hence suggests that the Myanmar Tamils belong to a transnational Tamil 'cosmopolis' – as theorized by Sheldon Pollock (2006) in his work on 'Sanskrit cosmopolis'. Belonging to the 'cosmopolis' confers the Myanmar Tamils an identity they are comfortable with.

Notes

1 Burma is used for the period before 1989, after which the name of the country is Myanmar.
2 Michael Symes was one of the first British envoys sent to Burma in 1795. From this experience he wrote 'an account of an Embassy to the Kingdom of Ava'. Ava was one of the royal centres of the Burmese Konbaung Dynasty (1752–1885), hence the British knew the Burmese kingdom as 'Ava'.
3 Interestingly J. S. Furnivall also adopted the term 'medley', arguing that in the 'plural society' the different communities 'mix but do not combine' (Furnivall 1948: 304).
4 Ruth Fredman Cernea (2006) reminds us that the Jews were regarded as 'Almost Englishmen' in British Burma. Same may have applied to the Armenians.
5 According to Harvey, 'Armenians first came to Burma in 1612' (Harvey 1925: 346fn).

6 Sangermano stayed in Ava from 1783 to 1806 and his book *A description of the Burmese Empire* was published in 1833. Niccolo de Conti had travelled in Southeast Asia already in the fifteenth century but was more interested in goods than souls.
7 See, for instance, 'Myanmar Tamil Catholics Reclaim Their Identity' in *ucanews.com* on 23 April 2018.
8 All details based on an interview with Reverend Jenson (13 May 2007).
9 Reverend Jenson reiterates that he was invited to Germany to study medicine. He studied German and received a degree in medicine. He returned from Germany in 1988.
10 Interview with Luke Andrew (16 December 2018).
11 A CD-ROM was produced from the first meeting.
12 Mara is one of the many subgroups of Mizo/Chin.
13 Interview with Reverend Martin Lalthangliana (11 August 2012).
14 www.lcamission.org.au/about-us/who-we-are/countries/myanmar-program-partners.
15 www.lcamission.org.au.
16 In a personal interview (17 August 2012).

References

Andrew, E. J. L. (1933), *Indian Labour in Rangoon*, Bombay: Oxford University Press.
Baxter, James (1941), *Report on Indian Immigration*, Rangoon: Government Printing and Stationery.
Bigandet, Paul (1887), *An Outline of the History of the Catholic Burmese Mission from the Year 1720–1887*, Rangoon: Hanthawaddy Press.
Brass, Paul (1991), *Ethnicity and Nationalism: Theory and Comparison*, New Delhi: Sage.
Cernea, Ruth Fredman (2006), *Almost Englishmen: Bagdhadi Jews in British Burma*, Lanham, MD: Lexington Books.
Chakravarty, Nalini Ranjan (1971), *The Indian Minority in Burma: The Rise and Decline of an Immigrant Community*, Oxford: Oxford University Press.
Coedes, George (1944), *Histoire ancienne des etats hindouises d'Extreme Orient*, Hanoi: EFEO.
Furnivall, John S. (1948), *Colonial Policy and Practice: A Comparative Study of Burma and Netherlands India*, Cambridge: Cambridge University Press.
Gheddo, Piero (2007), *Missione Birmania. I 149 anni del Pime in Myanmar 1867–2007*, Bologna: Editrice Missionaria Italiana.
Harvey, G. E. (1925), *History of Burma: From the Earliest Times to 10 March 1824: The Beginning of English Conquest*, London: Frank Cass.
Heikkilä-Horn, Marja-Leena (2009), 'Imagining Burma: A Historical Overview', *Asian Ethnicity*, 10 (2): 145–54.

Jayaraj, Daniel P. (2003), 'Lutheran Churches in Eighteenth-Century India', *Lutheran Quarterly*, X (vii): 77–97.
Khoo Thwe, Pascal (2002), *From the Land of Green Ghosts: A Burmese Odyssey*, London: HarperCollins.
Lehman F. K. (1967), 'Ethnic Categories in Burma and the Theory of Social Systems', in *Southeast Asian Tribes: Minorities and Nations*, ed. Peter Kunstadter, 93–123, Princeton: Princeton University Press.
Lintner, B. (1997), *The Kachin: Lords of Burma's Northern Frontier. Peoples and Cultures of Southeast Asia*, Chiang Mai: Teak House Books.
Mahajani, Usha (1960), *The Role of Indian Minorities in Burma and Malaya*, Bombay: Vora.
Majumdar, R. C. (1948), *Greater India*, Bombay: National Information.
Pearn, B. R. (1946), *The Indian in Burma*, Herefordshire: Le Play House.
Pollock, Sheldon (2006), *The Language of the Gods in the World of Men: Sanskrit, Culture, and Power in Premodern India*, Berkeley: University of California Press.
Sakhong, Lian H. (2003), *In Search of Chin Identity. A Study in Religion, Politics and Ethnic Identity in Burma*, Copenhagen: NIAS.
Sandhu, Kernial S., and A. Mani (eds) (1993), *Indian Communities in Southeast Asia*, Singapore: ISEAS.
Sarkissian, Margaret (1987), 'Armenians in Southeast Asia', *Crossroads*, 3 (43): 1–33.
Schönbeck, Oluf (2012), *All Religions Merge in Tranquebar: Religious Coexistence and Social Cohesion in South India*, Copenhagen: NIAS.
Shway Yoe ([1882] 1963), *The Burman: His Life and Notions*, New York: Norton.
Tin Maung Maung Than (1993), 'Some Aspects of Indians in Rangoon', in *Indian Communities in Southeast Asia*, ed. K. S. Sandhu and A. Mani, 585–623, Singapore: ISEAS.
Turnell, Sean (2009), *Fiery Dragons: Banks, Moneylenders and Microfinance in Burma*, Copenhagen: NIAS.

Websites

http://catholicmissionmm.blogspot.com/2007/6/history-of-myanmar-catholic-church.html (accessed: 1 October 2020).
https://www.lcamission.org.au/about-us/who-we-are/countries/myanmar/myanmar-program-partners/ (accessed: 1 October 2020).
https://www.ucanews.com/news/myanmars-tamil-catholics-reclaim-their-identity/82090 (accessed: 1 October 2020).

Problems and challenges facing ethnic diversity in Myanmar: A socio-historical analysis from a Christian perspective

Samuel Ngun Ling

A brief historical survey

Myanmar, formerly known as Burma, shares common borders with the two most populous, as well as technologically and economically emerging, countries in the world: India and China. As the largest country in Southeast Asia in terms of surface area, Myanmar also serves as a land bridge that connects South and Southeast Asia. Peace and stability in the region are therefore important not only for Myanmar but also for the Asian region as a whole.

The total population of Myanmar, according to the 2014 census, is about 51.4 million (51,486,253). Buddhism is practised by 87.9 per cent of the population; Christianity by 6.2 per cent, the majority of whom belong to the Baptist denomination; Islam by 4.3 per cent; Hinduism by 0.5 per cent; Animism by 0.8 per cent; other religions by 0.2 per cent; and those with no religion amount to 0.1 per cent of the population (Aung 2016). The 135 ethnic groups officially recognized in Myanmar are brought together into eight major ethnic groups: Burman, Karen, Kachin, Chin, Mon, Rakhine, Kayah and Shan. Although predominantly a Buddhist country, Myanmar is therefore multicultural and religiously diverse. Compared to other countries in Southeast Asia, Myanmar is unique in the sense of its long isolation from the world and international community. Some writers and international journalists have referred to the country as a hermit nation, a forgotten peninsular, or even a lonely planet. Kosuke Koyama, a well-known Japanese-Christian theologian, once described the isolation of Myanmar as 'the Burmese way to loneliness' (Koyama 1976: 29). Are we, the people of Myanmar, still to be considered strangers from a lonely planet?

Before discussing the problems and challenges of contemporary Myanmar, as seen from a Christian (Protestant) theological perspective, I will first provide some background information on Myanmar's development during the last millennium (Ling 2017: 34–9). So far, Myanmar has been through seven stages of political change.

First, large parts of what is now Myanmar had *monarchical rulers* from the early eleventh to the late nineteenth century. The end of this stage was marked by the three Anglo-Burmese wars from 1824 to 1885, which led to the dethronement of the last Burmese king, King Thibaw (r. 1878–85). The nineteenth century also saw the first Protestant mission with the arrival of the American Baptist mission in Myanmar on 13 July 1813.

Second, the country experienced *colonial rule* under the British Indian Empire from 1824 to 1947. The Buddhist nationalist movement was born from this long period of suffering under the colonial yoke. It perceived British colonial rule as Christian rule and therefore developed a strong anti-Christian voice. In part, Christian-Buddhist tensions also overlap with ethnic conflicts, such as the conflict between Karen and Burman. Such conflicts are considered to be also rooted in colonialism as a remnant of Western cultural expansionism, fuelling Buddhist nationalist resurgence against the Christian presence in Myanmar until today. Myanmar Christians came to be regarded with suspicion as pro-Western and disloyal to the nation. In 1965, as a result of such anti-Christian sentiments, Christian missionary schools, hospitals and properties were all nationalized by the new revolutionary government under General Ne Win in order to create a centralized socialist system under his control (Chain 2003: 10).

Third, *after independence*, Burma tasted a short-term parliamentary democracy for fourteen years from 1948 to 1962. This democratic system was actually stamped out by a kind of 'theocracy' – the attempt to make Buddhism the state religion under the then prime minister U Nu, which led to strong resistance among Christian ethnicities.

Fourth, General Ne Win took power under a military coup on 2 March 1962 and then introduced the 'Burmese Way to Socialism', which was pursued for twenty-six years from 1962 to 1988. For about three decades, this 'way' completely failed to maintain the country and turned it into one of the poorest countries in the world.

Fifth, a military coup took place again in 1988. The country was under the control of *military capitalism* for twenty years. Sociopolitical restrictions, economic crisis and religious oppression became common issues for the church and Christians in Myanmar.

Sixth, the same rulers of the military regime, under the leadership of General Thein Sein (prime minister: 2007–11; president: 2011–16), took off their military uniforms and dressed themselves as civilians instead, while continuing to rule the country under a *new constitution*, which they introduced in 2008 to protect themselves and the powers that they had against the will of the people.

Seventh, a *new government* led by Daw Aung Suu Kyi, State Counsellor, and her party, the National League for Democracy (NLD), emerged from the long political turmoil and tried to foster democratic values in the country. However, the 2008 constitution introduced by the military regime that guarantees the military a significant degree of political control remains as a stumbling-block to the full-fledged political freedom of the new government. Hence, there are actually two political powers in place, the military and the NLD, playing rather different political roles in the system of Myanmar and its development towards full democracy and stable peace.

Problems and challenges

Struggle for democracy

The struggle for democracy and freedom began with the so-called 1947 Panglong Agreement, signed by the major leaders of the ethnic minority groups at Panglong, Shan State, to form a federal union based on democratic principles and ethnic equality. However, as has been said, after regaining independence from British colonial rule in 1948, parliamentary democracy lasted only a short period, until 2 March 1962, when it was terminated by a military coup under General Ne Win. On seizing power, Ne Win nullified previous efforts to establish a genuinely federal Union State of Burma. Having claimed that he would safeguard the union from possible disintegration, Ne Win tried to isolate the country from the rest of the world throughout his period of rule (1962–88), eradicated all freedom of expression and association, restricted human rights and practised draconian economic policies. He also imposed systematic repression on ethnic minorities, including Christian ethnic minorities such as the Karen, Kachin and Chin, who had always fought hard for ethnic autonomy and equal rights.

The nationwide struggle for democracy and freedom became visible in Myanmar through the 1988 attempt to topple the country's dictatorship and put an end to totalitarian rule, often referred to as the '8888 Uprising' (= 8 August 1988). In its brutal reaction, the military regime also crushed church movements, with a number of Christians and church leaders being killed, and it murdered or arrested and imprisoned leaders of the democracy movement. The military junta named itself the State Law and Order Restoration Council in September 1988 and renamed Burma "Myanmar" in 1989. It set out to quell opposition by announcing that it would soon hold multiparty elections. The first general election was then held in 1990, and Aung San Suu Kyi's party, the NLD, won a landslide victory, securing 392 of the 485 seats. However, the military regime refused to relinquish its political power and placed Aung San Suu Kyi under house arrest for about eighteen years. She was awarded the 1991 Nobel Peace Prize for her non-violent struggle for democracy in Myanmar. It took almost another twenty years before the military regime called for a new general election in November 2010. Yet, the military leaders still hold the political power guaranteed to them by the 2008 constitution, which has not yet been amended.

Religious conflicts

Myanmar has experienced various ethnic conflicts and tensions rooted in the pre-independence period, especially between majority Buddhist and minority non-Buddhist ethnicities. A leading political figure who tried to make Buddhism the state religion was U Nu, who ruled as prime minister of independent Burma from 1948 to 1958 and from 1960 to 1962. When Buddhism was officially made the state religion in August 1961, there was strong opposition from ethnic religious minorities, especially from the Christian and Muslim minorities, leading to a certain degree of religious conflict. It was this conflict that led the Karen and Kachin ethnic Christians to form the Kachin Independence Army (KIA) and to wage the Karen National Union (KNU) insurgencies (see also Smith 1965; Mendelson 1975).

Officially, the primary purpose of the 1962 military coup led by General Ne Win was to prevent the further disintegration of the Union of Myanmar, which is comprised of majority Buddhists and minority non-Buddhists (Ling 1988: 173). A new socialist constitution, proposed in 1973 and confirmed in 1974, provided freedom of religion within the bounds of the law, guaranteeing all citizens protection against discrimination on religious grounds. This constitution was again abolished in 1989 and a new government, the State Law and Order Restoration Council (SLORC), was formed with the aim of wiping out all opposition. In 1993, SLORC was renamed the State Peace and Development Council (SPDC), with the hope of ensuring the continued influence of the military junta in a new constitutional government. Throughout these years under military control, the tensions surrounding religious issues in Myanmar's national affairs, especially in the sociopolitical relationship between the Buddhist majority and non-Buddhist minorities, remained an unresolved issue on the political agenda.

According to the 2008 constitution of the Republic of the Union of Myanmar, 'the Union recognizes Christianity, Islam, Hinduism and Animism as the religions existing in the Union on the day of the coming into operation of this Constitution' (Article 362). And 'the Union may assist and protect the religions it recognizes to its utmost' (Article 363). But, according to Article 361, 'the Union recognizes the special position of Buddhism as the faith professed by the great majority of the citizens of the Union' (printed edition: Constitution 2009: 151). What this special status or position of Buddhism means is the continuity of the sociopolitical power of Buddhism, pointedly sanctioned against the freedom and movements of other religions in the country. This concept of a favoured religion claims, on the one hand, to embrace all religions in the country so that they can flourish together peacefully and harmoniously, while, on the other, simultaneously minimizing the freedom of the unfavoured religions (Ling 2014: 12). The net result is that the concept of a favoured religion implicitly condones the idea of favoured adherents over the adherents of unfavoured religions, so that the whole concept brings about discrimination between religious peoples, at both the individual and the ethnic level. It is on the basis of such a concept that minority ethnic Christians and majority Burman Buddhists have confronted each other in a conflict leading to a breach of dialogue or communication between them. This conflict has resulted in turn in an identity problem for both Buddhist and non-Buddhist ethnic peoples. For an ethnically Burman Buddhist to become a Christian means abandoning his or her sociocultural identity, while for other ethnic religious minority groups (*Taing-zin-hta* = ethnic peoples) such as Christians and Muslims, not being a Buddhist is almost an act of disloyalty towards Buddhist society and the nation (ibid.: 13).

The Challenge of Buddhist nationalism

Since being given a special position in the Constitution of the Union of Myanmar, Buddhism and its religious activities have become a great challenge to other minority religions such as Christianity. The socialist government under General Ne Win began to practise a mechanism of cultural assimilation by using the Buddhist religion as its social and political tool to dominate ethnic minorities. Some considered this assimilation process to be 'Burmanization' or even a form of ethnic cleansing because it strongly advocated the early anti-colonialist and nationalist philosophy of Buddhism: namely, 'to be an authentic Burman is to be a Buddhist' (Brown 1926: 102; Pearn 1962: 20). This development created not only challenges but also negative reactions to the Christian mission movements in postcolonial Myanmar, as the Christian mission was viewed with suspicion as being a remnant of Western colonial rule as it had been practised in Myanmar in the early nineteenth and twentieth centuries. A Burmese Buddhist nationalist motto coined in the 1930s during the so-called peasants' revolution was '*Amyo, Barthar, Thatana*', meaning 'Race, Religion, Mission'. This motto reflected not only the resurgence of Burmese Buddhism and culture but also an emerging national ideology of post-independence Burmese Buddhist nationalists in Myanmar.

Buddhist nationalist ideology has had a negative impact on the non-Buddhist minority religions such as Christianity, Islam and Hinduism and has triggered restrictions on their freedom. Among Burmese Buddhist nationalist ideologists was also the famous Burmese writer U Po Latt, who explicitly endorsed the Buddhist philosophy of Burmanization. He wrote,

> The official view was that a unity of culture existed among the peoples of the Union and that existing differences are only expressions of the same culture at different stages of development. The Burman and Pyu peoples had long since amalgamated; the Mons had almost been absorbed, and Shan assimilation was in progress. The Karens, Kachins, and Chins were also mainly Tibeto-Burman, and all were allegedly suitable for becoming parts of a closely-knit cultural organization. (Latt 1952: 27–8)

This Burmese Buddhist philosophy tries to build a national identity based on Buddhism, with the result that ethnic minorities attempt to de-Burmanize themselves as a protection against the invasion of the predominant Buddhist religion, culture and civilization. Burmese Buddhist nationalism has resulted in various political restrictions being imposed on the religious and cultural activities of religious minorities such as Christians and Muslims. From the socialist period to the previous period of military rule (before 2010), all ethnic or indigenous dialects were prohibited from being taught at primary/elementary schools, and all schools in Myanmar were forced to teach in Burmese. The problem for ethnic minorities was not so much that Burmese was imposed as the common language of Myanmar, and more the fact that the military tried to eliminate by force the indigenous religions, cultures and languages of minority peoples living in the hilly areas of Myanmar. The NLD government has now partly solved the problem by allowing ethnic languages to be taught again at primary school.

The challenge of ethnic diversity

Strong ethnic diversity is a unique feature of Myanmar. Besides the 135 ethnic groups that are officially recognized and the eight major ethnic groups, there may also be, as a linguistic survey shows, more than two hundred sub-ethnic language groups in Myanmar (Linguistic Research Group 2003). The ethnic diversity of Myanmar, that is, the existence of multi-religious and multicultural diversity, demonstrates 'the interwoven nature of a community life' (Ling 2003: 63).

Myanmar is still entangled in two kinds of political struggle: striving for national reconciliation and peace and strengthening political dialogue to protect the rights and freedom of ethnic minority peoples. Decades-long fighting, political repression, human rights violations and the crises afflicting the economy, healthcare and education have impacted on minority people, in particular, leading to the modern phenomenon of internally displaced people within, and externally displaced people outside, the country.

This general situation affects Christianity in specific ways. Despite the fact that it has been present in the country for two centuries, Christianity is still marginalized in the larger Burmese society. Christian missions continue to be seen as part of the Western colonialist three-M scheme: Merchant, Mission, Military (Smith 1999: 45). This historical stigma has contributed to the deterioration of interreligious relations and has weakened interfaith cooperation at the national level. During the long period of military rule, Christian and non-Christian minorities, such as Muslims and Hindus, had to struggle to preserve and promote their ethnic and religious identities. If all religions were granted equal freedom of expression and worship, there would be the opportunity to establish interfaith harmony and peace. Yet, a climate of cultural domination and political suspicion fosters tensions and conflicts between diverse ethnic and religious groups. By redefining the meaning of national identity, Burmese Buddhist nationalism creates an identity crisis for all ethnic and religious (i.e. non-Buddhist) minorities, eventually leading to the social exclusion, marginalization and religious discrimination of minorities, pushing the poor, the powerless and the illiterate more and more to the margins of society.

The challenge of religious diversity

The challenge of ethnic diversity overlaps with the challenge of religious diversity. The dominance of Burmese Buddhism and especially the ideology of Buddhist nationalism lead to a paradoxical situation. The exclusion of ethnic and religious minorities from the mainstream of national development is in part based on the Buddhist principle of non-interference in other religions. 'Our religion is good for us, yours for you', as a Burman Buddhist once said to the wife of an American Baptist missionary (Knowles 1831: 137). Traditional Theravāda Buddhism teaches that one should neither propagate one's own faith by force nor colonize other faiths and traditions and strictly prohibits monks from participating in any kind of political or commercial activities. While this philosophy of non-interference can foster tolerance, it also fails to promote dialogue and cooperation between Buddhism and other religions. As a result, religions in Myanmar coexisted peacefully, but there was no interaction or cooperation between them.

In the context of Buddhist nationalism, however, the rights of minority religious groups such as Christians and Muslims were restricted, while the Buddhists enjoyed full freedom of expression. The constitutional favouring of Buddhism as the majority religion, combined with the traditional philosophy of non-interference, does not encourage Buddhists to promote dialogue with minority religions or interreligious cooperation but actually encourages them to be disinterested in minority religions and to treat interreligious understanding as unimportant. However, the lack of mutual understanding has often led to the increased and diverse repression of religious minorities, which shows how important dialogue and cooperation are for the common well-being of a society.

As far as Christian minorities are concerned, the Buddhist philosophy of non-interference is coupled with a deep suspicion rooted in the colonial past. Christians are viewed as pro-Western, pro-British, pro-American, as advocating a Western cultural dominance whose political presence and cultural intervention are often perceived as a cultural and social threat to Burmese Buddhist nationalism and to the solidarity of the whole nation. Non-interference therefore turns into strong opposition and negative reactions to Christianization, especially from the Buddhist side.

In this situation, one of the major tasks of the churches in Myanmar is to reconfigure the whole pattern of Christian religion, church and mission. This is true not only of Myanmar but globally, too. As Stanley J. Samartha has said, 'to reject exclusivism and to accept plurality, to be committed to one's faith and to be open to the faith communities of our neighbours, to choose to live in a global community of communities, sharing the ambiguities of history and the mystery of life – these are the imperatives of our age' (Samartha 1998: 193). In a multicultural and religious situation, engaging constructively with religious diversity does not necessarily mean losing one's own faith tradition, culture and identity. Rather, it can help enrich common life, community relationships and global ministry. Actually, it involves a critique of globalization, which is itself built on capitalism – the capitalist value of privatizing one's own space and property and zealously guarding them. But religious or cultural pluralism comes as a demand to open our private space to the other, a space where we jealously guard our God and religion. It requires an altogether new orientation. Religious pluralism provides us with an opportunity to speak out and be heard, and asserts that every view deserves to be heard, including those that are decidedly religious.

Generally speaking, a Christian living in the postmodern era is constantly engaged in a process of creatively aligning her faith commitments with the various other pluralisms that exist, be they religious, political, economic or social (McGowan 1991: 215), which requires not only discernment but also the ability to work for the common good of humanity. I therefore agree with Hans Küng's dictum: 'No survival without a world ethic. No world peace without peace between religions. No peace between the religions without dialogue between the religions' (Küng 1993: xv).

Concluding reflections

The current global situation is in urgent need of peace and security. Every society and nation need to make every effort to achieve peaceful and fruitful cooperation. Myanmar is a country where some of the world's most influential religious traditions are present and can enter constructive dialogue. Religions tend to become complacent and dominating when tied to political power, as was the case with Christianity and Buddhism in Myanmar. Under British colonial protection, Christianity appeared as an imperialistic force. Similarly, Buddhism seemed to be more aggressive when it was strongly tied to the military governments. Despite the military regime's assurance of religious freedom and non-discrimination, Buddhism has been favoured over other religions in all its activities. In such a religiously oppressive context, Christian minorities strongly believe that supporting democracy and freedom is necessary to nurture peace, justice and security in the country. In fact, the most appropriate way to help Myanmar become a true democracy is through the full and equal participation of all people, including all ethnic and religious minorities, in the process of building a new nation.

Unfortunately, religion is involved today in the global context in conflicts and violence, especially when it is co-opted by political, economic and even geopolitical forces. In fact, it would be a great mistake to link terrorism simply to a particular religion. Terrorism is often the result of discontent and frustration, which themselves are caused by extreme marginalization and poverty. The increasing gap between the rich and poor will continue to be the breeding ground for conflicts, and religion will be co-opted by forces fighting for their survival. No number of arms and ammunition will eradicate terrorism. Global justice is the only way to reduce conflict and terrorism. Terrorism should make us look afresh at the social and political dynamics of religious pluralism.

In order for a nation to develop peacefully and harmoniously, people of all faiths and ideologies need to work together to formulate common issues and to achieve common growth. I trust that common efforts will enable us to grow together as better Buddhists, better Christians, better Muslims and better Hindus. I am convinced that the indigenous peoples in Myanmar strongly support solidarity among religious groups to help strengthen the common struggle for the future of the common good. While I cannot speak for all Christians in Myanmar, I feel that, as ethnic Christian minorities, we should commit ourselves to the following:

- Supporting the non-violent actions of political movements that oppose the tyranny of dictatorships and fight for democracy, freedom and justice.
- Equipping people with the know-how to build a just and peaceful society in the context of ethnic conflicts and violence. The Myanmar Institute of Theology trains ethnic church leaders, teaching them through workshops and seminars about minority rights, human dignity, gender equality, peacebuilding and interreligious dialogue and cooperation.
- Promoting solidarity among ethnic-minority Christian churches, so that they can raise their common voices to the world and community surrounding them. The Myanmar Council of Churches and the Myanmar Baptist Convention are encouraging their member churches to promote solidarity among the churches and Christian leaders, especially in times of political transition.

- Promoting interfaith dialogue and cooperation both with the Buddhist majority and among minority religious communities such as Christians, Muslims and Hindus. Their cooperation in dealing with humanitarian issues such as supporting the victims of civil wars, natural disasters and a pandemic such as Covid-19 would help build a peaceful community for diverse religious and ethnic groups in Myanmar.

References

Aung, San Yamin (2016), 'Government Publishes Data on Populations of Religious groups', *The Irrawaddy News*, 18 December 2016. http://www.irrawaddy.com/news/burma/govt-publishes-data-on-populations-of-religious-groups.html.

Brown, R. Grant (1926), *Burma as I Saw It: 1889–1917*, London: Methuen.

Chain, Tun Aung (2003), 'The Christian-Buddhist Encounter in Myanmar', *Engagement. Judson Research Center Bulletin*, published by Judson Research Center of the Myanmar Institute of Theology, 1: 2–10.

Constitution of the Republic of the Union of Myanmar, 2008 (2009), Ministry of Information (Myanmar): Printing & Publishing Enterprise.

Knowles, James D. (1831), *Memoir of Mrs. Ann H. Judson: Late Missionary to Burmah*, Boston: Lincoln and Edmunds.

Koyama, Kosuke (1976), 'Theological Solutions in Asia and the Mission of the Church', in *What Asian Christians Are Thinking: A Theological Sourcebook*, ed. Douglas J. Elwood, 16–40, Manila: New Day.

Küng, Hans (1993), *Global Responsibility: In Search of a New World Ethic*, New York: Continuum.

Latt, U Po (1952), 'Union Culture: Its Sources and Contacts', *Burma Journal*, 3: 2–21.

Ling, Samuel Ngun (2003), 'The Encounter of Missionary Christianity with Resurgent Buddhism in Post-colonial Myanmar', *Quest, An Interdisciplinary Journal for Asian Christian Scholars: Religion and Globalization*, 2 (2): 63–74.

Ling, Samuel Ngun (2014), *Communicating Christ in Myanmar: Issues, Interactions and Perspectives*. 3rd edn, Yangon: ATEM.

Ling, Samuel Ngun (2017), *The Meeting of Christianity and Buddhism in Burma: Its Past, Present, and Future Perspectives*, Yangon: Ling's Family.

Ling, Trevor O. (1988), 'Religious Minorities in Burma in the Contemporary Period', in *Ethnic Conflicts in Buddhist Societies: Sri Lanka, Thailand and Burma*, ed. K. M. de Silva, P. Duke, E. S. Goldberg and N. Katz, 172–86, London: Pinter.

Linguistic Research Group (2003), *Myanmar Language Varieties, Government Classification, Location, and Status* (unpublished report), Yangon: Myanmar Institute of Theology.

McGowan, John (1991), *Postmodernism and Its Critics*, Ithaca, NY: Cornell University Press, 1991.

Mendelson, E. Michael (1975), *Sangha and State in Burma*, Ithaca, NY: Cornell University Press.

Pearn, B. R. (1962), *Judson of Burma*. London: Edinburgh House Press.

Samartha, Stanley J. (1998), 'Globalization and Its Cultural Consequences – a Theological Response', in *Ethical Issues in the Struggle for Justice: Quest for pluriform Communities. Essays in Honour of K. C. Abraham*, ed. M. P. Joseph and Daniel D. Chetti, 182–95, Tiruvalla: Christava Sahitya Samiti.

Smith, Donald E. (1965), *Religion and Politics in Burma*, Princeton: Princeton University Press.

Smith, Martin (1999), *Burma: Insurgency and the Politics of Ethnicity*. New York: Zed Books.

10

Burmanization and its effects on the Kachin ethnic group in Myanmar

Layang Seng Ja

Identifying the overall context and misery in Myanmar

In Myanmar, suffering has many faces. This chapter begins with a sketch of the context, followed by an analysis of the history of how the Kachin community, living in the northern part of upper Myanmar, close to China and Tibet, has been affected by Bamanization (or 'Burmanization'). 'Bama' is the name of the majority ethnic group in Myanmar, from which the Anglicized forms 'Burma' and 'Burmese' derive. Bamanization refers to the process by which other ethnic and religious minorities are forced to conform with the majority. Similar processes have taken place in European states, for example, the Norwegianization of the Sami and the earlier suppression of the Welsh language and identity by England. My chapter aims to offer, from a Christian perspective, an interfaith theology that provides practical norms for the harmonious coexistence of the various religious communities in Myanmar.

The misery of every Myanmar tribe, including the Bama, began with British colonization and continued with the rise of the military after 1948, when Myanmar began to go into decline. Today, despite all its natural resources, Myanmar is one of the poorest countries in Asia. Any Myanmar citizen who has to show his or her passport abroad risks being regarded with suspicion since the immigration officer will probably have heard about the notorious corruption of the Myanmar government and its military. Its resources are not used to develop the country for the benefit of all its citizens. Instead, the wealth accruing from these resources lands on the bank accounts of a few top military leaders and their 'cronies'.

Myanmar is also home to more than 135 ethnic groups, the largest of which is the Bama or Burmans, who comprise 60 per cent of the population and are mostly Buddhist. It is a country where the National League for Democracy (NLD) and the military are now ruling together for their own benefit. Ever since the Thein Sein government in 2010, the country has claimed to be moving towards a democratic system. In reality, though, the military still exercises control behind the scenes. This has continued under Aung San Suu Kyi's NLD government, and Myanmar citizens therefore continue to suffer. Minority ethnic groups continue to experience religious and ethnic discrimination, economic stagnation, exploitation and civil war. They continue to suffer arbitrary arrest, rape, sexual abuse and religious persecution. As a result, thousands of young people from all occupations have fled to neighbouring countries such as Bangladesh, China, India, Malaysia and Thailand in search of safety and a better future (Hang Do 2012: 76). Consequently, Myanmar remains a backward country and a symbol of disaster.

The Kachin ethnic community

The Kachin ethnic group is composed of six major tribes: Jinghpaw, Nung, Rawang, Zaiwa, Longwo and Lachit. They identify themselves in their own language as *Jinghpaw*, and they are the largest ethnic group in Kachin Land in the northern part of Upper Myanmar (Min Thu 2015: 9). It is bordered by China to the north and east and by India to the west. The Kachin population within Kachin State itself is over 1.2 million. The majority here are Kachin; the rest are Shan, Bama, Chinese and Indians. Before the arrival of the British, Kachin Land had been a separate territory. The Kachin regard this as the happy time when their ancestors ruled themselves, free of the deceitful intervention of the Burmese military. Ever since the Kachin consented to Kachin Land becoming part of the Union of Myanmar in the Panglong Agreement (1947), successive military regimes have pursued their policy of Bamanization and exploitation of the Land's natural resources – jade, timber, gold, platinum and amber. It has become increasingly clear that the military regimes had no intention of abiding by the Panglong Agreement (Layang 2016: 482).

For generations, the Kachin's livelihood has depended on the land, the forest and the rivers. Blessed by nature with an abundance of resources in their territory's natural forest ecosystem, the Kachin should be rich (ibid.). However, these resources have been plundered and the ecosystem destroyed as successive military regimes and now the present government have granted jade mining and logging concessions along with rights to refine and sell both at home and abroad. The elites who have been granted these concessions are only interested in self-enrichment. Their activities have led to widespread environmental degradation – air, ground and water pollution, massive soil erosion, sedimentation of rivers, increased flooding, acute water shortages in some areas in the dry season, and a considerable decrease in biodiversity. While some areas suffer low water levels, others suffer increases in flooding. In addition, the water contains diesel and mercury, which are harmful for drinking, bathing, washing clothes and fishing for food. In allowing this to happen, the present government is killing future generations of Kachin. They are selling and destroying the future of our children (Layang 2014: 44).

Before the Christian missionaries came, the Kachins were animists. But they had a strong belief in one powerful God above all. When a missionary arrived at a large Kachin village, he heard the people cry out, 'Oh, God help us! Oh God have mercy on us!' At first the missionary thought that the villagers were Christians, but, as he approached the village, he saw the people, gathered outside one of the houses, lifting their heads towards heaven, calling upon the Great God (*Karai Kasang*) to come and help them. Surprised by their strange behaviour, he asked whether they were Christians. The villagers (who were animists appealing to different kinds of spirits) shook their heads and said that they were crying out to heaven because they were at their wit's end and their Nat priest could no longer help them. The missionary discovered that the Kachins had a much higher and clearer conception of God than he had expected. They ascribe to God the creation of the world. For them, he is the all-knowing Karai Kasang, the Great Spirit who stands above all other spirits (Sword 1954: 63). Today, Christianity is the main religion in Kachin State and 98 per cent of the Kachin population are Christians. In general, they are an honest, simple, friendly and peace-loving people with a keen sense of justice.

Promoting Bamanization in the Kachin Land and its effects

The Burmese military forces and civil war

The permanent military presence in Kachin Land promotes Bamanization and ethnic cleansing. There is constant fighting between Myanmar's armed forces and the Kachin Independence Army. Prior to independence from British colonial rule, the Kachin, like the other ethnic minorities, agreed to become part of the Union of Myanmar on the understanding that they would have some degree of autonomy. However, this part of the agreement was never honoured. Thus, several Kachin independence movements joined together, becoming the Kachin Independence Army (KIA) to struggle for autonomy within a federal Union of Myanmar as promised in the Panglong Agreement. However, in 1994, the Kachin leaders agreed to a ceasefire with the military regime in order to build trust, with the organization's name then becoming the Kachin Independence Organization (KIO) (Layang 2016: 483).

The military constantly demanded that all ethnic armies disarm. Kachin leaders rejected this demand, knowing that, far from guaranteeing peace and ethnic autonomy, doing so would leave the Kachin people defenceless. Thus, the KIO remained firm, stating that, unless the regime and the present government fulfilled the promise made in the Panglong Agreement of 1947 to give the Kachin a place in a federal union and ethnic rights, they would not disarm (Fuller 2009).

Consequently, on 9 June 2011, the military broke a seventeen-year-old ceasefire and is now engaged in an aggressive war against the KIO (Hang Do 2012: 76). Sending thousands of troops into Kachin State to enforce a military solution has caused a massive displacement of civilians. Many Kachin people caught in the crossfire have either fled abroad or been internally displaced and have sought shelter in various Kachin local churches. The army has burned villagers' houses and churches down, destroyed farms, taken property, raped women and killed innocent civilians. The fighting has intensified every year since 2011. The military has used cluster bombs, phosphorous bombs and helicopter gunships to attack civilians and the Kachin army as if the Kachin were a foreign enemy (Layang 2017: 210).

In a blatant lie, the government has told the international media that there is peace in Myanmar. Whenever it can, the military government seizes new strategic sites and expands its military presence in Kachin areas (Layang 2014: 45), with 350 Kachin villages being affected and their inhabitants forced to flee. Most have lost family members and all their property. Some have made makeshift dwellings in the jungle, while others have sought refuge in various local churches in Myitkyina and other places where the Kachin army is in control in Kachin State and along the border with China (Layang 2014: 45). The military has targeted not only KIA posts but also civilian areas, including religious centres and villagers working on their farms (CSW 2018). The military and successive governments, including today's NLD and elite companies, have colluded in this. The result has been endless war, making thousands of innocent villagers homeless. The military and the present government have also blocked relief supplies by directing aerial bombing and heavy artillery fire at civilians. Now, Kachin Land has been flooded with more than 160,000 Internally Displaced Persons (IDPs), that is, Kachin people who fled their villages and live in 165 IDP camps spread across Kachin and Northern Shan (Williams 2018).

While international attention has focused mostly on the Rohingya of Rakhine State, the international community as well as other ethnic groups in Myanmar have neglected the fate of the Kachin (*The Guardian* 2018). Some aid has trickled through from international organizations, but mostly the Kachin, and particularly local Christian congregations, have been left to fend for themselves with what few resources they have. Kachin Land has been bled dry and its people made powerless and isolated. Many are refugees or internally displaced, which is all due to the military and its collaborators.

The enforcement of Burman religion and culture

By nature and culture, the Bama are a friendly, kind-hearted people who are generous and ready to help others in need. The Buddha teaches them to love peace. In contrast to Buddhist teaching, an extremist Buddhist nationalist group called MaBaTha spreads hate speech and incites Buddhists to acts of violence. MaBaTha is led by prominent Buddhist monks who have the support of the military and the elites. They exert more influence on many Myanmar Buddhists than the government itself. Their main goal is to promote Bama culture and Buddhism at the expense of ethnic and faith minorities (International Crisis Group 2017). They demand that children be taught only about Bama history and Buddhism in government schools. Thus, they force Bama culture on minorities and try to erase ethnic identity. From the age of five, it is obligatory for pupils in government schools to learn only about the triumphs of Bama kings and heroes, to recite Bama poems and to perform Bama dances at school ceremonies. Stall Naw, a Kachin girl, has said that, 'what was missing from my childhood was a chance to learn the culture and history of my own people, the Kachin' (Gray 2018). These monks also pursue a politics that encourages xenophobia and regards non-Bama and non-Buddhists as the enemy.

The military and MaBaTha also use Buddhist religious symbols as a tool for political gain. They mark their ownership of Kachin land by building their pagodas wherever there is a hill, big or small. For instance, on a hill near Machanbaw (Putao district), the northernmost town in Kachin State, there is a natural rock formation that resembles a giant dragon. The rock is subject to a popular Kachin folktale, which says that a grandmother was washing clothes in the sea with her grandson playing nearby (or, according to another version, a mother was breastfeeding her child), when a dragon appeared, lured the infant to it and dragged him into the sea. The grandmother then beat her breast and implored the lord of thunder to save her grandson and to punish the dragon. The thunder deity then looked for the dragon to kill it. The dragon tried to shelter in a cave, but the lord of thunder struck the dragon into seven pieces before its whole body could enter the cave. Over time, the remains of the dragon's body gradually turned into stone. In 2016, MaBaTha and the military put up a pagoda there, turning the dragon into a Burmese pagoda symbol. The presence of an army post makes the point even clearer. Bama culture and religion are trying to replace Kachin culture and religion and to claim ownership of the land (Layang 2019: 101). The Kachin people's beautiful hills, valleys, plains and mountains have to bear the symbols of their domination. Thus, the beauty of nature has been abused and plundered.

The regime's policy of Bamanization is at the expense of the minorities. To establish Buddhism as the state religion, the military is spending a considerable amount of the country's income on building and renovating Buddhist temples and images while neglecting the development of the country and harmonious existence with minorities. Whoever protests against the unjust deeds of the military and the government, whether in speech or writing, risks ending up in prison or worse. Since the government uses physical force and bullying tactics to quell all opposition, most people are forced to stay silent to survive. Consequently, minority ethnic groups are oppressed, and their very existence is challenged (Layang 2016: 482). For, the same military troops that purged Southwest Myanmar have moved north to another beleaguered religious and ethnic minority, the Kachin Christians (William 2018).

In addition, the military regime has a deliberate policy of ethnic cleansing. The authorities have allowed Chinese business people to plant poppy fields in Kachin majority areas and to sell drugs very cheaply in Kachin villages and towns, including near Kachin Theological College and Seminary (Myitkyina), targeting Kachin youth. Destroying the future of the Kachin with drugs is one of their ways to sustain their rule over the Kachin and their land. So far, there has been no change under the new NLD government. Instead, the State Counsellor Aung San Suu Kyi has become a living shield for the military, as has been stated by Dennis Gray (2018):

On taking power in early 2016, Suu Kyi declared that national reconciliation and a federal constitution would be high priorities. Instead, the transition to democratic rule and its greater freedom has come with a rise in nationalism and radical Buddhism. Suu Kyi has not condemned continuing military atrocities against the Kachin and others, and her stock with ethnic minorities has plummeted. Many say she is first and foremost a Burman. … It was also the duty of the government, the official says, duty to promote Buddhism and build Buddhist pagodas everywhere in the country […]. … Kachin State, where more than 90 percent of the Kachin people adhere to Christianity, has among the highest concentrations of pagodas in the country. The government continues to pursue a 'forced assimilation and indoctrination program'.

As a result, the Kachin people constantly experience physical, spiritual and mental challenges and struggles to survive in their own land.

A challenge to participate in active resistance to the unjust policy of discrimination

Learn to accept differences and ethnic rights

Although Aung San Suu Kyi and her NLD promised change, in reality their government seems to be collaborating with the military in the slow genocide of the Kachin people. Aung San Suu Kyi has shielded the military by keeping silent about the genocide of the Rohingya in Rakhine State and the actions of the army against the Kachin in Kachin State. Myanmar military rulers, through past and present Myanmar governments, have oppressed and exploited the Kachin. They have done so in collusion with the mining and logging companies and the Chinese opium barons. They have been abetted by the silence of the Bama Buddhist majority and the international community. What kind of interfaith theology can meet the challenges of this situation?

First, we need to ask why there is no peace, love and joy but only conflict and disaster in a Buddhist country full of pagodas, religious symbols of peace. The main obstacle is the dominant regime's unjust propaganda and policy of Bamanization. The majority Bama ethnic group has failed to accept the identity of other ethnic groups, as well as their right to their homelands and right to head the government. Minority ethnic Christians are often regarded as second-class citizens. Many conservative Bama people, MaBaTha, and the military believe that only Buddhists are qualified to lead the government. One good example is Henary Van Tio, an ethnic Chin Christian who was chosen as vice president of Myanmar but who has been constantly opposed by Burmese nationalists. There were rallies against his appointment on 2–3 April 2016, with Burmese nationalists and twelve Buddhist monks leading the campaign. Thousands called for him to be removed from office simply because he was neither Bama nor Buddhist (Min 2016).

Since national identity is tied to Buddhism and to Bama language and culture, there are many groups who fall outside; hence the many conflicts with those with a different identity to the majority – Rakhine, Kachin, Karen, Wa and Shan. Some of these ethnic minorities are Christians, such as Kachin and Chin, some may be both Christian and Buddhist, such as Karen, while many Rakhine are Muslims. Such groups are pressured to conform to the majority religion and culture. If Christians remain faithful to their identity in Christ, they are likely to suffer various forms of discrimination and persecution. The majority Bama see ethnic Christians as betraying national identity because Christians share the religion of our former colonial masters.

If Myanmar is to emerge from this nightmare of interethnic and interfaith conflict, national identity can no longer be the prerogative of the Bama-Buddhist majority. All its citizens must be accepted regardless of their religion or ethnicity. Moreover, the government should be for the good of all its citizens and not just the privileged few. As has been stated above, the Kachin, like the other ethnic minorities, agreed to become part of the Union of Myanmar on the understanding that they would have some degree of autonomy, which was never realized. However, this part of the agreement was never honoured. Even under the present (2020) government, the policy in practice is that the old power elite retains its control over the country through a ruthless process of Bamanization, the suppression of minorities and the exploitation of their resources. It is a trick to maintain the support of the majority, but the majority should realize that they are being deceived. Present policies are not in their interest, either. These policies conflict with true Buddhist values and are used solely for the benefit of the political, military and economic elite and at the expense of the poor majority of whatever religion or ethnicity.

As I have discussed above, even though Myanmar claims to be moving towards a democratic system, the military still pulls the strings. With a quarter of the seats in the national assembly and control of three key ministries (Ministry of Border Affairs, Ministry of Defence and Ministry of Home Affairs), the continued power of the military is guaranteed. The NLD stays in government as long as it suits the armed forces. Since Myanmar is home to different ethnic groups, unless majority Bama people learn to acknowledge, respect and accept differences and ethnic rights, there will always be conflict and misery. If we are called to be agents of peace and harmonious existence for humanity on earth, it is also the duty of religious leaders to take a stand against ethnic discrimination, which is what Bamanization is. It is not wrong to want to become a great nation, but we need to recognize that, as a nation, we are not one ethnic group but many, not of one faith but of several. Any attempt to impose a single ethnic identity and a single faith identity can therefore only be divisive. National unity can only be achieved through mutual acceptance and recognition and through devotion to a common goal of promoting the welfare of the whole people, not just a privileged few.

Hungering for what is right

According to Jesus's teaching, we are called to manifest our identity as the true children of God by hungering for what is right (Matthew 5). Buddha's teachings also emphasize that, when a person has right thoughts, 'his thoughts will become increasingly benevolent, harmless, and selfless and filled with love and compassion' (Dhammananda 1993: 81). Thus, Buddhism has its five precepts to hunger for what is right: (1) not to harm or kill, (2) not to steal or cheat, (3) not to harm others by sexual wrongdoing, (4) to avoid false speech, and (5) to avoid intoxicants and anything that hinders right-mindedness. While the precepts may be somewhat different from the Ten Commandments, there are significant similarities – enough for there to be some consensus on right action between the two faith communities. Thus, especially the two religious communities should be able to cooperate in resisting the destructive policies of the military and their collaborators in government. In neglecting to do so, Buddhist and Christian leaders have failed in their duty to guide the people. Silence has made possible the chaos that has engulfed the country.

For instance, during the Saffron Revolution of 2007, not all monks took part in the demonstrations against military tyranny. Far from it. Most of those who did were junior monks and amounted to less than 2 per cent (Zahler 2010: 118) of the estimated total of 560,000 monks and nuns in the country (The Republic of Union of Myanmar: The State Samgha MahaNayaka Committee: 2016). Only tens of thousands of Buddhist monks and nun marched peacefully in the stress during this crisis (Clements 2008: 16). Ross and Abrams also report that 'by September 24th citizens and monks in 25 cities throughout Burma were taking part in marches, with 100,000 people participating in Yangon and 30,000 in Mandalay' (Ross and Abrams 2007). In contrast, the *Sayadaw Gyi*, that is, the higher and senior monastic ranks who could have had a greater impact on the regime and the masses, kept silent on what was so vital for the entire nation. Rather than marching with their fellow monks, they provided spiritual guidance and comfort to the military generals who were inflicting poverty and suffering on the nation. It was the junior monks who acted rightly and fought for justice (Hang Do 2012: 79). But it was not just the *Sayadaw Gyi* who failed to take part in demonstrations – Christians, Muslims, Hindus and the masses (*Ludtu*) were just spectators (Hang Do 2012: 79). We all failed. We should have joined hands with the junior monks. Then we would have acted rightly. Then we would have shown that we truly hungered for justice. Consequently, we are challenged to resist the regime's oppression and discrimination with regard to ethnic and religious minorities. This is not just for our own sake. The oppressors also need liberation. They need to be enlightened about themselves and their own selfish destructiveness. It is easy to see the chains that bind their victims. But they are also enchained, imprisoned in their false ideas.

As Buddhism has five precepts to guide its followers to right action, so Christianity also has its principles to guide all who hunger for righteousness:

1) To stand up for justice without picking up the sword.
2) To rise above the world without abandoning the oppressed and the poor.
3) To seek the humanity of the oppressor without collaborating or losing one's integrity.
4) To be loyal to our own faith without descending into sectarianism or fanaticism (Duaybis 2015).

The five precepts and these four principles do not contradict but rather complement each other. The land of Myanmar has never been a monolith with a single ethnic and religious identity. Nonetheless, justice, peace and prosperity are possible. To achieve them requires us to be bold and to act. We should be out there encouraging the struggle and sharing tears. We should be out on the street with the IDPs, engaged in the work of restoring humanity and hope, cleaning out the forces of evil to create a place where God's children can dwell. We are called to be friends with the common people and especially with those who are oppressed, the lowly, the weak and the ignorant. The goal is to work for a better society. This requires radical political action. Justice demands that our natural resources benefit us all. It demands an inclusive society that grants full citizenship and identity to us all. We have reached a point where 'we must learn to live together as brothers or we will perish together as fools', as Martin Luther King Jr. pointed out in his speech in St Louis on 22 March 1964. Unless we do so, we shall never achieve ethnic reconciliation, and our dream of a genuine federal union will never be realised.

Compassion as a way to heal misery and a norm for harmonious existence

To heal the wounds of Myanmar, we need to adopt Jesus's model of compassion and put it into practice. The gospels show that there was much suffering in Israel at the time of Jesus, and there are certain parallels to the situation in Kachin State. Israel was an occupied country. Hellenization and Romanization were strong. The majority of Palestinian Jews suffered crippling poverty. Some owned and worked their own land while, in other cases, wealthy landholders with large estates rented out land to tenant farmers, who paid them with part of their produce. At the top of society, the ruling classes such as the Sadducees, High Priests and a handful of the Herodian governing class made the decisions (Burkett 2002: 28). Beneath the ruling elite, there were a few groups that had some wealth and influence: retainers (scribes, bureaucrats and generals serving the ruling elite) as well as merchants and priests. However, the bulk of the population, the common people, had little access to wealth or power. This class consisted primarily of farmers but also included artisans (weavers, builders and potters) and even less reputable classes (prostitutes, outlaws, beggars and underemployed itinerant workers) (Burkett 2002: 28).

Another heavy burden was taxation to fund Herod's building projects. Ever since the Jews lost their land to Gentile rulers, it was the vulnerable peasant community who paid a disproportionate share of taxes. After Herod's death, his son Herod Antipas continued the building projects in Galilee. These projects drained the material and human resources of the region and had a serious impact on economic, social and ecological life in Galilee (Freyne 2004: 134). More important, though, was his introduction of a new element in the population, with Herod Antipas replacing the old Hasmoneans, who had resisted Herod, with a new elite and retainer classes. Even though the majority of the inhabitants were Jewish, the new cities were alien to the surrounding territory and flooded with newcomers (Freyne 2004: 134). Moreover, Roman rule and urbanization introduced new types into the population – scribal administrators, military personnel and others in various retainer roles, acting on behalf of the ruling elite and the native aristocracy. There were new demands for goods and services, which therefore increased the burden of taxation on the peasantry. As always in such situations, it is the poor who are most vulnerable (Freyne 2004: 134), and the majority of Jewish peasants, supposedly the owners of the Promised Land as God's chosen people, were in reality oppressed and exploited, a conquered people. None of the parties of their own elite showed any interest in lifting their burdens or relieving their sufferings.

Unlike some authority-minded and party-affiliated Jews, Jesus felt compassion for the peasant community and whoever else might be considered outsiders – the sick, the disabled, the poor, prostitutes, tax collectors, even Roman officers. Matthew 6.34 says, 'When Jesus landed and saw a large crowd, he had compassion on them, because they were like sheep without a shepherd.' Jesus knows the sufferings of his fellow humans well because he lived in a world where Gentiles ruled their land. He respected the twofold law – *the written and oral law* – of the Pharisees but quarrelled with them for neglecting the weightier matter, which was the command to 'love your neighbour' (Sanders 1990: 97). Jesus focused more on the core Biblical demands and value of love, justice and mercy. His position on Mosaic laws and the practices of Jewish oral traditions emphasizes the humanitarian side of Judaism (Flusser 1993: 24). For him, what counts is not so much ritual observance as the love of justice, mercy and faith that God desires (Hosea 6.6). The need to apply compassion as a means to heal the community's disaster is emphasized repeatedly. 'But go and learn what this means: "I desire mercy, not sacrifice"' (Matthew 9.13; 12.7) (Marshall 2014: 97). Jesus gives the Torah a humanitarian interpretation, taking the view that love and compassion are the greatest commands (Flusser 1993: 24). Therefore, he also sought community with the 'tax collectors', those collaborating with the oppressors, and he was condemned for being friends with them. Jesus heals, saves and enlightens the nations with his compassion (Bauckham 2008: 360–1).

As in Jesus's world, there are many parties in Myanmar. Civilians are caught between Aung San Suu Kyi's puppet government and the military, the real rulers. Besides, many Myanmar citizens are torn between various political and religious factions that usually only promote their own interests and leadership. Their idea of leadership is deeply rooted in the military authoritative style. Thus, older leaders have become so possessive that they do not want any change and pay no heed to the voices of the vulnerable community. Consequently, many church leaders see themselves as being in a position of political or cultic power rather than understanding the need to practise the Biblical values of love and compassion.

In such circumstances, the situation of the Kachin people resembles that of the common people in Roman Israel. Its natural resources and the welfare of the people are under threat from outside rule and exploitation. Indeed, their very identity is at risk. As in Jesus's time, civilians are caught between rival political and religious factions and those in power, each promoting their own special interests. Today, Burmese refugees are fleeing to various neighbouring countries, hoping to resettle in a third country to rebuild their lives (Hang Do 2012: 71–2). Many others have fled the fighting to seek refuge within Myanmar.

What now? Is it right to wait for Myanmar to have effective leaders who have a heart? We need to be convinced now that Jesus's model is the way to build a Myanmar that is home to all its peoples, regardless of religion and ethnicity, social status and wealth. Compassion moves us to be with the needy, the suffering and the exploited. Compassion drives us to journey with the victims, to accept differences and to hunger for what is right. Our tears and misery will not be wiped away by Aung San Suu Kyi's party or the military regime, not by the KIA or the rich. It is God's compassion within each of us that will enable us to build a home where we can live together in harmony. Do we, as an interfaith community, have this compassion? Can we respond to the misery by acting to end it? The present refugee situation is not just a humanitarian concern or a matter of human rights. It is also a theological issue. As an interfaith community, we must attend to what God is calling us to do. God's compassion calls on us to journey with those suffering and stand up for justice (Longchar and Gordon Cowans 2011: iii). To paraphrase Cedar Duaybis, we should not let theology be just talk – ideas in our heads that never result in action. It is all about solving humanity's problems. It is a practical issue about how humans can exist with dignity (Duaybis 2015).

References

Bauckham, Richard (2008), *The Jewish World around the New Testament*, Grand Rapids, MI: Baker Academic.
Burkett, Delbert (2002), *An Introduction to the New Testament and Origin of Christianity*, Cambridge: Cambridge University Press.
Clements, Alan (2008), *The Voice of Hope*, New York: Seven Stories Press.
CSW (2018), 'Burma Army Target Kachin Christian Mission School', 14 May 2018. https://www.csw.org.uk/2018/05/14/press/3971/article.htm (accessed: 1 August 2020).
Dhammananda, K. Sri (1993), *What Buddhists Believe?*, Taipei, Taiwan: Corporate Body of the Buddha Educational Foundation.

Duaybis, Cedar (2015), Notes taken from class lecture (powerpoint slides) given by Duaybis at Swedish Theological Institution, Israel. February 27.

Flusser, David (1993), *Jewish Sources in Early Christianity*, Tel-Aviv: MOD.

Freyne, Sean (2004), *Jesus a Jewish Galilean: A New Reading of the Jesus Story*, London: T&T Clark.

Fuller, Thomas (2009), 'Ethnic Groups in Myanmar Hope for Peace, but Gird for Fight', *The New York Times*, 10 May 10 2009. https://www.nytimes.com/2009/05/11/world/asia/11iht-myanmar.html#:~:text=Now%2C%20as%20they%20have%20many,battle%20with%20Myanmar's%20central%20government.&text=Gam%20Shawng%20Gunhtang%2C%20the%20chief,since%20its%20founding%20in%201961 (accessed: 1 September 2020).

Gray, Dennis D. (2018), 'Myanmar Forces Burman Culture on Minorities, Erases Identity', *AP News*, 16 March 2018. https://apnews.com/249d72db491a47a79886c43b6085b6d2/Myanmar-forces-Burman-culture-on-minorities,-erases-identity (accessed: 1 August 2020).

Hang Do, Lian (2012), 'Life as Refugees Was Not a Choice: The Burmese Refugees Plight', *CTC Bulletin*, 28 (1) December: 68–80.

International Crisis Group (2017), *Buddhism and State Power in Myanmar*, Report V 290/Asia, 5 September 2017. https://www.crisisgroup.org/asia/south-east-asia/myanmar/290-buddhism-and-state-power-myanmar (accessed: 1 August 2020).

Layang Seng Ja (2014), 'Establishing a Peaceful Reign of God according to John 18:1–11', in *Conversations with Biblical Texts: In God's Image. Journal of Asian Women's Resource Centre for Culture and Theology*, 33 (3): 36–49.

Layang Seng Ja (2016), 'The Aggressive Brothers versus the Victimized Orphan', in *Voices from the Margins*, ed. R. S. Sugitharajah, 481–94, 25th edn, Maryknoll, NY: Orbis.

Layang Seng Ja (2017), 'The Role of Jesus for the Kachins: Understanding Jesus from the Present Kachin Context', *Theology Under the Bo Tree*, 2: 202–23.

Layang Seng Ja (2019), 'Civil War, Refugees, Disability and Theology', in *Disability Theology from Asia: A Resource Book for Theological and Religious Studies*, ed. Anjeline Okola and Wati Longchar. PTCA Study Series, No.17, 97–111, Kolkata: Edan-WCC.

Longchar, Wati, and Gordon Cowans (eds) (2011), *Doing Theology from Disability Perspective*, Manila: ATESEA.

Marshall, Mary (2014), *The Portrayals of the Pharisees in the Gospels and Acts*, Göttingen: Vandenhoeck & Ruprecht.

Min Thu, Z. (2015), *The Kachins: Their Unique Traditions & Customary Laws*, Myitkyina: LS Saing Kham

Min, Awng Kyaw (2016), 'Myanmar Times: Nationalists Rally against Both Vice Presidents', *Myanmar Times*, 5 April 5 2016. https://www.mmtimes.com/national-news/19820-nationalists-rally-against-both-vice-presidents.html (accessed: 1 August 2020).

Ross, Alexa, and Evan Abrams (19 August–29 September 2007), 'Burmese (Myanmar) Monks Campaign for Democracy (Safron Revolution), 2007'. https://nvdatabase.swarthmore.edu/content/burmese-myanmar-monks-campaign-democracy-saffron-revolution-2007 (accessed: 1 November 2020).

Sanders, E. P. (1990), *Jewish Law from Jesus to the Mishnah*, London: SCM.

Sword, Gustaf A. (1954), *Light in the Jungle*, Chicago: Baptist Conference Press.

The Republic of Union of Myanmar: The State Samgha MahaNayaka Committee (2016), *The Account of Wazo Monks and Nuns in 1377(2016 years)*, http://www.mahana.org.mm/en/religious-affairs/the-account-of-wazo-monks-and-nuns-in-1377-2016-year/?fbclid=IwAR2ci7HR4JdKlT62OumQT8FhpblIIcJ_jUyE2GLEX7R9G4QSCX2BVrbxTY8 (accessed: 1 November 2020).

The Guardian (2018), 'Myanmar Army Killing the Civilians in Escalating Conflict in Kachin'. https://www.theguardian.com/global-development/2018/may/01/myanmar-army-escalating-conflict-kachin-un-united-nations (accessed: 1 August 2020).

Williams, Lee (2018), 'Burma's Beleaguered Baptists: Rohingya Muslims Aren't the Only Religious Minority under Fire in Myanmar', *Christianity Today*, 19 October 2018. https://www.christianitytoday.com/ct/2018/november/kachin-christians-burma-myanmar-baptists-rohingya.html (accessed: 1 August 2020).

Zahler, Diane (2010), *Than Shwe's Burma*, Minneapolis: Twenty First Century Books.

Part 4

The Case of Islam

11

Islam and ethnic diversity in Myanmar

Myint Thein (Nyeinchan Lulin)

Myanmar, formerly known and often referred to as 'Burma', is situated in Southeast Asia. Its estimated population of 51.5 million (2014) belongs to hundreds of different ethnic groups and practise various religions. The majority Bamar (Burman) ethnic group makes up about two-thirds of the population and also dominates the military and the government sector. The other ethnic nationalities, making up the remaining one-third, live mainly in seven states.

After the assassination of the national leader General Aung San, the Union of Burma achieved its independence from Britain in 1948. However, more than sixty years of conflict between the Myanmar army and armed ethnic groups have left the country with a multitude of problems. After the military coup in 1962, General Ne Win's 'Burmese Way to Socialism', based on a centralized, one-party system, replaced General Aung San's policy of 'Unity in Diversity'. Moreover, under Ne Win, several ethnic groups were removed from the list of those given official recognition.

Myanmar's first democratically elected, civilian-led government since 1962 took office in March 2016. The World Report 2017 of the Human Rights Watch points out that the National League for Democracy (NLD), headed by the State Counsellor Daw Aung San Suu Kyi, controls a majority of seats in both parliamentary houses. However, the new government inherited deep-rooted problems, including the constitutional power of the military, repressive legislation, the weak rule of law and the deeply corrupt judiciary. Moreover, a new strain of ethno-nationalism and anti-Muslim propaganda have been parts of the transition in Myanmar.

Although – as I will show in this chapter – Muslim and other ethnic minorities in Myanmar continue to be subjected to severe and systemic human rights violations, Muslims in Myanmar have always shown loyalty to the state throughout the history of Burma (Myanmar) and have always faced the challenges peacefully to maintain harmony with the Buddhist majority.[1] Therefore, minority rights must be protected in Myanmar; otherwise, majority rights would lose their meaning.

The origins and development of Islam in Myanmar

Myanmar (Burma) is a Buddhist-majority country that was an independent kingdom before being annexed by the British and made a province of India in 1886. The Japanese invaded and occupied the country during the Second World War, but it was returned to British control and finally regained its independence in 1948. Although the country has no official state religion, the government continues to show preference for Theravāda Buddhism. According to the 2014 nationwide census, there are 2.2 million Muslims in Myanmar. However, Muslim leaders estimate that there are in fact four to five million Muslims in Myanmar and two million Muslims living as immigrants in other countries such as Thailand, Malaysia, Indonesia, Bangladesh, India, Pakistan and Saudi Arabia.

Kingdoms before the colonial period

Islam has flourished in Myanmar since the eighth century CE (Smart 1917: 20; U Kyi 1962: 160–1).[2] Islam arrived in Myanmar via three main routes: (1) by sea route through Muslims from Arabia, Persia and India; (2) by land through Yunnanese and Tartars from Yunnan, China; and (3) through Afghans, Indians and Persians from Bengal (Gaur Kingdom) and India (Moghul Empire). Moreover, there are Malay Muslims in the southernmost part of Myanmar.

The early Muslims arrived in Myanmar as traders, travellers, sailors, soldiers, adventurers, saints and preachers, prisoners and slaves, and mercenaries in the service of Burmese and Rakhine kings in various periods and were well settled before 1823 (the First Anglo-Burmese War) (Ministry of Defence 1997: 65–73). Due to their loyalty to the Burmese kings, Muslims were sometimes given high-ranking positions in administration, economic activities and the military, including forming special bodyguard units for the king. Moreover, the three Pa-thi (Muslim) kings reigned in Pathein (Delta) during the thirteenth century. Kamans (Muslim) also became the kingmakers who had the authority both to enthrone and dethrone kings during the Mrauk-U period in Rakhine.

New Muslim communities emerged in precolonial times due to their intensive exchange and communication with many ethnic groups and especially through intermarriage with local non-Muslim women, as well as intermarriage between different races among the Muslims. They are the following:

1. Pa-thi, Myedu and Kala-pyo (Burman Muslims) in Burma Proper.
2. Rohingya, Ka-man and Rakhine Muslims in Rakhine region.
3. Panthay (Myanmar-Chinese Muslims) mainly along the Myanmar-China border and main cities such as Yangon and Mandalay.
4. Pashu (Myanmar-Malay Muslims) in Thaninthayi region, the southernmost part of Myanmar, near the Thai border.

More Muslim groups arrived from India during and after the colonial period, some maintaining their Indian ancestral names, such as Surti, Memom, Quliya, Bengali, Narsapuri, Pa-than and Kaka. A few Muslims belong to the officially recognized ethnic nationalities such as Kachin, Kayah, Kayin, Chin, Mon, Shan and Pao. After the Burman Muslim Congress (BMC) was dissolved by the ruling Anti-Fascist People's Freedom League (AFPFL) party in September 1956, the Rohingya tried to stand as a separate community both politically and racially, by which time the government and the Burmese military also recognized them as Rohingya.

Muslim minorities during the British colonial period

The term *Pa-thi* was officially used for Burmese Muslims during the reign of Burmese kings (U Tin [1962] 1973: 176). During the British rule, the population census taken in Burma in 1891, which was the first census to cover the whole of Burma, used the term *Zer-ba-dee* for Burmese Muslims (both the descendants of Burmese Muslims from the days of Burmese kings and the progeny of mixed marriages between Muslim Indians and Burmese since the period of British conquest) (Yegar 1972: 33). However, Burmese Muslims did not like the term and opposed its use. In Notification No. 1112, dated 9 August 1941, the government announced its decision to respect the Muslims' demand and replaced the term *Zer-ba-dee* with *Burman Muslim* (Yule and Burnell 1903: 984). 'Burman' refers to the ethnic group, while 'Burmese' refers to all citizens of Burma, as well as the language spoken by Burmans.

During the struggle for independence, the convention of the AFPFL held in Rangoon (Yangon) in January 1946 and led by the national leader General Aung San affirmed the loyalty of Burmese Muslims to the country and applauded the statement 'Burmese Muslims are Burmans' made by the BMC, led by Sayagyi (= Great Master) U Razak. In proposal no. 6, the convention also gave national minority rights to Burmese Muslims if demanded (*Deedok Journal Weekly* 1946: 15–16, 31).[3] According to section 10 of the Constitution of the Union of Burma (1947), there was only one type of citizenship throughout the Union. According to subsections (i), (ii) and (iii) of section 11 of the Constitution, Myanmar Muslims (both the descendants of Burmese Muslims, from the days of Burmese kings, and the progeny of mixed marriages between Muslim Indians and Burmese, from the period of British conquest) were already citizens of the Union (Constitution 1948). Moreover, any person who is entitled under subsection (iv) of section 11 of the Constitution to be given citizenship and who has been granted a certificate of citizenship under the Union Citizenship (Election) Act 1948 shall continue to be a citizen of the Union.

The BMC helped unite the Burma Proper (majority Burman) and the Frontier Areas (ethnic minority groups) and to sign the Panglong Agreement in February 1947 to form the Union of Burma. U Pe Kin of the BMC became the most important and prominent negotiator in the Panglong Agreement. National elections for a constituent assembly were held in April 1947, when the AFPFL, led by General Aung San, won the majority of seats. However, on 19 July, nine persons, including General Aung San and Sayagyi U Razak, were assassinated during a ministerial meeting by a group of armed men. Of the nine, Sayagyi U Razak and Ko Htwe (the former's bodyguard) were Muslims. The Union of Burma became an independent nation on 4 January 1948, and U Nu became the country's first prime minister (U Pe Kin 1990: 19, 90, 132–4).

Muslims in post-independence Burma

After the 1947 Constitution of Burma and the nation's independence in 1948, there were four Muslim ministers (U Pe Kin, U Khin Maung Lat, U Raschid and Sultan Mahmood), with many Muslims serving as members of parliament or as high-ranking officials in the government and military. Muslim communities enjoyed the same status, rights and privileges as all other citizens in Myanmar.

During a meeting with representatives of the Burman Muslim Congress at the City Hall in Rangoon on 29 December 1955, the prime minister, U Nu, and the then leader of the ruling party, the AFPFL, affirmed that Burmese Muslims are Burmans. However, he demanded that the Congress be dissolved and urged Burmese Muslims who wished to continue their political careers to join the AFPFL as Burmese nationals and those who wished to practise their religion officially to join the Islamic Religious Affairs Council (*Hanthawaddy Daily Newspaper* 1955).

However, after the military coup led by General Ne Win in 1962, not only Muslim communities but all ethnic minority groups gradually lost their legal status, rights and privileges, due to Ne Win's ideology of the 'Burmese Way to Socialism' and 'Anti-Federalism with Burmanization process' (*The Times*, 3 March 1962; Silverstein 2004 77). The regime's violation of human rights and international norms sparked long-lasting conflicts, insurgencies and civil wars.

According to the Instruction Book 'How to fill in the form' that the Ministry of Home and Religious Affairs issued on 9 December 1972 for the 1973 population census, there were at that time 144 national races in Burma, including Rakhine-Chittagong (referring to Rohingya), Myanmar Muslim, Rakhine-Kaman, Myedu, other Burmese-Indians (except Chittagong, Hindustani. Tamil, Talegu, Dai-net, other Indians and Pakistanis) and Burmese-Chinese (including Panthay, except Yunnan, Canton, Fukan and other Chinese) (Ministry of Home and Religious Affairs 1972: 45). Moreover, according to the government newspapers, which quoted the Immigration and Manpower Department, there were 143 ethnic races, including the six ethnic races mentioned above, that professed Islam as their faith (*Botahtaung Newspaper* 1973: 11). Therefore, these Muslims gave their 'affirmative-confirmatory' votes for the new Constitution of the Socialist Republic of the Union of Burma (1974) as officially recognized national races and citizens of Burma.

Under subsections (i) and (ii) of section 145 of the Constitution, any person who was a citizen of the Union before the 1974 Constitution of the Union was deemed to be a citizen of the Union. According to the 1947 constitution, there is only one class of citizen across the country, but, according to the new constitution of 1974, there are two categories of citizen, 'Citizen by Birth and Citizen by Law'. However, under the dictatorship of General Ne Win, the Burma Socialist Programme Party (BSPP) proclaimed the 1982 Burma Citizenship Law, which excluded these Muslim ethnic groups (with the exception of Rakhine-Kaman) and recognized only 135 ethnic groups (*Working People's Daily* 1990: 7).

The new law created three categories of citizen (Citizen, Associate Citizen and Naturalized Citizen) and denied citizenship to many Muslims, openly declaring that only people of *pure blood* should be called nationals of Burma (*Working People's Daily* 1982). Since then, Muslim communities in Myanmar have been referred to as mixed-blood people, migrants and *Ka-las* (aliens or undesirable Indians who do not belong to Myanmar). Moreover, Muslim minority communities are told that they do not have their own state and that no race can be formed on the basis of religion. Therefore, they neither belong to the national ethnic groups of Myanmar nor are even eligible to be citizens. Some Burmese leaders blindly or unwittingly followed General Ne Win's words and identified themselves as *pure race*, while condemning those who were the products of interbreeding as *impure race* (*Working People's Daily* 1991).

The old BMC was dissolved on 30 September 1956 by the pressure of the AFPFL. Nevertheless, many members who wished to continue their political careers joined the AFPFL by their own choice, while other members established the new BMC. The names 'Burman Muslim' and 'Rakhine Muslim' as ethnic designations then became a problem in the political arena.[4] Therefore, the Rakhine Muslims chose 'Rohingya' instead of 'Rakhine Muslim' as their ethnic name. The new BMC, which was formed on 1 October 1956, one day after the dissolution of the old BMC, also chose 'Pa-thi' instead of 'Burman Muslim' as their ethnic designation, and it changed the party's name to the 'All Burma Pa-thi National Congress' on 1 October 1961 (Lay 1999: 254–6, 266–7, 320). With the term 'Pa-thi', it renewed the demand that the Myanmar Muslim community be granted the status of a recognized national minority, similar to the Kachin, the Karen and the Chin (Report 1960). Many founding members of the Pa-thi National Congress had supported 'Burmese Muslims are Burman' in the 1946 BMC conference but later realized that the AFPFL had changed its attitude. Meanwhile, some other ethnic minorities, Rakhine and Mon, struggled for 'statehood'. It is worth noting that neither the democratic nor the military governments ever saw the term 'Pa-thi' as being religiously affiliated like the term 'Burman Muslim', and it was accepted in the political arena as an ethnic term. The military government's policy of allowing only the BSPP throughout the country led to the abolition of all other political parties, including the Pa-thi National Congress, in March–April 1964 (Lay 1999: 338). The Mayu Frontier District (north of Rakhine State), where the Rohingya formed the majority of the population, was also dissolved in 1964.

Under the military junta (1988–2011)

An uprising occurred in 1988 as a result of the withdrawal of currency notes without compensation, economic mismanagement, the failure of the Burmese way to socialism, police brutality, corruption and military dictatorship. However, agents of the socialist government managed to incite anti-Muslim riots in Taung-gyi (Shan State), Mye-dae (Magway Division), and Pyay (Bago Division), where

Muslims were killed, properties looted or destroyed, and mosques, religious schools, houses, shops and even orphanages razed to the ground. Due to the Burman-Buddhist ultranationalism rooted in the colonial period, anti-Indian and anti-Muslim sentiments are not new in Myanmar, but the anti-Muslim riots of 1988 were incited with the clear political aim of diverting people's attention from a particular political issue to a religious issue. Nevertheless, successful anti-government demonstrations all over the country led General Ne Win to relinquish his control, which eventually led to another military coup on 18 September 1988, which was orchestrated by General Saw Maung, who took power and promised a democratic election. The military then formed the State Law and Order Restoration Council (SLORC) and governed the country.

Some Muslims and Muslim organizations supported the military junta, while others actively participated in the democratic movement. The two late Muslim leaders, Saya Chai and U Kyaw Nyunt, were among the five members of the junta's Multi-Party Democracy General Election Commission and the international community recognized the 1990 general election as being 'free and fair'. Two other prominent Muslims, Major Ba Thaw (retired) and U Aung Maytu of Minhla, were among the top leaders of Daw Aung San Suu Kyi's NLD. Both died in prison. Many pro-democracy Muslim leaders, students and politicians were also detained. During the SLORC reign, there were about twelve Burmese-Muslim-based and Rakhine-Muslim-based political parties, which tried, but failed, to regain their original national identity and status in Myanmar. The SLORC even refused to transfer power to those elected to parliament in the 1990 elections.

An important issue discussed by the Myanmar-Muslim-based political parties before and after the Multi-Party Democracy General Election period (May 1990) was that of Muslim identity in Myanmar. Put simply, there are two different concepts: 'Burmese Muslims are Burmans, which means merging with the Burmese majority', and 'Burmese Muslims are a national minority group in Myanmar'. The debate still continues today among Myanmar-Muslim communities and organizations. However, in contrast to the past, immigration officers now no longer recognize Burmese Muslims as ethnically Burman.

Regarding citizenship, the 2008 Constitution of the Republic of the Union of Myanmar, passed under the military junta, replaced the 1974 constitution, but the 1982 Burma Citizenship Law is still in force, and Muslims in Myanmar continue to suffer from the same inhuman treatment as before. Over time, the Burmese military and political leaders changed their attitude towards Muslim minorities, ignoring the historical facts and laws. The concept formulated by the Burman Muslim Congress in 1946 ('Burmese Muslims are Burmans'), and the affirmation of their identity by the National Leader General Aung San, by the AFPFL and by the 1947 and 1974 constitutions of Myanmar no longer seem to be working.

Although struggling shoulder to shoulder with their Burmese Buddhist brothers and sacrificing their ethnic minority rights for the goal of independence, Muslim communities gradually lost their citizenship rights after independence and were unjustly rejected even in their civil and communal identity. Today, the legal status of the vast majority of Muslims in Myanmar is described as 'suspicious' by immigration officials, who refuse to issue them with a Citizenship Scrutiny Card, claiming that Muslims are not qualified to have such a card according to the Burma Citizenship Law of 1982. Rohingyas in Rakhine (Arakan) State are commonly referred to as 'illegal migrants' and are therefore ineligible even for National Registration Cards (*International Religious Freedom Report 2010 – Burma*). Some are treated as refugees in Bangladesh, India, Saudi Arabia, Thailand, Malaysia and Indonesia.

Muslim graduates who do not have a Citizenship Scrutiny Card cannot obtain their degree/certificate and then face difficulties when progressing to further studies or entering employment and when applying for a passport to travel abroad. Even though there is no written directive that bars Muslims from jobs or promotion opportunities in government services, this is what happens in practice (*The Irrawaddy*, January 2006: 17).

Moreover, there were anti-Muslim movements and riots in many cities during this period, such as in Hin-tha-da, Taung-gyi, Yangon, Mandalay, Mawla-myaine, Bago (Pegu), Pyay (Prome), Kyauk-pyu, Sit-twe (Akyab), Toung-oo, Kyauk-se and Chauk, with many Muslims being killed or having their property taken away from them and many being imprisoned for defending themselves. Mosques and madrasahs (religious schools) were destroyed and copies of the Quran burnt or treated in an insulting way. After the riots, some mosques and religious schools were allowed to rebuild or reopen in some but not all places (e.g. not in Toung-oo or Chauk). Such information is never allowed to appear in the media in Myanmar but is found in the US State Department's annual International Religious Freedom Reports, which talk of an 'abuse of religion' in Myanmar. After Buddhist monks attacked a number of mosques in 1997, the military junta tried to calm the situation by demonstrating its commitment to all religions in a book published in 1998 in two volumes, *Sasana Yaung-war Htun-se-boh* (To Enlighten the Glory of Religion), and by claiming that the monks who had attacked the mosques were not real monks. But this was hardly more than a political stratagem.

In 1983, some extremists declared certain townships in Rakhine State such as Gwa and Taung-gote to be 'Muslim-free zones', with Muslims no longer being permitted to live there (*International Religious Freedom Report 2005*). Man-aung Island (Cheduba) in Rakhine State and Kyauk-padaung (Mandalay Division) were also declared 'Muslim-free zones'. It was very difficult for Muslims in Rakhine State to travel, do business, marry and study without an identity card. The government claimed that this policy was for reasons of security, but Muslims feel that it is a form of ethnic cleansing (*The Irrawaddy* 2006: 18).

As a result, many Muslims try to escape the country. Today, the problem of Myanmar Muslim refugees extends not only to bordering countries like Bangladesh and Thailand but also to Saudi Arabia and ASEAN countries, with refugees also arriving as boatpeople since 2009 (*Jakarta Globe*, 17 February 2009). Therefore, the problem of national identity of the Burmese Muslim community is important not only for Myanmar but also for the world community, including ASEAN, the United Nations (UN) and the Organization of the Islamic Conference (OIC).

Civilian governments since 2011

Myanmar held its first election in twenty years on 7 November 2010, with the ruling junta stating two days later that the junta-backed Union Solidarity and Development Party (USDP) had won 80 per cent of the votes. The majority of the democratic forces, including the NLD, had boycotted the elections. No Myanmar-Muslim-based political party had registered for the elections but two Rakhine-Muslim-based political parties had – namely, the National Democratic Party for Development (NDPD), a Rohingya party, and the Kaman National Progressive Party (KNPP). The new civilian government took office on 1 April 2011. There were only three Rakhine-Muslim MPs, who represented the USDP. They tried to represent the cause of the Muslim community in Rakhine by cooperating with the ruling party (the USDP), but none of the USDP's Muslim members, including the three MPs, were nominated as candidates for the 2015 general election.

The military-backed USDP government assumed power in 2011. From the beginning of 2012, there were new anti-Muslim actions and further violence in Rakhine State, which then spread across the country, such as killings, the destruction of mosques and religious schools, as well as houses and shops, and different forms of discrimination. In 2015, the government, in cooperation with some extremist Buddhist monks and leaders, adopted a package of four laws aimed at the 'Protection of Race and Religion' and targeting Muslims and Christian minorities. These laws infringed upon the exercise of freedom of worship, conversion, marriage and other human rights (Protection of Race and Religion 2019).

Although the NLD party led by Daw Aung San Suu Kyi won a landslide victory in the November 2015 general election, Myanmar still faces many obstacles to becoming a democratic country. There is not a single Muslim MP in either of the two new houses of parliament. Myanmar now has two parallel governments: an elected civilian government and the military. The constitution gives the military power over key institutions such as defence, home affairs and border areas and also over the police and general administrative departments that control bureaucracy at almost every level. The elected civilian government does not have sufficient authority to act in areas related to security and policy.

Current issues

The 2008 constitution

Since independence, Myanmar has had three different constitutions: a federal democratic constitution (1947) proclaimed in 1948, a socialist constitution under the one-party system in 1974 and the third and current constitution promulgated in September 2008 after a referendum.

On taking power in September 1988, the military junta (State Law and Order Restoration Council) suspended the 1974 constitution. The Constitution of the Republic of the Union of Myanmar 2008 was drafted and approved during the rule of the military junta, and the opposition sees it as a tool for the continuing military control of the country, because it still grants the military significant control over the country. Yet, there are additional problems, such as religious equality and the issue of citizenship. The 2008 constitution provides that every citizen be equally entitled to the right to 'freely profess and practise religion' (Article 34). It recognizes 'Christianity, Islam, Hinduism and Animism as the religions existing in the Union' (Article 362) and prohibits discrimination based on religion (Articles 348, 352, 368). The great majority of Myanmar's citizens are Buddhist, and the state recognizes Buddhism as the most eminent religion. The constitution therefore grants it a 'special position' (Articles 361, 363). Legally, the use of religion for political purposes is forbidden (Article 364), and the practice of religion is under the control of the Union within the purview of 'public order, morality or health and other provisions of the Constitution' (Article 34) (Constitution 2008: 9, 149–52). However, in reality, the minority religions face restrictions on certain religious practices.

According to section 345 (a) and (b) of the 2008 constitution, any person previously deemed a citizen of the Union shall also be deemed a citizen of the Union. Yet, as has been said above, after the 1982 Burma Citizenship Law, the government reduced the number of officially recognized ethnic groups from 144 to 135 by excluding most of the Muslim ethnic groups. While the Bamar (Burman) form the largest ethnicity, Myanmar's other ethnic groups prefer the term 'ethnic nationality' over 'ethnic minority', as the latter term increases their sense of insecurity in the face of what is often described as 'Burmanization'.

The ruling party, the NLD, as well as ethnic nationalities and the majority of the population, wants to change the current 2008 constitution, which was drafted and adopted during the rule of the military junta. U Ko Ni, a prominent Myanmar-Muslim legal expert and the legal advisor to the ruling party, was cold-bloodedly shot dead outside Yangon International Airport on 29 January 2017 for advocating change to the constitution. The killer, Kyi Lin, tried to flee but was caught by a number of taxi drivers, one of whom, Ko Ny Win, he shot. According to the president's office, U Ko Ni's murder was intended to destroy the peace and stability of the country. It was a political assassination, and many international and regional organizations have called for a transparent investigation into the murder. In February 2019, two men were sentenced to death and two others jailed. However, one of the masterminds behind the killing, former Lt. Col. Aung Win Khine, absconded, and not all of those behind the killing have yet been identified.

The 2014 census

After the Buddhist-Muslim violence in Rakhine in 2012, ultranationalists claimed that the growth of the Muslim population due to high birth rates justified their campaigns to 'protect' race and religion in the country. As there are no reliable statistics on the population, no one knows exactly how many ethnic and religious groups there are in Myanmar. The last comprehensive, although controversial, census was conducted by the British in 1931. Between 29 March and 10 April 2014, the government conducted a Population and Housing Census in cooperation with the United Nations Population Fund (UNFPA), with the

Department of Population and the Ministry of Immigration and Population publishing provisional results in August 2014. These results recorded a total of 51,419,420 people, including an estimated 1,206,353 persons who were not counted in parts of Arakan, Kachin and Kayin States. Numerous ethnic, civil organizations criticized the ethnic coding used in the census, claiming that it had been designed without proper consultation and calling for the census to be postponed until there was peace in the country. Furthermore, despite initial promises to the contrary, over one million Rohingya were counted as 'other' or 'Bengali', and therefore not as Myanmar citizens. The census also did not count the millions of people from Myanmar who were then living outside the country. Trusting government figures remains problematic particularly with regard to the size of ethnic populations.

According to the CIA World Factbook, the majority group (Bamar or Burman) make up 68 per cent of the country's population of 51 million, with the Shan (9 per cent), the Kayin (7 per cent), the Arakanese (Rakhine) (4 per cent) and the Mon (2 per cent) comprising the largest ethnic nationality groups after the Bamar. Others estimate that the percentage of ethnic nationality groups is much higher. Many have argued that the breakdown of population by ethnicity is dubious and that the central government has consistently underestimated the size of non-Burman communities. Official demographic figures and indicators are likely to be particularly flawed in relation to border areas, many of which remain inaccessible to the government as well as international agencies. Given the anti-Muslim attitude of nationalist Buddhists, data regarding the Muslim population are especially controversial. The often quoted figure of 1.1 million Muslims apparently excludes the Rohingya. According to the 2014 census, 4.3 per cent of Myanmar's population of 51 million are Muslim, which would be 2.19 million Muslims and hence include around 1.2 million mostly Rohingya Muslims in north-western Rakhine State. However, drawing on statistics at township level and on information provided by mosque trustees and social-welfare organizations, analysts and Muslim leaders estimate the overall Muslim population of Myanmar to be even larger.

Issues to do with the Identity Card for National Verification (NVC)

One very significant issue is that of citizenship. Rohingya and other Muslim communities in Myanmar have been continuously denied their rights to citizenship and other rights. The 1982 Burma Citizenship Law not only targeted

Rohingyas, making them stateless or illegal immigrants, but also Myanmar-Muslim communities, making them second- or third-class citizens. Since 2015, the immigration department has been issuing the Identity Card for National Verification (NVC), a card that grants residency but not citizenship, with the effect that non-Buddhists can be declared non-citizens. In line with the 1982 Burma Citizenship Law, persons who had previously held the National Registration Card (NRC) had to return the card to the appropriate township immigration office, which in turn issued them with a Citizenship Scrutiny Card (CSC), an Associate Citizenship Scrutiny Card (ACSC) or a Naturalized Citizenship Scrutiny Card (NCSC). However, instead of one of these citizen cards, most Rohingyas in Rakhine State were given a 'white card' (Temporary Registration/Identification Certificate, TRC/TIC) or later an NVC.

Since the introduction of the Burma Citizenship Law in 1982, persons who do not hold any card were scrutinized under the articles of this law until 2014, with the personal data of the applicant, his/her parents and four grandparents (i.e. the data of seven persons) being verified. If the applicant is entitled to be a citizen of the Union, then he or she is issued one of the three citizenship cards mentioned. According to notification 19/2015 dated 11 February 2015 and signed by the president, those still holding temporary identity certificates ('white cards') issued under the 1982 Burma Citizenship Law are now required to surrender their temporary certificates as they expired on 31 May 2015. The 'white cards' are to be replaced by the new NVC.

Of the 759,672 temporary certificates issued, only 469,183 have been surrendered. According to a news release by the State Counsellor's Information Committee, those who have failed to surrender their temporary certificate include those who have received a different kind of identity card, who have lost their card, who have a card that is damaged, who have died and who have failed to surrender the document because they live outside the region. From 1 June 2015, the temporary certificates have been gradually replaced by the new NVC, the main objective being to scrutinize whether people are entitled to become a citizen in accordance with the 1982 Myanmar Citizenship Law and to recognize them as residents in Myanmar.

The Department of Immigration continues to issue NVCs even to Myanmar-Muslim applicants whose parents both hold the Citizenship Scrutiny Card in mainland Myanmar (= Myanmar except Rakhine State), prompting the five Islamic organizations officially recognized by the government to issue a joint statement to Muslims 'not to apply for or accept NV cards' until further notice. In 2017, the Immigration Department declared that there would be no discrimination based on religion regarding qualification for citizenship. However, nobody knows what new strategy or procedures will be introduced in the future.

U Thein Swe, the Union Minister for Labour, Immigration and Population, held a meeting in Yangon on 21 January 2017, to which he invited twenty-five Muslim leaders, including leaders from the five recognized Islamic religious organizations, as well as politicians, businesspeople and social activists. He explained the process of issuing National Verification Cards and declared that Myanmar-Muslim applicants from the mainland would not be issued with an NVC. Instead, their nationality would be scrutinized in accordance with the 1982 Burma Citizenship Law. The process of issuing NVCs had been delayed in Rakhine State, and the minister urged the Muslim leaders to cooperate with the ministry.

The Muslim leaders urged him to scrutinize nationality in accordance with the 1982 Burma Citizenship Law, even though they had previously criticized this Law. They rightly pointed out that Rohingyas in Rakhine State are not undocumented people; they could be scrutinized under the 1982 Burma Citizenship Law, because, like other citizens prior to the issuing of white cards, they had previously held the NRC. They had to hold their white cards for twenty years (1995–2015) without any road map or guarantee. As a result, they and their children lost their citizenship rights, a situation that continues until today. The real author of the 1982 Burma Citizenship Law, General Ne Win, intended for everyone in the third generation to become a full citizen of the Union automatically. However, instead of becoming citizens, Muslims in Myanmar have had bitter experiences regarding the temporary card (the white card), and now another new process, the issuing of NVCs without any road map or guarantees, has started again.

However, the issuing of NVCs to Muslims continues in Rakhine State, although most Rohingyas do not apply for an NVC. Unfortunately, diplomat circles in Myanmar were falsely informed that Myanmar-Muslim leaders would not cooperate with the civilian government, and the Turkish ambassador to Myanmar met with some Muslim leaders in Yangon on 5 April 2017 to discuss the matter and clear up the misunderstanding. For Muslim leaders in Myanmar, the 1982 Burma Citizenship Law contradicts the basic principles and spirit of the United Nations Charter and international norms and should either abolish its unfair requirements for citizens or include the various national races and ethnic minority groups so that they can enjoy political, economic and social opportunities equitably.

The Rohingya issue

The effective denial of citizenship to the Rohingya has facilitated rights abuses, including restrictions on movement, limitations on access to health care, livelihood, shelter, education, arbitrary arrests and detention, and forced labour. Travel is severely constrained by authorization requirements, security checkpoints, curfews and strict control of access to Internally Displaced People camps.[5] Such barriers compound the health crisis caused by poor living conditions, severe overcrowding and limited health facilities. Currently, the Union government is urging people to avoid the term 'Rohingya', the term by which the group self-identifies. Ultranationalist Buddhists reject the term in favour of the term 'Bengalis', which implies the status of illegal migrants, and the State Counsellor (Aung San Suu Kyi) refers to the group as the 'Muslim Community in Rakhine State'.

On 9 October 2016, nine police officers were killed in coordinated attacks on three border outposts in Maungdaw District along the border with Bangladesh. Asserting that both the initial and subsequent attacks had been carried out by armed Rohingya militants, the government launched military-clearance operations to locate the alleged attackers, which led to numerous reports of serious abuses of Rohingya villagers by the army and police. The UN Office for Human Rights alleged in a report issued in February 2017 that Myanmar security forces, army and police had killed hundreds of people and gang-raped women and girls, forcing up to ninety thousand Rohingya Muslims from their homes. The ongoing Rohingya crisis in Myanmar has thus become a domestic issue with serious implications for the region, since thousands of Rohingyas have fled the country. The UN has also repeatedly called for the international community to urge Myanmar's civilian government to end the military crackdown on this minority group. Some human rights groups have even accused the Myanmar government of genocide. According to a report by Yale Law School and researchers at the International State Crime Initiative at Queen Mary University, London, there is 'strong evidence of a genocide perpetrated in Myanmar against the Rohingya people by the government' (Queen Mary University 2015). However, a permanent solution to the Rohingya issue rests in the hands of Myanmar.

In 2016, the current Myanmar government established three bodies to address sectarian tensions in Rakhine State: a government committee led by the State Counsellor for the Development of Rakhine State, an investigation committee led by Vice President U Myint Swe and a nine-member national/international advisory commission led by the former UN secretary general Dr Kofi Annan, the latter beginning its work in September 2016.

However, the government has continually failed to investigate abuses against the Rohingya adequately and has not acted on recommendations to seek UN assistance to investigate the violence. In November 2019, Gambia filed an application before the International Court of Justice (ICJ) alleging that the violence committed by the Myanmar government against the Rohingya violated the Convention on the Prevention and Punishment of the Crime of Genocide. On 23 January 2020, the ICJ issued a provisional order asking Myanmar to implement an emergency measure to save the Rohingyas from genocide and to preserve evidence of acts of genocide. The ICJ also ordered Myanmar to submit a report on its compliance with the order on 23 May 2020 and every six months thereafter until the case is decided.

A regional solution should be found quickly to prevent the humanitarian crisis in Rakhine State from worsening, and ASEAN member states should create favourable conditions in which discussion can take place on how to address the problem.

Education

As far as access to education is concerned, there are serious security issues for Muslim students and discrimination due to the lack of valid citizenship cards. For example, Muslim students who pass the matriculation examination in Thandwe township, Rakhine State, are instructed to join universities in Taung-goke and Sit-twe, where Muslims have been killed, thus making it impossible for them to do so; in various cases, Muslims have been barred from enrolling at a university because they do not have a citizenship card, and not having a valid citizenship card has also prevented Muslim graduates from obtaining their graduation certificate.

Interfaith issues

The various conflicts in Myanmar, such as the conflict between Rakhine Buddhists and Rohingya Muslims, the interethnic fighting in Shan State between different armed ethnic groups and the conflict between the ethnic Arakan Army and the Myanmar military (Tatmadaw), have caused great hatred in the country. After the anti-Muslim violence in Myanmar between 2012 and 2014, interfaith dialogue became a crucial mechanism of conflict resolution. Although the NLD government has largely eliminated the Buddhist nationalist groups such as 969 and the Association for the Protection of Race and Religion (MaBaTha), Buddhist identity politics remains influential and may come back in different forms. As a result, interfaith activities led by Muslim groups have been targeted and attacked by so-called Buddhist nationalists. Exploiting the absence of the rule of law, Buddhist extremists have even established some 'Muslim-free zones', as has already been mentioned, leading to such incidents as the one concerning a Muslim named Kyaw Min, who was arrested and fined Kyats 500,000 for taking a Buddhist friend to Mu-ta-khwe village in Pa-an township, Kayin State, on 28 December 2016 – the village is a so-called Muslim-free zone.

The freedom to practise their faith is under severe pressure for Muslims. For example, in 2017, a mob led by some Buddhist monks belonging to the extremist Myo-chit Yahan group stopped Islamic religious gatherings, including interfaith programmes that had been given official approval by the Yangon regional government.[6] The police apparently had no power to intervene. This shows that even Muslims in downtown Yangon have no security, and the attention of the international community is urgently required. Moreover, Buddhist extremists and hooligans have claimed on Facebook that 'we will wash our feet with the blood taken from the throats of kalars' (here, 'kalar' signifies undesired aliens or Indians) and will prevent any Islamic gathering in the country.

In 2017, the Buddhist monk U Wirathu published the book *African Catfish* in Burmese. This book compares Muslims to African catfish, who live by eating other fish, and claims that Buddhists and Muslims can never coexist peacefully. Such hate speech has been propagated by ultranationalists led by extremist Buddhist monks. Although Muslim organizations have informed the authorities, no proper action has been taken. As a result, non-Muslims often think that Islam, the Quran and the Prophet Muhammad are the roots of terrorism and consider mosques to be terrorist centres.

There are also more positive examples, though. In 2016, the well-known Buddhist monk Ven. Myawady Mingyi Sayardw wrote a foreword to my book *Pyidaungsu Muslims* [Citizen Muslims of Myanmar], which presents strong evidence of the full citizenship of Muslim communities in Myanmar and corrects misunderstandings of Islam. The book was welcomed by elites, politicians, historians and even Buddhist monks. However, journals belonging to the leading Buddhist extremist group (MaBaTha) condemned the book as an insult to the history of Myanmar and declared its author to be a liar. In 2019, interfaith activists launched the White Rose Campaign in response to the events in three Muslim areas of South Dagon township in Yangon on the nights of

13–15 May, when two hundred ultranationalists led by Michael Kyaw Myint and some Buddhist monks forced temporary Muslim prayer sites to shut down during Ramadan. Buddhists among the interfaith activists gave white roses to Muslims leaving mosques in Yangon after prayers as a sign that they rejected violence and encouraged solidarity, love, kindness and harmony among the followers of different religions in Myanmar. This campaign quickly spread to the main cities of Myanmar. The Yangon regional government took action against Michael Kyaw Myint and other extremist leaders, and anti-Muslim activities have gradually stopped since then. In 2016–17, the lower house (Pyithu Hluttaw) and the State Counsellor drafted a bill on hate speech, but this has not yet (in September 2020) been implemented.

Islamic organizations

Muslims in Myanmar have not been able to centralize their efforts properly. Every organization and group – whether big or small – has its own leaders and muftis. There is no such religious authority as a body recognized by the government or approved by the whole community. Successive governments have never allowed the appointment of a Shaikhul Islam or Grand Mufti for the whole country, which would have been possible under the Kazi Act of 1880. However, there are currently five Islamic organizations[7] which have formed a committee to administer an annual government fund of Kyats 500,000 (= USD 320). The directorate of the government's Department of Religious Affairs deals with these organizations regarding Islamic affairs. These five organizations have formed the 'All Myanmar Islamic Organization' to discuss and decide on some important and common religious issues such as Hajj, Qurbani and the Eidul Adha festival.

In addition, there are some other important Islamic organizations, centres and institutions pursuing various charitable and educational activities. In Yangon, the Myanmar Muslim Women's League runs a girls' orphanage and a Muslim women's religious centre that organizes religious events for women. Also based in Yangon, the Al-Azhar Islamic Institute of Myanmar and the Islamic Centre of Myanmar run courses on Islam and offer Arabic and English classes, interfaith and Da'wah programmes, education and social-welfare activities, training in leadership and capacity-building and so on. The Islamic Centre of Myanmar, the Islamic Religious Affairs Council, the Muslim Central Fund Trust and the Jamiyatul Ulema al-Islam are the member organizations of the Regional Islamic Da'wah Council for Southeast Asia and the Pacific (RISEAP). In Mandalay, teachers and ulemas of Jami'ah Arabiyah, Kant-Balu, Sagaing Region, have formed an organization called 'Salahiyatul Ulemah'. A group of ulemas have broken away from the Jamiyatul Ulema al-Islam and formed a new organization called 'Myanmar Muslim Ulema Organization', based in Yangon. Two popular civil-society organizations led by Muslims are the Myanmar Muslim Network and the Peace Cultivation Network.

Under the present circumstances, Muslims cannot do anything to have their grievances addressed. Muslim organizations have to be very careful when dealing with such problems and usually have to deal with the director general of the Department of Religious Affairs and sometimes with the Union Minister of Religious Affairs and Culture, meaning that they are sometimes unable to report the true situation of an emergency issue involving Muslims to the highest authorities in time or to deal with these authorities directly.

Myanmar Muslims are an integral part of Myanmar society and can be seen in all economic strata. Funds locally raised from the community support mosques and madrasahs, as well as the activities that they run, and most imams, madrasah teachers, muazzins and other Islamic workers in mosques are poorly paid, especially in poor and remote areas. Islamic Da'wah workers, such as writers, teachers and orators, usually do voluntary work.

The government used to allow the Burma Broadcasting Service to broadcast a ten- minute programme every year for Muslims during the two Eid festivals and the Prophet Day, but this is no longer the case.

Conclusion

In March 2017, the UN Human Rights Council once again adopted its resolution on Myanmar and extended the Special Rapporteur's mandate, requesting that she identify benchmarks for reform. However, the EU decided not to introduce a resolution at the UN General Assembly in November, underscoring the fact that the international community's approach is softening. The UN Human Rights Council held interactive dialogue with the Special Rapporteur in September 2020 on human rights in Myanmar. Presenting his progress report, Thomas Andrews dealt with the forthcoming elections and stated that the 'results of an election could not accurately reflect the will of the people, when the right to vote was denied because of a person's race, ethnicity or religion'. According to Andrews, there is 'no evidence that the Government was willing or prepared to facilitate the right to vote for hundreds of thousands of voting age Rohingya located in Rakhine state or in refugee camps in Bangladesh'.

The Myanmar representative promised that the election would 'be free, fair, transparent and reflective of the desire of the people'. The discussion focused on reports of ongoing human rights violations and the fact that these violations were not investigated seriously.[8]

Myanmar has faced grave human rights violations for decades. All violations of human rights and international norms in Myanmar occur within a culture of impunity, due to the government's failure to provide accountability and justice. To prevent further violations, the new democratic government should form a commission to make appropriate recommendations based on its findings. In doing so, we need to address the root causes of the problem, such as the following:

- General Aung San's policy of unity in diversity as opposed to General Ne Win's policy of the Burmese way to socialism and a centralized one-party system before 1988.
- The extension of military power and the government's process of centralization after the 1988 military coup.
- State nationalism as opposed to the emergence of ethnic nationalism to protect identity, language, culture and natural resources.
- Emergence of ultranationalism and religious persecution without the rule of law.
- The ongoing armed conflicts and relocation of populations.

There can be no real peace, development or national unity for the country, or justice and freedom for all people in Myanmar, unless

- the concept of diversity and pluralism is recognized;
- a culture of tolerance and commitment to dialogue emerges both administratively and in civil society; and
- visionary leadership and systematic administration are properly established, and the rights of individuals and every ethnic group are guaranteed in accordance with the constitution and other laws.

Moreover, the struggle for self-determination by any ethnic group cannot be separated from the mainstream of democracy and the human rights movement. Myanmar must recognize and embrace its diversity in order to create a federal country and to ensure a stable and secure future. 'Unification through diversification' should be the notion used in the current situation to overcome the enormous huddles related to ethnic Muslim rights on the road map to federalism.

Notes

1. There have been a few armed Muslim groups in the past, such as the Mujahid movement (along the Myanmar-Bangladesh border), the 786 movement (Myanmar-Thai border) and the Kawthoolei Muslim Liberation Front, which mainly fought alongside the Karen National Liberation Army (KNLA); in the present, there is the so-called Arakan Rohingya Salvation Army (ARSA). None of them represented the Muslims of Myanmar and their total numbers are less than 1 per cent of the total Muslim population of Myanmar. Moreover, they have never been able to attract much support, either internally or internationally, even among Muslim nations. Yet, with the exception of the Mujahid movement in the past and the ARSA in the present, even armed Muslim groups generally seek a federal democracy.
2. U Kyi (B. A.) had formerly been a lecturer in the history department of the University of Rangoon.
3. This journal was published by one of the National Martyrs, Deedok U Ba Cho.
4. However, after the military coup in 1962, the immigration department permitted the use of 'Burmese Muslim' or 'Myanmar Muslim' as a racial name for the NRC and household population lists. The term 'Myanmar Muslim' was included in the Immigration Department's list of national races of Burma in 1972 for the 1973 population census. After 1990, the Immigration Department gradually prohibited the term 'Myanmar Muslim' again as a racial name, although the term was and still is officially accepted and widely used in social and religious fields.
5. According to the UNHCR report of 2014, there are about 140,000 internally displaced people in Rakhine State. They are victims of the communal violence which broke out in 2012 amongst the Rakhine and Rohingya communities. Although they have been provided shelters, food and medicine by the UNHCR and other NGOs, they face hardship in the camp such as a lack of healthcare support and education for their children.
6. For example, in Thaketa township, Yangon, on 5 January 2017, and at the YMCA Hall, Botataung township, Yangon, on 8 January 2017. A few extremist monks threatened Muslim wards (Bengali-su) on 7 January 2017, and an Islamic gathering to be held in Myanmar Medical Association Hall on 14 January 2017 had to be cancelled for the same reason.
7. These are the following:
    1. Islamic Religious Affairs Council H.Q. (IRAC),
    2. Jamiyatul Ulema al-Islam,
    3. Myanmar Muslim (Religious) Youth League (Ma-Ma-La),
    4. All Myanmar Maulavi Organization, and
    5. Myanmar Muslim National Affairs Organization (Ma-Ah-Fa).

8 https://reliefweb.int/report/myanmar/human-rights-council-holds-dialogue-special-rapporteur-myanmar-and-starts-dialogue (accessed: 1 September 2020).

References

Burma/Myanmar Library (2019), 'Protection of Race and Religion Laws and Discrimination against Women from Religious Minorities'. https://www.burmalibrary.org/en/protection-of-race-and-religion-laws-and-discrimination-against-women-from-religious-minorities (accessed: 1 August 2020).

Constitution of the Union of Burma (1948), Rangoon: Government Printing and Stationery.

Constitution of the Republic of the Union of Myanmar (2008).

International Religious Freedom Report 2005 – Burma, US Department of State. 'Abuse of Religious Freedom.'

International Religious Freedom Report 2010 – Burma, US Department of State.

Lay, Pathi U Ko Ko (1999), *Myanmar Naing-ngan hnit Islam Thar-tha-nar* [Myanmar Naing-ngan and the Religion of Islam], Mandalay: Limited circulation for researchers by Author.

Ministry of Defense, ed. (1997), *Sasana Yaung-war Htun-se-boh* [The Glory of Religion to be Enlightened], vol. 1, Yangon: Office of the Director of Rehabilitation, Ministry of Defence.

Ministry of Home and Religious Affairs (1972), *Pone-san Phyae-swet-yan Hnyun-kyar-chet* [The Instruction How to Fill up the Forms], Rangoon: Immigration and Manpower Department, Ministry of Home and Religious Affairs.

Queen Mary University of London (29 October 2015), 'Campaigns of Violence towards Rohingya Are Highly Organised and Genocidal in Intent'. https://www.qmul.ac.uk/media/news/2015/hss/campaigns-of-violence-towards-rohingya-are-highly-organised-and-genocidal-in-intent.html (accessed: 1 August 2020).

Report of the General Secretary of the New BMC to the General Assembly to Discuss the Burman Muslim Affairs and the Issues of Burmese Politics, Mandalay, Upper Myanmar, March, 1960.

Silverstein, Josef (2004), 'Burma's Struggle for Democracy: The Army against the People', in *The Military and Democracy in Asia and Pacific*, ed. R. J. May and Viberto Selochan, 69–87, Canberra: Australian National University E Press.

Smart, R. B. (1917), *Burma Gazetteer: Akyab District*, vol. A, Rangoon: Government Printing and Stationery.

U Kyi (1962), *Myanmar Yazawin Thi-at-phwe-yar Ah-phyar-phyar* [Various Notable Facts in the Chronicle of Myanmar], Rangoon: University of Rangoon.

U Pe Kin (1990), *Ko-twe Pinlon* [Pinlon, An Inside Story], 6th edn, Yangon: Ministry of Information.

U Tin ([1962] 1973), *Myanmar-min Oke-choke-pone Sartan hnit Bo-daw-pha-ya-i' Ya-za-that khaw-thaw ah- maint-taw taan-gyi* [Thesis of the Administration of Burmese Kings and Criminal Law Royal Decree of Bodawpaya], part 2 (1965), part 4 (1973), Rangoon: Government Printing Press.

Yegar, Moshe (1972), *The Muslims of Burma: A Study of a Minority Group*, Wiesbaden: Otto Harrassowitz.

Yule, Col. Henry and A. C. Burnell, eds (1903), *Hobson-Jobson: A Glossary of Colloquial Anglo-Indian Words and Phrases, and Kindred Terms, Etymological, Historical, Geographical and Discursive*, new edn, London: John Murray.

Newspaper References (in chronological order)

'The AFPFL Solved the National Minority Problem', *Deedok Journal Weekly*, vol. 19, no. 26, 4 February 1946).

Harry Priestley, 'The Outsiders', *The Irrawaddy*, vol. 14, no. 1, January 2006, 17.

Hardyanto, 'The Rohingya Question, a True Test for Asean' (Opinion), *The Jakarta Globe*, 17 February, 2009.

Myanpyithar, 'Our Union of Myanmar Where 135 Ethnic Groups Reside', *The Working People's Daily*, 26 September, 1990, 11.

'The Prime Minister U Nu's Speech', *The Hanthawaddy Daily Newspaper*, 30 December, 1955.

The Times, 3 March 1962.

'There are 143 National Races in the Union, Already Prepared to Take Population Census', *Botahtaung Newspaper*, 23 February, 1973, 11.

The Working People's Daily, 9 October, 1982.

The Working People's Daily, 22 February, 1991.

12

Civil documentation and discrimination against religious and ethnic minorities in Myanmar

Myo Win

The mass displacement of at least six hundred thousand Rohingya from Rakhine State, Myanmar, to Bangladesh in late 2018 brought to the attention of the international community the historical and ongoing persecution, as well as statelessness, of Rohingya in Myanmar. However, as this chapter will outline, Rohingya are not the only religious and ethnic minority group in Myanmar who may be, or risk becoming, stateless.

In 2016 and 2017, SMILE Myanmar, a non-profit NGO based in Yangon and Mandalay, carried out two studies that investigated the risk of statelessness amongst religious and ethnic minorities in Myanmar, beyond the experiences of the Rohingya community.[1] The studies also considered the relationship between access to civil documentation and the enjoyment of fundamental rights in Myanmar. This chapter reports on both studies, documenting the experiences of practising Muslims, Hindus and Buddhists of various ethnicities in Bago, Yangon, Mandalay, Pathein and Mawlamyine.

Civil documentation and statelessness in Myanmar

Statelessness occurs when a person is unable to realize the right to nationality. The right to nationality is often an essential prerequisite to accessing other fundamental rights such as healthcare, education and employment opportunities. While the lack of documentation may not result directly in statelessness, populations that are stateless are often undocumented and face huge barriers to accessing documentation and protection services. On the other hand, undocumented populations can be at a higher risk of statelessness, if they are unable to obtain and provide the documentation required to confirm their citizenship.

The United Nations High Commissioner for Refugees (UNHCR) estimates that there are at least ten million stateless people worldwide.[2] To date (2020), there has been no comprehensive study that provides an accurate baseline figure as to the size and profile of the stateless population in Myanmar and those at risk of statelessness. However, the UNHCR estimates that there are six hundred thousand stateless people in Rakhine State alone.[3] The total numbers are likely to be greater given the discriminatory nature of Myanmar's Citizenship Law, policies and procedures and the significant barriers that various populations face in accessing civil documentation and other forms of legal identity.

Since Myanmar's independence in 1948, nation-building has increasingly focused on building a national identity that excludes ethnic and religious minorities and fosters division amongst them. Restricting the right to a nationality and access to documentation is one way in which this policy has been implemented. For example, attempts by successive governments to 'scrutinize' the population living within the territory of Myanmar has resulted in the creation of numerous forms of documentation and processes for obtaining documentation that clearly exclude a number of ethnic and religious minorities.

Framework of civil documentation in Myanmar

After independence there were two Acts on citizenship, the 1948 Union Citizenship (Election) Act and the Union Citizenship Act. Both were replaced by the 1982 Citizenship Law and its 1983 Citizenship Procedures, which codify the acquisition, confirmation and loss of Myanmar citizenship. The 1982 Citizenship Law introduced three types of citizenship, 'citizens', 'associate citizens' and 'naturalized citizens', whereas previously there had only been one type of citizenship in Myanmar.

Each type of citizenship pursuant to the 1982 Citizenship Law is afforded different entitlements and is evidenced by specific documentation: the Citizenship Scrutiny Card (CSC), the Associate Citizenship Scrutiny Card (ACSC) and the Naturalised Citizenship Scrutiny Card (NCSC). Dual citizenship is prohibited under the 1982 Citizenship Law.

Eligibility for citizenship in Myanmar primarily follows ethnic and descent-based (*jus sanguinis*) criteria. The descent-based criteria for acquiring citizenship require individuals to produce documentary evidence to substantiate their claim for citizenship. Such documentation can include birth certificates, household lists and documentation proving residency or citizenship on the part of both biological parents and all four grandparents. However, in practice, many individuals are unable to produce the necessary documentation to support their claim for citizenship.

Since 1982, Myanmar's government has issued numerous types of identity documentation in varying colours that show different classes of citizenship or residency status, as well as corresponding rights. This system of documentation is complicated, and obtaining information on the eligibility of each piece of documentation is beyond the reach of the majority of the Myanmar population.

In situations where an individual has either lost or does not have access to the supporting documentation (e.g. children of undocumented parents or individuals who have lost documents due to displacement or natural disaster), he or she can apply for a letter of recommendation from the village head or from the ward or township administrator. Whether such a letter is forthcoming depends on the willingness of the village head or township administrator and on the type of document that an individual is trying to acquire.

The following provides a brief overview of the various forms of civil documentation and other forms of legal identification in Myanmar:

- *National Registration Card (NRC)*, also called 'three-folded card', is green for men and pink for women. Issued pursuant to the Residents of Burma Registration Act of 1949 and the Residents of Burma Registration Rules of 1951, the majority of NRCs were collected by the government in the late 1980s and often replaced by Citizenship Scrutiny Cards (CSCs). However, findings from research as recent as 2016 show that NRCs are still being issued.
- *Citizenship Scrutiny Card (CSC)*, 'pink card' or '*naing* card' as it is also called, indicates full citizenship and is issued under the 1982 Citizenship Law and 1983 Citizenship Procedures. Under the 1983 Citizenship Procedures, children apply for a CSC at the age of 10, and CSC holders must then renew their cards at the ages of 18, 30 and 45. As a result, CSCs are sometimes referred to according to the age at which the applicant is supposed to apply for the card, for example, a ten-year card.[4] While the

1982 Citizenship Law does not restrict freedom of movement based on citizenship, the cards distributed under the law (CSCs, NCSCs, ACSCs) say that one 'must carry this card when travelling'.[5]

- *Naturalised Citizenship Scrutiny Card (NCSC)*, or 'green card', indicates naturalized citizenship and is issued under the 1982 Citizenship Law and 1983 Citizenship Procedures. Persons can apply for an NCSC if they have resided in Myanmar since 1948 or were born outside Myanmar but have at least one parent who has citizenship status. According to the law, they must also be at least eighteen and able to speak one of the national languages of Myanmar well. A foreign spouse can only obtain naturalized citizenship if the marriage was entered into before 1982.

- *Associate Citizenship Scrutiny Card (ACSC)*, or 'blue card', indicates associate citizenship and is issued under the 1982 Citizenship Law and 1983 Citizenship Procedures. Those who had applied for citizenship under the 1948 Citizenship Act – prior to the passing of the 1982 law – may be eligible for associate citizenship. The 1948 Act had looser criteria and allowed foreigners to become citizens if they had resided in Myanmar for five years, spoke one of the national languages well and respected the laws.

- *Foreign Registration Certificate (FRC)* is issued, pursuant to the 1940 Registration of Foreigners Act and Rule 6 of the 1948 Registration of Foreigners Rules, once a foreigner informs the authorities of his or her address and provides proof of identity. A foreigner is a 'person who is not a citizen of the Union' as defined under the 1864 Burma Foreigners Act.

- *Temporary Registration/Identification Certificate (TRC or TIC)*, also referred to as 'white card', was issued pursuant to section 4 of the 1949 Registration of Residents Act and section 13(1)(c) of the 1951 Resident Registration Rules to various Muslim groups and populations of Chinese and Indian background in the early 1990s after their NRCs had been collected. TRCs do not indicate citizenship status and only provide proof of identity and residence. TRCs were invalidated by Presidential Notification No. 19/2015 on 11 February 2015.

- *Identity Card for National Verification (INVC/NVC)*, or 'turquoise card', was introduced as of 1 June 2015 and later issued pursuant to State Counsellor's Office Notification dated 27 December 2016 based on the 1949 Registration of Residents Act Section 5(2)(d). NVCs are often issued to former TRC/TIC holders and FRC holders.

- *A Household List*, that is, a household registration form or family registration list, also known as 'Form 66/6', records the biographical data of

the *registered* residents who are part of a given family and is issued under the 1949 Residents of Burma Registration Act.
- A *Birth Certificate* issued by the Ministry of Health upon the birth of a child.

Methodology of the studies

Religious and ethnic minorities

It is common for minorities in Myanmar to experience discrimination on the basis of their belonging to a minority ethnicity and/or religion. While all Muslims in Myanmar are generally identified as being from a religious minority background and experience discrimination as a result, Muslims of particular ethnicities are often subject to heightened discrimination in comparison to others. At the same time, individuals who practise the majority religion, Buddhism, but who also identify as belonging to a minority ethnic group, such as people of Kachin ethnicity, may too face discrimination on the basis of their ethnicity. Therefore, the research that we undertook in 2016–17 included participants who identified as belonging to either religious or ethnic minorities, as well as participants who identified as belonging to both. However, in the context of heightened religious tensions in Myanmar, this research focused particularly on individuals who identified as belonging to a minority religion.

Every effort was made to include as diverse a range of participants as possible. The five locations are geographically spread but within reasonable travelling distance from Yangon. Travel to remoter areas was not feasible due to the budget limitations of the research project.

Yangon, Mandalay and Bago

In the 2016 study, three focus group discussions (FGDs) were undertaken in each location – Yangon, Mandalay and Bago – with a total of 255 participants. Participants were identified through SMILE's existing networks. Due to restrictions, the project was not able to hire translators of the ethnic languages of all the participants. The FGDs were conducted by our SMILE staff in Burmese, limiting potential participants to those who spoke Burmese. The notes of the FDGs were later translated into English.

All participants were informed of the purpose of the FGDs and of the research more broadly. They all gave their oral consent before starting the FGDs and were informed that they had the freedom not to answer questions and to leave at any time. The names of the participants have been withheld to prevent any reprisals or discriminatory acts against them. FGDs were conducted in hotels that our staff judged to be safe and secure.

The study also involved semi-structured interviews with individuals and key informants in Yangon, Mandalay and Bago. Key informants included officials from the Ministry of Labour, Immigration and Population (MoLIP), as well as lawyers and religious leaders. In terms of the religious make-up of the participants, the majority identified as Muslim (81 per cent), while other participants identified as Buddhist, Hindu-Buddhist, Hindu or Christian.

Pathein and Mawlamyine

Building on the 2016 study, we conducted FGDs in 2017 with 179 individuals (87 in Pathein and 92 in Mawlamyine). FGD participants were from non-Bamar (= non-Burman) ethnic and religious minorities living in and around Pathein and Mawlamyine. In addition, thirteen semi-structured interviews with key individuals, such as MoLIP officials, faith leaders, lawyers and brokers, were carried out in and around the areas of Pathein and Mawlamyine. These interviews were also conducted in Burmese.

SMILE employed local coordinators for each of the locations to recruit participants, handle logistics and co-facilitate the semi-structured interviews. The local coordinators were selected based on their community networks and relationship to religious leaders. To ensure the quality and credibility of the FGDs, we conducted interactive training to familiarize facilitators and local coordinators with conflict sensitivity, consent, types of civil documentation in Myanmar and facilitation techniques. As this training used the specific questionnaire designed for the FGDs, it helped improve upon particular questions by, for example, standardizing the words used to discuss marriage registration. We also trained note-takers on certain skills, such as organizing notes and fully capturing participants' answers.

At the beginning of every FGD, our facilitators explained the meaning of consent and stressed that the identities of participants and identifying information would remain confidential and any information used in the report would be presented without disclosing identifying information.

Limitations and challenges

Yangon, Mandalay and Bago

Tensions and violence in northern Rakhine State feed hostile sentiments against Muslims and other religious minorities throughout Myanmar. The FGDs took place in this tense atmosphere and were therefore affected by it. Some individuals contacted to engage in the FGDs – particularly in Bago – refused to participate because they feared reprisal and/or did not want to endanger their ongoing citizenship applications. Whilst our facilitators adopted various strategies to build trust and rapport with participants, it is likely that the latter may not have shared all details about their experiences. This sometimes led to a lack of detail in some accounts of their experiences of acquiring documentation.

Despite our attempt to include a large number of participants with diverse backgrounds, we cannot claim that the results obtained can be generalized to represent all religious minorities in the whole Union. Similar and additional FGDs would have to be conducted throughout Myanmar in order to broaden and deepen our findings.

Additionally, the semi-structured interviews only targeted faith leaders, MoLIP officials and Myanmar lawyers. The research would have benefitted from interviewing a wider range of key informants, notably from the health and education sectors.

Pathein and Mawlamyine

Every effort was made to ensure that the FGDs included a diverse range of individuals. However, since participants were invited through community and religious leaders based on pre-existing relationships and connections through those contacts (based on contacts in each location), certain minority groups (such as those practising Islam) may have been over-represented. As with all social research of this nature, the data gathered may be subject to the bias either of the interviewers or respondents.

Some potential participants were concerned about their safety and thus did not attend, such as individuals from a village named Kaw Kani in Mawlamyine, most of whom did not hold any civil documentation. SMILE and Justice Base did not turn away participants who attended even if they did not fit into the category scheduled for that day; thus, for example, some participants on 'young people' days were older than twenty-four.

In some cases, responses by participants were incomplete or lacked specifics. Some participants repeated exactly what other participants had said, and it is unclear whether they had had the same experience, were confused or afraid to speak honestly. At times, participants relayed experiences without saying whether it had happened directly to them, a member of their community or whether it was based on knowledge learned from others through stories or rumours.

The questions used in the interviews also gave rise to some ambiguity. Some questions were compound questions (e.g. 'Were you able to self-identify your ethnic group or was this allocated to you?'), and at times participants gave 'yes' or 'no' responses, making it difficult to determine which part of the question they were referring to. In response to compound questions, the clearest answers again came from those participants who had strong opinions or direct experience with regard to imposed identity. Often those who had suffered more egregious challenges gave longer explanations of what had occurred, and these explanations may not be generalizable to all minorities.

While we trained note-takers and facilitators on the types of identity documents that exist in Myanmar, and asked participants to identify their documentation using a pre-established list, some participants used inconsistent terminology such as referring to a CSC and an NRC interchangeably. Participants also said that they held a 'pink card', which at times meant a CSC but in other cases meant a threefolded card or NRC for females. For the purpose of the analysis below, individuals who used the term 'pink' or '*naing*' without also saying 'NRC' or 'threefolded' were coded as holding a CSC. Similarly, participants and those interviewed individually used the terms 'identity card' or 'ID' without explaining exactly what card they were referring to. In such cases, facilitators and note-takers missed opportunities to clarify participants' answers.

Finally, local coordinators attempted to interview particular key individuals but were sometimes unable to do so. In Mawlamyine, for example, the local coordinator tried to interview an immigration officer but was eventually only able to interview one of the officer's assistants. In Pathein, the local coordinator wanted to interview brokers (intermediaries between immigration officials and the public), as they were frequently identified by participants as playing a significant role in the application process, but, when asked for contact information, participants responded that they did not know any brokers.

Access to civil documentation

Quantitative findings

During the 2016 study in Yangon, Mandalay and Bago, around one-third (36 per cent) of the participants were holders of civil documentation (i.e. a CSC), another third (33 per cent) did not have any form of documentation and 18 per cent did not give information on their documentation status or gave answers that we could not use.

Across these three research locations, the percentage of men and women who did not hold civil documentation was equal (i.e. 27 per cent), except in Bago, where 39 per cent of women and 25 per cent of men did not hold such documentation. Forty-nine per cent (in Bago, 61 per cent) of young people (participants aged between fourteen and thirty) said that they did not have any documentation.

During the 2017 study in Pathein and Mawlamyine, nearly half of the participants (49 per cent) stated that they held a CSC, the other 51 per cent being composed of the following: 4 per cent held an NCSC; 28 per cent, an NRC; 2 per cent, an FRC; 4 per cent were still in the process of applying; 2 per cent had unknown documentation; and 11 per cent had no documentation at all. Forty-three per cent of the young people in the study (i.e. those under twenty-five) did not have civil documentation or were waiting for their application to be processed. The four FRC holders were all male, Hindu and from Pathein. One of these participants said that his FRC had been taken away by an immigration officer and not returned. He received a slip of paper instead, which he now uses as his identification.

Qualitative findings

Across both the 2016 and 2017 studies, we can see that there are two main barriers to accessing civil documentation: limited knowledge on the part of the Myanmar population when it comes to the legal framework governing citizenship in Myanmar (including the criteria for acquiring, confirming and retaining citizenship pursuant to the 1982 Citizenship Law); and the actual process of applying for civil documentation. The 2016 study revealed that knowledge barriers are more prevalent amongst women and amongst young people from rural areas.

- 'I don't understand how to become a Myanmar citizen' (female, Yangon).
- 'Immigration officers oppress us if they think we are uneducated. Some uneducated people are really afraid to go to the Immigration Office' (female, Bago).

Another barrier described by participants is the often arbitrary, lengthy and complicated application process. Several participants expressed difficulties in obtaining the many documents required when applying for civil documentation. For example, a number of participants said that they had no civil documentation or were unable to renew their documentation at the ages of 18, 30 and 45 because they had lost their civil documentation or other form of legal identification.

Participants also highlighted that the arbitrary nature of decisions made about applications for documentation can further confuse applicants regarding the actual legal criteria and process for obtaining civil documentation. Another factor compounding this problem is that the public has no access to informal directives and procedures regarding the application process.

- '[The process] is time consuming, expensive and tiring' (female, Bago).
- 'When we go to the Immigration Office to apply for an ID card, they tell us that the school will do it for its pupils. When we go to the school, they say that the ward will do it. Finally, the ward says that we have to go to the INRD Office' (female, Mandalay).
- 'Although I submitted my grandparents' documents, showed my parents' pink cards, they rejected my application. I now have a National Registration Card. I refused to take it at first, but it is still better than nothing' (female, Mandalay).

A further barrier discussed by participants was that those applying for documentation are often required to pay 'tea money' or 'unofficial fees' (i.e. bribes). Participants reported that the ability to pay such bribes is frequently the determining factor as to whether someone can obtain documentation. Participants reported that it was also common for people to pay dealers (also known as brokers) who serve as intermediaries between immigration officials and the public when it comes to obtaining civil documentation. The use of brokers often expedites the process. The costs associated with using a broker or paying a bribe directly to MoLIP, and the success of using either or both, varied significantly amongst participants and depended on the applicant's existing documentation, his or her perceived ethnicity or religion and/or the position of the immigration officer. For example, a Muslim religious leader interviewed in Pathein stated that, if members of his community did not pay unofficial fees, they would not receive any documents. In his experience, the amount varies – from 30,000 to 100,000 MMK (22 to 73 USD).

However, the majority of participants highlighted that the most significant barrier to accessing civil documentation was ethnic and religious discrimination, with such discrimination often raising the barriers mentioned above. A young man from Pathein, who self-identified as Myanmar Muslim, applied for his CSC when he was eighteen and was forced to wait for three years. When he asked INRD officials why it was taking so long, they told him directly that it was due to his religion. He then agreed to change his religion to Buddhism and was then issued a card 'within fifteen minutes'.

- 'We found out that [the INRD Office] had thrown away our documents. They told us they couldn't do anything as there were no senior staff' (young person, Mandalay).
- 'In our district, there are twenty-four villages altogether. Every villager was given an ID card except people from two Muslim villages. They took pictures of these people but refused to give them ID cards.'
- 'Even though I had submitted all the documents required, officers told me I couldn't have an ID card because of my race' (young person, Bago).
- 'I lost my ID card and it was really difficult to apply for a new one. It took ages to check my family history. They asked me for 30,000 MMK. I went to the office very often in Chan Mya Thar Si Township. Officers told me they were not allowed by superiors to issue cards to Muslims' (male, Mandalay).
- 'I have already spent 300,000 MMK for my younger son and he still does not have an ID card. We have been trying to get one for four years. Even though we submit all the documents required, they refuse, saying that we are Muslims. For my second daughter, I have spent 200,000 MMK. They gave her a CSC,[6] but they wrote Indian as her "race". I have given up the idea of getting an ID card for my younger son because it is pointless even though we give them a lot of money.'
- 'As soon as they saw that we are Muslims, they suspended the procedure for my son's ID card – even though we had all the documents required. They asked for one lakh per person. I have four children and I cannot afford this amount for all of them.'[7]

Participants indicated that, when obtaining or renewing their documentation, immigration officials often did not allow individuals to list the ethnicity by which they self-identify. The findings indicated that this was more likely to be linked to religion than ethnicity, with Muslims most commonly reporting that they, or members of their community, were unable to list the ethnicity with which they identified. Participants who identified as practising Muslims described being designated ethnic identities such as 'Indian', 'Pakistani' or 'Bengali/Bangladeshi' by the authorities, whereas previously it had been possible to self-identify as 'Bamar' while simultaneously being a practising Muslim. Participants also explained that officials had often said that Muslims could not have 'Myanmar' as their civil identity.

- 'My race is Kayin. But on my NRC, it is written Kayin, Bengali, Indian and Islam' (young person, Bago).
- 'When I put Myanmar-Muslim, they changed it to "Bengali"' (female, Mawlamyine).
- 'They said if I am a Muslim, I could not put "Burma". I can only get an NRC if I put "Bengali" under Ethnicity/Nationality. They refused when I told them to change it. I was very upset, and I told them to put whatever they wanted under Ethnicity/Nationality' (male, Mawlamyine).
- 'I am Karen, my grandparents are Karen . . . they did not let me put "Karen". They only let me put "Bengali" if I am Muslim' (female, Mawlamyine).

As a consequence of such discriminatory practices against Muslims, some participants reported that they had engaged in self-censorship by writing a religious or ethnic identity that they thought MoLIP would be less likely to reject.

- 'I put my religion as Buddhist in my application even though I am Muslim' (young person, Bago).

Some Muslim participants explained that they were afraid to approach MoLIP to obtain their civil documentation as they had previously been verbally abused or ignored by MoLIP officials. They believed that they had been treated this way because they were Muslims. The majority of participants who complained of such discrimination did not know of the complaint procedures when it came to discrimination on the part of officials.

It was also common for participants to reveal their concerns about renewing their civil documentation. Because of their ethnicity and religion, they feared that renewing their documentation would result in a decline or loss of their status in Myanmar. For example, participants described fearing that, when applying to renew their documentation, they would be given a residency document instead of a new civil document or that their civil documentation would be confiscated, and they would not receive any documentation to replace it.

- '[When people] renewed [their] 10-year-old card, sometimes [they] got back white cards and sometimes [they did] not get back any card' (young person, Mawlamyine).

Participants also said that it had become common practice for MoLIP officials to label persons as 'mixed blood' if they were not considered to be members of only one of the recognized national ethnic groups. It was reported by participants that different procedures for processing 'mixed-blood' applications would then be followed, including separating out non-Buddhist children in school campaigns that issue CSCs to children who have turned ten.

Finally, some of the programmes designed to address citizenship challenges, such as having immigration officials enter communities and accelerate the application process for identity documents, have resulted in divisions between and among different ethnic and religious groups. For example, according to participants, immigration officials refused to process applications at schools, in wards/villages and at immigration offices for those perceived or labelled 'mixed-blood'. If applications from minority religious or ethnic groups were processed, then applicants were given TRCs or INVCs rather than the documentation to which they were entitled under the 1982 Citizenship Law. In another example, an immigration official refused to go to any locations where individuals of Tamil ethnicity or those who practised Christianity resided.

Civil documentation and the enjoyment of rights

Property rights

In the 2016 and 2017 studies, participants said that civil documentation is often required to purchase property or land. A woman in Bago explained that holding such documentation was necessary to complete Form 7 relating to property rights and conveyance of land. People without this documentation often use someone else's documentation or name to buy property. However, this can leave people vulnerable to exploitation. For example, one woman in Bago described a situation where an undocumented person had given money to a documented person to purchase a property; when the transaction fell through, the documented person did not return the money. Participants without civil documentation also reported difficulties in renting or leasing properties.

In the 2016 study, participants also said that not having civil documentation made it difficult to borrow money from the formal financial sector for the purpose of buying/leasing property. A number of participants reported difficulties in selling property if they did not have civil documentation, with one woman in Yangon saying that she could not sell her house because, since buying the property, she had seen her white card become invalidated.

Freedom of movement

One of the biggest challenges articulated by participants across both studies was travelling within Myanmar without intimidation or restrictions. Civil documentation or travel recommendation letters were described as necessary for travel, but even the possession of such documentation did not necessarily prevent intimidation or restrictions when travelling. For example, in the 2016 study, participants reported that religious minorities faced additional scrutiny by authorities when travelling, despite the fact that they held some form of civil documentation.

- 'We go for a trip; immigration officers check our ID card. Even if they don't check others' cards, they check ours. Even though we hold pink cards, they ask for money, saying that our cards are fake' (male, Bago).
- 'If "Bengali" is mentioned in the ID card, you cannot buy the bus ticket' (male, Yangon).

In the 2017 study, participants reported that such treatment was largely linked to religious identity as those who expressed difficulties held a combination of NRCs, CSCs and, in some cases, no card. For example, almost all participants who said that they had experienced travelling difficulties were Muslims, with the exception of two Hindu participants and one Christian. This aligns with participants' perceptions of why their movements are restricted, for most said it was either due to their appearance or religion.

Right to education

Lack of civil documentation was reported in both studies as particularly problematic when accessing tertiary education, which also limited the employment opportunities of those affected. Civil documentation is often required to enrol in university.

- 'I don't have a CSC card, so I cannot attend university. Even if we get a high mark, we can't enrol at an institute university' (female, Pathein).

In other cases, students without civil documentation were not permitted to graduate or receive their degree certificate, even if they had finished the relevant course of studies. One man in Yangon had studied medicine up until the final year but would not be awarded his degree certificate because he did not have civil documentation. Similarly, one female participant from Mawlamyine explained that she had attended university until the final year, but she could not obtain the degree certificate because she did not have civil documentation. Her family had lost the supporting documentation necessary, so that she could not apply for civil documentation.

Conclusion and recommendations

A large proportion of participants in both studies did not hold any civil documentation, which, according to the participants, resulted from various barriers, including religious and ethnic discrimination. Participants also revealed that civil documentation is often essential to enjoying fundamental human rights in Myanmar such as the right to own property, the right to an education and the right to move freely. These findings may reflect broader trends in Myanmar.

On the basis of our findings, we recommend that key stakeholders take a number of measures to address the risks of statelessness detailed here.

In order to *empower minority communities*, we need to formulate a better information policy. We therefore recommend holding information-sharing sessions and workshops with individuals in minority communities to impart knowledge of the 1982 Citizenship Law, including information on how to apply for identity documents and on the individuals and organizations that may be able to assist when it comes to obtaining identity documents, such as religious leaders and the Norwegian Refugee Council.

To facilitate inter- and intra-community engagement and solidarity among ethnic and religious minorities, we also recommend disseminating research findings amongst and between minority communities on the key barriers faced by minorities in obtaining civil documentation. To this end, we suggest that minority communities identify individuals who have dealt with immigration officials and/or been involved in the process of obtaining documentation for individuals in some manner. Such individuals should be given special training that provides them with information along the lines of what our findings imply and also regarding the scope and application of the 1982 Citizenship Law and its key procedures and good practices in legal empowerment generally. All relevant laws, directives, regulations, guidance and procedures should be made publicly available and disseminated amongst those populations affected.

Most desirable would be a *reform of citizenship law, policy and practice*. The 1982 Citizenship Law should be amended to reintroduce only one category of citizenship. Furthermore, citizenship should be given to all children born in the territory of Myanmar who would otherwise be stateless. Any reference to a person's ethnic or religious identity should be removed from identity documents. The application process for civil documentation needs to be simplified and streamlined. Special measures should be taken to improve procedures and remove blockages that prohibit the efficient processing of applications. This may include training officials in relevant areas and having such officials process applications at the community level, which includes minorities, to remove practical restrictions such as the costs incurred by travelling.

The Citizenship Law in Myanmar has become a mechanism of systematic religious and ethnic discrimination. Using this discriminatory law to deny citizenship rights amounts to a bureaucratic cleansing of minorities in Myanmar. Any serious process of democratization should immediately overturn the practice and its legal basis.

Notes

1 SMILE, December 2016, 'Assessing the Risks of Statelessness for Religious Minorities in Myanmar', undertaken with UNHCR funding and technical support. SMILE and Justice Base, December 2017, 'Access to Documentation and Risks of Statelessness', undertaken with Justice Base and UNHCR funding and technical support. Justice Base is a UK NGO which has supported lawyers and civil society in Myanmar since 2012.
2 UNHCR (December 2017), 'Figures at a Glance'. http://www.unhcr.org/figures-at-a-glance.html.
3 UNHCR (September 2019), 'Myanmar Fact Sheet'. https://reporting.unhcr.org/sites/default/files/UNHCR%20Myanmar%20Fact%20Sheet%20-%20September%202019.pdf.
4 Typically, a citizen receives their first civil document at the age of ten. This is facilitated by the child's primary school. However, in practice, minority populations are often required to apply directly at an office of the Ministry of Labour, Immigration and Population (MoLIP). Citizens are required to renew their cards at a MoLIP office at the age of 18, 30 and 45. However, in practice, if this is not written

expressly on the back of the card, there is no consequence for not renewing the card. This discrepancy allows the authorities to implement the law arbitrarily.

5 See 1983 Procedures Relating to Myanmar Citizenship Law, Form Associate 8(a) and Form Citizen 6(a) (see also the directions to Form Citizen 6, noting that the holder 'must produce this certificate upon request by an official for inspection'); 1983 Procedures Relating to Associate Citizenship, Form Associate 4(a) and 8(a) (see also the directions to Form Associate Citizen 4, noting that the holder 'must produce this certificate upon request by an official for inspection'); 1983 Procedures Relating to Naturalized Citizenship, Form Naturalized 6(a) and 8(a) (see also the directions to Form Naturalized Citizen 6, noting that the holder 'must produce this certificate upon request by an official for inspection').

6 Here, the respondent said 'CSC', but it is unclear whether it was perhaps a different type of identification such as an NRC, NCSC, ACSC, FRC or TSC.

7 'One lakh' is another term for 100,000 MMK, which is equivalent to about 73 USD.

13

Being a Mon: Buddhist–Muslim relations

Madlen Krueger

Being a Mon is determined by a person's perpetual struggle against losing their identity. The story of being a Mon is told as an everlasting struggle both against being assimilated by the Bamar and for being recognized as different from them.[1] The focus on being different from the Buddhist Bamar affects how Buddhist Mon narrate their dealings with the Muslim community in their region. Muslim–Buddhist relations in Mon State are defined by the narrative that the situation is handled differently and more successfully than in other regions. In this chapter, though, I will argue that the conflicts are in fact the same as in other regions in Myanmar and that the Muslim community is oppressed and excluded there, too. However, the conflict is narrated as being between the Muslim community and Buddhist Bamar rather than Buddhist Mon.

I will first give a critical-historical overview of the Buddhist Mon narrative and describe what Michael A. Aung-Thwin calls the 'Mon Paradigm', before providing an overview of the Muslim community in Mon State. This chapter is based on interviews with representatives of Muslim and Buddhist communities in Mon State during one of my research stays in 2019.[2]

Mon identity – the category of ethnicity

Ethnic Buddhist minorities like the Mon, Shan and Rakhine fear losing their language, culture and history. Like the majority Buddhist Bamar, the ethnic Buddhist minorities are concerned with their own ethnic historiography and with affirming their legitimacy through non-Burmese sources. This has been demonstrated by Patrick McCormick (2014) in his article on 'modern' historiography in Myanmar, where he argues that ethnic minorities look for external sources to have a history told independently of the Bamar language, culture and Buddhist practice and to be perceived as not merely imitating the Bamar. Preserving the linguistic heritage is one of the key factors underlining independence from Bamar culture. As guardians of religion and culture, Buddhist monks are the main contributors to establishing or retaining the cultural heritage, which they do by publishing and printing manuscripts on cultural, literary and historical themes (McCormick 2014: 307–9).

The concept of ethnicity is given quite an important place in Burmese life. But it is still a concept that the British imposed and as such is part of the British legacy. That does not mean, however, that the Burmese themselves had no conception of making differences.[3]

> Rather, the concept of 'ethnicity', with its boundaries and intellectual heritage in romantic nationalism, is a different ordering and way of making sense of difference from what went before. The concept of an 'ethnic group' has an exclusive, reified quality that earlier conceptions did not. … Following popular conceptions in current English usage, ethnicity often refers to a constructed identity based on shared markers, such as language and cultural and religious practices. (McCormick 2014: 317)

Viktor Lieberman points out that in the middle of the eighteenth century, during the reign of Alaungphaya (r. 1752–60), cultural factors of identity formation moved into the centre, alongside the usual political categorization and distinction between Mon and Bamar. He sees periods of upheaval and uncertainty as primarily responsible for this. The period around Alaungphaya's rule was marked by numerous revolts in Lower Burma against the expansion of the rule of the Kongbaung dynasty (1752–1885) that Alaungphaya founded. The link between cultural aspects, political loyalty and ethnicity were nevertheless fluid and differed from region to region. As an example, Lieberman compares the uprisings in the eighteenth century with those after 1947. The former aimed to increase regional influence and were more inclusive in nature, while ethnic affiliations in the provinces did not matter. In contrast, the latter were guided by the demand for recognition and autonomy for individual nation states and territories that clearly belonged to one ethnicity (Lieberman 1978: 480). Referring to the two rival empires of the fourteenth and fifteenth centuries, the Bamar Kingdom of Ava (Upper Burma) and the Mon kingdom of Pegu (Lower Burma), Lieberman concludes,

> The wars between Ava and Pegu, therefore, were not 'racial' or 'national' struggles *per se*, but regional and dynastic conflicts in which cultural traits could

be made to serve as a public badge, a visible emblem, of political loyalty. To some extent, 'Mon' was a role filled by people loyal to Pegu, while 'Burman' was the role accepted by people loyal to Ava. (Ibid. 458)

The construction of ethnicity as something that excludes other identities makes the idea of multiple or shifting identities impossible. The national discourse insists on the uniqueness of ethnicity, which collides with the recognition that people can have multiple alliances, for example, religious, linguistic and cultural. Mon nationalists construct Mon ethnicity as bounded and foreclosing, as representing one nation with a shared history (McCormick 2014: 318–20). This contradicts reality and everyday practice, since the Mon also have inter-religious and interethnic relationships. Inalterability and homogeneity are an intellectual construction that creates a narrative of the ethnic Mon as being distinct from the Bamar. The narrative is part of a centuries-long struggle for supremacy between the two ethnic groups, a struggle that the Bamar were finally able to decide for themselves but only due to their aggressive Burmanization policy. The relationship between the Mon and Bamar can be depicted as ambivalent. On the one hand, they are opponents in the nationalist discourse, in which unique characteristics and demarcations prevail. On the other, the Mon have a unique position in modern Burmese historiography, since they are the people who brought Buddhism to Myanmar and who thus represent the cultural heritage of the Bamar. McCormick speaks of an 'enshrining of the Mons in the Burmese national historical narrative as religious and cultural donors' (ibid.: 311–12). He draws attention to the fact that, with an ethnic lens, history is narrated as being based on ethnic conflicts. In the context of multiple ethnic minorities and their own histories, the historical framework is limited and does not accept different or contradictory narratives (ibid.: 322–4).

Mon nationalism and the depiction of Mon history

The following brief historical account of Mon history is taken from the article 'The Mon History', published by the Mon Unity League (MUL), which was founded in 1996 to present a united Mon front. It is a synopsis from the book *Discovery of Rehmonnya* that was published later in 2007 (MUL 2004). It covers the classical period in the history of the Mon people, from the early first millennium until 1757, when the last Mon ruler of Pegu (Bago) was defeated by the warrior King Alaungphaya, forcing many Mon into exile in the Thai border region. As Ashley South points out, the Mon civilization was among the most influential in precolonial Southeast Asia. They are considered transmitters of Theravāda Buddhism and Indian political culture. In hindsight, Mon nationalists have interpreted this classical period as a golden age (South 2010: 150–2).

The historical milestones presented in 'The Mon History' are partly based on the *Glass Palace Chronicle of the Kings of Burma*,[4] and begin with the Mon kingdom around the fourth century BCE until the eleventh century CE and its capital Thaton, which is believed to have been the centre of Theravāda Buddhism in Southeast Asia at the time. Bamar and Mon chronicles both claim that this kingdom is Suvaṇṇabhūmi (Pāli) – The Golden Land – as mentioned in the Mahāvaṃsa. This ties the Mon strongly to the kingdom of Ashoka, as it is believed that, according to the Mahāvaṃsa, Ashoka sent missionaries to a so-called Suvaṇṇabhūmi.[5] Thus, the high civilization of the Mon existed long before that of the Bamar, which began in the ninth century with the rise of Bagan and is now considered the epitome of Buddhist culture in Myanmar. The rise of Bagan led to the downfall of the Thaton Kingdom in 1057. The MUL refers to the rise of the first Bamar empire as a unity created by force. It was only through the influence of the Mon that Bagan could become a cultural centre. Therefore, the Mon are the true origin of Buddhist culture in Myanmar. After the fall of Thaton, the Mon brought forth more 'golden ages of Mon culture'. One such golden age began with the transfer of the capital of the independent Mon kingdom to Pegu and lasted from 1365 to 1533. The last began in 1740 with the fall of the second Bamar empire and with the conquest of the Bamar capital Ava (Inwa) in 1752, when the Mon ruled over almost the whole of Myanmar. But, in 1757, King Alaungphaya, the founder of the Kongbaung Dynasty that ushered in the third Bamar empire, drove the Mon out of Upper Burma. Since then, as the MUL puts it, the Mon have been a people without a country, the MUL describing this process as ethnic cleansing (MUL 2004).

After the Bamar empires, the British colonized Lower Burma in 1824. Both the Bamar and the British are described as 'colonizers'. 'Until and except the periods when they were colonized by the two alien nations, the Burman and British, the Mon had exercised full rights of self-determination for many centuries' (ibid.).

The key historical data foregrounded here underpin the image of the Mon as culturally superior to the Bamar and as being constantly in dispute with oppressive Bamar empires over the issue of sovereignty. The significant points in Mon history depict the Mon kingdoms as golden ages, wise rule, a coexistence of happy and prosperous people with peaceful ties to neighbouring countries. Not only are the Mon presented as culturally superior to the Bamar; they are also presented as a people who have always lived together harmoniously as one ethnic group.

However, highlighting the cultural and political domination of the Mon also makes clear their demand for recognition as an ethnic group in its own right and thus their right to their own Mon State. While the Mon's precolonial history is characterized by regional battles between different empires (Upper Burma versus Lower Burma), conflict in the postcolonial period is marked by the struggle against assimilation into Bamar culture. Numerous examples in Burma's cultural history confirm the Mon's fear of assimilation. For example, today's icon of Burmese Buddhist culture, the Shwedagon Pagoda in Yangon, was built by a Mon ruler. Yet, it has been a symbol of the Bamar since the eighteenth century and is therefore deemed lost to Mon culture.

The post-independence history of the Mon is marked by this struggle for their own identity, since the first post-independence prime minister, U Nu (1948), did not recognize the Mon as a distinct ethnic group. Ashley South calls this the 'obliteration of the Talaing' (synonymous with Mon), which continued with General Ne Win. In 1962, Ne Win denied that there was a need for a state-approved, separate Mon culture, claiming that the Mon tradition had been absorbed into the Burmese national culture and that there was therefore no reason to acknowledge an autonomous Mon identity. As South has shown, political reasons drove the military to reject a separate Mon identity, since such an identity would support demands for self-government (South 2003: 31-2). Mon nationalists took up arms shortly after independence and in 1958 founded the Mon National Liberation Army (MNLA), the armed wing of the New Mon State Party (NMSP). By 1995, the NMSP had been forced to agree a ceasefire with Yangon. The party had no other choice because it no longer had the backing of the Thai military. The MNLA gave up its arms under the 1995 agreement (South 2003: 3-4, 2010: 161).

With the 1974 constitution, the Burma Socialist Programme Party (BSPP) (1962-88) officially recognized Mon and Rakhine States with an official Mon State Day on 19 March. But, unlike the Mon National Day held in February, this official holiday is not popular among the Mon. The former has symbolized Mon independence since 1947 and celebrates the mythical foundation of Pegu. Introduced as an expression of ethnic nationalist sentiments during the final days of colonial rule, it now functions as a display of strength and unity and as a symbol of linguistic and cultural revival, celebrating the inception of the Mon kingdom and commemorating the fall of the kingdom in 1757 (South 2003: 36-9).

Historical narratives – the 'Mon Paradigm'

In his book *The Mist of Rāmañña: The Legend That Was Lower Burma*, Michael A. Aung-Thwin analyses the historiographical background of what he calls the 'Mon Paradigm', which comprises two main narratives of Mon supremacy. First, the Mon people introduced Theravāda Buddhist culture. Second, they civilized the Burmese-speaking people of the hinterlands in former Upper Burma by introducing to the kingdom of Bagan writing, architecture, the arts and the social structures of kingship. Aung-Thwin shows how these narratives involve two different historical stages and were finally codified as an important ideology in the historiography of early Burma: (1) As the bringer of Theravāda Buddhist culture, there was a Mon kingdom in Lower Burma prior to Bagan. (2) The civilization of Upper Burma was initiated with the conquest of Thaton, the capital of the Mon kingdom Rāmañña or Rāmaññadesa, the land of the Mon, in 1057 by the Bamar King Anawrahta (Aung-Thwin 2005: 1–12).[6]

As Aung-Thwin shows, the foundation of the ideology of the Mon story is to be found in the fifteenth century, when the Mon King Dhammazedi (r. 1472–92) sought to legitimize the dominance of the Mon over the Bamar by creating a narrative of Mon supremacy. The best way for a Buddhist ruler to achieve legitimacy is to establish a connection to the Indian Emperor Ashoka (3rd century BCE). Dhammazedi linked Lower Burma with the classical age of Ashokan India through identifying Lower Burma – Rāmaññadesa – as Suvaṇṇabhūmi. Drawing on the event of the Third Buddhist Council in the third century BCE, when two arahants (Pāli), Uttara and Sona, were sent to Suvaṇṇabhūmi, Dhammazedi was able to claim that the Mon were the earliest recipients of Buddhist orthodoxy in Southeast Asia, a Buddhist orthodoxy purified by the continuous mission of and connection to Sri Lanka (ibid.: 67–78, 113–17).

U Kala, a Burmese historian, wrote the first national chronicle of Burma's monarchy, *The Great Chronicle*, in the early eighteenth century, where he describes in detail Anawrahta's conquest of Thaton. In this story, the Burmese King Anawrahta (r. 1044–77) converted to the orthodox version of Theravāda, and, in order to promote this religion, he wanted to obtain its canonical texts, which were said to be in Thaton. The king of Thaton was not interested in sending the texts, which led Anawrahta to conquer Thaton. He took the entire population with him to Upper Burma, which benefited from the expertise of craftsmen and clergy from Lower Burma. Despite being a Bamar, U Kala promoted Dhammazedi's claims of Mon cultural primacy and thereby established the narrative of a Mon kingdom and its cultural supremacy (ibid.: 136–9). According to Aung-Thwin, U Kala reproduced the narrative because it allowed U Kala to link Anawrahta to the Buddhist emperor Ashoka and draw on the Buddhist principle of a 'righteous victory' – *dhammavijaya* – which ends the reign of rulers who have become 'heretic' kings through the victory of a righteous Buddhist king.[7] After Dhammazedi and U Kala, the British reinforced the narrative. Dhammazedi created and invented the narrative to legitimize his rule and that of the Mon. By promoting the narrative, U Kala was responsible for making it popular and for depicting a Burmese king as a rightful Buddhist king. The British endorsed the narrative, and colonial scholars actually merged the two narratives of the cultural supremacy of Lower Burma and the Mon's civilization of Upper Burma.

According to Aung-Thwin, this narrative served the British in several ways. First, by depicting the Mon people as the carriers of the cultural heritage, it reduced the claim of historical pre-eminence made by the Bamar. Second, by comparing the glorious past of the Mon with its current state, it showed the oppressive nature of Bamar rule with regard to the Mon and ethnic minorities in general. Yet, the ulterior motive was to weaken the Bamar ethnic majority (ibid.: 282–94). The British Government of India was interested, especially during the First Anglo-Burmese War (1824–6), in establishing a counterforce to the Burmese monarchy by depicting an ancient Mon kingdom. In sum, according to Aung-Thwin, what was responsible for the 'Mon Paradigm' under the British was the view of ethnicity as a precise entity in an age of ethnic nationalism, the focus of scholars on antiquity, their interest in preserving what they considered to be an ancient culture and the political reasoning and interests of the colonial administration (ibid. 297–8).

It should not be forgotten that the narrative of the Mon's cultural supremacy has always been accompanied by a story of its decline, deprivation and ongoing struggle for survival. The story of the conquest of Thaton is the beginning of the oppression of the Mon people by the Bamar. The fall of Thaton serves as a symbol of the tragedy and highlights the suffering of the Mon people. According to Aung-Thwin, the British are responsible for the motif of the victimized Mon people. He also calls it a politico-intellectual scheme that influenced how Mon intellectuals of the twentieth century viewed the past (ibid.: 261–80).

As should have become clear, one crucial aspect of Mon identity is its distinction from the Buddhist Bamar. The perennial struggle for identity and recognition runs through contemporary history. A second important aspect of Mon identity is preserving its language, with Mon nationalist movements quickly establishing schools to teach the Mon language. (Min Zin and Sangkhlaburi 2003). Under the leadership of Ashin Thilasara, a well-known Dhamma lecturer, and members of Ramonnya Dhammasariya Mon Sangha Association, Rāmaññaraṭṭha Buddhist University was founded in Mawlamyine in May 2012. One of my interview partners there said that the decision to found the University was motivated by the fact that government schools excluded the Mon language, leading to its gradual decline over the years. Monks did not have the opportunity to learn their own traditional language or to take their exams in the language. Lay people and monks can both study at the University, which places special emphasis on the subjects Mon History, Mon Literature and Mon Buddhism. Teaching is in English or Mon only, and the University does not accept those who cannot speak English or Mon, meaning that other ethnic groups cannot enter the University.[8]

The Muslim community in Mon State – Mawlamyine

According to the 2014 census, 92.6 per cent of those living in Mon State are Buddhists, 5.8 per cent are Muslims and 0.5 per cent are Christians. As a result, Mon State has the second largest population of Muslims after Rakhine State (35.1 per cent) and before Yangon (4.7 per cent) (Census Atlas 2014: 26–7). Mawlamyine, the capital of Mon State, is known for its strong nationalism and for being the birthplace and stronghold of the Buddhist nationalist 969 movement, which in 2013 gave rise to the Buddhist Association for the Protection of Race and Religion (MaBaTha).[9] The movement is very active in the area and celebrated the passing of the four 'Race and Religion Protection Laws' in 2015. However, in my interviews, civil society leaders repeatedly pointed out that, despite the provocative behaviour of MaBaTha monks, communal leaders had been able to maintain harmony. For example, when MaBaTha members threw stones at mosques, riots could be prevented because mediators from interfaith groups rapidly appeared at the scene to defuse the situation.[10]

With a population of three hundred thousand, Mawlamyine has an ethnically and religiously mixed population. Buddhist Bamar and the ethnic Mon majority still live alongside a large population of Muslims and Hindus around the old colonial town centre at the port. While Mon are more numerous in Mawlamyine district, especially in the lower townships, Indian and Chinese communities are found all over the state but particularly in the city of Mawlamyine itself.[11]

According to J. A. Berlie, the history of the Muslim community in Mawlamyine began during colonial times. Besides Yangon and Mandalay, Mawlamyine is famous for the quality of its *hāfiz* education – knowledge of texts. Berlie ascribes this to the fact that during the colonial era the city was the capital for twenty-six years, when it attracted Indian Muslims, including many scholars. There are thirty-three mosques still open today, which were built at the end of the nineteenth and beginning of the twentieth century (Berlie 2008: 66–7). The historical background of Muslims in Mon State is thus linked to the history of Indian Muslims in Myanmar.

In his essay on the perception of Indian Muslims in Myanmar, Renaud Egreteau shows that Islamophobia has its origins in anti-colonial Indophobia. During the colonial period, the immigration of Indian communities supported by the British and Indian communities always shaped the area, including Mawlamyine. Indian migration first began in 1826 in the coastal areas of Arakan and Tenasserim. Indian immigrants were religiously and ethnically diverse and included Sunni Bengalis, Sikh Punjabis and Christian Telugu speakers, who usually formed their own religious communities within Burma.

Alongside Chinese and European communities, Indian communities controlled trade and banking and dominated the military ranks and other social sectors such as education, health and administration. The migrants were already familiar with the British system and were therefore favoured. Before the Japanese invasion in 1942, there were 1.1 million Indians living in the country (Census 1931; approx. 1.017 million of 14.7 million). The end of the nineteenth century saw the growth of xenophobia, which was directed mainly against Europeans, Chinese and Indians and was linked to nationalist tendencies. This xenophobic nationalism was increasingly directed against Indian communities, as they were more visible. In contrast, Chinese communities had assimilated quickly (Egreteau 2011: 35–7). As Egreteau writes,

> The Burman-dominated elite despised the lack of inclination (or even willingness) for assimilation in to the Burmese Buddhist society that the Hindu or Muslim Indian migrants had shown. Many indeed had brought to Burma their faith, cultural organisations, societal stratification, matrimonial customs and intra-cast marriage obligations, and even families. This was contrary to the Chinese, for example, who mostly took wives within the Burmese society and thus became integrated to a far greater extent. (Ibid.: 36–7)

The first anti-Indian riots began in the first half of the twentieth century. The 1920s and 1930s saw a series of anti-Indian riots led by a Burmese mob in

Yangon. The May-June clashes of 1930 took place in the wake of the rural-based Saya San rebellion (1930–1), which was defeated by British forces. Explicitly calling for action against foreigners, this rebellion resulted in outrages against Indians. From then on, the struggle for independence was accompanied by a greater willingness to use violence. As early as 1938, there were increasingly anti-Muslim undertones alongside the strong anti-Indian and anti-Western resentment of Burmese leaders. Egreteau calls this the colonial trauma, and it has influenced how Indian and Chinese communities have been perceived ever since (ibid.: 39–41).

The violence in the 1920s and 1930s was followed by the first wave of emigration during the Japanese invasion. While U Nu was pro-Buddhist in his policies but neutral towards other religious communities, Ne Win (1962–88) exacerbated the tensions in the 1960s through his restrictions on citizenship and his open xenophobia and devaluation of Indian communities. In Egreteau's words,

> Expressions of 'indophobia' [sic] range from the spread of popular anti-Indian racist stereotypes within a society, prejudiced beliefs and derogatory terms insulting the Indian people targeted, to daily social segregation, racial state-sponsored policies, riots and pogroms, or even ethno-religious cleansing. (Ibid.: 34)

Until 1988, Ne Win used an open anti-Indian rhetoric, which was also explicitly directed against India. It was not until the mid-1990s that the anti-kala rhetoric disappeared and was replaced by an openly anti-Muslim rhetoric (ibid.: 49–50).

Thus, Indian communities have since the 1940s either migrated due to the political situation, displacement and stigmatization, or assimilated. Burmese Indian communities that are still recognizable as such and have not assimilated are still stigmatized today. This is especially true of the Muslim community, as anti-Muslim undertones in particular have persisted alongside anti-Indian resentment, which have turned into outright Islamophobia. Egreteau speaks of a 'dormant Islamophobia' during colonial times, which, however, has now become open. He also speaks of a trauma caused by the British colonial period that has shaped views of India and, subsequently, of Indian communities in Burma.

> Nevertheless, it appears that the hostile Burmese perceptions of the *'Kalas'* developed through old colonial-rooted resentments tend now to be more and more articulated around anti-Muslim sentiments, as most of the Burmese Muslims – including the Rohingya minority – happened to share the same Indian origins. (Ibid.: 52)

Beyond Yangon, Burmese Indians are still visible communities with large settlements in port cities like Mawlamyine and Sittwe. As in other regions and places in Myanmar, Mawlamyine, the capital of Mon State, also reflects the diversity of Muslim communities. Here, the Indian Muslim communities dominate the city. However, there are also the *Pati*, who refer to themselves as Burmese Muslims, both to distinguish themselves from the Indian Muslims and to underline their claim to have lived in Myanmar for generations (Berlie 2008: 6–12).[12]

While the Yangon region is depicted as ridden with violence, due to its separated communities in wards and its history of conflict, Mawlamyine is depicted as a tolerant region with a good network of social cohesion. More than five hundred to six hundred civil society groups were mentioned in my interviews with civil society leaders and representatives of civil society organizations. These groups are well connected with each other and contribute much to peaceful coexistence. They do not want tensions between Buddhists and Muslims like in Mandalay in 2016, since such tensions would encourage the government to impose travel restrictions and would weaken the economy. As soon as religious and civil society leaders or government representatives see the potential for conflict between the different communities, they intervene and mediate, thereby resolving conflicts from the very beginning. However, my interview partners emphasized that control within neighbourhoods is better in religiously and ethnically diverse wards, while a network of security control is active in exclusively Muslim wards, as more conflicts are expected to emanate from these regions. This statement seems to be based on the assumption, and presumably prejudice, that possible conflicts emanate from the Muslim community and that Muslims tend to be radical. The vaunted peaceful coexistence, however, comes at the expense of Muslim communities, which face constant surveillance from the neighbourhood or civil society.[13]

In my interviews, Buddhist Mon, both monks and lay people, emphasized that there are no ethnic or religious conflicts in Mawlamyine. Interfaith groups and civil society seem to have built up a well-functioning network that can act quickly. I was also told that the clashes which do occur are either between different Muslim groups or, if there are any between Muslims and Buddhists, they are caused either by Muslims or by Bamar Buddhists but not by the Mon.

As in other parts of Myanmar, there is anti-Muslim resentment and institutionalized discrimination against the Muslim community in Mon State, making the discrimination and injustice faced by the Muslim community in Mawlamyine a major theme during my interviews. Muslim life and practice are hindered, and there is a sense of constant scrutiny, hostility and powerlessness within Muslim communities. Leases for land with mosques are not renewed, or mosques that were built during the colonial period are not listed on official registers and thus declared illegal and demolished. Closed mosques cannot be reopened, nor can old mosques be renovated or new mosques built. Any religious event, no matter how small, has to be reported to the authorities months in advance. Friday prayers have to be registered and approved every week. Visible displays of Muslim identity are increasingly sanctioned, with women wearing the hijab being prohibited from entering the grounds of state schools. Muslim leaders say that the pressure exerted by the authorities on the Muslim community has increased since 2011 and that there has been an increased feeling among the Muslim community of fear and helplessness with regard to decisions made by state institutions. Moreover, the Muslim community in Mawlamyine is also confronted with the problem of being unable to obtain an ID card and citizenship. As a recorded Muslim, a person is not accepted as belonging to any indigenous ethnic group and can therefore only register as Bengali, Pakistani or Indian, which in turn means that the person is not recognized as a citizen, even if her parents are Mon. Being officially counted as a Muslim Mon is therefore institutionally impossible.

Muslim leaders point out that the discrimination and marginalization to which their community is subjected is an institutional problem driven by the state, and one that is increasingly affecting and hampering neighbourhood coexistence. Until the beginning of the Thein Sein government (2011–16), interaction among people in Mawlamyine was described as peaceful and harmonious, with the different religious communities still participating in each other's festivals. Nowadays, however, the Muslim community is increasingly seen as a threat to peaceful coexistence between the different communities. The Muslim community is portrayed as foreign and incompatible with the local cultures and customs. As a result, Muslims are increasingly ostracized in Mawlamyine, too.[14]

The different communities in Mawlamyine are well informed about the open conflicts in other regions, which makes the Muslim community feel tremendous pressure to avoid any conflicts. As Annika Pohl Harrisson (2018: 81) states, an 'absence of (visible) violence does not mean that there is no structural violence'. She also argues that Muslims in Mawlamyine have developed subjugation as a strategy to prevent conflict. Coexistence, peacefulness and harmoniousness are only on the surface, and Mon State is a region where violence has not erupted yet (ibid.: 69).

Conclusion

As the entanglements of religion and ethnicity have resulted in the notion that a Bamar is exclusively Buddhist, it is impossible for a Muslim to be a Bamar. Similarly, being a Mon implicitly means being Buddhist. The ethnic category of being a Mon is strongly influenced by the notion of not being a Bamar. Therefore, being a Mon is negotiated in distinction to being a Bamar. This distinction influences how Muslims and Buddhists interact in Mawlamyine. Thus, conflicts between Buddhists and Muslims in Mon State are described as conflicts between Bamar and Muslims. MaBaTha is perceived as a Bamar organization that has its roots in Mon State but lacks the support of the Mon people. People tend to distance themselves from MaBaTha and try to avoid any conflicts. This, however, does not imply tolerant and harmonious interaction between Buddhists and Muslims in Mon State. The same discrimination against Muslims takes place as in other regions regarding the obstruction of religious practice and citizenship issues. Muslims in Mon State are connected and have developed strategies to avoid conflicts. They accept discrimination and engage in intrafaith discussion about ways to integrate all Muslim communities in Mawlamyine. This intrafaith dialogue is still in its early stages but is in a more advanced state in Mawlamyine than in other regions in Myanmar.

Notes

1 I use the term 'Bamar' for the ethnic group and 'Burmese' for the people living in Burma/Myanmar.
2 I conducted fieldwork in Myanmar in 2016–19. This chapter draws especially on fieldwork conducted in Mawlamyine in March 2019, which included expert interviews, key informant interviews and informal discussions with locals.
3 A number of studies have problematized the concept of ethnicity in the context of Myanmar. See, for example, Thant Myint-U (2001); Gravers (2005); Gravers (2007); Charney (2009); and Ferguson (2015).
4 Especially on the journey of King Anawrahta to Thaton (Tin and Luce 1923).
5 The Mahāvaṃsa is the Great Chronicle of Sri Lanka and addresses the arrival and spread of Buddhism in Sri Lanka and the chronology and actions of Buddhist kings. See Geiger (2006: 82–7).
6 Aung-Thwin scrutinizes these claims by analysing historiographical sources and basically rejects them as false. He argues that the 'Mon Paradigm' was part of the British divide-and-rule policy that supported minorities, oppressed majorities by

disparaging their cultural achievements and thereby divided people along ethnic lines. Therefore, the British helped create a narrative of the historical and cultural dominance in precolonial times in Burma. Furthermore, he argues that Bagan was the predominant culture and that it was only after it began to decline in the late twelfth century that Lower Burma gained in importance. For Aung-Thwin, not even a polity or state structure existed in Lower Burma prior to Bagan (Aung-Thwin 2005: 8–12).

7 For an analysis of Anawrahta's story in the light of an invented tradition, see Aung-Thwin (2005: 104–53).
8 Interview at Rāmaññaraṭṭha Buddhist University on 2 March 2019 with a Mon Buddhist monk who teaches Mon language and belongs to the unofficial Rāmañña nikāya. That means the nikāya (a section of the Buddhist monastic order) is not one of the nine nikāya stated in the State LORC Law No. 20/90 of 31 October 1990. The majority of monks in Mon State belong to the Rāmañña nikāya.
9 For an extensive discussion of MaBaTha and the consequences of its anti-Muslim propaganda, see, for example, Walton and Hayward (2014); Walton (2017); and Holt (2019).
10 The interviews were conducted on 1 April 2019 with three representatives of a civil society group. All three identify themselves as Mon. The group is mainly active in interfaith dialogue, organizes peace events and has numerous youth programmes. During the time of my interview, they were organizing an event to bring communities together and distribute food over the Buddhist New Year. However, the group were the only ones who were openly critical of MaBaTha.
11 Mon are a minority in the Thaton area of Mon State, where Kayin and Bamar and Pa-O form the majorities (Phyo Thiho Cho 2015).
12 For a detailed analysis of the diversity of the Muslim community, see Chapter 11 in this volume. For a critical analysis see Khni Maung Yin (2005).
13 Interviews with civil society leaders and Muslim leaders on 1 April 2019.
14 Interview with three Muslim leaders on 2 April 2020. All had reservations about meeting for an interview, and there were long negotiations over where to meet, with a hotel seeming too suspicious and a private house being ruled out on account of the neighbours.

References

Aung-Thwin, Michael A. (2005), *The Mists of Ramanna: The Legend That Was Lower Burma*, Honolulu: University of Hawai'i Press.

Berlie, J. A. (2008), *The Burmanization of Myanmar's Muslims*, Bangkok: White Lotus Press.

Charney, Michael W. (2009), *A History of Modern Burma*, Cambridge: Cambridge University Press.

Egreteau, Renaud (2011), 'Burmese Indians in Contemporary Burma: Heritage, Influence, and Perceptions since 1988', *Asian Ethnicity*, 12 (1): 33–54.

Ferguson, Jane M. (2015), 'Who's Counting? Ethnicity, Belonging, and the National Census in Burma/Myanmar', *Bijdragen Tot De Taal-, Land- En Volkenkunde*, 171: 1–28.

Geiger, Wilhelm ([1912] 2006), *The Mahāvaṃsa or the Great Chronicle of Ceylon*, New Delhi: Asian Educational Services.

Gravers, Mikael (2005), *Nationalism as Political Paranoia in Burma: An Essay on Historical Practice of Power*, rev. and exp. 2nd edn, London: Taylor & Francis e-Library.

Gravers, Mikael (2007), 'Introduction: Ethnicity against the State – State against Ethnic Diversity?', in *Exploring Ethnic Diversity in Burma*, ed. Mikael Gravers, 1–33, Copenhagen: NIAS Press.

Holt, John Clifford (2019), *Myanmar's Buddhist-Muslim Crisis: Rohingya, Arakanese, and Burmese Narratives of Siege and Fear*, Honolulu: Hawa'i Press.

Khin Maung Yin (2005), 'Salience of Ethnicity among Burman Muslims: A Study in Identity Formation', *Intellectual Discourse*, 13 (2), 161–79.

Lieberman, Victor B. (1978), 'Ethnic Politics in Eighteenth-Century Burma', *Modern Asian Studies*, 12 (3): 455–82.

McCormick, Patrick (2014), 'Writing a Singular Past: Mon History and "Modern" Historiography in Burma', *SOJOURN: Journal of Social Issues in Southeast Asia*, 29 (2): 300–33.

Min, Zin and Sangkhlaburi (2003), 'Mon Culture: Dying or Reviving?', *The Irrawaddy Magazine*, 11 (8). https://www2.irrawaddy.com/article.php?art_id=3124 (accessed: 20 December 2020).

Mon Unity League (MUL) (1 April 2004), 'The Mon History – an Article Collected from the Book "Discovery of Rehmonnya"'. http://monnews.org/mon-people/ (accessed: 20 December 2020).

Phyo Thiha Cho (04 November 2015), 'As Polls Near, Attacks in Mon State Capital Raise Fears of Communal Violence'. https://www.mizzima.com/news-election-2015-election-features/polls-near-attacks-mon-state-capital-raise-fears-communal (accessed: 20 December 2020).

Pohl Harrisson, Annika (2018), 'Everyday Justice for Muslims in Mawlamyine: Subjugation and Skilful Navigation', *Independent Journal of Burmese Scholarship*, special issue on everyday justice, 1 (2): 57–85.

South, Ashley (2003), *Mon Nationalism and Civil War in Burma: The Golden Sheldrake*, London: RoutledgeCurzon.

South, Ashley (2010), 'Ceasefires and Civil Society: The Case of the Mon', in *Exploring Ethnic Diversity in Burma*, ed. Mikael Gravers, 149–77, Copenhagen: NIAS Press.

Thant Myint-U (2001), *The Making of Modern Burma*, Cambridge: Cambridge University Press.

Tin, Pe Maung, and G. H. Luce (1923), *The Glass Palace Chronicle of the Kings of Myanmar*, London: Oxford University Press.

UNFPA (2015), *Census Atlas Myanmar: The 2014 Myanmar Population and Housing Census*, Department of Population, Ministry of Labour, Immigration and Population.

Walton, Matthew J., and Susan Hayward (2014), *Contesting Buddhist Narratives: Democratization, Nationalism, and Communal Violence in Myanmar*, Honolulu: East-West Center.

Walton, Matthew J. (2017), *Buddhism, Politics and Political Thought in Myanmar*, Cambridge: Cambridge University Press.

Postscripts

14

Tatmadaw's coup in 2021: The return of totalitarian rule?

Mikael Gravers

Most states possess an army – in Myanmar, the military believe they possesses the state. The Military Defence Services – Tatmadaw – believe that they are the only rightful organization to rule Myanmar. This perception derives from the first coup in 1962, ostensibly aimed at preventing Shan and Kachin leaving the Union of Burma and fighting ethnic armed organizations. Since then, Tatmadaw has claimed that it not only defends the nation's sovereignty but also prevents the disintegration of Myanmar. Their nationalist slogans are still visible in the 'Basic Principles' of the 2008 constitution: 'non-disintegration of the Union', 'non-disintegration of national solidarity' and 'perpetuation of sovereignty'. It emphasizes 'flourishing of a genuine, disciplined multiparty democratic system; enhancing the eternal principles of Justice, Liberty and Equality in the Union and; enabling the Defence Services to be able to participate in the National political leadership role of the State'. The last words explain the idea purported by Tatmadaw that it has a legitimate right to play a dominant role in the political leadership.

Thus, behind the façade of parliamentary elections is the premise that Tatmadaw can declare a state of emergency when these 'principles' are endangered. That is what happened on 1 February 2021.[1] The following is a brief preliminary analysis of why Tatmadaw acted and what their strategy is, as of March 2021.

Min Aung Hlaing, senior general and chief in command of Tatmadaw, made it clear in January that he might stage a coup. Few believed that the threat would materialize. However, before the threat, he said that it might be necessary to change the law and even the constitution. Why? After the general election in 2020, Tatmadaw had discovered two 'flaws' in their 'disciplined democracy'. First, the Tatmadaw chief complained that electoral rolls contained spurious names. Later the claim rose to ten million false names. He accused the Union Election Commission (UEC) of mismanagement, but observers had not found any irregularities during voting. Ethnic areas including approximately 1.5 million voters had been excluded due to ongoing security problems. A new rule gave voters living outside the township where they were born[2] the right to register, and military personnel had to cast their votes – uncontrolled by officers – outside army camps. In short, the Tatmadaw had no say in these changes because the National League for Democracy (NLD) government controlled the UEC. UEC and Aung San Suu Kyi rejected an investigation of the elections. It seems as if the Tatmadaw chief asked for a deal, including that she somehow changed the outcome of the elections. Tatmadaw had lost almost half of its elected seats. She refused this 'deal'. Then the army tried the option of declaring a state of emergency using the provisions in chapter 11 of the constitution. The president is the only person who can convene the eleven members National Defence and Security Council with six officers in majority. The president refused. This was the second 'flaw' and the last straw for Min Aung Hlaing. Not that the nation was in danger – but that Tatmadaw had lost influence and power while Aung San Su Kyi had not only gained more seats in the parliament but also gradually gained more influence in and control over the state administration, as will be explained below.

First, a brief flashback is necessary, because recent events were a culmination of previous military frustrations.

Events leading to the coup

During the Rohingya crisis, Tatmadaw had asked Aung Sang Suu Kyi to convene the Defence and Security Council. She refused. When the Covid-19 crisis began in 2020 and the government initiated restrictions, Tatmadaw demanded that the council convened. Once again, she refused. Tatmadaw then formed their own Covid-19 committee headed by the vice president, a general who is now acting president. This indicates that Tatmadaw has been contemplating to resume full power before the recent crisis in the uneasy entente with the NLD.

In 2019, Aung Sang Suu Kyi's defence at the UN International Court of Justice in The Hague further angered the Tatmadaw. She dismissed that an intentional genocidal act had been committed but admitted that if the military had committed war crimes these would be dealt with at military courts in Myanmar.

This near admission of crimes was regarded as a humiliation by Tatmadaw and may have been the reason why Min Aung Hlaing surprisingly promised to let the Rohingya return in a speech after the coup. He even accused her of the expulsion of the Rohingya.

The expanding powers of Aung San Suu Kyi had generated a growing paranoia within the top ranks. It is likely that some officers supported her, as did the former junta member Shwe Mann since 2015. Min Aung Hlaing acted in order to maintain the loyalty within the ranks and to secure Tatmadaw's control over politics, state administration and the economy. The military is a tightly controlled corporate order where loyalty upwards in the hierarchy is rewarded with promotion, protection, economic opportunities, jobs and free health care – a privileged nationalist brotherhood. A patron should not be forgotten or let down, and Min Aung Hlaing is known to consult his patron, former senior general Than Shwe, who ruled from 1989 to 2010. Tatmadaw is also a huge patron-client system of favours, presents and bribes. It includes businesspersons ('cronies'), nationalist monks and local militia.

Tatmadaw's new ruling body, the State Administrative Council (SAC), is now working to dismantle Aung San Suu Kyi's power base and her NLD. A new UEC has been appointed, and it has annulled the 2020 elections. SAC has announced that they will change the electoral law to have proportional representation in order to keep the NLD and its leader out of power.

They are investigating Aung San Suu Kyi's charity foundation named after her late mother Daw Khin Kyi. The foundation/Aung San Suu Kyi is accused of having received illegal foreign funding. The constitution states that it is illegal for political parties to receive foreign money – but not for charities. The foundation has also received money from former military cronies. One military crony, convicted for drug trafficking, has 'confessed' that he gave her 1.5 million dollars cash. This could mean two to three years in jail for Aung San Suu Kyi. However, the most serious charge is that she has violated the Official Secret Act – a law from colonial rule, which can give up to fourteen years in jail.

In 2018, Aung San Suu Kyi managed to move the powerful General Administrative Department (GAD) from the Home Affairs Ministry to the ministry headed by the president. This was an important move, because GAD controls immigration law, as well as the local administration of townships, wards, districts and village tracts. The Tatmadaw is now dismissing GAD staffs in the whole system and replacing them with their own loyal staff – a clear sign of Tatmadaw's fear of losing control. However, some replacing staff from the military proxy party Union Solidarity and Development Party (USDP) have declined to take over because of widespread protests from civilians in their own neighbourhoods.

Min Aung Hlaing is head of SAC, and according to the emergency articles in the constitution, he has sovereign power over the legislature, the executive and the judicial system. The laws on sedition and on defaming the government, nos 121, 124 and 505 in the penal code, have been tightened with drastic increases in sentences up to twenty years. The laws will be used against the NLD, the Civil Disobedience Movement's (CDM's) activists and officials who will be 'disciplined' for opposing the new regime. The regime has accused Aung San Suu Kyi of 'causing fear and disturbing public tranquillity' with reference to article 505. It can mean two years in jail added to other sentences and barring her from future elections.

These and other laws are remnants from colonial rule. NLD's plan of reforming the law system never really materialized when her main judicial advisor, the Muslim lawyer U Ko Ni was assassinated in front the Yangon Airport by former officers in 2017. This came after fervent critique from nationalist monks who blamed Aung San Suu Kyi for allowing Muslims' influence and claimed she was going to repeal the so-called four race protections laws.[3] The assassination was a serious warning and demonstrated that killing of civilians was still part of Tamadaw's thinking.

Besides killing and beating demonstrators, Tatmadaw has also revived its force of thugs (formerly called Swan Arr Shin, 'Masters of Force'), convicts released after the coup – often drug addicts on methamphetamine equipped with iron rods and knives. These groups were active during the anti-Muslim riots in 2012–13. After the coup, when they began terrorizing during the night, vigilante groups caught thugs while they were poisoning water tanks. They are now also visible in daytime attacking demonstrators brutally.

Ultranationalist monks have attacked cars sporting photos of Aung San Suu Kyi. However, the state monastic council (Ma Ha Na; Sangha) has urged the military, NLD and Aung San Suu Kyi to negotiate and compromise, as well as protecting the civilians. The Sitagu Sayadaw, one of the most influential monks and member of the ultranationalist organization MaBaTha, has endorsed the coup. As patron of the project, he helps Min Aung Hlaing in constructing the world's largest marble Buddha statue. The general is obviously in need of doing 'meritorious' acts now.

Tatmadaw seems ready to lift the Covid-19 restrictions – probably because they harm their economic interests. However, with Covid-19 out of control, the

CDM actions and gradual withdrawal of international assistance may cause a drastic decline in the economy.

Why are the generals able to maintain totalitarian-like rule?

In the years after the 1962 coup, Tatmadaw not only took the role of politicians in the Burma Socialist Programme Party but also began to enter the civil services. Military personnel entered positions in the state administration creating a powerful Bamar patron–client (*saya-tapyit*, 'teacher–pupil') network into the entire society. This network based on absolute loyalty and a flow of services and 'gifts'/bribes produced a unique cohesion as well as opportunities for those who had the best navigation skills.[4] This meant that the elites emerging during General Ne Win's dictatorship became integrated in this Tatmadaw controlled network. It served to secure economic security after retirement and promotion for Tatmadaw personnel, as well as control over the emergence of fractions – but also relative wealth for higher ranks. Over the years, it developed into a strong system of corporate interests, identity and privileges.

Moreover, Tatmadaw founded the Defence Services Institute in order to secure its personnel's welfare. It developed into a large business enterprise, and Tatmadaw gained increased control over the economic activities. In 1990, the Myanmar Economic Holdings Ltd. was founded, and in 2008 the Myanmar Economic Corporation was organized. These military controlled organizations are engaged in almost all parts of the economy, for example, in mining, gem trade, tourism, construction and external trade. Military business dominated even after the economy was somehow liberalized after 2010. Meanwhile, privatization made the use of bribes flourish even more than previously, and Myanmar saw an increase in the number of tycoons. At the same time, Tatmadaw secured an unlimited budget at the expense of health, education, agricultural modernization and so on. The military has expanded to about four hundred thousand people since the 1988 uprising.[5]

Tatmadaw became an experienced counter-insurgency force fighting about twenty ethnic armed organizations and had a psychological warfare department as early as 1954. They have learned to control subversive elements not only by the use of force but also by creating instant fear and deep anxiety using false information and censure, as well as by the use of numerous informers. They have used agents in monk's robes, as well as the criminal thugs mentioned above. This regime of profound anxiety seems to return in 2021.[6]

During the past years, Tatmadaw developed a huge Military Intelligence Services (MIS), which kept surveillance of civil society with thousands of informers, and penetrated some of the ethnic armed organization. They managed to split the Karen National Union (KNU) and supported the formation of the Democratic Karen Buddhist Army in 1994-9. The MIS also spied on student activists and on officers getting too corrupt or too ambitious and undermining the morale.

As mentioned above, since the 1962 coup, Tatmadaw's ideology is a nationalism claiming to defend race, religion and culture from 'neocolonial' and communist enemies. Bamar culture and Buddhism were regarded as being endangered by these forces. Their nationalism may look as a mere façade but has been an important part of Tatmadaw's totalitarian strategy. It has been used in Tatmadaw's propaganda and constituted the legitimizing rhetoric of military rule. Time will show if the new rule will use nationalist rhetoric. It may perhaps not sound as persuasive as in 1962!

Monks have a long tradition of demonstrating and or even entering rebellions since colonial rule. Tatmadaw has regarded monks as a potential influential and oppositional force since 1960. Thus, Ne Win managed to secure control of the Sangha (the monastic organization). During the 2007 uprising of monks, Tatmadaw arrested and disrobed many monks while issuing new ID cards with photos. They even raided monasteries and killed some monks.

Soldiers live in closed camps and lead a strictly controlled and secluded life. They are indoctrinated to believe they alone are able to guard the country and that protesters and non-Bamar ethnic people are disruptive criminals and stooges of foreigners. This distorted view of civil society makes it possible to order soldiers to kill and destroy civilian property, as we have seen on numerous videos.

The sum of the controlling measures used by the Tatmadaw is the reason for their ingrained and lasting power. However, the generals have failed to secure a popular following since their 'disciplined democracy' began, and citizens are again regarded as enemies of the 2008 constitution, which the generals themselves have violated. Tatmadaw's control has been eroded since 2015, alarming the commanding officers. In other words, what we have seen since 1 February 2021 is based on decades of the military's experience. They are prepared to survive sanctions and isolation, as the Vice Senior General Soe Win has stated.

The NLD is a much looser network based on loyalty to Aung San Suu Kyi, non-violence and democracy. It has no collective leadership or vice leader and no control of means of force. It has a considerable wide and deep civilian support.[7] However, there has also been criticism of Aung San Suu Kyi's failure to listen to advice that contradicted her opinion and of promotion of ministers and staff based on loyalty more than on qualifications.

***

The generals obviously feared the competition from the NLD and realized they were losing control. Therefore, Tatmadaw has returned to its totalitarian measures. In order to maintain their imaginary of being the 'only legitimate national power', they use propaganda with misleading information such as 'demonstrators use violence and democratic rights as excuses for disrupting the social order' or 'henchmen of foreigners have misled them'. They use draconic laws, terror and wage war on civil society; they close media and arrest journalists. They claim to 'join hands with the people in defence of democracy'. Instead, the country is descending into a humanitarian disaster. In all, paraphrasing Hannah Arendt, they deprive the civilians the right to claim democratic rights.

Generations Z will not listen to Tatmadaw's propaganda – and Tatmadaw, blinded by their own ideology, do not understand Generation Z and its fierce resistance. But will all Tatmadaw personnel continue to accept the killings, economic chaos and an imploding state – or begin questioning the tactics and defect? At the time of writing, the opposition is mounting an organized challenge to military rule. The generals have clearly underestimated the opposition, and a costly civil war might unfold.

Notes

1 For details on the coup, I refer the readers to *The Irrawaddy, Frontier Myanmar, Myanmar Now* and *Asia Times* and the military *Global New Light of Myanmar* among many other sources, e.g., the *East Asia Forum* blog at the Australian National University. I have also obtained information from contacts in Myanmar.
2 Household lists controlled by the General Administrative Department are crucial in terms of obtaining ID cards and other legal papers and registrations.
3 See above Chapter 1, p. 29, note 12.
4 See the important study by Yoshihiro Nakanishi (2013). See also the fine analysis by Prager-Nyein (2011) and Min Win (2010).
5 See Lintner (1989) on the 1988 uprising and the atrocities committed by Tatmadaw.
6 I have described this as 'political paranoia' (Gravers 1999): Every person is a potential enemy; all foreigners are enemies. Totalitarian domination induces a total political and almost ontological fear pervading the entire society including

the inner circles of the Tatmadaw. Totalitarian measures were repeated during the demonstrations of Buddhist monks in 2007 (Gravers 2012).
7 The underground NLD parliamentarians are working to establish a coalition with the ethnic armed ceasefire groups in a National Unity Consultation Council promising a new federal constitution and a federated army. However, it will take time to overcome a long history of interethnic mistrust.

References

Gravers, Mikael (1999), *Nationalism as Political Paranoia in Burma: An Essay on the Historical Practice of Power*, London: Curzon Press.

Gravers, Mikael (2012), 'Monks, Morality and Military: The Struggle for Moral Power in Burma – and Buddhism's Uneasy Relation with Lay Power', *Contemporary Buddhism*, 13 (1): 1–33.

Lintner, Bertil (1989), *Outrage: Burma's Struggle for Democracy*, Hong Kong: Review.

Nakanishi, Yoshihiro (2013), *Strong Soldiers, Failed Revolution: The State and Military in Burma, 1962–88*, Singapore: NUS Press, Kyoto: University Press.

Prager-Nyein, Susanne (2011), 'The Armed Forces of Burma: The Constant Sentinel', in *The Political Resurgence of the Military in Southeast Asia: Conflict and Leadership*, ed. Marcus Mietzner, 12–44, New York: Routledge.

Win, Min (2010), 'Looking Inside the Burmese Military', in *Burma or Myanmar? The Struggle for National Identity*, ed. Lowell Dittmer, 155–84, Berkeley: University of California.

15

Ethnic and religious diversity

Hans-Peter Grosshans

The essays in this volume analyse ethnic and religious diversity in Myanmar from various perspectives and from within the framework of different academic disciplines, such as religious studies, cultural studies, social anthropology and theology. Furthermore, some contributions analyse the theme in view of three religions: Buddhism, Christianity and Islam. And, finally, some contributors come from or live in Myanmar and belong to a specific ethnicity and a specific religion there; other contributors come from other parts of the world but have a unique expertise in regard to Myanmar and its ethnicities and religions or have a knowledge of interfaith issues and religious plurality with regard to Myanmar and worldwide. Belonging to the latter category, I want to conclude this volume by adding some general reflections on ethnic and religious diversity in societies and states from a global perspective. The form of this postscript will be an essay, which will allow me to connect observations on ethnic and religious diversity in Myanmar to similar constellations in other parts of the world but also to reflect on and draw some general conclusions about the link between ethnicity and religion.

Multi-ethnic and multi-religious coexistence in Mynamar

Living together in multi-ethnic and multi-religious contexts now seems to be normal for many people all over the world. This coexistence is usually peaceful, but it is occasionally tense and creates conflicts. In many societies of the world, people who belong to or come from different ethnic groups and who belong to different religions (or have no religion at all) live together and cooperate constructively with each other. Generally, we can say that at present most societies comprise a diversity of ethnicities and religions.

These situations of ethnic and religious diversity are often seen as something special and new and are compared to earlier times, when a particular region, country or society had an ethnically and religiously homogeneous population. At least, it seems to us that this was the case (until historians eventually proved us wrong). Today, however, we have religious and ethnic diversity almost everywhere in the world. However, this situation is not really new. Almost everywhere there has always been ethnic (and often religious) diversity in societies. Throughout the history of religion as we know it, there has always been an awareness that other people worshipped God differently and also worshipped other gods – whether these people lived close to home or far away. Therefore, in the relationships of families and ethnic groups, of peoples and societies, religious aspects also had to be negotiated or were part of conflicts. The same applies to ethnic plurality in societies. In many societies and states, people from different ethnic groups contributed to the general well-being of society and the functioning of the state. This coexistence of people from diverse ethnic backgrounds also needs to be constantly renegotiated, including in families, but can also contribute to conflicts.

Good and harmonious coexistence in multi-ethnic and multi-religious societies is often threatened by the imperial interests of ethnic and religious groups striving for dominance in a society or state. Then the guiding idea in a multi-ethnic and multi-religious society is no longer 'unity in diversity' but 'unity in uniformity'. Myanmar is a good example of this, since, as some of the studies in this volume show, the country has seen massive state and state-supported attempts at Bamanization and Buddhization. Even the country's name, 'Myanmar', just like the earlier name, 'Burma', is an expression of the dominance of the largest population group, the Bamar or Burmese.

The guiding idea of 'unity in uniformity' is unfortunately still widespread in the contemporary world. It is realized in corresponding practices of ethnic and religious homogenization of populations in societies and states. This guiding idea has often been present in human history in different forms and intensities. If we follow Robert Bellah, who in his book *Religion in Human Evolution: From the Paleolithic to the Axial Age* (Bellah 2011) analysed religions as part of the history of evolution in general and the evolutionary history of humanity in particular, then religions with their rituals and festivals are a core element in the homogenizing formation of families, groups and societies. In this function, they played an important role in the formation of some great empires and imperial societies in many parts of the world. Thus, some religions established themselves as world religions in the so-called Axial Age (a term used by the German philosopher Karl Jaspers (1949) for the period between 800 and 200 BC, when some empires were formed such as in China, Persia, Egypt, Greece, Rome and Central America), which led to the overriding of traditional family and tribal religions that had contributed to the diversity of the religious field. A common religious practice and shared religious beliefs were essential to the formation of such empires and imperial societies and provided the ritual and symbolic forms for internal coalescence and cohesion in these empires and societies. Robert Bellah already conducted extensive research in the 1960s on religion in Asia. The more important for the identity and social cohesion of a society or state religions were and are the more relevant they were and are for contacts with people in other societies, be they friendly and peaceful or unfriendly and aggressive.

In the analyses provided by Robert Bellah and others, then, we can observe how the world religions were able for various reasons to bind people beyond their original societies and contexts by uniting people in a common religious practice and common religious beliefs, even though they originally belonged to different societies and ethnic groups with different languages and cultures. These differences then articulated themselves within the world religions on a subordinate level in the form of denominations, schools and currents. Interestingly, these different realizations of the world religions sometimes exist today in specific combinations with ethnicities or ethnic groups. Examples of such specific connections of denominations, schools or currents of the world religion – sometimes in clear opposition to the mainstream in the respective religion – can be observed worldwide and also in Myanmar. I want to mention here only a few selected examples from Myanmar. Jane M. Fergusson describes in her chapter in this volume the significance of the Buddhist monk Sao Myat (1943–1980), who is still revered in Myanmar by many Shan people in Southern Shan State, particularly by some groups of Shan separatists. He was a Theravāda Buddhist practitioner, but his spiritualism also incorporated elements of Tantrism. Fergusson shows that Sao Myat's non-orthodox qualities (besides his other skills) gave him his special strength and significance and in turn reaffirmed the position of Buddhism in Shanland – and this despite its being an exception on the fringes of 'orthodox' forms of Theravāda Buddhism, as can be found especially among the dominant ethnicity in Myanmar, the Bamar. It was especially the fact that Shan State Army soldiers revered Sao Myat that made his significance for the question of Shan sovereignty all the greater. Similar observations can be made in regard to Christianity in Myanmar, which takes the form of many denominations there (Baptists, Methodists, Anglicans, Catholics, Lutherans, Pentecostals and others), these denominations often being related mainly to specific ethnicities. As the largest Christian denomination in Myanmar, the Baptists have a strong presence especially in Chin State and Kachin State. Or, to give another example, Lutheran Christians can mainly be found among former immigrants from India and among the Mara people (in Chin State). The strong connection of Sunnite Islam with the ethnicity of the Rohingya people in Rakhine State is well known, as is the conflict over their citizenship status in Myanmar (which also affects the small number of Christian Rohingyas, too).

There is religious diversity in almost all states and societies in the world today: there is not only one religion but a plurality of religions, which are even more plural since each one comprises various denominations, schools and currents. This is the case even in societies that seem at first sight to be religiously homogeneous. Even if the vast majority of a society's population belongs to a single religion, there may be small minorities practising other religions. Unfortunately, sociological analyses of the presence and significance of religions in societies and states worldwide usually pay little attention to this, since they often focus only on the larger picture and on the dominant and historically significant religions in a country.

Myanmar is a very clear example of how a state has attempted – between 1960 and 2010, and partly still today – to make an ethnically and religiously diverse population ethnically and religiously homogeneous (through Bamanization and Buddhization).[1] Likewise, how the country that is now Myanmar was in the period before independence in 1948 is also a clear religious-sociological example of an ethnically and religiously plural society. Today's Myanmar was then described as the very opposite of an ethnically and religiously homogeneous society.

We can find such a description in *Colonial Policy and Practice: A Comparative Study of Burma and Netherlands India* (1948), the classic study on ideological-religious pluralism in Indonesia and Myanmar by the British colonial official John S. Furnivall, who used the concept of a 'pluralistic society' to characterize the societies of the former Burma and Indonesia in the first half of the twentieth century (Furnivall 1948: 303–12). According to Furnivall, different groups in Burma and Indonesia lived together constructively and without ultimately uniting with each other in the sense of forming a homogeneous society. Each of these groups held onto its own religion, its own culture and language, its own ideas and ways of life. In a sense, there was no explicit common social will among all people. Besides being members of ethnicities and religions, people encountered each other as individuals and members of families. This happened mainly in the marketplace, with economic exchange uniting people. 'In the plural society the highest common factor is the economic factor, and the only test that all apply in common is the test of cheapness' (Furnivall 1948: 310). People interacted with each other primarily as business partners and as competitors, or as buyers and sellers. In these interactions, they formed a liberal society that was ethnically, religiously and ideologically plural. However, Furnivall also noted that the pluralistic societies of Burma and Indonesia lacked a common social will, that is, the will to form and be part of a joint society, which he attributed primarily to the colonial situation and the fact that the populations in these countries were prevented from becoming independent societies.

Society in Myanmar has changed more than once since Furnivall's time. Colonialism ended and Myanmar became independent; there then followed several decades of military socialism, which was only transformed into a civilian government in 2011. Furnivall's concept of a 'pluralistic society' is therefore not a description of Myanmar today but a reminder that Myanmar, like Indonesia, is a historical paradigm of positive coexistence among members of an ethnically and religiously diverse population. Why is such a liberal and pluralistic concept of society no longer seen as an option at all today?

After Myanmar became independent in 1948, there were attempts at 'nation-building', which were (and are) by no means unproblematic, as Myanmar is a state with many ethnic groups, languages, cultures and religions. Thus, attempts to build a homogeneous nation in Myanmar were (and are) subject to strong criticism and opposition, especially on the part of ethnic (but also religious) groups, who consider the 'pluralistic society' described by Furnivall to be much more appropriate and attractive than a culturally, linguistically and religiously homogeneous Myanmar.

Politically, in all its attempts at nation-building, Myanmar lacks a true federalist concept of the state. The concept of non-territorial federalism that Nehginpao Kipgen proposes in this volume seems to be intelligent and balanced given the ethnically and religiously diverse situation in Myanmar. It is based on the one hand on the principle of subsidiarity, which means that political responsibility for questions of education (schools and universities), culture and religion, but also of land use (use of raw materials, settlement policy, infrastructure, etc.) and of internal security (police), remains in the country's seven states and seven regions (and probably even in their respective districts) and therefore with the ethnic groups in their traditional settlement areas. On the other, Kipgen's proposal goes beyond this classical model of federalism by arguing for the preservation of cultural, ethnic and religious identities throughout the whole of Myanmar – for example, through appropriate services and opportunities in the education sector (schools with classes in the various ethnic languages of the pupils).

How urgent it is to establish an effective federalism in Myanmar is shown above all by analyses from the perspective of individual ethnic groups, such as the *Karen* or *Kachin*. In Seng Ja Layang's analysis, critique of the abiding colonial structures in Myanmar should extend to the writing of history, which is presented only from the perspective of the largest and most dominant ethnic group, the Bamar. The Kachin have a quite different history of their country (Kachin State) and of today's Myanmar. The plurality of historical narratives is reminiscent of similar constellations in other parts of the world, such as the Balkans, where neither the Austrian Habsburg monarchy nor the South Slav movement or the state of Yugoslavia succeeded in uniting the peoples there into a homogeneous society or a nation, with the ethnic and cultural (but also religious) narratives proving stronger than the homogenizing state orders.

In Myanmar, it is also easy to observe that in attempts to form a nation and become a state, the distinction between majority and minorities in the overall population and society creates its own problems. Given this distinction, it seems impossible to form a state or nation in the sense of a union or federation, which is after all the claim that the state of Myanmar makes in its constitution: to be a union of the peoples of Myanmar. An alternative to the distinction between majority and minorities could be the establishment of a strong federalism (as conceived by Nehginpao Kipgen, for example). Another alternative could be to regard the individual ethnic groups as equal regardless of their size – to see them in a sense as nations – and then to build a union or federation of the peoples of Myanmar on this basis (which could be similar to the European Union).

On its path to becoming a union of its peoples, Myanmar needs strong political and legal protection for minorities, so that citizens throughout the country can live their ethnic, cultural and religious identity without restriction. The fact that this is not possible everywhere is particularly evident in the highly problematic situation of the Rohingya in Rakhine State,[2] whose ambiguous status under the citizenship law demonstrates that human rights are not sufficiently anchored as fundamental law in Myanmar and are thus not able to give the relevant protection to all minorities.

Broad ethnic diversity has manifold consequences for coexistence in a multi-ethnic state. Politically, a strong federalism should give effective protection to minorities, which of course should not result in the dominance of minorities. Politically and socially, this also means making possible in the country as a whole the practices of the diverse cultures and the cultivation and preservation of the ethnic languages, including in the education system. It also means communicatively that a uniform administrative and legal language holds together the diversity of ethnic groups, languages and cultures.

The willingness to implement a consistent and consequent federal constitution in Myanmar increased vehemently among the population of Myanmar in 2021. This new acceptance of federalism results from the strong resistance of an overwhelming majority of Myanmar's population to the military's – the Tatmadaw's – coup d'état on 1 February 2021.[3] In the attempts to make the resistance against the new military junta effective, new alliances are emerging in Myanmar's population between ethnic groups and also religions. In this, a rethinking among the people of Myanmar, and especially among the younger generation, the Generation Z (Gen Z), is becoming apparent with regard to the fundamentally and consistently federal design of the Union of the Peoples of Myanmar. The Committee Representing Pyidaungsu Hluttaw (CRPH), a parliamentary representative committee made up of a few parliamentarians elected in November 2020 primarily from the National League for Democracy (NLD) – an underground government of Myanmar, so to speak – and other actors are trying to form a national alliance of resistance to the military junta and possibly even something like a federal army made up of the various underground armies of diverse ethnicities with strong participation of volunteers from the Bamar ethnicity.

The CRPH has declared that the problematic 2008 constitution is null and void as of 31 March 2021. At the latest since the beginning of March 2021, a new federal constitution has been drafted by the CRPH, representatives of the ethnic groups and other stakeholders. Admittedly, not all ethnic groups and their military actors are involved in this process, because among them the NLD also stands for the Burmese attempts of ethnic and religious homogenization. Despite similar reservations, other ethnic groups have nevertheless decided to resist the military junta because for them any form of oppression is an evil. Thus, many young Burmese/Bamar recognize that up to now the various other ethnic groups have not been adequately respected politically and socially and that they themselves have been misled by negative state propaganda. Indeed, the ethnic groups' interest in more self-determination and more political participation is also their interest, which at present can possibly be asserted only with the help of those who had been denounced as 'rebels'.

Similarly, there is also a rapprochement between the religions. The realization that members of all religions present in Myanmar have very similar social ideas, represent similar political values and are willing to risk their lives for them leads to a fresh perception of the other religions. This is particularly true with regard to the religious communities' potential for resilience and resistance. The image of a Catholic nun kneeling before soldiers and begging them to shoot her and spare the demonstrators has become iconic. Among the Kachin, who are predominantly Baptist Christians, the German resistance fighter and Protestant theologian Dietrich Bonhoeffer serves as a role model and motivation for resistance against the military junta in their own country. Similar examples can be found throughout Myanmar in various religious traditions. If the spook of the military Junta is eventually over, these experiences can be built upon in a new attempt to form a true federal union of the peoples of Myanmar.

Opposing homogenization: Religious diversity in modern societies

Religious diversity in Myanmar is part of the broader diversity (of ethnicities, cultures and languages) with which people in Myanmar live and which need to be integrated into a society and state without their being homogenized.

Robert Bellah's reconstruction of the historical development of religions shows that, from an evolutionary perspective, a group of persons (family, clan, ethnicity) originally coincided with a religion. In particular, religious practice strengthened the inner cohesion of a social group and set it apart from other groups due to its specific characteristics. According to Bellah's analyses, these positive evolutionary functions of religion were also adopted by most empires formed in the so-called Axial Age, when many ethnic groups were forcibly united. These religions, which thus developed into so-called world religions, detached themselves from their exclusive assignment to a certain ethnicity or whatever kind of social unit. Their significance lay precisely in the fact that they (mostly forcibly) united people from different ethnic groups and social units into an imperial state with a common religious practice.

We find this hope in the unifying power of a common religion formulated particularly impressively in Europe at a time when there was no longer any common religion at all. This loss of religious unity in Europe only took place within Christianity in the schism between Byzantium and Rome in 1054, when European Christianity separated into Western European and Eastern European Christianity, and in the Reformation in the sixteenth century, when Western European Christianity was further pluralized. But, writing in his well-known text of 1799, *Christendom or Europe*, the German poet Novalis ([1799] 1981) lamented the loss of religious unity in Europe brought about by the Reformation and the Protestantism to which it had given rise.[4] What Novalis longed for – possibly with some irony – is what lives on to the present day in talk of the 'Christian West', which may conceal the hope that a unified Christian religion in Europe will provide its various peoples and states with a common spiritual foundation that can foster reconciliation and peace in the midst of all the political, economic, social and cultural differences in Europe. In contrast to this idea of the Christian religion as a unified European house of peace, Protestantism has developed a more open and plural conception, one that argues that peace in Europe cannot be secured by sacrificing the freedom of the individual or the self-determination of groups and peoples. Rather, peace and reconciliation are only possible with such freedom.

Such a plural conception then also corresponds to the more recent history of religion in Europe. The religions of Christianity, Judaism and Islam, which originated in Western Asia, have been joined by other religions in modern times, especially since the nineteenth century: Hinduism, Buddhism, religious movements from Japan, China, Korea, America and Africa. Mainly due to colonialism and then to global migration movements, there has been an increased migration of Hindus, Buddhists, Sikhs and Muslims to Western Europe from the nineteenth century onwards, so that a multi-religious and multicultural society has now emerged in parts of Western, Northern and Central Europe. Some major cities in Europe have almost all religious traditions present: Mosque communities, Hindu temple communities, Buddhist pagoda communities, Sikh Gurdwara communities, African and Indian traditions, the so-called Youth Religions, esoteric groups and so on contribute to religious life in Europe's major cities alongside Christian and Jewish communities.

However, this is the case not only in Western Europe but also in other parts of the world. The vast majority of the world's religions are present today even in societies that appear to be very homogeneous in terms of religion, if often only as small minorities. As a consequence, ethnic groups and societies can often no longer simply be identified with a particular religion. The reverse is also true: religions can no longer simply be identified with certain ethnic groups and societies. Of course, there are still ethnic groups and societies that are strongly influenced by a single religion, be it because of its historical role and cultural significance. Sometimes a state or a society is linked almost ideologically to a single religion, so that the freedom of religious practice of members of other religions is not respected and they are sometimes treated as second-class citizens and discriminated against in political and civil life.

Religious diversity is a defining feature of the world at the present time. With their dynamism and vitality, religions in their diversity shape the present at least as much as economic globalization and global migration movements – even if this can be observed with varying intensity in the different regions of the world. The religious situation worldwide is characterized by a diversity of vital religions in many places. Everywhere in the world, globalization – with the global exchange of goods, services and information but also global travel and migration movements – is bringing with it a variety of new encounters with religions practised worldwide, and therefore also a dramatic increase in the extent to which issues of religion are being discussed. There is therefore also a need everywhere in the world to deal with religious developments worldwide but also at the local and regional level. This requires expanding the disciplines of religious studies and theology in universities and including the subject of religion in school curricula in order to raise the level of knowledge and competence in issues to do with religion.

One characteristic of (so to speak: modern) societies today is their broadening of horizons compared to pre-modern societies (Pollack 2009). This applies geographically but also with regard to the entire horizon of knowledge and experience available to people. With the broadening of their horizons, people have become acquainted with and confronted by a plenitude of possibilities of understanding themselves, which powerfully relativize their values, convictions (including religious convictions) and worldviews, thereby calling into question traditional certainties. Traditional *religious* certainties can also be liquefied in this way: they now appear as contingent and dependent on certain contextual conditions. However, the relativization of values, convictions and worldviews in the global horizon also strengthens the fundamentalist tendency towards safeguarding them in the sense of making them into ultimate truths and certainties. Thus, as people's global horizons expand, fundamentalist and realistic forms of religion are also strengthened. Religious certainties are then not liquefied but, conversely, solidified in such a way that they appear like a rock in the surf of the zeitgeist. Nonetheless, although this may seem counter-intuitive, we should regard fundamentalist and realistic forms of religion as indicators of a modern society. But this paradox is part of the ambivalences of modernity.

The broadening of horizons is accompanied by individualization in the field of religious affiliation and religious practice. 'Less than in pre-modern societies, what an individual thinks, feels and believes is determined by origin and milieu' (Pollack 2009: 72, my translation). Individuals now find less support in their religious orientations, actions and affiliations in contemporary societies than in pre-modern societies, where religious affiliation was determined by family or ethnicity and its tradition. As a result, religious ideas and actions are not necessarily weaker and less present in the individual. However, they are less visible because they correspond less to a social, communal religious practice. At the same time, religious orientations, actions and affiliations are more mixed interreligiously and interdenominationally, because individuals on their own combine elements from diverse religious traditions (Dalferth 1997).

In this respect, the broadening of horizons in modern societies is also accompanied by a 'pluralization of cultural orientations and identities' (Pollack 2009: 73, my translation). This is especially true with regard to their social acceptance, which means in concrete terms that a plurality of religious and denominational communities in the same place is becoming increasingly accepted and taken for granted. This may be the greatest challenge facing traditional religions and denominations that strive for religious homogeneity (and so for their own dominance) in a geographical area or in an ethnic group. For, merely tolerating religious minorities will then no longer be sufficient or acceptable. Tolerance towards those of other faiths, which the vast majority of religious communities and denominations practise, must then be replaced by the principle of recognition at the societal level and by mutual respect between diverse religious communities and denominations (Grosshans 2010).

It follows from the religious diversity that can be found everywhere in the world that the religions (their leaders and teachers and adherents) talk to each other and cooperate. Interaction and dialogue are to be understood in an open-ended way. It does not have to be about dissolving boundaries and differences between religions; it can also be about defining the boundaries more clearly and understanding the differences better (Grosshans 2014). A boundary does not have to be only a barrier and a lack; it can also be something praiseworthy. Admittedly, though, it is only by being beyond a boundary that one can judge whether it can still be something other than a restriction and a lack, or whether it can also yield, to use Pierre Bourdieu's formulation, a *gain in distinction* (Bourdieu 1979). Borders between religions and denominations are important to bring peace to human life. Clear borders are just as much a blessing as a civilized way of dealing with religions and denominations. The wish to transcend borders in the field of religion does not necessarily mean dissolving these borders. A civilized approach to religious boundaries presupposes their recognition as well as acceptance of and respect for people from other religious affiliations and their religious practices beyond the respective boundaries. Such a way of overcoming religious boundaries is the opposite of an imperial usurpation of others and strangers. Rather, it involves allowing others and strangers to be others and strangers. It also includes being able and wanting to remain different and foreign even to others and strangers in the field of religion.

Either way, it follows that religions and their members need to learn about other religions, to study their respective teachings and practices in detail, and then to improve their own teachings about other religions in such a way that they also correspond to how the other religions understand themselves. This requires theologies in the religions that reconstruct the practice and teachings of the religions in the past and present *emically*, that is, from within the religions themselves, while also taking into account the results of *etic* religious research in an interreligious and intercultural horizon. Under these conditions, the individual religions can define their respective theology of religions, which corresponds to the religious diversity in the present and then also leads to constructive dialogue and cooperation between the religions.

The diversity of religions in the present has manifold consequences for the coexistence of people in their societies. In their search for meaning, individuals can come to terms with a diversity of religious concepts offering meaning to their lives. Families are increasingly challenged by interreligious constellations and have to learn to deal with the different religious affiliations of family members – for example, they then have to deal with new festivals and rituals. Societies have to come to terms with the increasing diversity of religious life. They must help end the widespread religious illiteracy and radically increase religious education, so that people can learn about their own religion and about the religions of their fellow citizens. Politicians are challenged to regulate the diverse religious activities of individuals, groups and organizations within a legal framework that is both binding and liberal. A central part of these regulations has to be the human right of religious freedom, which needs to be anchored as a fundamental right in the constitutions of individual states in order to protect both individual and communal religious practice.

The Impact of Religions for Ethnicities

What is the link between ethnic and religious diversity? In contemporary societies, both types of diversity present similar challenges for living together. In a multi-ethnic state like Myanmar, ethnic and religious diversity is a fact that cannot be ignored. There are various combinations of ethnic and religious diversity. It is also the case at the ethnic level that there is religious diversity within an ethnicity. In conclusion, let me therefore address the question of how a constructive and positive connection between religions and ethnicities can be imagined. As I have pointed out, the special connections of religions with ethnic groups, peoples, nations or states (and vice versa) are increasingly dissolving or at least becoming looser. However, in Christian theology, the contextual theologies of recent decades have made it clear that there are also deep internal connections between Christianity (and, indeed, all other religions) and the experience and situation of ethnic or social groups. Religions are very concerned with the existential, economic, political, cultural and social situations of people and their communities. The more specifically religions relate to these life situations, the more intensively they identify with the respective people and communities. This is true simply because religions essentially consist of communities and individuals that belong to concrete groups, which are often ethnic groups.

Within Christianity, Protestantism in particular has done much to preserve the identity of ethnicities through translating the Bible into many ethnic languages, some of which were written down for the first time as a result. In the Reformation of Western Christianity in the sixteenth century, Martin Luther's translation of the Bible into German gave rise to many other translations into European vernacular languages. This attention to vernacular languages has survived in Protestantism to this day. Since then, the Bible has been translated into several hundred national and ethnic languages around the world, thereby preventing the disappearance of many languages: in 2018, translations of the whole Bible existed in 674 languages and translations of parts of the Bible in 3,324 languages. These translations help preserve the languages, each of which is at the core of an ethnic identity and helps it to survive and transmit itself even in a globalized world with very few dominant world languages or in a society where state authorities seek to impose homogeneity in the name of 'nation-building'.

If religions see themselves as concrete communities of believers on the ground, then there is necessarily a large intersection between the religious communities and the different areas of social life. If ethnic plurality is of importance socially (e.g. due to migration), then this is also an issue for the religious communities, which also have to clarify for themselves how to deal with ethnic diversity in their own practice. The contextual theologies of recent decades in particular have drawn attention to the fact that a religion can make the concerns of an ethnic group or even a social class entirely its own in order to stand up for an ethnicity or a social class as a whole – for example, by calling for justice or for self-determination – and thus help fight the injustice and lack of freedom that befall a people or a social class. In Christian theology, one speaks of 'empowering' people affected by injustice and a lack of freedom through the practice and teaching of a religion, in order to strengthen them in their resilience but also in their struggle for justice and self-determination.

Despite all the differences between religions on this issue, it is extremely difficult to conceive of a religion that lacks deep solidarity with all aspects of the concrete life of the people belonging to it. From the perspective of ethnic diversity, this can mean that religions play their part in ensuring that the concrete coexistence of people with different ethnic affiliations or origins succeeds for the benefit of all. However, this solidarity of a religion with all aspects of the concrete life of the people belonging to it can also mean from the perspective of ethnic diversity that it again and again supports with its spiritual means the efforts of an ethnic group to preserve its identity or to fight for its self-determination and even sovereignty.

Notes

1 Since 1999, Myanmar has been designated by the US Department of State as a 'Country of Particular Concern' under the International Religious Freedom Act of 1998 for having engaged in or tolerated particularly severe violations of religious freedom. For details about these ongoing violations of religious freedom in Myanmar see the '2019 Report on International Religious Freedom: Burma' of the Office of International Religious Freedom of the US Department of State (https://www.state.gov/reports/2019-report-on-international-religious-freedom/burma/).
2 For an excellent reconstruction of the history of the Rohingya and the conflict between Buddhists and Muslims in today's Myanmar, see Zöllner (2018).
3 See Mikael Graver's clear and convincing analysis of the coup and the Tatmadaw's self-image in Chapter 14.

4 For an English translation of Novalis's *Christendom or Europe*, see http://ghdi.ghi-dc.org/sub_document.cfm?document_id=3619.

References

Bellah, Robert (2011), *Religion in Human Evolution: From the Paleolithic to the Axial Age*, Cambridge, MA: Harvard University Press.

Bourdieu, Pierre (1979), *La distinction. Critique sociale du jugement*, Paris: Ed. de Minuit.

Dalferth, Ingolf U. (1997), '"Was Gott ist, bestimme ich!" Theologie im Zeitalter der "Cafeteria-Religion"', in *Gedeutete Gegenwart*, ed. Ingolf U. Dalferth, 10–35, Tübingen: Mohr Siebeck.

Furnivall, John Sydenham (1948), *Colonial Policy and Practice: A Comparative Study of Burma and Netherlands India*, Cambridge: Cambridge University Press.

Grosshans, Hans-Peter (2010), 'Toleranz. Ein umstrittenes Konzept im Umgang mit religiöser Pluralität', in *Integration religiöser Pluralität. Philosophische und theologische Beiträge zum Religionsverständnis in der Moderne*, ed. H.-P. Grosshans and M. D. Krüger, 15–29, Leipzig: Evangelische Verlagsanstalt.

Grosshans, Hans-Peter (2014), 'Grenzziehung und Grenzüberwindung zwischen Religionen und Konfessionen. Eine theologische Reflexion', in *Grenzziehungen und Grenzüberwindungen. Philosophische und interdisziplinäre Zugänge*, ed. Bärbel Frischmann (Studia philosophica Iaderensia 3), 231–45, Hannover: Werhahn Verlag.

Jaspers, Karl (1949), *Vom Ursprung und Ziel der Geschichte*, Munich: Piper Verlag.

Novalis ([1799] 1981), 'Die Christenheit oder Europa. Ein Fragment [1799]', in *Werke in einem Band*, ed. Novalis, 525–44, Munich/Vienna: Hanser-Verlag.

Pollack, Detlef (2009), *Rückkehr des Religiösen? Studien zum religiösen Wandel in Deutschland und in Europa II*, Tübingen: Mohr Siebeck.

Zöllner, Hans-Bernd (2018), *Das Totenschiff – die Tragödien der Rohingya. Eine historische Collage*, Berlin: regiospectra Verlag.

Index

786 movement (Myanmar-Thai border) 211n.1
969 movement 4, 90n.1, 126, 137n.2
8888 Uprising (8 August 1988) 78, 163

Abrams, Evan 181
accommodation 3, 59–61
Adas, Michael 13
Afghanistan 75–6
Africa 265
African Catfish (U Wirathu) 207
Agra, India 148
Ah Myo Pyauk Mar So Kyauk Hsayar 66n.11
Akbar (Mughal emperor) 148
Alaungmintaya (King) 96
Alaungphaya (Burman King) 13, 232–4
Al-Azhar Islamic Institute of Myanmar 208
Alexandra of Denmark (empress) 78
alienation 3, 52, 54, 56–7, 61–3
All Burma Council of Young Monks 15
All Burma Students' Democratic Front (ABSDF) 42
All Mon Region Democracy Party 41
All Myanmar Islamic Organization 208
American Baptist Foreign Mission Society 151
American Baptist Missionary Press 152
American Deep South 75
American Lutheran Church (ALC) 154
Amish movement 76
Amporn, Jirattikorn 88
amyo kabia ('mixed races') 18–19, 24–5, 27
analysis of identity 111–14 (*see also* identity)
Anawrahta (King) 81–3, 89–90, 236–7, 243n.4
Anderson, Benedict 28n.4, 52–3, 59, 63
Anderson, Johanna 151
Andrew, E. J. L. 142

Andrew, Jenson 154–5, 159n.8–9
Andrews, Thomas 209
Anglican Church 149, 155
Anglo-Burmese 162
war 37, 96, 142
Annan, Kofi 206
Anthony Cathedral 153
anthropology/anthropologists 9–10, 15–16, 28n.1–2, 59, 257
Anti-Fascist People's Freedom League (AFPFL) 17, 39, 193–4, 196, 198
Arabia 192
Arakan Army 64, 206
Arakan Buddhist 132
Arakan Liberation Party (ALP) 42
Arakan Mohammedans 14
Arakan Rohingya Salvation Army (ARSA) 20, 26, 30n.22, 211n.1
Armenian Church 147, 157
ASEAN 199, 206
Ashoka 234–7
Asia 37, 148, 173
Asia Times 255n.1
Askari, Hasan 108
Assam, India 152
Assembly of God (AoG) 154
assimilation 3, 52, 54, 58–9, 165–6, 235, 239
associate citizenship 18, 217
Associate Citizenship Scrutiny Card (ACSC) 203, 215, 217
Association for the Protection of Race and Religion 30n.25, 207
Aung Htoo, U. 63
Aung Maytu, U. 197
Aung San Suu Kyi 2, 16–18, 26, 31n.34–5, 38–9, 43–5, 50, 52, 57, 61, 65n.6, 123, 126–7, 163–4, 174, 178–9, 184–5, 191, 197. 200, 250–1, 254–5
Aung-Thwin, Michael A. 231, 236–7, 243–4n.6–7
Aung Win Khine 201

Australian National University 255n.1
Austria 137n.4, 262
Ava (Upper Burma) 143, 150–1, 158n.2, 159n.6, 232–4
Axial Age 259, 264
Ayatham (monk) 87–8

bad blood 19
Bagan 53, 65n.5, 81–3, 90, 234, 236, 244n.6
Bago (Pegu) 13, 198, 214, 218–19, 220, 222–7, 233
Bagyidaw (King) 53
Baha'i 130
Balibar, Étienne 12, 26
Bama/Burman group 36–8, 46, 173–4, 177–80
Bamar (or Burman) 2, 13, 110, 133, 202, 243n.1, 244n.11
  Buddhism 51
  community 58
  culture 55, 232, 235, 254
  customary law 29n.11
  empire 234
  ethnic 56–7, 122, 237, 263
  kingdoms 54
  labour 131
  language 53, 60, 63, 232
  military 64
  mob 133
  Myanmar's population 52
  nationhood 55
  organization 243
  patron–client 253
  population 50
  soldiers 16
Bamar Buddhists 55, 110, 130–1, 241
Bamar Kingdom of Ava (Upper Burma) 232
Bamar Sar 58
Bamiyan Buddha 75–6
Bangkok 84, 158
Bangladesh 20, 30n.22, 62, 64, 126, 130, 174, 192, 198–9, 205, 209, 211n.1, 214, 225
Baptist Christians 264 (*see also* Christians)
Baptist Missionary Magazine 14
Barth, Fredrik 11

Bartholomeusz, Tessa 117
Ba Thaw 197
Bauckham, Richard 184
Baxter, James 142
Bayinnung (King) 79
Bechert, H. 74
Beech, Hannah 21
Bellah, Robert 258–9, 264
Bengal (Gaur Kingdom) 23, 60, 192
Bengal (India)
  immigrants 23
Bengala Kayin Islam 24
Bengalis 14, 20–1, 145, 205, 239 (*see also* Rohingya)
Berkwitz, Stephen C. 118n.1
Berlie, Jean A. 15, 62, 239, 241
Berlin Wall 154
Bethlehem Lutheran Church in Yangon 154–6, 158
Bhikkhu Buddhadāsa 117
Bible 269
Bigandet, Paul (Bishop) 14, 151
Big Chiang Tung Buddha statue 80
birth certificate 218
blue card. *see* Associate Citizenship Scrutiny Card (ACSC)
blue socialist books 59
Bo, Charles Maung 153
Bogin, Benjamin 101
Bombay 143
Bonhoeffer, Dietrich 264
Border Area Development Programme 78
Border Areas and National Races 78
Border Guard Force (BGF) 40
Boshier, Carol Ann 16, 29n.13, 65n.1
Botahtaung Newspaper 195
Botataung Daily Newspaper 61
Bourdieu, Pierre 268
Boutry, Maxime 57, 60
Bowie, Katherine A. 84
Brac de la Perriere, Benedicte 95
Brass, Paul 158
Bray, J. 39
British Burma 94, 97, 131, 144, 158n.4
British Burma Army 16
British East India Company (EIC) 148–9, 151–2
British Empire 77, 131
British Government of India 237

British India 14–15, 147, 162
British Oil Company (BOC) 150
Brohm, John 95
Brown, R. Grant 166
Brubaker, Roger 11
Buddha Dhamma Charity
   Foundation 129
Buddhasasana 111
Buddhism 1–3, 15, 21, 31n.35, 55, 64,
   101–2, 161–2 (see also Theravāda
   Buddhism)
  anti-Muslim 21
  Chiang Tung 83–9
  danger/threat to 31n.31, 118, 124
  homogeneity 18
  minority and 21
  Ne Win's new ideology 55
  political monks 123
  precepts 181–2
  promotion as dominant religion 64
  protection 123, 125
  race and 27
  sociopolitical power 165
  state religion 164
Buddhists 1, 16, 23, 270n.2
  culture 3
  loyalty 14
  migration of 265
  monarch 2
  monks 25, 74, 76–7, 102, 124 126,
    134, 177, 180–1, 198, 200, 207–8,
    232, 256n.6
  mutual mistrust Muslims 20
  nationalism 4, 124–30, 165–7
  and non-Buddhists 115, 164
  no role of violence among 21
  protectionism 4, 124
  religious exclusivism 4
  riots with Muslims 20
  saṅgha 83
  shrines 24
Buddhist Asia 103
Buddhist Association for the Protection of
   Race and Religion (MaBaTha) 238
Buddhist Bamar 5, 125–6, 231, 237–8
Buddhist/Hindu 101
Buddhist Karens 22–3, 28n.7, 31n.29,
   64, 131
Buddhist Mon 5, 231, 241

Buddhist-Muslim 5, 118n.1, 201
Buddhist–Shan 73, 131
Buddhist University 135
Buddhist Women Special Marriage and
   Succession Act (1939) 15, 129
Buddhist Women's Special Marriage
   Law 29n.12
Buddhization 258, 260
Burkett, Delbert 183
Burma Act of 1935 147
Burma Army 97
Burma Broadcasting Service 209
Burma Citizenship Law (1982) 59, 195,
   197–8, 201–4
Burma Foreigners Act (1864) 217
Burma Independence Army 57
Burma Karen National Association 17
Burman (Scott) 144
Burman Buddhists 165, 168, 197
Burmanization (Bamanization) 2–4, 13,
   44–5, 65n.1, 173–85
  Burman religion and culture 177–9
  Burmese military forces 175–9
  civil war 175–9
  compassion 183–5
  differences and ethnic rights 179–81
  discrimination 179–85
  Kachin ethnic community 174–5
Burman Muslim Congress (BMC) 193–4,
   196, 197
Burma Socialist Programme Party
   (BSPP) 51, 64, 66n.11, 195–6,
   235, 253
Burmese Buddhism 79, 82, 90, 92, 94
Burmese Buddhist 55–6, 61, 74–5, 97
Burmese Communist Party 65n.4
Burmese Days (Orwell) 19
Burmese Independence Army 57
Burmese Konbaung Dynasty 158n.2
Burmese Muslims 193–4, 196–7, 199,
   211n.4, 240–1
Burmese Socialist Programme
   Party 58–61
Burmese Supremacy (*Mahar Bamar*) 57
Burmese Translation Association 58
Burmese Way to Socialism 51–2, 59, 162,
   191, 195–6, 210
Burnell, A. C. 193
Byzantine 75, 265

Cady, John F. 29n.10
Callahan, Mary P. 30n.20
capitalism 56, 169
Carey, Felix 151
Carey, William 151
Carlo, Padre 150
Carson, Arthur 152
Carson, Laura 152
Catholic Church 79, 150, 153, 157
Catholic St Xavier's Church 153
Catholicism 141, 151, 153, 157
census 201–2
   British 14, 16, 30n.2, 144, 193
   Census of India 143, 145
   colonial administration 9
   global 37, 192
   illegal invasion 21
   Rohingyas not being counted 128
Center for Southeast Asian Studies (CSEAS) 47n.2
Central America 259
Central Europe 265
central government 3, 20, 36–7, 39, 46, 62, 202
centralization of the economic system 56–7
Cernea, Ruth Fredman 158n.4
Chain, Tun Aung 162
Chakravarti, Nalini Ranjan 142–5
Chan Mya Thar Si Township 224
Charles Bo (Catholic Cardinal) 135
Charney, Michael W. 55
Chatterjee, Partha 28n.4
Chauk 198
Cheesman, Nick 19, 30n.18, 122, 124, 128
Chettiar caste 14, 146–7
Chiang Dao District (Chiang Mai Province, Thailand) 92
Chiang Hung (Sipsong Panna) 85
Chiang Mai (Thailand) 10, 77, 100
Chiang Tung 74, 77–8, 85
   Gold stencilling 87
   Temple banners 86
   Temple drum 86
Chiang Tung Buddhism 81, 83–9 (*see also* Buddhism)
Chiang Tung Buddhist 85, 87 (*see also* Buddhists)
Chiang Tung Chronicle 81
Chin (ethnic minority) 13, 130
China 50, 56, 60–1, 74, 79, 130, 150
Chin Christians 157, 178–9 (*see also* Christians)
Chinese 19, 23, 56, 60–2, 77, 85, 104, 128, 130–1, 174, 178–9, 195, 217, 238–40
Chin Lutheran Churches 141, 156–7
Chin National Front (CNF) 42
Chin National League for Democracy 44
Chin State 16, 37, 260
Chittagong/Chittagonians 14, 20, 195
Cholas 14
Christianity 4, 74–5, 130–1, 141–59
   Christianity in Indian 'Province of Burma' 150–2
   Christianity in Indian subcontinent 147–50
   Eastern European 265
   European 265
   history 142–7
   Indian churches in Burma 153–5
   Non-Indian Lutherans 156–7
   xenophobic prejudices 64
Christianization 168
Christians 17, 58, 182, 227, 238, 260
   Asian 141
   Buddhist 162
   Catholic 141, 157
   Chin 58, 163, 180
   churches 4, 133, 158
   colleges 136
   communities 23
   congregations 177
   empowerment 4
   ethics 134
   ethnicities 162, 179
   gospel to India 147, 149
   history 75
   identity 4
   immigrant groups 150
   Indian 141, 150
   Japanese 161
   Kachin 5, 58, 163–4, 175, 178, 180
   Karen 14, 16, 30n.26, 58, 64, 131, 163–4
   Karenni 58
   Lutheran 260
   military officers 59

minorities 4, 164-5, 168-70
mission 3, 166-7
missionaries 13, 55-6, 58, 152, 175
Muslims and 128, 155
pastors 131
in postmodern era 169
priests 134
Protestant 162
as scapegoat 128
schools 58
Tamil 142, 149, 155, 157
theology 135, 269-70
Christian West 265
Chulalongkorn (King) 84
CIA World Factbook 202
cis-Salween Shan States 94
citizenship
cards 26, 30n.23, 203, 206
denial of 62, 205
division in Burma 18
documentation. 5
dual 215
eligibility for 216
identity and 182
law 11, 18, 62, 262
naturalized 19, 24, 217
rights 22, 125, 198, 202, 204, 229
Citizenship Act (1948) 217
Citizenship Law (1982) 13, 18-20, 59, 195, 197-8, 201-4, 215-17, 222, 226, 228-9, 230n.5 (*see also* Burma Citizenship Law (1982))
Citizenship Procedures (1983) 215-17
Citizenship Scrutiny Card (CSC) 198, 203, 215-17
Civil Disobedience Movement (CDM) 252-3
civil documentation and discrimination 214-30
access to 222-6
Bago 218-19, 220
framework of 215-18
freedom of movement 227
Mandalay 218-19, 220
Mawlamyine 219-21
Pathein 219-21
property rights 226-7
qualitative findings 222-6
quantitative findings 222

religious and ethnic minorities 218
rights 226-8
statelessness and 214-15
Yangon 218-19, 220
civilian governments 199-200
civil war 65n.3, 175-9
Clark, T. 64
Clarke, Sarah L. 55, 60
Coedes, George 142
coexistence 122-37
Buddhist nationalism 124-30
diversity and its denial 130-2
minorities 124-30
pluralism 132-5
collective identity 4, 6, 108-10, 114 (*see also* identity)
Collins, Steven 95, 113
colonial administration 9, 13, 15, 237
colonial governance 16
colonialism 13, 15, 22, 261, 265
British 1, 56
Western 84
Colonial Policy and Practice: A Comparative Study of Burma and Netherlands India 260
colonial rule 9, 17-18, 20, 27, 28n.8, 65n.5, 131, 162-3, 166, 176, 235, 251-2, 254
colonization 3, 12, 31n.27, 84-5, 173
Commission for National Identity 53
Committee Representing Pyidaungsu Hluttaw (CRPH) 263
communal violence 20, 122, 211n.5
communitarian ideology 12
compassion 183-5
love and 181
lovingkindness and 113
conflicts
resolution 110, 133
violence and 9
constitution 200-1
democratic reforms 127
election law and 27
empowered military (*Tatmadaw*) 2
favouring Buddhism 168
federal 10, 27, 263
legal aspects 11, 165, 251-2
military 43-4, 164, 191, 200
principles 249

to protects religious
    minorities 123, 136
  right 25–6, 269
  voting for 195
Convention on the Prevention and
    Punishment of the Crime of
    Genocide 206
Council of Elders *(Mahathera
    Samakhom)* 84–5
covenantal pluralism 122–3, 127, 136
Covid-19 157, 171, 250, 252
Cowans, Gordon 185
Cowans, Longchar 185
Crouch, Melissa 29n.11, 29n.14, 128–9
cultural homogeneity 18

da Gama, Vasco 148
Dalferth, Ingolf U. 267
Dalla 153, 155, 157–8
Dalla Catholic 153
Danish Burma Committee 28n.3
Danish Foreign Affairs Ministry 28n.3
Danish Institute for International Studies
    (DIIS) 133
Dark Age 77
Da'wah workers 209
Daw Khin Kyi 251
de Albuquerque, Afonso 148
de Conti, Niccolo 159n.6
Deedok, Ba Cho, U. 211n.3
Deedok Journal Weekly 194
Defence and Security Council 250
Defence Services Institute 253
Delhi Durbar 78
Delta 14, 135, 153, 192
democracy 2–3, 27, 39–41, 45–6,
    128, 163–4
Democratic Karen Buddhist Army
    (DKBA) 31n.29, 41–2, 254
democratization 36–47, 129, 229
demographic changes 11
Denmark 11
Department for the Propagation of
    Religion 131
Department of Immigration 203
Department of Population 202
Department of Religious Affairs 208–9
Description of the Burmese Empire, A
    (Sangermano) 159n.6

Dhamamyal (anti-communist
    ideology) 58
Dhamma 21, 30n.24, 115–17, 126,
    133, 137n.2
Dhammantaraya Rohingya 30n.24 *(see
    also* Rohingya)
Dhammapada 291 113
Dhammazedi (King) 236–7
Dictionary of the Kachin Language, A
    (Hanson) 152
Di Di 45
Dīghanikāya 115
Dikshit, Shivangi 47n.2
Dīpavaṃsa 115
'discipline-flourishing democracy' 40
Discovery of Rehmonnya 233
discrimination 5, 15, 179–85
diversity and its denial 130–2
divide-and-rule 64
  administration 3
  policy 13
  by racial categorization 15–17
Doh Bamar Association 65n.7
domestic violence 129
Duaybis, Cedar 182, 185

East Asia 103, 142
East Asia Forum 255n.1
Eastern Shan State 73–90
  Chiang Tung Buddhism 83–9
  material religion 74–7
  visual Burmanization of Buddhist
    community 77–83
  visual culture 74–7
education 206
  monastic 87
  opportunities 125
  policy 84
  promotion 62
  right to 227–8
Edward VII (emperor) 78
Egreteau, Renaud 29n.9, 29n.12, 239–40
Egypt 259
Ein Du 31n.29
empowering minority communities 228
England 148, 173
'ERASMUS +' exchange program 136n.1
Ethnic Affairs and Internal Peace
    Committee 42

Index

ethnic and religious diversity 257–71
   homogenization 264–9
   impact of religions for
     ethnicities 269–70
   multi-ethnic coexistence 257–64
   multi-religious coexistence 257–64
ethnic armed groups 39–43, 57, 62–3
ethnic armed organizations 10, 12, 18, 63, 131, 249, 253–4
ethnic autonomy 16, 163, 176
ethnic boundary making 12
ethnic categorization 9, 11–12, 17
ethnic conflicts 4, 12, 162, 164, 170, 233
ethnic cultures 10–11
ethnic difference 10
ethnic disunity 18
ethnic diversity 2, 4, 9–10, 161–71
   Buddhist nationalism 165–7
   challenges 167
   religious conflicts 164–5
   religious diversity 168–9
   struggle for democracy 163–4
ethnic identities/identification 1–3, 9–11, 13–14
ethnic identity 3, 10, 13, 74, 83, 89, 95, 114, 177, 181, 225, 269
ethnicity 3, 9–28, 36–8, 73, 231–3
   British administration 15–17
   discourse on 10
   divide and rule by racial categorization 15–17
   Hindus 22–6
   Karen Muslims 22–6
   nationalism 12–15
   of reification 9
   religion and 5
   religions for 269–70
   Rohingya crisis 20–2
   theory 11–12
ethnic markers 10
ethnic minorities 3–5, 10, 13, 36–47, 64, 82, 88, 123, 128, 130, 165–6, 170, 178, 195, 196, 198, 218
ethnic nationalities 10, 18, 37, 191, 193, 201–2, 237
ethnic/racial categorization 19
ethnic rights 179–82
ethnic stereotypes 10
ethnographic race 16

Ethnographic Survey of Burma 15
ethnographic surveys 16
ethno-nationalism 10, 17, 95 (*see also* nationalism)
ethno-religious hierarchy 3
Europe 265
European Union (EU) 11, 262
Evangelical Lutheran Church in Myanmar (ELCM) 257
Everyday Justice and Security in the Myanmar Transition 28n.1

Facebook 207
Farrelly, Nicholas 124
Ferguson, Jane M. 59, 95, 103–4, 243n.3, 259
fieldwork 28n.1, 243n.2
Fink, Christina 123
First Anglo-Burmese War 192, 237
First World War 16
Flusser, David 184
focus group discussions (FGDs) 218–19
foreign agents 128
Foreign Registration Certificate (FRC) 217
Form 66/6. *see* household list
Four Cuts Policy 62–3
four race protection laws 15
fourth dynasty 65n.6
Frazer, James 15
Frederik IV (King) 148
Frederiksnagar in Serampore 151
freedom of movement 227
Freyne, Sean 183
Friedenlund, I. 110
Frontier Areas 16–17, 78, 85, 94, 96
Frontier Areas Administration (FAA) 16
Frontier Myanmar 255n.1
Frydenlund, Iselin 110, 118n.1, 124–5, 128–9
Fuller, Thomas 176
Furnivall, John S. 17, 158n.3, 260–1

Galache, Carlos Sardina 122, 125
Galae 30n.27
Galilee 183
Galtung, Johan 1
Gambia 125, 206
Ganjam 145

Geiger, Wilhelm 243n.5
Gellner, David N. 101
General Administrative Department (GAD) 31n.28, 251
Generation Z (Gen Z) 255, 263
Gerin, R. 46
German Research Foundation (DFG) 6
Germany 149, 159, 159n.9
Gheddo 150
Ghosh, N. 42
Glass Palace Chronicle 116
Glass Palace Chronicle *(Hmannan Yazawin)* 53
Glass Palace Chronicle of the Kings of Burma 234
Global New Light of Myanmar 255n.1
Goa, India 148
Godvari 145
Gola 30n.27
Gombrich, Richard 101, 118n.4
Gravers, Mikael 27, 28n.7, 29n.16, 30n.25, 31n.29–30, 31n.33, 31n.36, 118n.1, 118n.5, 131, 243n.3, 255–6n.6, 270n.3
Gray, Dennis D. 45, 177–8
Great Britain 28n.6, 37, 52, 58, 144
  administration 15–17
  colonial law 29n.11
  colonial rule 1, 9, 65n.5, 163
  colonies 142
Great Chronicle, The 236
Great God *(Karai Kasang)* 175
Greece 259
Green, James H. 28n.2
green card. *see* Naturalised Citizenship Scrutiny Card (NCSC)
Grosshans, Hans-Peter 5, 6, 267
Guardian, The 177
Gupta, Megha 47n.2
Gwa (Rakhine State) 199

hāfiz education 239 (*see also* education)
Hague, The 125, 250
Hang Do, Lian 174, 176, 182, 185
Hanson, Minnie 151
Hanson, Ola 151–2
Hanthawaddy Daily Newspaper 195
Harari, Yuval Noah 76
Hare Krishna movement 76
Harris, Elizabeth J. 116

Harrisson, Annika Pohl 31n.32, 242
Harvey, G. E. 14–15, 158n.5
Harvey, Peter 113–14
Hayami, Yoko 94
Hayward, Susan 118n.1, 244n.9
Heikkilä-Horn, Marja-Leena 144
Hellenization 183
Henry Van Thio 45
Herod Antipas 183
Hindu(s) 9, 14–15, 18, 22–6, 30n.27, 31n.31, 141, 143, 152, 155, 167, 265
Hindu Buddhist Missionary Association 31n.31
Hinduism (or Brahmanism) 64, 102, 108, 130
Hindu Mahasabha 146
Hindu Tamil 146
Hin-tha-da 198
Historical Research Committee 64
History of the Catholic Burmese Mission (Bigandet) 151
Hitler, Adolf 52
Hkun Htun 96
Hlaing, A. H. 38
Holt, John Clifford 2, 110–11, 115, 118, 118n.5, 244n.9
Home Affairs Ministry 31n.28
homogenization 264–9
Hong Kong 142, 155
Hoover, Dennis 122
Hosea 184
household list 217–18
Houtman, Gustaaf 19, 52
Hpa-an 31n.29, 153
Htay, H. H. 43
Human Rights Watch 191
Hutchinson, John 28n.4

iconoclasts 75–6
identity (*see also* visual culture)
  analysis of 111–14
  Buddhist 27, 55
  Buddhist Mon 5
  Burmese 50, 74
  cards 22, 221
  Christians 4
  citizenship and 182
  collective 4, 6, 108–10, 114
  communal 198

contested 2
cultural 54
defined 73
diverse 2, 124
documentation 216, 221, 228–9
ethnic 1, 3, 10, 13, 74, 83, 89, 95, 114, 167, 177, 181, 225, 229, 269
individual 4
Karen 13
legal 215
Mon 235, 237
Muslim 197, 242
national 10, 17, 21–2, 27, 55–6, 83, 89, 110, 166, 180, 197, 199, 215
papers 20, 23–4
politics 3, 9–10, 15, 20, 26, 207
proof of 217
religious 1–4, 27, 74, 83, 89, 108, 111, 114–18, 144, 167, 182, 227, 229
rights 37
self-ascribed 19
shifting 233
sociocultural 165
Tamil 157–8, 165
temporary certificates 203
Identity Card for National Verification (NVC) 202–4, 217
illegal migrants 198, 205
Imagined Communities (Anderson) 28n.4
immigration 11, 14
   from British India 14–15
   illegal 20
   Indian 3
   law 251
   officers 24, 222, 226
Immigration Department 203, 211n.4
independence 38–9
   movements 146–7
India 14, 22, 29n.9, 29n.12, 50, 56, 60, 78, 130, 192
   churches in Burma 153–5
   immigration 3
   migrants under British administration 142–6
   races 9, 14–16, 28n.28
India(n) 3, 15, 141–58, 174, 192, 217, 224, 225, 234, 240–1, 265
   ancestral names 193
   British Empire 162
   churches in Burma 153–5
   groups from Bengal 60
   immigrants 14, 62, 239
   Lutherans 156–7
   madrasa 25
   Muslim 193–4, 239
   Muslim identity papers 125
   partition 108
   races 9, 14, 15, 28n.30, 29n.10, 29n.12
   replace Bamar labour 131
   riots 3, 14–15, 131
   sentiments 197
   Tamils 154
   yogi 103
Indian/British 19
Indian National Congress (INC) 146
Indigenous Burmese races 16
indigenous groups *(taing-yintha)* 11, 16, 64, 104, 111, 130, 132, 166, 170, 242
individual identity 4, 108–9
Indo-China 84
Indonesia 192, 260
Indophobia 239–40
Inn National Development Party 44
Insein Baptist Church 155
Instruction Book 195
insurgents 39, 56, 62
inter-communalism 122
interfaith 5, 29n.12, 133–4, 167, 171, 180, 185, 206–8, 238, 241
Internally Displaced People (IDP) 125, 177, 205
International Court of Justice (ICJ) 125, 206
International Criminal Court in The Hague 26
International Crisis Group 177
International Religious Freedom Act of 1998 270n.1
International Religious Freedom Report 2005 199
International Religious Freedom Reports 198
International State Crime Initiative at Queen Mary University, London 205
Interreligious Dialogue Training Centre 134
Irrawaddy, The 198–9, 255n.1

282 Index

Islam 74, 108, 128, 130–1, 157, 161, 165, 265
  Bengala Kayin 24
  Christianity and 55, 64, 74, 111, 117, 125, 134, 257
  conversion to 129
  groups 30n.22
  Islamophobia 27, 132, 239–40
  madrasah 136
  monk 125
  mosque 133
  organizations 208–9
  radical 25
  self-identification 25
  Sunnite 260
  terrorism 20, 22
  xenophobic prejudices 64
Islam and ethnic diversity 191–212
  civilian governments 199–200
  current issues 200–9
  military junta (1988–2011) 196–9
  origins and development 192–6
Islamic Centre of Myanmar 208
Islamic Religious Affairs Council 195, 208
Islamophobia 27, 132, 239–40

Jain 142
Jakarta Globe 199
Jami'ah Arabiyah 208
Jamiyatul Ulema al-Islam 208–9
Japan 29n.12, 97, 192
Jaspers, Karl 259
*jātaka*s 85
Jenkins, Richard 11, 27
Jerryson, Michael 110, 118n.1
Jerusalem Church 148
Jesus 184
Jeyaraj 148
Jinghpaw (tribe) 174
Joffe, Ben Philip 101
Jørgensen, Anders Baltzer 28n.1, 31n.30, 31n.33
Judaism 130, 184
Judson, Adoniram 151
Judson Church 151

Kachin (ethnic minority) 4, 10, 13, 16–17, 36, 130, 174–5

Kachin Baptist Church in Burma, The (Tegenfeldt) 152
Kachin Christians 178
Kachin Independence Army (KIA) 42, 61, 64, 65n.4, 164, 176
Kachin Independence Organization (KIO) 41
Kachin Land 152, 174, 175–9
Kachin State 39, 44, 174–6, 178–9, 183, 260, 262
Kachin Theological College and Seminary (Myitkyina) 178
KAICIID. *see* King Abdullah bin Abdulaziz International Centre for Interreligious and Intercultural Dialogue
Kala, U. 236–7
Kalar 14, 22–7, 30n.27, 132
Kalar Gyi 31n.27
Kalaymyo 152
Kama 61
Kaman 60, 195
Kam Mueang 85
Kant-Balu 208
Karai Kasang 175
Karekin II (Armenian Catholicos) 157
Karen (ethnic minority) 13, 17, 29n.16, 36, 130–1, 150–1, 155–6, 180
Karen/Bamar 19
Karen/British 19
Karen Christians 131
Karen Hindus 3
Karen Muslims 3, 14, 22–6, 31n.33
Karen National Association 13
Karen National Defence Organization 65n.4
Karen National Democratic Party 44
Karen National Liberation Army (KNLA) 211n.1
Karen National Liberation Army-Peace Council (KNLA-PC) 42
Karen National Union (KNU) 12, 16–17, 29n.16, 42, 61, 164, 254
Karenni 36
Karenni National Progressive Party (KNPP) 61
Karen State 3, 14, 21–3, 30n.26, 31n.31
Karen Youth Organization 17
Karlsson, Klemens 83

Kataoka, Tatsuki 94
Kataragama, Sri Lanka 101
Kaw Kani 220
Kawthoolei Muslim Liberation Front 31n.29, 211n.1
Kayah State 16–17, 36–7, 150, 153
Kayah State Democratic Party 44
Kazi Act of 1880 208
Kelsay, John 110
Keng Tung 97 (*see also* Chiang Tung)
Keng Tung in Eastern Shan State 96
Kerala, India 147–8
Keyes, Charles F. 84, 95, 102–3, 118n.1
Khammai Dhammasami 84
K. H. Aung 45
Khine Lin 55
Khin Maung Kyaw 62
Khin Maung Lat, U. 194
Khin Nyunt 78
Khin Yi 15, 29n.10
Khmer 85
Khni Maung Yin 244n.12
Khola Engelai 30n.27
Khola Wa 30n.27
Khruba Bunchum 81–2, 88
Khuen Buddhist 88
Khun Leng 96
Khun Num 96
Khwe Char Nyin Pae Chin 61–2
King, Martin Luther 182, 269
King Abdullah bin Abdulaziz International Centre for Interreligious and Intercultural Dialogue 134, 137n.4
kingdoms before colonial period 192–3
Kipgen, Nehginpao 3, 6, 37–40, 42–3, 261–2
Knowles, James D. 168
Ko Htwe 194
Ko Ko Gyi 132
Konbaung Crown 96
Kònbaung dynasty 13, 65n.5, 96, 232, 234
Ko Ni, U. 127, 201, 252
Ko Ny Win 201
Korea 265
Koyama, Kosuke 161
Krueger, Madlen 5–6
Krummel, John W. M. 103
Kukai 103

Küng, Hans 169
Kuomintang (Communist Party of Burma) 97
Kuppuswamy, C. 39
Kya Khun Sar 43
Kyauk-padaung (Mandalay Division) 199
Kyauk-pyu 198
Kyauk-se 198
Kyaw, Nyi Frieden Lund 118n.5
Kyaw Hpyo Tha 31n.34
Kyaw Min 207
Kyaw Nay Min 61, 66n.11
Kyaw Nyunt, U 197
Kyaw Thet 51
Kyaw Win 55
Kyed, Helene Maria 27, 132–3
Kyi, U. 192, 211n.2
Kyi Lin 201
Kyi Sein Win 52, 65n.9
Kyi Win Sein 55–6

Lachit (tribe) 174
Lahu (minority) 17, 30n.20
Lahu Democratic Union (LDU) 43
Lall, Marie 19
Lal Sawi Thanga 156
Lalthangliana, Martin 156, 159n.13
Lang, Karen 102
Lan Na (Northern Thailand) 77, 79, 83–5, 87, 92, 96
Lan Na Buddhism 85
Laos (Northern Thailand) 74, 92
Lashio 127, 133, 153, 157
Layang Seng Ja 174–6, 178, 262
Leach, Edmund 10, 28n.2, 73, 102, 104
Learman, Linda 125
Lehman, F. K. 152
Leider, Jacques 20, 30n.21
Leipzig Mission 154
liberalization 126, 128–9
Lieberman, Victor B. 13, 232
Linguistic Research Group 167
Lintner, Bertil 152, 255n.5
London 17, 148
Lone, Andrew Mang 156–7
Longwo (tribe) 174
Lower Burma 234–6, 244n.6
Loy, David 114
Lua ethnic group 90n.2

Luce, G. H. 116, 243n.4
Lung Sayay Gaw Ya 98
Lutheran Christians 260
Lutheran Church of Myanmar (LCM) 148, 156
Lutheran Protestantism 141
Lutheran World Federation (LWF) 156

MaBaTha movement 4, 21, 23, 25, 30n.25, 31n.29, 126, 128, 131–2, 135, 137n.3, 177–9, 207, 238, 243, 252
Machanbaw (Putao district), Kachin State 178
Madras, India 147, 154
Madurai in Tamil Nadu 155
Mae Hong Son Province (Northwest Thailand) 95
Mae Sai 79
Mahādukkhakkhandha Sutta (Majjhimanik ā ya 13) 113
Mahajani, Usha 142–3, 1467
Mahāmuni *(Maha Myat Muni)* Buddha sculpture 82–3
Ma Ha Na 252
Mahāvaṃsa 234, 243n.5
Mahmood, Sultan 194
Mainland Southeast Asia 95
Majjhimanikāya 22 118n.2
majoritarianism 2
Majumdar 142
Malaysia/Malaya 142, 155
Man-aung Island (Cheduba) 199
Mandalay 96, 132–3, 136n.1, 144, 153, 198, 218–20
Mandalay Region 37
Mang, P. Z. 38
Mangrai of Chiang Rai/Chiang Mai (King) 77
Manipur 102
Mara Evangelical Church (MEC) 156–7
Maraland 156–7
Maramargyi 60–1
Marshall, Mary 184
Marston, John 104
martial races 16
masculinity and sexuality 102
material religion 74–7
Maung Aung Myoe 63
Maungdaw District 205

Maung Maung 30n.17, 65n.3
Maung Maung Gyi 51, 65n.3
Mawlamyine/Mawla-myaine 198, 219–21, 238–42
Maymyo (Pyin Oo Lwin) 153, 157
Mayu Frontier District (Rakhine State) 196
McCormick, Patrick 231–3
McDaniel, Justin 104
McGowan, John 169
Mekthila 127, 132–3
Mendelson, E. Michael 15, 103–4, 164
Methodism 141
mettābhāvanā 118
Middle East 16, 130
military *(Tatmadaw)* 78
military capitalism 162
military coup 3, 5, 17, 38–40, 78, 154, 162–3, 195, 197, 211n.4
Military Defence Services. *see* Tatmadaw
military forces 175–9
Military Intelligence Services (MIS) 254
military junta (State Law and Order Restoration Council) 196–200, 263–4
military rule 10, 18, 20, 23, 26, 40, 51, 64
military socialism 261
Milne, Leslie 102
Min, Awng Kyaw 180
Min, Zin 238
Min Aung Hlaing 43, 249–52
Mindon (King) 150
Ministerial Burma 16
Ministries of Border Affairs and Ethnic Affairs 28n.2
Ministry of Education 58
Ministry of Immigration and Population 202
Ministry of Labour, Immigration and Population (MoLIP) 37, 219, 223, 225–6
minorities 124–30
Min Thu, Z. 174
Min Win 255n.4
Mist of Rāmañña: The Legend That Was Lower Burma, The (Aung-Thwin) 236
mixed race marriages 14
Mizoram, India 156

modernization 126
Moken (or Salon) 60
Mon 231–44
   Bamar 19
   ethnicity 231–3
   history 233–5
   identity 231–3
   kingdom 13
   Mawlamyine 238–42
   Muslim community in Mon
      State 238–42
   nationalism 233–5
   paradigm 236–8, 243n.6
Möng Nai 96
Möng Pan on the Shan Plateau 3, 93, 96–8
monk 98–100
Mon-Khmer 59
Mon King Dhammazedi 236
Mon National Day 235
Mon National Liberation Army
   (MNLA) 235
Mon New State Party 65n.4
monogamy 30n.25
   law 29n.12
Mon State 31n.32, 55
Mon State Day 235
Mon Unity League (MUL) 233
Mon Unity Party 44
Morgan, David 74–6
Moulmein (Mawlyimyine) 150, 153
Mrauk-U period in Rakhine 192
Mro (Khume) 60
Mujahid movement 30n.22, 211n.1
multiculturalism 122, 136n.1
multi-ethnic coexistence 257–64
Multi-Party Democracy General Election
   Commission 197
multi-religious coexistence 257–64
Murakami, Tadayoshi 89
Muslims 1, 9, 14, 15, 20–2, 29n.12, 58, 61,
   90n.1, 117, 127, 131, 191, 196–9, 202,
   206, 208, 240–1, 244n.9, 252
   challenges 5
   community in Mon State 238–42
   funeral places 25
   India(n) 193–4, 239
   informants 24
   inheritance 15
   invasion of 21
   issuance of 'White Card' to 20
   Karen Muslims 22–6
   minorities during the British colonial
      period 193–4
   mutual mistrust Buddhists 20
   in post-independence Burma 194–6
   Rakhine 195, 196–7, 199
   riots with Buddhists 20
   Rohingya 1, 29n.12, 64, 125
   savage 125
   social rights of 26
Muslim Buddhism/Muslim-
   Buddhist 3, 21
Muslim Central Fund Trust 208
Mussolini, Benito 52
Mwe Taw temple 98, 100
Mya Han, U. 56
Myanmar
   Burma renamed as 47n.1
   constitution 25
   history 12–15
MyanmarAlin News 58
Myanmar Baptist Convention 170
Myanmar Buddhism 94, 117
Myanmar Buddhists 177
Myanmar Christians 162
Myanmar Citizenship Law (1982) 203
Myanmar Council of Churches 156, 170
Myanmar Economic Corporation 253
Myanmar Economic Holdings Ltd. 253
Myanmar Indian Churches (MIC) 155
Myanmar Institute of Theology (MIT) 6,
   134, 157, 170
Myanmar Lutheran Church 156–7
Myanmar Medical Association
   Hall 211n.6
Myanmar Muslim Network 209
Myanmar Muslims 209
Myanmar Muslim Ulema
   Organization 209
Myanmar Muslim Women's League 208
Myanmar Now 255n.1
Myanmar Tamils 158
Myanmar Universities Historical Research
   Centre 29n.16
Myawady Mingyi Sayardw 207
Mye-dae (Magway Division) 196
Myint, Michael Kyaw 208
Myint Swe, U 205

Myitkyina 176
Myo-chit Yahan 207
Myo Nyunt 44
Myo Oo 54
Myo Pya 61
Myo Win 30n.23

Naga (minority) 16–17
Nakanishi, Yoshihiro 255n.4
Nam Kham 102
Nanda 44
Nang Oo 98
Nang Sapphires Tinilar Win 28n.1
National Convention 40
National Defence and Security Council (NDSC) 43, 250
National Democratic Alliance Army – Eastern Shan State 41
National Democratic Force 41
National Democratic Party for Development (NDPD) 199
national identity 10, 22, 55–6
nationalism 3
  aim of 10
  Buddhist 124–30
  ethnicity 12–15
  Mon 233–5
  populism and 11
National League for Democracy (NLD) 2, 22, 26, 31n.35, 36, 40, 42–4, 50, 126, 128, 163, 174, 191, 250, 263
national races 11, 18, 30n.20, 37, 59
National Registration Card (NRC) 20, 203, 216, 223
National Unity Consultation Council 256n.7
National Verification Card 24, 204
Nationwide Ceasefire Agreement (NCA) 42, 50
native races 9, 28n.8
Naturalised Citizenship Scrutiny Card (NCSC) 203, 215, 217
naturalized citizenship 18–19, 24, 217 (*see also* citizenship)
Nay Yar Pay Ah Thi Ah Hmat Pyut Chin 59–61
Ne Win 3, 13, 15, 17–18, 50–64, 65n.2–3, 65n.6, 65n.10, 66n.11, 97, 130, 162–3, 195, 204, 240, 254

Citizenship Law from 1982 18–20
  core procedures of regime 57–62
  ideological foundations of regime 54–7
  narrative for Burma 53–4
  negative effect Burmanization policy on peacebuilding 63–4
New Jerusalem Church 148
New Mon State Party (NMSP) 41, 43, 61, 235
New Testament 148, 152
New York Times 21
Ngun Ling, Samuel 4, 6, 130, 157, 162, 165, 167
Nitta, Y. 44
non-Bama 37
Non-Indian Lutherans 156–7
Northeast India 152
Northern Europe 265
Northern Myanmar 130
Northern Shan 177
Northern Thailand 88, 100
Norwegianization 173
Notes & Queries on Anthropology 15–16
Not-Self teaching 112
Novalis 265
Nu, U. 39, 51, 55–6, 58, 65n.9–10, 146, 162, 164, 194, 235, 240
Num Serk Harn 104
Num Suek Harn 98
Nung (tribe) 174
Nyi Nyi Kyaw 26, 30n.24

Obeyesekere, Gananath 101–2
Official Secret Act 251
Old Testament 152
Organization of the Islamic Conference (OIC) 199
Orwell, George 19
Ottama, U. 146

Pacification 14, 28n.6
Pakistan 30n.22
Pali 85
Palihawadana, Mahinda 116
Panglong Agreement (1947) 16–17, 38–9, 163, 174
Pa Nyo 98
Pa-O (minority) 17, 30n.20, 60

Pa-O National Liberation Organization (PNLO) 42
Parsis 143, 145
Pascal Khoo Thwe 150–1
Passayana (Vajrayana Buddhism) 101
Pathein (Delta) 192, 219–21
Pa-thi (Muslim) 192
Pa-thi National Congress 196
Paung Daw Oo International University in Mandalay 135
peacebuilding 63–4
Peace Cultivation Network 209
Peano, Bartolomeo 150
Pearn, B. R. 142, 166
Pegu (Bago) 150, 233
Pe Kin, U. 194
Persia 148
Philip, Jan 155
Philippines 148
Phyo Thiho Cho 244n.11
pink card. *see* Citizenship Scrutiny Card (CSC)
P. Kyaw Han 52
pluralism 132–5
pluralistic society 261
Plütschau, Heinrich 148
Po Kan Kaung 62
Po Latt, U. 166
political categorization 11
political identification 14
political paranoia 255n.5
political violence 11
Pollack, Detlef 266–7
Pollock, Sheldon 158
polygamy 15, 128
polygyny 129
Pope Francis 153
Population Control Law 29n.12
populism 11
Prager-Nyein, Susanne 255n.4
preventative counter-violence 26
preventive repression 12, 26
primordial heritage 18
primordialism 12
Procedures Relating to Associate Citizenship (1983) 230n.5
Procedures Relating to Myanmar Citizenship Law (1983) 230n.5
Procedures Relating to Naturalized Citizenship (1983) 230n.5
property rights 226–7
Prophet Day 209
Prophet Muhammad 207
Protestantism 269
public categorization 11
Pwo Karen 13–14, 17, 23, 30n.27
Pwo Karen Buddhist 23
Pyay (Bago Division) 196
Pyidaungsu Muslims [Citizen Muslims of Myanmar] 207
Pyi Daung Su Thar 58
Pyithu Hluttaw 40, 208

qualitative findings 222–6
quantitative findings 222
quasi-democracy 3, 37, 41–2
quasi-military government 57, 65n.2
Qur'an 133, 207

Race and Religion Protection Laws 238
race/ethnic group 16–17, 27, 30n.19
racial categorization 3, 15–17
racial names 16
Rakhine (Arakan) 20, 26, 29n.12, 36, 60–1
Rakhine Buddhists 64 (*see also* Arakan Buddhist)
Rakhine Investigation Commission 132
Rakhine Kingdom 60–1
Rakhine Muslim 193, 196–7, 199
Rakhine Nationalities Development Party 41
Rakhine State 30n.22, 60, 62, 132, 198–9, 262
Ramadan 208
Rāmaññaraṭṭha Buddhist University 238, 244n.8
Ramberg, Lucinda 101
Ramnad 145
Ramonnya Dhammasariya Mon Sangha Association 238
Rangoon. *see* Yangon
Rangoon Arts and Sciences University 59
Rangoon University 28n.2
Raschid, U. 194

Ratanaporn Sethakul 84–5, 87
Rawang (tribe) 174
Razak, U. 194
Regional Islamic Da'wah Council for Southeast Asia and the Pacific (RISEAP) 208
Registration of Residents Act Section 5(2)(d) (1949) 217
reified identities 10
relics 90n.4
religion and culture 177–9
Religion in Human Evolution: From the Paleolithic to the Axial Age (Bellah) 258
Religions for Peace Myanmar 135
religious and ethnic minorities 218
religious belief 62, 75, 259
religious conflicts 164–5
Religious Conversion Law 29n.12
religious diversity 2–4, 6, 9, 168–9, 260, 264–9
religious freedom 123, 128
religious identity 1–4, 27, 114–18
religious minorities 5, 123, 125, 133, 136, 164–5, 168, 170, 227–8, 267
religious tensions 66n.11
Residents of Burma Registration Act of 1949 216
Residents of Burma Registration Rules of 1951 216
Review of Faith & International Relations, The 30n.25
right to education 227–8 (*see also* education)
Robinne, François 89
Rogers, Benedict 59, 123
Rohingya 10, 65n.10, 205–6
  crisis 3, 13, 20–2
Rohingya Muslims 1, 29n.12, 64
Rohingya Solidarity Organization 30n.22
Roman Catholic Barnabite Mission 150
Roman Catholic Church 141, 148, 153
Roman Catholics 152
Romanization 183
Rome 259, 265
Ross, Alexa 181
Royal Danish Missionaries 148
royal palace *(haw)* 78
Rozenberg, Guillaume 104

Russia 148

Sacks, Jonathan 109
Sadan, Mandy 16, 122
Saffron Revolution of 2007 124, 181
Sagaing Region 152, 208
Sai Ga Kham 98
Sai Kam Mong 95
Sāimong Mangrāi 81
Sai Sai 92
Sakhong, Lian H. 28n.3, 152
Salahiyatul Ulemah 209
Sallman 76
Salvation Army 155
Salween District 16
Salween River 92
Samartha, Stanley J. 168–9
Sandhu, Kernial Singh 142
Sangermano, Vincenzo 150, 159n.6
saṅgha 77, 83–5, 87, 95, 105, 254
Sangha Act (1902) 84–5
Sangha Administration Act of 1902 84
Sangkhlaburi 238
Sang Nanta 98
San Nyein 56
Sanskrit 85
Santasombat 73
San Yamin Aung 31n.35
Sao Kham Sai 98
Sao Mahakhanan 77
Sao Myat (monk) 3–4, 92–3, 100–4, 259
Sao Myat (Lord Pinnacle) *Kon Ho Yao* 100
Sao Myat Portrait 99
Sao Shwe Thaik 45
Sargent, R. 43
Sasana Yaung-war Htunse- boh (To Enlighten the Glory of Religion) 198
Saudi Arabia 30n.22, 192
Saw Augurlion 56
Saw Eh Dah 28n.1
Saw Maung 52
Saw Mutu Say Poe 42
Saw Say Wah 28n.1
Saya Chai 197
Saya San rebellion 14, 240
Schmidt-Leukel, Perry 4, 6, 112, 115, 117
Schober, Juliane 122
Schönbeck 148, 150

Schonthal, Benjamin 111, 118n.5
Scott, J. George 144–5
sea gypsies. *see* Moken (or Salon)
Sebastian Manrique 150
Second Anglo-Burmese War 143
Second World War 20, 192
secularization 126
Seekins 41
Seiple, Chris 122
self-ascribed identity 19
self-identity 45
self-mummify 94
Seng Ja Layang. *see* Layang Seng Ja
Sevitabbā sevitabha Sutta (Majjhimanikāya 114) 113
Sgaw 17
Shaikhul Islam 208
Shan Buddhism 94–5
Shanland 93
Shan Nationalities Democratic Party 41
Shans at Home (Milne) 102
Shan State 3, 16–17, 36–7, 38, 44, 60–1, 92, 163 (*see also* Eastern Shan State)
Shan State Army 65n.4
Shan State Army – South (SSA-S) 42
Shan-Tayouk 61
Shan United Revolutionary Army (SURA) 102
shaving act 101
Shils, Edward 28n.5
Shin Arahan (King) 81–3, 89–90
Shingon Buddhism 103
Shneiderman, Sara 74
Shu Maung 52
Shway Yoe. *see* Scott, J. George
Shwedagon Pagoda 235
Shwedagon Paya 79, 83, 89–90
Shwe Lu Maung 53, 65n.3
Shwe Mann 251
Shwe Pay Lwa 66n.11
Siamese Thai language 85
Siddhartha (Prince) 102
Sikhism 108
Sikh men 76
Silverstein, Josef 195
Simms, Sao Sanda 96
Singapore 142, 156
Singaporean Tamil 155
Sinhalese 115

Sino-Burmese 128
Sino-Tibetan 60
Sitagu Sayadaw 252
Sitha Kywe Village 104
Sit-twe (Akyab) 198, 206, 241
Skilling, Peter 115
Slodkowski, A. 42
SMILE Myanmar 214
Smith, Anthony D. 28n.4
Smith, Donald E. 164, 167
Smith, Martin 10, 30n.22
social cohesion 6
social justice 133
Soe Win 254
Songkran *(Thingyan)* 82–3
South, Ashley 19, 73, 234–5
Southeast Asia 37, 73, 77, 94–5, 100, 103–4, 130, 141–2, 146, 159n.6, 234, 236
Southern Burma in Tenasserim 142
Southern Chin State 156
Southern India 101, 141, 157
Southern Shan State 3, 95, 259
South Slav movement 262
Southwest China 130
Southwest Myanmar 178
Spiro, Melford E. 95, 103, 105
Sri Lanka 77, 111, 117, 236, 243n.5
St Anthony in Yangon 153
State Administrative Council (SAC) 251
State Counsellor's Information Committee 203
State Law and Order Restoration Council (SLORC) 23, 47n.1, 78, 130, 164, 197
statelessness 214–15
State Peace and Development Council (SPDC) 40, 164
Steinberg, David I. 52, 59
Stevenson, Noel 16–17, 28n.2
Stewart, Christopher 122
St John's Cathedral in Rangoon 151
St Mary Orthodox Church 148
struggle for democracy 163–4
Sunnite Islam 260
Suttanipāta 705 113
Suvaṇṇabhūmi (Pāli) 234, 236
Swan Arr Shin 252
Swearer, Donald K. 84–5

Symes, Michael 142, 158n.2
Syriam (near Yangon) 150
Syrian Orthodox Church in India 147

Ta'ang 60
Tachileik 79
Tai-Chinese 59
Tai Khuen 77, 81–2, 85
Tai Loi 83
taing-yin-tha ('original people') 19–20
Taing Yin Thar See Lone Nyi Nyut Yae 58–9
Tai Yuan 85
Taliban 75
Tambiah, Stanley J. 30n.25
Tamil Christians 155
Tamil Hindu 14
Tamil identity in Myanmar 157
Tamil Lutheran Church 141
Tamil Methodists 155
Tamil Nadu, Southern India 147–8, 150
Tamil Nadu Theological Seminary 155
Tamils 14, 145
  immigrants 4
Tanjore 145
Tantrism 3, 92–105
  exception 104–5
  Möng Pan on the Shan Plateau 96–8
  monk 98–100
  Sao Myat 100–4
  Shan Buddhism 94–5
Tatmadaw 206, 249–56
  coup 250–3
  totalitarian-like rule 253–5
Taunggoke 206
Taung-gote (Rakhine State) 199
Taunggyi (Shan State) 153, 196, 198
Taungoo dynasty 65n.5
Taung Tan Tharthnar Pyut 58
Taylor, Robert H. 9, 14, 29n.9, 39, 55, 57
Tegenfeldt, Herman 152
Telugus 145, 154
Temporary Registration/Identification Certificate (TRC or TIC) 217
Ten Commandments 181
Thailand 13, 24, 50, 53, 55, 65n.8, 74, 79, 88, 97, 111, 130
Thai Myanmar 82
Thaketa township, Yangon 211n.6

Thakin (master) 15, 65n.7
Thanlwin River 14
Than Shwe 18–19, 251
Than Tin 62
Thant Myint-U 13, 30n.19, 65n.3, 243n.3
Than Tun 53
Tharaphi Than 59
Thaton 234, 236
Thawnghmung, Ardeth M. 12
Thein Sein 20, 30n.25, 41–3, 79, 163, 174, 242
Thein Swe, U. 204
Theravāda Buddhism 2, 4, 77, 82–3, 89–90, 92–3, 95–6, 104, 108–18, 168, 192, 234, 236, 259 (*see also* Buddhism)
  analysis of identity 111–14
  problem 108–11
  religious identity as problem 114–18
Thet 60
Thibaw (King) 162
Thich Nhat Hanh 114
Thilasara, Ashin 238
Third Buddhist Council 236
Thongchai, Winichakul 52–3, 55, 59, 62, 65
Thuzana, U. 31n.29
thway-naw ('pure blood') 18–19
Tibet 102
Tibeto-Burman 59
Tiloka, U. 25
Tiloka Bhiwuntha, U. 21
Tin, Pe Maung 116, 243
Tin, U. 193
Tinker, Hugh 29n.16
Tin Maung Maung Than 144
Tio, Henary Van 179
Tonkin, Derek 20, 30n.21, 59
totalitarian-like rule 253–5
Toungoo dynasty 79, 151, 198
Tranquebar 148
Triangle Regional Military Command 79
Turnell, Sean 146
turquoise card. *see* Identity Card for National Verification (NVC)
Twiss, Sumner B. 110
Tylor, Edward 15

undocumented populations 215

UNESCO World Heritage Site 75
UN Human Rights Council 209
UN International Court of Justice 250
Union Citizenship Act 215
Union Citizenship (Election) Act 215
Union Day 38
Union Election Commission (UEC) 44, 250
Union Minister of Religious Affairs and Culture 209
Union of the Peoples of Myanmar 263
Union Solidarity and Development Party (USDP) 20, 22, 27, 31n.32, 41, 44, 46, 129, 199, 252
United Nationalities Alliance (UNA) 40
United Nations (UN) 137n.4, 199
United Nations Charter 204
United Nations High Commissioner for Refugees (UNHCR) 211n.5, 215
United Nations Population Fund (UNFPA) 201
United States 58, 265
United Wa State Army (UWSA) 41
University of Mandalay 136n.1
University of Yangon 59
UN Office for Human Rights 205
Upagupta (or Shin Upagutta) 90n.3
Upaniṣad 112
Upper Burma 235–6
US Department of State 198, 270n.1

Vedic Rishis 115
Ven Keum Vang (Cambodian monk) 104
Vienna 134, 137n.4
Vihāra, Wat In, Chiang Tung 88
Village Tract Administrator 23
visual culture 74–7, 83
Visuddhimagga 113–14
Vizagapatam 145

Wa (minority) 17, 30n.20, 60, 90n.2
Wade, Francis 19, 30n.21, 122–3, 125–6
Walton, Matthew J. 29n.15, 39, 57, 118n.1, 125, 128, 244n.9
Waters, Tony 53
We-self vs. Others 55, 57
West, David 6
Western Asia 265
Western Europe 265

Western European Christianity 265
Western Myanmar 123
white card. see Temporary Registration/ Identification Certificate (TRC or TIC)
White Rose Campaign 207
Wichirayan (Prince) 84
Williams, Lee 177–8
Win Tint Tun 63
Wirathu, Ashin (monk) 90n.1, 111, 207
Women's American Baptist Foreign Mission Society 151
Workers Daily (newspaper) 19
Working People's Daily 195–6

Xavier, Francois 148
xenophobia 22, 239

Yale Law School 205
Yangon 6, 14–15, 29n.12, 58, 79, 123, 127, 130, 133, 136n.1, 143, 145, 153, 156, 181, 193, 198, 204, 207, 218–20, 241
Yangon Airport 252
Yangon Armenian Church 157
Yangon Heritage List 154
Yangon International Airport 201
Yangon Railway Station 154
Yangon University Campus 151
Yanyaungung 15
Yawnghwe, Chao-Tzang 28n.3
Yay, Patrick 55
Yegar, Moshe 14, 20, 28n.8, 29n.9, 30n.21, 193
Ye Hein Aung 64, 66n.11
Yellamma (goddess) 101
'yesterday Rohingya' 21 (see also Rohingya)
Young Sone Thabone 65n.4
Youth Religions 265
Yule, Col. Henry 193
Yunnan (China) 92

Zahler, Diane 181
Zaiwa (tribe) 174
Zer-ba-dee. see Burmese Muslims
Zerbadi 14, 28n.8
Ziegenbalg, Bartholomäus 148
Zöllner, Hans-Bernd 270n.2
Zothan Mawia 157

www.ingramcontent.com/pod-product-compliance
Lightning Source LLC
Chambersburg PA
CBHW052151300426
44115CB00011B/1618